Beyond Atlanta

Beyond Atlanta

The Struggle
for Racial
Equality
in Georgia,
1940–1980

Stephen G. N. Tuck

The University of Georgia Press

Athens and London

© 2001 by the University of Georgia Press

Athens, Georgia 30602

All rights reserved

Designed by Betty Palmer McDaniel

Set in 11/14 Monotype Janson by G&S Typesetters

Printed and bound by Maple-Vail

The paper in this book meets the guidelines for
permanence and durability of the Committee on
Production Guidelines for Book Longevity of the
Council on Library Resources.

Printed in the United States of America

05 04 03 02 01 C 5 4 3 2 1

Library of Congress Cataloging-in-Publication Data
Tuck, Stephen G. N.
Beyond Atlanta : the struggle for racial equality in Georgia, 1940–
1980/Stephen G. N. Tuck.
p. cm.
Includes bibliographical references and index.
ISBN 0-8203-2265-2 (alk. paper)
1. Georgia—Race relations. 2. Afro-Americans—Civil
rights—Georgia—History—20th century. 3. Civil rights
movements—Georgia—History—20th century. I. Title.
F295.N4 T83   2001
305.8′009758—dc21   00-053656

British Library Cataloging-in-Publication Data available

Contents

Acknowledgments

Many people have helped to make this book possible. In England, numerous academics have shared insights and given advice along the way. I am particularly grateful to Tony Badger for his unstinting enthusiasm and encouragement. Bill Dusinberre first pointed me toward the civil rights movement in Savannah. John Thompson has been a much appreciated and meticulous reader of the manuscript at various stages. Adam Fairclough, whose work shaped my own thinking, has been extremely generous in his time and advice. I would also like to thank my American history colleagues at Cambridge University.

In America, Dan Carter made my stay at Emory University possible. Cliff Kuhn, who knows more about black protest in Georgia than anyone I know, was kind enough to share some of this knowledge with me. John Dittmer gave me important advice at an early stage and has read a large proportion of the manuscript. Thanks are also owed to John Bertrand in Rome, Edward Cashin in Augusta, John Lupold in Columbus, John Inscoe at the University of Georgia, Paul Bolster, Lawrence Hanks and Joan Browning.

I had the privilege of meeting and interviewing hundreds of people who had been involved in the struggle for racial equality in Georgia. Most were activists, some were observers, and some were opponents. I am very grateful to all those who gave their time and who helped me to discover the salient issues in each community. I learned far more from them than they will know. I am particularly grateful to W. W. Law and Warren Fortson.

I spent almost two years in America, and many people housed, fed, and befriended me in that time. I thank the Heads in Savannah and Moultrie, the Devers in Washington, D.C., the Greers in Rome, John Lupold in Columbus, Koinonia Farm in Americus, and above all the King family in Atlanta. Also many thanks to Jon,

Johanna, Eric, Christian Evangelical Fellowship, Vinnie (a superb drama teacher!), and the Roots United Soccer team.

Without exception, the staff of every library and archive I visited aided greatly in my research. The staff at Howard University, the Auburn Avenue Research Library, the APEX Museum, and the University of Pennsylvania were helpful beyond the call of duty.

This research would not have been possible without generous funding from the British Academy and the Fullbright Association. During this time, I was fortunate to be based at Trinity College in Cambridge, Emory University in Atlanta, and Gonville and Caius College in Cambridge. I have been very lucky to have had such supportive colleagues in each community.

In England, I have been surrounded by some wonderful friends and an ever-expanding family, who have unwittingly helped see this book to completion.

Above all, I thank my wife, Katie, for her extraordinary patience, support, and good humor. The last twelve months of writing this book coincided with the first twelve months of our marriage. I am so glad that one is over and the other is just beginning. This book is dedicated to her, with all my love.

Abbreviations

ACCA   Atlanta's Committee for Cooperative Action
ACHR   Atlanta Council on Human Relations
ACLU   American Civil Liberties Union
ACPL   Atlanta Civic and Political League
ACRC   All-Citizens Registration Committee
AFL   American Federation of Labor
ANVL   Atlanta Negro Voters League
AU   Atlanta University
AUL   Atlanta Urban League
BCCC   Bibb County Coordinating Committee
BCIA   Burke County Improvement Association
CCCV   Chatham County Crusade for Voters
CIO   Congress of Industrial Organizations
COAHR   Committee on an Appeal for Human Rights
CORE   Congress on Racial Equality
FEPC   Fair Employment Practice Committee
GCHR   Georgia Council on Human Relations
GCL   Georgia Voters' League
GTEA   Georgia Teachers and Education Association
HCDC   Hancock County Democratic Club
HEW   Department of Health, Education and Welfare
HOPE   Help Our Public Education
ILA   International Longshoremen's Association
MCHR   Macon Council on Human Relations
NAACP   National Association for the Advancement of Colored People
NUL   National Urban League
SCEF   Southern Conference Educational Fund
SCHW   Southern Conference on Human Welfare
SCLC   Southern Christian Leadership Conference

SCOPE	Summer Community Organizing Project
SNCC	Student Nonviolent Coordinating Committee
SRC	Southern Regional Council
SUMMIT	Atlanta Summit Leadership Conference
TIC	"To Improve Conditions" Club
UAW	United Auto Workers
UGA	University of Georgia
UNIA	Universal Negro Improvement Association
UPWA	United Packinghouse Workers of America
VCC	Vine City Council
VCIA	Vine City Improvement Association
VEP	Voter Education Project
WPA	Works Progress Administration

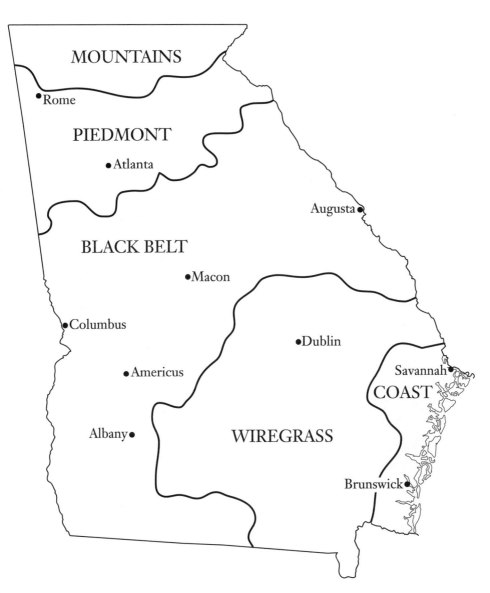

City map of Georgia with geographical regions (From Dittmer, *Black Georgia in the Progressive Era,* page 4, copyright 1977 by the Board of Trustees of the University of Illinois Press. Redrawn by University of Georgia Graphics and Photography with permission of the University of Illinois Press.)

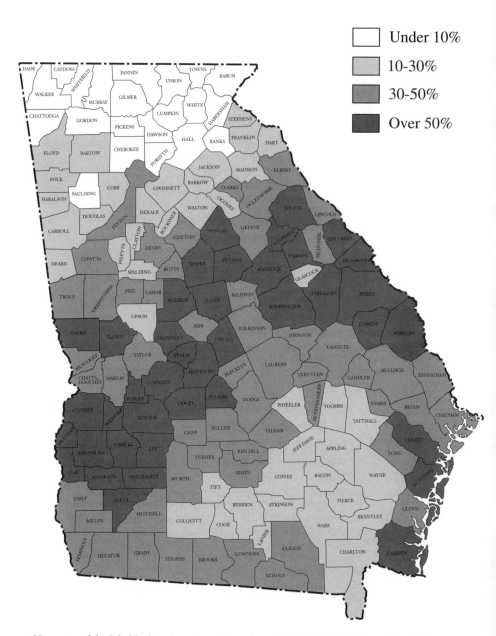

How powerful might black voting strength have been in 1946 if all black Georgians had been registered to vote? This map shows the proportion of black adults among each county's adult population. (From appendix II of H. C. Owen's Master's thesis, "The Rise of Negro Voting in Georgia." Redrawn with permission of H. C. Owen and the American Map Company.)

Beyond
Atlanta

Introduction

W. E. B. Du Bois wrote of Georgia at the start of the century that in many respects, "the Negro problems have seemed to be centered in this state." No doubt this claim is applicable to many states, but to Du Bois it was particularly evident because he lived and worked in Atlanta, as progressive a city as one could find in the South, but a day's journey by train took him to Albany, in the heart of the rural black belt.[1]

Unwittingly, Du Bois highlighted the cities that were to become Georgia's two most well-known (and well-documented) scenes of civil rights activity. Atlanta, the "city too busy to hate," was the southern base for the Student Nonviolent Coordinating Committee (SNCC) and the Southern Christian Leadership Conference (SCLC) and home to one of the South's first black mayors. By contrast, Albany, in Dougherty County, had a reputation for intransigent white supremacy. During 1961–62, Albany was the scene of the major setback for Martin Luther King Jr. and the base for SNCC's Southwest Georgia Project, the intended twin of the Mississippi Project. But between these two extremes Georgia witnessed a wide range of local protests showing in high relief the diversity of the southern civil rights struggle.

This book traces the struggle by black Georgians for racial equality from the pre–World War II era of unfettered, often violent, white supremacy to the modern period of federally guaranteed racial integration first welcomed officially into Georgia by Governor Jimmy Carter in 1971. The history of protests across Georgia confirms that the story at the local level was very different from the national one. Robert Norrell wrote in 1985 that "each community now has a story to tell about the movement, and only when many of those stories are told will the South's great social upheaval be understood."[2] Certainly in Georgia, the movements in Atlanta and Albany during the 1960s were only one part of a far wider picture.

It was not simply that local movements were shaped primarily by local people, or that they acted as a microcosm of the whole, but that the struggle for black equality was played out differently in each locality. After interviewing almost two hundred activists throughout Georgia, I was struck by the differing perceptions of the salient racial issues, not to mention the diverse nature and outcome of local movements. The contrast between black activism in rural and urban areas was especially striking. But even within communities, the efforts to effect racial change took different forms. In Atlanta, the strategies and aspirations of the traditional leadership differed vastly from the attempts to raise the standard of living and expunge exploitative landlords in the poorer areas of Atlanta's Vine City.

Local and state studies have conclusively shown that the classic paradigm of a civil rights movement orchestrated by Martin Luther King and other high-profile leaders reflects contemporary media headlines rather than the reality of black activism in southern communities.[3] In Atlanta King was urged to keep out of local protest by some black community leaders, including his father. One survey in rural Georgia during the mid-1960s showed that some black teenagers had not even heard of Martin Luther King.

Community studies have also pointed out that black activists were influential long before the so-called King years of civil rights protest. Adam Fairclough concluded that in Louisiana black activism in the generation before King was "more than a prelude to the drama proper; it was the first act of a two-act play."[4] The history of the Georgia movement reinforces this view. Rev. Ralph Mark Gilbert is barely mentioned in the history books, but during the early 1990s he was still remembered admiringly by some veterans of Georgia protest as the "preacher" and the "dramatist" who led a movement some fifty years previously. But if there was a first act of protest before the King years, there was also a third act afterward. In Georgia's major towns and cities, protest after the federal acts of 1964–65 was not simply a mopping-up exercise. The removal of legal segregation raised new questions about the meaning of racial equality at the local level. In many smaller communities, organized challenges to white supremacy occurred only after Lyndon Johnson had signed the Civil Rights Bill.

When one views the civil rights movement in a longer-term perspective across the entire state, it is clear that the struggle for racial equality does not follow one normative pattern. For example, integration, one of the shibboleths of the modern civil rights movement, was not always the primary goal of black activists in Georgia. Lonnie King led the student demonstrations against segregated lunch counters in

Atlanta in 1960. Just over a decade later, he engineered a settlement in Atlanta's educational system that provided for improved funding and increased black control but left the majority of black children in segregated schools. For King, it was time to "get out of court and move on to the more important issue of educating kids."[5]

Similarly, nonviolent direct action, the classic tactic of mass protests, was one tactic among many used by black Georgians. Registering to vote, casting a ballot, lobbying, making legal challenges, applying economic pressure, staying away from school, and, at times, undertaking violent action were other overt strategies that were employed. Indeed, the very idea of successful protest covered a wide range of perspectives. Charles Sherrod, the leader of the Southwest Georgia Project, argued that "our criterion for success is not how many people we register, but how many people we can get to begin initiating decisions solely on the basis of their personal opinion." For Sherrod, civil rights activism was "a psychological battle for the minds of the enslaved."[6]

Of course, a concentration on local initiatives at the expense of the national picture also distorts the history of civil rights protest.[7] Grassroots protest was influenced by national organizations and headline-grabbing confrontations. During the early 1960s, the template of nonviolent direct action campaigns was copied and adapted by activists in communities throughout Georgia. As James Brown, the state National Association for the Advancement of Colored People (NAACP) youth secretary, told a mass meeting in Savannah in November 1960, Georgia's youths "could not see the struggle for freedom without participating themselves."[8]

But even during the classic years of mass protest, black activists in Georgia's rural black belt and city slums were involved in markedly different freedom struggles. The history of black protest in Georgia provides a reminder, too, that the race issue was not simply a battle royal of nonviolent black activists against southern crackers. It involved complex interactions between black and white Georgians, with numerous dissenters on both sides. One of the central features of the black protest in Atlanta was the struggle for leadership among different sections of Atlanta's black community. Across the state, black activism was not simply about racial confrontation but often focused on the development of black community institutions.

Taken as a whole, the history of community protest in Georgia highlights several key themes. The NAACP, which is receiving increasing scholarly attention, was the dominant protest organization in the state. The NAACP's legal efforts not only provided the background for direct action protest, but local branches and at times the state chapter spearheaded black activism throughout the period. In both urban and rural Georgia, women played crucial, albeit often unheralded, roles. While college students spearheaded the leading direct action movements of the 1960s, high school students were responsible for the numerous school boycotts in smaller communities. Across the state, the Masons, unions, neighborhood clubs, black-controlled media, and businesses rivaled the church as the crucial building blocks of the nascent civil rights movement.

The history of black activism during the 1940s underscores the impact of the war, especially in the behavior of soldiers based in Georgia and veterans returning to the state. After the "King years," the race issue was increasingly intertwined with the struggle against poverty and the more widespread issues of education and employment. Throughout the period, the history of protest in Georgia emphasizes the paramount importance of local contexts in determining the nature and outcome of local protests.[9]

A statewide study has a twofold purpose, however, distinct not just from the national picture but from the local one as well. A state is a helpful canvas on which to paint local detail, bridging the gap between overgeneralization and emphasis on localism. At the same time, studying the entire state forces the historian to consider the faltering or unsuccessful struggles across Georgia's 159 counties and investigate why often there was little obvious protest activity at all. Thus the statewide survey provides a narrative of one of the more remarkable social movements in the history of the United States. Certainly many of the grassroots activists in Georgia believed that their efforts were part of a broader social movement. For example, on the eve of World War II, Josephine Wilkins, a board member of the Southern Conference on Human Welfare's Committee on Georgia, urged fellow activists to think about the wider significance of their work: "The little stage on which we are performing is Georgia. Well what of it? Some would say it is just one of the 48 other states. But isn't it more than that? Isn't it recognized that Georgia is the seat of the southern situation? And the South the key to the national solution? And when we go on to think of the place that the United States holds in the family of nations—is it far-fetched to conclude that we Georgians play an important role? I think not."[10]

Recent statewide studies of civil rights protests have shown the advantages of trying to relate local detail in a more general synthesis.[11] It would be an overstatement to claim that the story of the civil rights movement in Georgia parallels the movement as a whole, for each state has a different story to tell. Taken together, though, the histories of the individual southern states should provide one way to gain an overview of the national civil rights movement that takes full account of the perspectives of both the national leaders and the local activists.

But the danger of a state study is that it produces a multiplicity of micro-histories and a proliferation of detail. It begs the question whether there is a distinctive state pattern, and if so, what it adds to our understanding of the movement. In Georgia, it was not a distinctive state culture but the state political structure that bound together local protests, especially in the years before the direct action mass movement. As a result, Georgia had a distinctive civil rights history during these years, one characterized by an unprecedented rise in state voter registration based on highly developed local movements in Georgia's leading cities.

No distinctive cultural thread set Georgia apart from other southern states. While Mississippi may have been "the most Southern place on earth" and Louisiana had its creole influence, Georgia was characterized, if anything, by its diversity. A *New York Times* reporter, Claude Sitton, who covered much civil rights activity during the 1960s, reflected "that there were many Georgias," and as a result, "there were many Georgia civil rights movements." [12]

Atlanta had its own unique style, in stark contrast to most other areas in the state (not to say the South). But it was not simply a case of an Atlanta-rural cleavage in Georgia because many of the cities and rural regions also differed markedly from each other. Savannah had its own style; one commentator observed in 1960 that "Savannah society is traditionally self-contained and aloof from the rest of Johnny-come-lately Georgia, nodding coolly to Atlanta . . . but bowing only to London and Florence." [13] Albany and Columbus followed the general pattern of black-belt towns; Athens was a university town; and coastal Brunswick and Rome in the northern mountains were historically more moderate. The rural areas contained two distinct areas of majority black population, the southern black belt and the coastal counties, while the proportion of black Georgians decreased markedly toward the northern mountains.

As Sitton has pointed out, there were many civil rights experiences in Georgia. Atlanta had a story of its own, and David Garrow has described it as "the centerpiece for the southern black freedom struggle of the 1950s and 1960s." [14] But though Atlanta was Georgia's leading city, Savannah was, in many ways, the leading city of protest. Some urban movements, such as those in Macon, Savannah, and Atlanta, were very active and some, especially those in Rome, Savannah, Macon, and Brunswick, were particularly effective. In the rural black belt, the outright intimidation experienced by SNCC workers was different from the more manipulative behavior of local sheriffs in Georgia's coastal counties so clearly depicted by Melissa Fay Greene in *Praying for Sheetrock.* Across the state, protests were on a different time scale, relied on different participants and networks, and often had differing tactics and goals.

When taken in aggregate, therefore, there was no all-pervasive Georgian pattern during the years of mass direct action protest. Each community may have had its own story to tell, but the state as a whole did not. From the 1960s onward, local movements in Georgia were not particularly linked either. Protesters in middle Georgia joked ruefully that the civil rights movement stopped in Perry, one hundred miles to the south of Atlanta. Meanwhile, Savannahians attested to their independence from Atlanta as a point of pride.[15] In the black belt, SNCC workers never intended to extend their project beyond the fifteen counties of southwest Georgia and felt ignored by the Atlanta office.[16] The tumult in Albany served as a warning rather than a prototype both for agitators and for city officials in other cities in Georgia.

Of course, there were numerous connections between local protests within the state. It was Atlanta students and advisers who precipitated the integration of the University of Georgia in Athens. Lawyers C. B. King and Donald Hollowell handled many Georgia civil rights cases after 1955, and Frances Pauley, the head of the Georgia League of Women Voters, was also widely involved. The state conference of the NAACP sought to initiate action in several localities, especially under the leadership of Robert Flanagan during the 1970s.[17] The state Baptist Union, Georgia Masons, and numerous informal state networks all played important roles at times. But overall there was no equivalent of the church network in Alabama, let alone a Mississippi summer.

After *Brown* and Montgomery the interplay between local protests and broader changes was not confined to the state but extended across the South. Southwest Georgia Project workers traveled to Mississippi and Selma. The Albany movement was triggered by the Freedom Riders, while students in Rome, Macon, and other towns reflected later that they drew their inspiration from Greensboro and Montgomery rather than Savannah and Atlanta. During the 1970s and 1980s, local movements involved in voting registration, economic uplift programs, and legal challenges sought help from out-of-state organizations such as the Voter Education Project (VEP), financial foundations, and the American Civil Liberties Union (ACLU).

What is abundantly clear is that there is no seamless narrative for Georgia during and after the so-called King years. The movements and developments in Atlanta and Savannah (and to a lesser extent Macon) were often out of step with those in the rest of the state. And while it is interesting to contrast the story in southwest Georgia with that of Atlanta, it is also instructive to compare the Southwest Georgia Project with its twin in Mississippi and to compare Atlanta with other leading industrial or liberal cities. In similar vein, Savannah invites comparison with Charleston and the coastal counties with similar ones in South Carolina.

But if there was no cohesive Georgia culture, the importance and distinctiveness of Georgia's political structure, particularly until the end of the 1950s, does make the state framework in this case an apposite context in which to place local protests. This was a period, of course, before *Brown,* Little Rock, and the Civil Rights Acts of 1964–65, when the enforcement of segregation was dependent on action at the state level and the attitude of the governor. Georgia's county-unit voting system, which gave disproportionate power to rural areas, gave the state a particularly distinctive political framework. V. O. Key rightly described Georgia politics as the "rule of the rustics," never more so than during the years 1933–37 and 1941–43, when Eugene Talmadge, the "last of the southern demagogues," was governor.[18] The county-unit system ensured that in the state's growing rural-urban political cleavage, Georgia's major cities, which were the strongholds of civil rights activism, remained marginalized.

While Georgia had a distinct political structure, the state also witnessed a vigorous black voter registration campaign out of step with the pace of change in the rest of the South. The registration figures speak for themselves. While Mississippi had 5,000 registered black voters and Louisiana had 7,000 by 1946, nearly 125,000 black Georgians were registered to vote, comfortably the highest number of any southern state.[19] Behind these figures was a coalition of local movements seeking to effect change within both their respective localities and the state as a whole.

Changes in the South and political changes within the state provided a window of opportunity for this new phase of black protest. What set Georgia apart was the existence of unusually developed urban movements, preeminently in Savannah and Atlanta, that had already forced changes in racial mores in their respective localities. And in the context of 1940s Georgia, these local movements were forced by the strength of state authority and rural political domination to be linked into the rest of the state and laid the platform for a statewide challenge to the Talmadge regime.

Largely because of the registration of black voters, the "nigra issue" dominated Georgia politics in the gubernatorial elections of 1946 and 1948. The eventual victory by ardent white supremacist politicians precipitated a violent backlash against black activists across the state. In response, black Georgians sought to create a single statewide organization. In the event, the severity of the supremacist backlash proscribed the continuation of such an overt challenge to Jim Crow.[20] But if heightened supremacist violence was particularly prevalent in Georgia during the end of the 1940s, it was a pattern common to southern states during the 1950s.

By the time of the upsurge of direct action protest during the 1960s, local protests in Georgia were stimulated by broader influences such as the high profile of Martin Luther King Jr. and highly publicized set-piece confrontations across the South. The final removal of the county-unit system by 1962 and the assertion of federal influence after the Little Rock crisis and the Civil Rights Act made the state political framework less significant for local movements.

Nevertheless, the state context remained significant if less distinctive. In the wake of the *Brown* decision, Georgia did not follow the pattern of massive resistance. The prospect of Atlanta's schools integrating in 1961 while Georgia's statutes ruled that any integration prohibited funding for the state school system threatened public schools across Georgia. Both the Sibley Commission, set up by Governor S. Ernest Vandiver to investigate public opinion, and the Help Our Public Education (HOPE) campaign, which successfully kept the schools open, were statewide affairs.[21] The ACLU, VEP, and NAACP organized their activities on a state-by-state basis. But in general, civil rights struggles remained in the locality, from the issues of affirmative action and control of education in Atlanta to those of redistricting and poverty in rural Georgia.

Overall, the movement in Georgia highlights the full diversity and complexity of the struggle for racial equality. It reaffirms the significance of Atlanta as a center-piece city for southern protest and highlights the vigor of black activism in Savannah. But before the King years in particular, the dominance of state politics and the idiosyncrasy of Georgia's county-unit voting system tied the movements in Atlanta and Savannah to the rest of the state. The history of Georgia's protest demonstrates that during these years, the state perspective is not merely a midpoint between the local and national ones but that it can be the only one that provides a real understanding of events.

1

First
Challenges
to Jim Crow
after 1940

The "greatest film ever made" premiered to rapturous acclaim in Atlanta on 1 December 1939. At Loew's Grand Theatre, costars Clark Gable and Vivien Leigh mingled with over two thousand of Georgia's white glitterati, including Mayor William B. Hartsfield, Governor Eurith Rivers, and former governor Eugene Talmadge. For those fortunate enough to acquire a ten-dollar ticket, *Gone with the Wind* rekindled memories of a long-lost antebellum world of plantation life and the unhindered pursuit of the southern way. For black Georgians, however, the southern mores of white supremacy were still very much in existence, and for some blacks the film's positive publicity countered their attempts to expose the cruel realities of life under Jim Crow. In his 1940 Emancipation Day address, leading Atlanta insurance broker and NAACP branch president T. M. Alexander lambasted that "recent premiere when we went mad with the wind and all that was accomplished was torn down."[1]

NAACP officials in New York attacked the euphoria surrounding the film by asking, "Has slavery gone with the wind in Georgia?" Its *Crisis* magazine high-

lighted the ironic timing of the screening of *Gone with the Wind* in the same month
that a young Georgia black man was tried in federal court on the charge of fleeing
peonage. Robert Parker, a descendant from a slave family, had twice tried to leave
his landlord's farm in central Georgia during 1939. On each occasion his landlord
brought him back forcibly. Initially he was punished with thirty to fifty strokes of a
plowline. The second time, his punishment was so severe that the attending physi-
cian reported that Parker was in a "horrible condition." "The only difference between the two systems" of peonage and slavery, wrote the reporter, "is that in *Gone
with the Wind* days the Negro was bound to the landlord by a legalized property
system, while today it is the simple device of being in debt that binds him to the
soil." The first black newspaper in Atlanta, the *Daily World,* reported in 1940 that in
Georgia "there are more Negroes held by these debt slavers than were actually
owned as slaves before the War between the states. The method is the only thing
which has changed."[2] In a manner that became a hallmark of Atlanta's civil rights
protest during the ensuing decades, the city's black leadership was bitterly divided
in its response to *Gone with the Wind.* During the 1930s, Rev. Martin Luther King Sr.
had gained preeminence among Atlanta's black pastors by reinvigorating Ebenezer
Baptist Church on Auburn Avenue. Although an outspoken critic of segregation,
King had attended the premiere to watch his choir perform four spirituals. At a
meeting of the Atlanta Baptist Ministers' Union the following week, fellow ministers
formally censured King's behavior. Rev. William Holmes Borders, King's rapidly
ascending rival and pastor of neighboring Wheat Street Baptist Church, denounced
King's participation at an event that was otherwise segregated and promoted the sins
of dancing and drinking. Other ministers expressed anger at the spectacle of choir
members performing while dressed in aprons and "damn-bannas." Meanwhile, King
and T. M. Alexander engaged in a public slanging match in the lobby of a black-
owned Auburn Avenue bank, ending with Alexander telling King to "take your
business and go to hell."[3] In fact, such internecine struggle had little impact outside
Atlanta's black leadership, who remained publicly united in their opposition to
continued white supremacy in Georgia.

Of course, not all of Georgia's 159 counties were home to plantations reminiscent
of Scarlett O'Hara's beloved Tara. History and topography dictated that the southern cotton belt cut a swath across central and southwest Georgia on the lower
piedmont. Here, in 1940, the prevalence of large-scale plantations, although declin-
ing, meant that blacks formed the majority in nearly a third of Georgia's counties.[4]
The size and concentration of plantations gradually decreased away from this so-

called black belt. Further inland, the upper piedmont gave way to the mountainous north, where traditionally subsistence agriculture and small-scale mining predominated and black Georgians formed a very small minority. To the southeast, the Atlantic coastal plain stretched as far as the six coastal counties and the sea islands, home to descendants of the self-sufficient Gullah people whose tuneful language still remained a curious mix of English and native African tongues. By 1940 black Georgians constituted one-third of Georgia's population.[5]

These regions were by no means homogenous. In the countryside the majority of black Georgians were renters or laborers. Six percent were independent landowners, although black farmers owned on average less than a fifth of the amount of land held by their white counterparts. By 1940 most counties had a town, and a third of Georgia's one million blacks lived in towns of over five thousand people. Atlanta was rapidly emerging as the unofficial capital of the South, with ties to the North closer than those of almost any other southern city. Coastal Savannah, as a *New York Times* reporter concluded, had "always seen itself as a semi-autonomous republic in relation to the rest of the state." While most urban blacks were classified in census reports as unskilled laborers, the larger cities also included small groups who were classified as professional workers, particularly funeral directors, insurance agents, and federal employees.[6]

In the rural areas, too, life varied even within counties. During a field trip in 1940, state Extension Service official Z. T. Hubert was "struck by the general appearance of the men as to size, show of intelligence and sense of cooperation" in the village of Sand Hill, Long County, one of the many exclusively black settlements in the state and the South. Through the efforts of one man, Henry Porter, agricultural methods were advanced, and a school with a lunch kitchen was under construction. But this was "so different from the . . . other localities in this low county district," Hubert continued. In a neighboring black settlement he "could not find one home with a garden, and no attempt at home ownership. School was taught in an old abandoned church building."[7]

Despite these local variations, each region had its own distinctive character that would later shape the struggle for black civil rights in Georgia. "The very expression, 'South Georgia,'" suggested the historian Jerah Johnson, for example, "often connotes cultural particularities of the region." But in 1940, both cultural and especially political ties meant that each county, however diverse, faced inward toward the state capital in Atlanta. And for all black Georgians in each region of the state, whether in peonage, independent farmer, or urban worker, the common denominator was Jim Crow, buttressed by violence. "Negroes born in Georgia," Malcolm X reflected later, "had to be strong just to survive."[8]

In his study of black Georgia in the early twentieth century, John Dittmer concluded that "if there was such a thing as a typical lynching it took place in a rural south Georgia county during the summer." But the records of the NAACP reveal that lynchings could and did occur at any location across the state, both in towns and the countryside, and more often in Georgia than in any other state except Mississippi. Generally the pretext for a murder without trial was the threat of miscegenation. The assistant police chief in Macon, Georgia's third largest city, even dressed up as a woman in an attempt to discover any sexual miscreants. On one occasion this led to the fatal shooting in the back of one black man who reacted violently on discovering the ruse. More often than not, lynchings followed unsubstantiated rumor. In May 1940, for example, a black man and white woman were seen together in the woods outside Social Circle to the east of Atlanta. The Ku Klux Klan sought reprisal by lynching two black men entirely unconnected with the incident, one of whom was a pioneer resident of the community.[9]

Lynchings, however, represented only the most extreme form of violent white supremacy that was ubiquitous across the state. Any regional variation in racial mores lay within this context. The southern Georgia plantation black belt, including the counties nicknamed "Terrible Terrell" and "Bad Baker," earned notoriety for singularly oppressive race relations. Baker County's sheriff Claude Screws conducted a campaign of terror renowned even in Georgia for its racial barbarity. The story of Screws's treatment of Bobby Hall in 1948 was still told a generation later. Hall, a local black mechanic, resisted arrest for allegedly stealing an engine gasket. After beating Hall, Screws tied him to the back of a car and dragged him around the county seat before beating him again and pouring acid on his face. Less than a decade later, Screws was elected to the state senate.[10]

In contrast, the northern Georgia mountain region around Rome had a reputation for more tolerant race relations. Yet in 1940, Atlanta's black newspaper the *Daily World* reported the first racial incident "in this otherwise peaceful community [of Rome]" in years. A tenant, John Turner, along with his son, was shot by a white mob merely for being a "hardworking farmer who had amassed some degree of success from the sweat of his brow." Such incidents, the newspaper argued, forced people into the relatively safer haven of towns.[11]

The towns did provide large black neighborhoods often free from daily white interference. John Calhoun, an Atlanta black community leader and businessman, described his city in the 1940s as an "oasis in Georgia. When you went outside the city limits of Atlanta you were in danger." Nevertheless, the Klan dominated Georgia's city police forces, and hate organizations were concentrated in urban areas. Consequently, the major difference between the towns and the countryside was that urban racial violence was more often indiscriminate and generally limited to boundaries of racial contact, particularly on buses or on streets dividing racial neighborhoods.[12]

Police brutality was so familiar that only a particularly gruesome or unusual offense made the front pages of the black press. The *Pittsburgh Courier*'s headline story for June 1940 combined both. "When the hot iron came off my arm," recalled Quinter South, a sixteen-year-old Atlantan (arrested for burglary), "the skin came off with it. Then [the policeman] poked the hot iron into my neck and against my lips. I didn't want to get burned up any more, so I told him I was the one who broke into the gym." The twist came when the white Atlanta press and a federal grand jury briefly took up the case. But the real tragedy of such an incident, wrote one Atlanta reporter, was that it represented the "same old story" of "police brutality among Negroes and various incidents of brazen insults and attitudes." The reporter felt that the deeper problem was that even in the capital city there seemed no end in sight. "I am certain vengeance will be meted out to the offender by the Holy One," he continued. "But isn't there some way that we can be spared such gross impositions?"[13]

Violence by a minority reflected an entrenched white supremacist mind-set throughout Georgia. Travelers' diaries and scientific surveys showed that while justification for segregation varied from person to person, the vast majority of even peaceably minded white Georgians believed in the innate inferiority of blacks. A city carpenter was typical of those interviewed by Fisk University sociologist C. S. Johnson, who explained that "you know the old saying, 'he'll show the nigger in him?' It can be proved." Religious groups were no exception. A rabbi in Macon blamed white hostility on body odor. "If a Negro has been that way fifteen minutes before I can tell it." And at a revival meeting in 1935 for both races, the famous evangelist Gypsy Smith Sr. told the black Atlantans in the gallery that they could respond to the gospel message and come downstairs only "after other Christians and sinners had been served."[14]

The many legal aspects of Jim Crow reinforced such attitudes. Initially these laws ensured the discriminatory separation of the races after Reconstruction. "During the first two decades of the twentieth century," Dittmer concluded, "segregation in

Georgia reached a new plateau: the color line gave way to a color wall, thick, high, almost impenetrable." Nearly all towns had passed municipal ordinances requiring separation in restaurants and public amenities, and in many cities barbers had to choose whether to serve black or white customers. Even Atlanta, despite its image as a New South leader, was as segregated as any city in Georgia. Black Atlantans had to leave by the back door of the rail terminal, black criminals were transported in separate prison vehicles, and the Carnegie Public Library opened in 1902 to white patrons only.[15]

A proliferation of new legislation during the decade after the Great Depression paralleled the collapse of the plantation system, reflecting the need to introduce new forms of racial control in an urbanizing society. After 1940, for example, black Georgians faced a curfew in the major cities, and bus conductors throughout the state were empowered to move the compulsory racial dividing line on municipal buses if white passengers were forced to stand.[16] During the 1940s, Atlanta's parks were segregated and the city codified the custom of segregated theaters and halls. A new city ordinance also specified that white taxi drivers could carry only white passengers and "colored drivers" were restricted to carrying "colored passengers." In Albany after 1945, black and white theatergoers had to buy tickets at separate booths. By 1945, black and white witnesses used different Bibles for court swearings.[17]

Black and white Georgians viewed white supremacy from different perspectives. A comprehensive questionnaire by researchers in Georgia's Fort Valley region during the 1940s revealed that whites believed the most important benefits of Jim Crow were protection from intermarriage, social mixing, and equal representation in court. Blacks, by contrast, saw Jim Crow primarily as a barrier to improved employment, equal justice, and the freedom to manage their own affairs; to them, the issue of social contact was far less important. After interviewing black Georgians for several months, C. S. Johnson came to the same conclusion. "The two universally tabooed practices are intermarriage and interdependency," he wrote, but for black Georgians it was "not so much segregation that was resented as economic suppression and insults."[18]

Economic indexes demonstrated the pernicious effects of white supremacy from the black perspective. In the cities the rate of black unemployment was on average double that for the white working population.[19] The type of job opportunities available to black Georgians was also inferior. Although carpentry and blacksmithing had been the most important trades for freed blacks after Reconstruction, by 1940 only one-fifth of Georgia's carpenters and one-sixth of Georgia's blacksmiths were black.[20] Even black and white Georgians ostensibly employed in the same trade received differential pay. For example, the average annual salary for black teachers was less than half the average salary for white teachers. Similarly, the average white-owned farm dwelling was worth $851 in Georgia in 1940, compared with $366 for black-owned farms. Overall, black Georgians earned an average salary of $403 in 1939–40, less than half the $901 average for white Georgians and the fourth lowest state average for black southerners.[21]

Economic discrimination was mirrored by inequality in education and health. The state allocated less than $10 per head for each black pupil, the lowest of any southern state, in contrast to over $40 for each white child. In practice, the fraudulent spending of such grants by county authorities further broadened the divide.[22] The State Agricultural and Industrial Board reported in 1945 that 95 percent of black schools were unfit for use and the majority were one-teacher establishments. By 1940, black pupils completed a mere four grades of schooling on average, less than half that of their white counterparts, and a lower proportion of black than white children attended school. The infant mortality rate of sixty-seven per thousand for black Georgians was almost double that of thirty-nine per thousand for white Georgians in 1940. Black Georgians were three times more likely to die from influenza or pneumonia than their white counterparts.[23]

Statistical indexes alone, however, do not show the personal impact of such discrimination. In 1941, the American Council on Education commissioned a study of black youth in eight counties across the South, including Georgia's Greene County, a typical decadent plantation county located in the east of the state. It was a county in which "the traditions of the plantation system have collapsed with nothing to replace it," leaving a median black income of $329, the lowest of all the counties studied. The report made stark reading. "I'd like to have a house that don't leak, a house with no leaks in it anywhere," said one teenager. "It must be nice to have enough to eat every day." Schooling was even worse. Most black parents in Greene County faced extreme economic hardship, and the statement of one sixteen-year-old was typical: "My father wished he could let me go but I had to help on the farm." As a result, children attending school reached only the fifth grade on average. Diet and schooling had a shocking effect on IQ test scores, with both male and female adults averaging lower than eighty points. The economic consequences of such a start in life were clear even to the youth. Only 2.2 percent of girls wanted to go into domestic service, yet over 15 percent expected they would have to. Actually, nearly 70 percent of women who did not work on farms were domestics.[24]

The investigators in Greene County were more alarmed about the psychological effects of segregation. The fear of being attacked by white neighbors because of being successful underwrote farmer Harvey Goodson's philosophy to "go on getting what you can slow and be quiet about it." Greene County's black youth also had low self-esteem. Teenagers believed that their attractiveness was dependent on the lightness of their skin color. One girl remembered an incident when "this man was brighter [in color] than my uncle and he was making fun of my uncle's color. Uncle told him to leave him alone or there'd be trouble," and later the uncle killed him.[25]

While violence and economic inequality consolidated white supremacy, the exclusion of black Georgians from politics removed any hope of effecting change. As Clarence Bacote, a university lecturer and leading Atlanta black political activist, remembered, "Politics? There wasn't any in Georgia before 1946." For Bacote, these years were the "dark ages as far as Negro political participation" was concerned.[26] Legal requirements for registration, notably the need to pay a poll tax and to have a character deemed suitable for voting, excluded most black Georgians. Primarily, though, the ambiguity of the voting requirements gave local white officials the power to choose who could register. "I can keep the president of the United States from registering in Macon if I want to," the Bibb County tax collector told an interviewer in 1939. He would ask any black inquirer about the Supreme Court jurisdiction clause of the Constitution (Article III). "God himself couldn't understand that. I myself is the judge." If "in practice a Negro tried to vote in a Macon primary, he would be asked what in hell he wanted."[27]

In 1940, a white Georgia editor told the story of a young black Georgian who had attended school long enough to become interested in government:

> He reaches twenty-one and decides to register to vote. He goes to the awesome courthouse, where the tribunals grind away most of the time they are not in session on cases against Negroes. He's a little ill at ease....
>
> "What do you want boy?" someone on the inside of the tax collector's office asks.
>
> "I just want to register so I can vote."
>
> Then he gets the works. Since he is only twenty-one, he doesn't have to pay poll tax. He says he has no criminal record—so far so good. But wait.
>
> "Do you understand the duties and obligations of citizenship under a republican form of government?" he hears.
>
> "I don't know exactly...."

"Well do you own forty acres of land or $500 worth of property?"
"No sir."
And if that isn't enough to discourage the applicant, he gets another test.
The man behind the counter is the sole judge of his success or failure.
"You can't qualify," he is told.

A black Harvard graduate failed a Georgia test.[28]

The cornerstone of Georgia's white political supremacy was the Democratic Party's white primary.[29] Even where blacks were registered, particularly in the larger cities, they were legally restricted to voting only in the general elections or in special elections such as local bond issues. In a state that was the exclusive domain of the Democratic Party, being excluded from the primary was tantamount to being denied the franchise. The Republican Party in Georgia, which had been controlled by blacks until the presidency of Herbert Hoover, was at one time very strong in national affairs. But the spirit of "lily-whiteism" had driven out black involvement, and the party was so often torn by factional strife that it rarely offered candidates in local elections. By the end of 1937, according to one Republican leader interviewed by black political scientist Ralph Bunche, the Republican Party in Georgia was as "dead as a doornail."[30]

The county-unit system of counting votes, a method unique to Georgia, further entrenched a particularly rural form of white supremacy, giving rise to what V. O. Key described as "the rule of the rustics."[31] Since 1917, state law had mandated that the total popular vote be ignored, and that votes in primary elections be tabulated on a county-by-county basis. Each county received twice as many unit votes as it had representatives in the lower house of the legislature. The 8 most populous counties received six unit votes and thus three representatives each, the next 30 counties had four unit votes each, and the remaining 121 counties each received two unit votes. In practice this meant that the distribution of unit votes bore only the faintest resemblance to the distribution of the population, especially because the apportionment system had not been altered since its introduction in 1868. Thus the sparsely populated rural counties of Seminole, Decatur, and Colquitt, home to fewer than ten thousand Georgians, had as much representation as Fulton County in Atlanta, which had a population of over two hundred thousand people.[32]

The county-unit system ensured that in the state's growing rural-urban political cleavage, Georgia's major cities, which were the strongholds of civil rights activism, remained marginalized. At the same time, the county-unit system engendered statewide political machines and campaigns characterized by their backwoods appeal. In his survey of Georgia politics, Charles Pyles observed that "more than in any other southern state the rural elements dominated state politics for two decades" before 1948 and that it was the "county-unit system which largely accounts for the accentuation of rural-urban differences in Georgia." Ralph McGill, editor of the *Atlanta Constitution,* asserted that forty counties in Georgia were dominated by a courthouse ring and could be bought before any election. Each of these was a rural two-unit county.[33] Ralph Bunche concluded more succinctly that "Georgia's politics is largely a matter of factions and a great deal of debauchery." [34]

Such conditions were most obvious during the years 1933–37 and 1941–43, when Eugene Talmadge was governor. By keeping a cow on the lawn of the state capitol in Atlanta and refusing to campaign in any settlement that had a streetcar, Talmadge identified himself with the poor white farmer, even while his conservative economic outlook guaranteed him the support of Atlanta's business elite. By placing striking textile workers behind barbed wire in a concentration camp in 1935 and reading *Mein Kampf* to them aloud each afternoon, Talmadge also demonstrated his opinion of any resistance to the Georgia way. Above all, Talmadge's frenzied attacks on the dangers of a "Nigra takeover," and his links with the Ku Klux Klan set the tone for white supremacy across the state. At the famous "grass-roots convention" for southern leaders at Macon in 1936, Talmadge had even assumed sectional leadership as the guardian of white supremacy in the South by forming the "Southern Committee to Uphold the Constitution." [35]

By 1941, Talmadge and his faction came to personify Georgia's national reputation for demagogic "wool hat" politics, racism, and backwardness. His biographer, William Anderson, observed that "he became typecast for his regressive politics as a backwater southern demagogue, a ranting antique who represented all that had been wrong with traditional southern economics and morality . . . his was the mold from which demagogic stereotypes were made for Central Casting." [36] The northern press lampooned Talmadge as a comical cracker, going from stump to stump dressed in his famous red galluses. Even the *Crisis* joked that "we hope nothing happens to Governor 'Gene Talmadge of Georgia. He is the finest living reason why Negroes should not feel inferior to white people." [37]

For black Georgians, however, the rule of the Talmadges had far more serious consequences. This was a period, of course, before *Brown,* Little Rock, and the Civil Rights Acts of 1964–65, when the enforcement of segregation was dependent on action at the state level and the attitude of the governor. In Georgia, Talmadge had established black voting as the major issue in political campaigns, not so much because it posed a serious threat but because it assured him the mantle of protector of white Georgia. The racist hysteria gave carte blanche to violent racial acts. Talmadge's implacable opposition to black voting, the changing social mores of the cities, and out-of-state organizations seemed to proscribe any chance that Georgia blacks might effect change.

The race issue impinged on numerous areas of state politics. In June 1941, Talmadge reacted furiously to the appointment of Iowa-born Walter D. Cocking as dean of the University of Georgia College of Education. In an attempt to remove "foreign professors trying to destroy the sacred traditions of the South," Talmadge demanded the resignation of three of the regents who had elected Cocking. Talmadge even threatened to cut off money from the University of Georgia because a few Negroes had attended summer school. The reorganized board proceeded to dismiss both Cocking and President Marvin S. Pittman of Georgia Training College. Both these men, as pro-Talmadge regent James Peters explained, had allowed the book *Brown America* to be in the college library at one stage of their careers. According to Peters, the major theme of *Brown America* was to "erase the feelings of superiority of the white man." The obvious conclusion, continued Peters, was that the dismissed presidents "want Negroes to use the same schools, ride in the same trains and sit side by side. . . . It means they want intermarriage, that's what it means."[38] In response to such overt political interference, the Southern Association of Colleges and Secondary Schools removed accreditation from Georgia's ten state-supported white colleges in December 1941.

The "Regents' crisis," with its mix of vitriolic racism and xenophobia toward northerners, exemplified the extent of Talmadge's determination and ability to stifle the "furriners" and to uphold white supremacy. A *New York Times* editorial pointed out that Talmadge's attitude must reflect white opinion, especially that of the countryside, because "Georgia didn't have to have Mr. Talmadge for governor if it didn't care for him." Above all, the Regents' crisis demonstrated unequivocally that black Georgians could expect nothing short of continued racial suppression while Talmadge was governor. Talmadge repeatedly insisted that Jim Crow was to be protected whatever the cost and any black who was unhappy with that should "stay out of Georgia." As the *New York Herald Tribune* concluded, "Citizens of Georgia who have been under the illusion that Georgia is one of the United States must begin to feel rather limited by the special set of ideals their governor has proclaimed for them." [39]

Black Protest before 1940

Yet alongside Georgia's history of Jim Crow lay a remarkable tradition of black resistance, dating back to slavery. A Miss Deveraux of Savannah, for example, secretly taught school lessons to blacks from 1838. Mass boycotts in the same city thwarted the first attempts to introduce racial segregation on the buses in the 1890s, leaving Savannah as one of the last bastions of integrated public transport in the South until 1907. Hancock County in the rural black belt in eastern Georgia was one of many counties to have a reputation for being home to some "crazy niggers," the term referring to any blacks who refused to accept Jim Crow. At the start of the century, one visiting preacher in Talboton in west Georgia backed up his belligerent rhetoric by shooting dead a number of his Klan adversaries.[40]

Georgia's major cities also witnessed some organized protests in the early twentieth century. By the end of World War I, black Georgians had established sixteen branches of the NAACP. In Georgia, most branches sought to highlight cases of racial injustice and lobby city governments for improved amenities. The Savannah NAACP obstructed plans to relocate the city's red-light district to a black residential area, while the Augusta branch sponsored a drive to register black women to vote. Under the leadership of Rev. R. H. Singleton of Big Bethel AME Church and local insurance agent Walter White, who was later to become the president of the national NAACP, the Atlanta branch's membership surged to over two and a half thousand by 1920. In the same year, Atlanta hosted the first southern annual convention of the NAACP. Enthusiasm for Atlanta's NAACP centered on the efforts to vote down two education bond issues that had made no provision for black schools. The third, and successful, bond proposal in 1921 allocated funds to build Booker T. Washington Junior High School for black children. The National Urban League (NUL) also founded branches in Savannah, Atlanta, Augusta, and Albany during the World War I years, although only the Atlanta branch survived the Depression.[41]

Postwar pressure from white Georgians, including a spate of lynchings, curtailed the activities of most NAACP branches. The Thomasville branch in southwest Georgia disbanded in 1920 when local whites threatened to kill the branch president. Even in Atlanta black political protest was largely restricted to individual incidents. After reaching the age of twenty-one, Martin Luther King Sr. tried to register to vote, only to find that the "colored" freight elevator was broken and that he was barred from using the whites-only elevator or stairs. Writing of the black experience in Georgia, Donald Grant concluded that protest after World War I was an "often disheartening struggle." In any case, Grant continued, most protest was restricted to persuasion because "most blacks were generally so conservative that they were considered the despair of radicals, even of liberals." [42]

The dearth of overt protest after World War I, however, did not reflect a passive acceptance of white supremacy by black Georgians. In her study of the United Negro Improvement Association (UNIA) in Georgia, Mary Gambrell Rolinson highlights the largely unknown rise of Garveyism in the state during the 1920s. The Jamaica-born Marcus Garvey, based in Harlem, was renowned for his appeal to disadvantaged blacks in northern cities, emphasizing black pride, economic uplift, and the redemption of Africa. In fact, Garveyism also attracted support in the South after World War I, and there were at least thirty-four UNIA divisions in Georgia by 1926. [43]

Although there were branches in both Savannah and Atlanta, Rolinson noted "Garvey's remarkable penetration of rural Georgia and his popularity with share-croppers." The vast majority of UNIA divisions were in settlements of less than three thousand people. All but two of the branches were in the southernmost third of the state, and there were at least thirteen branches even in southwest Georgia, including two in Baker County. The majority of UNIA leaders identifiable in the 1920 census were tenant farmers. In many cases, UNIA divisions were able to penetrate some of the rural areas of the state that would not tolerate the NAACP, which emphasized integration. Garvey himself met with the Imperial Wizard of the Georgia Klan in 1922 and found common ground regarding his "back to Africa" plan. [44]

The UNIA divisions appear to have been centers of black activism. Much of this activity was focused on supporting the controversial figure of Garvey himself. Local meetings included a reading of Garvey's address from the first page of his newspaper, the *Negro World.* After Garvey was jailed for three months in 1923 for using the mail to mislead potential stock purchasers for his Black Star Steamship Line, the Baxley division held a mass meeting, sent a petition of protest with over two hundred signatures to the federal government, and contributed to the Marcus Garvey Defense Fund. Donations to the fund also came from many counties without UNIA divisions, indicating a wider support for Garveyism. [45]

Garvey's doctrine of black nationalism and separatism gained support in rural

Georgia. As well as writing in support of Garvey himself, correspondents to the *Negro World* from Georgia espoused the cause of "freeing the Motherland" of Africa. During the 1920s, three thousand farmers from Hancock County in the lower piedmont paid $1 each to return to Africa, albeit to a confidence trickster. Fifty-three blacks from Irwin County were more successful and boarded ship, although they had to return after twenty died of fever en route. Garvey's influence in Georgia was to have a longer legacy for black separatism in America as a whole. Elijah Muhammed, the son of a rural pastor and the future founder of the Nation of Islam, lived and worked in Macon during the 1920s.[46] Malcolm Little, later Malcolm X, was the son of an itinerant minister in Taylor County who was murdered for his outspoken propagation of Garveyism.

Garveyism existed only briefly in Georgia, however. The NAACP, which opposed black separatism in general and Garvey's opportunism in particular, prevented the UNIA from gaining a foothold in towns that already contained NAACP branches. Meanwhile, in the countryside, Rolinson concluded, "no doubt many younger Garvey sympathizers moved North to escape debt peonage." After Garvey's reimprisonment for fraud in 1925 and his subsequent deportation to England two years later, the UNIA lost impetus in Georgia.[47]

Although different in tenor from Garveyism, the more durable black organizations during the 1920s and 1930s also focused exclusively on black self-improvement rather than integration. The major churches on Auburn Avenue established the forerunner of insurance schemes, whereby hundreds of members from each congregation would pay an annual subscription both to provide poverty relief and housing and to insure themselves against disaster. The National Youth Administration and the National Urban League jointly sponsored a postwar program to help black youths "become efficient in the trades of the hand," a program that claimed to have trained over fifty thousand young people in Georgia by the end of the 1930s. Masonic lodges grew parallel with industrial development. As early as 1917, over two thousand members of the Society of Odd Fellows attended an address by Walter White. The Atlanta NAACP initially met in the Odd Fellows Building.[48]

During the Depression of the 1930s, the Communist Party temporarily came to prominence, with a vocal attack on racial discrimination in southern justice. In the early Depression years, Communists organized interracial activity, calling for "full racial, political and social equality." The labor historian Michael Honey commented that in Atlanta, as in Birmingham, Communist Party activists "sparked unprecedented interracial working-class activity."[49] Communist protest in Georgia even achieved national attention after the sentencing of Angelo Herndon to twenty years on the chain gang. Herndon was a nineteen-year-old black Communist who came to Atlanta to organize the unemployed during the Depression. Soon afterward, Herndon led a hunger march of a thousand Atlantans. According to the historian Charles Martin, it was "the biggest biracial demonstration in the South in several decades." In response to the march, Atlanta officials approved $6,000 for additional emergency relief. Herndon was subsequently convicted for distributing Communist literature, which the prosecution asserted was intended to incite rebellion and therefore warranted the death penalty under an 1833 law. The historian Taylor Branch commented that the "Herndon sedition case became second only to the Scottsboro rape case as the most sensational and prolonged racial trial of the depression." After numerous appeals, Herndon was eventually released in 1937, but in Georgia and across the South, the Herndon case marked the apogee, rather than the beginning, of Communist protest, as the party never gained more than three thousand black members in America.[50]

The more durable black protest after the Depression received little publicity and came from a cadre of indigenous black leaders in Georgia's major cities. In Savannah, the Young Men's Civic Club, which formed in 1938, was a working-class association that aimed to double black registration, particularly among longshoremen.[51] In Atlanta, such leaders were economically independent and generally prosperous. A. T. Walden, a Democrat activist and Atlanta's first black lawyer, was head of the Atlanta branch of the NAACP when he organized citizenship schools in 1932 for registered black voters. A graduate of Atlanta University, Walden had studied law in Michigan before serving in France during World War I. During the 1930s most black political protest developed outside the auspices of the NAACP. Largely as a rival to Walden, a federal postal employee and Republican activist, John Wesley Dobbs, organized the Atlanta Civic and Political League (ACPL) in 1934. Atlanta's factions did unite in response to city bond proposals and major issues, such as the meeting of over one thousand black Atlantans in 1933 to denounce the discriminatory implementation of the New Deal National Recovery Administration codes.[52]

Although organized protest was largely restricted to Atlanta and Savannah during the 1930s, reports of individual acts of protest abounded even under Talmadge's governorship, particularly in urban areas. One northern visitor told of a white agent selling bedspreads at the home of a "Negro bricklayer." "What's the matter with your hat," asked the bricklayer, "glued to your head?" The agent insisted that he would be fired if the company knew he "took off his hat in a nigger's home." Replied the bricklayer, "Well I'm firing you right now."[53] Many black Georgians recalled later that the segregated buses and streetcars were a regular cause of racial friction.[54] An Atlanta domestic worker, Alice Adams, for example, recalled that "sometimes we'd have arguments, little specks on the bus or the streetcar . . . sometimes we had flare-ups." Occasionally protests against white control took a more violent turn. In August 1940, Alonzo Pierce challenged his boss from Swainsboro Resin Company to a pistol duel when he was forced to work when sick. Both men shot successfully and killed each other.[55]

More often resistance took the form of avoiding the worst excesses of discrimination. Over one-quarter of a million black Georgians left the state between 1940 and 1960. For those who remained, resistance took a variety of subtle forms. In his inaugural presidential address at the all-black Morehouse College in Atlanta in 1940, Benjamin E. Mays discouraged students from using segregated facilities, insisting that "I wouldn't go to a segregated theater to see Jesus Christ himself." His wife, Annie Mays, always signed her name Mrs. Benjamin Mays in downtown Atlanta to force shopkeepers to call her by the courtesy title Mrs. Mays rather than the customary Annie. Martin Luther King Sr. refused to use segregated buses, and black Atlanta lawyer Peyton Allen bought a bicycle to avoid sitting at the back of the bus.[56]

Protest often took the form of mental resistance to segregation because the repercussions of physical resistance could be fatal. After two dangerous incidents while he was sitting in the white sections of public transport, Benjamin E. Mays accepted that he must sit at the back of streetcars but determined that "my body was there but not my mind." Contemporary poetry such as that of Atlanta's Alex Schmidt reflected this mind-set.

> Get back, take as little room as you can,
> Up front is for your betters, they sit tight,
> and spread their arrogance as peacocks fan
> their tails; whose fault that you were not born white?
>
> Unwanted by your kind who let you in,
> Contained, alone, you find your grudged spare place,
> And turn your thoughts maybe upon God's skin,
> Hoping that He like you has a black face.[57]

Robin Kelley has argued that the historiographical concentration on political civil rights protest overlooks the equally important issue of individual personal acts of defiance. For Kelley, the purposeful destruction of one of her employer's shirts by an Atlanta domestic servant should be considered alongside the formation of black protest organizations.[58] Similarly, many individuals may not have registered to vote but challenged white supremacy by refusing to step off a sidewalk, buying a copy of a black newspaper, or wearing a flashy suit.[59] "It is time to reject the artificial divisions between political history and social history," Kelley concluded. "Infrapolitics and organized resistance are not two distinct realms of opposition to be studied separately and then compared; they are the two sides of the same coin that make up the history of working class self-activity."[60]

The experience of Georgia by 1940 confirms much of Kelley's argument. In a period when most organized protest would result in violent retribution and usually no option of organized protest was available, any single act of defiance was an important demonstration of black protest. This social resistance by individuals also represented the desire for black equality that gave rise to organized protest later. The leading role of Benjamin E. Mays in Atlanta during the 1960s, for instance, was presaged by his earlier refusal to accept Jim Crow on the buses. Even before 1940, however, there remained a qualitative difference between the impact of individual defiance and organized protest. In 1938, for example, the ACPL organized enough voters to defeat a proposed $7.5 million bond that was designated for white schools only. The modified bond provided for a third of the money to be spent on black schools.[61] During the same period, a Baker County farmer, John Miller, sought to organize a local NAACP chapter, only to suffer a beating of such severity from local sheriff Claude Screws that he never again dared to question Screws publicly.[62] The bond protest involved far less personal cost than Miller's individual protest, but defeat of the proposed bond forced the issue of black education onto Atlanta's political agenda.

World War II, Operation Dixie, and Urbanization

Both nascent black organization and individual racial incidents were characteristic of early twentieth-century Georgia. Clearly, however, during the early 1940s, only social protest on a widespread scale or political or organized action could shake the solidity of Jim Crow across the state. Building on the tradition of sporadic black defiance, dynamic changes swept across the South after 1940 that heralded the beginning of a concerted drive for racial change in Georgia and the entire South. Accelerated urbanization and industrialization, the southern organizing drive of labor unions, the intrusion of the federal government in southern life, and the growth of white liberal opinion all affected race relations. These changes created a new situation in Georgia in which black groups emerged whose sole raison d'être was to attack white supremacy.

Chief among these forces invading the South was World War II. Georgia received more than one hundred thousand black men and women in military service, who quickly became acquainted with the state's racial mores. In 1941, a black private was found in his uniform, gagged and hands tied, hanging from a tree in the woods near Fort Benning, outside Columbus. An official investigation reported it as suicide.[63] But in common with military personnel across the South and in contrast to civilian Georgians, many black soldiers adamantly refused to accept discrimination.

The black press reported race riots at Camp Gordon, near Augusta, Fort Benning, and bases across the South, but it was the mutiny of black troops at Camp Stewart near Savannah leading to the death of a military policeman that gained national headlines. The *New York Times* concluded that violence in early June 1943 erupted in response to rumors that "colored girls" were being molested. In reality, as a local NAACP investigation had revealed merely a week before, conditions in the camp had been so bad that black soldiers were perpetually on the verge of mutiny. The camp commander was committed to keeping what was officially a U.S. reservation strictly segregated. The inadequate black recreational facilities, including a USO that could hold only a minority of the soldiers at any one time, were accentuated by the proximity of white clubs "equipped with everything for which the heart could wish." Some of the officers were "Georgia crackers, meaning everything that the term implies." But most contentious was the fact that only white soldiers were given accommodations when visiting nearby Savannah, leaving their black counterparts to sleep on the sidewalks. Animosity and fear caused rumors to proliferate, including false stories that black soldiers were dying each month from disease and officer brutality.[64]

Such frequent and determined outbreaks of racial defiance on Georgia soil were unprecedented in the history of the state. The soldiers' militancy often spilled over from the bases into the surrounding cities too. For many local black Georgians, watching soldiers refuse to sit at the back of the bus or habitually scorn the authority of local policemen were the first acts of racial defiance they had seen.[65]

Black residents of Savannah's West Broad Street were able to watch a version of the Camp Stewart mutiny from their own front rooms. Tempers had flared initially after a black soldier intervened in what he considered an unfair arrest of a female bystander at a drunken skirmish. He then vigorously defended himself by seizing the onrushing policeman's baton and, according to witnesses, "beat him to a pulp." The struggle escalated in the evening when, in a quite remarkable city scene, a large detachment of black soldiers, armed with guns mounted on trucks, confronted the full quota of Savannah's riot policemen.[66]

The militancy of the military became further entrenched in Georgia life when soldiers and civilians intermingled. Army friends of Auriel Brewer in Columbus spent a night protecting her father, the local NAACP leader, from the Ku Klux Klan. Soldiers from Fort Benning constituted the overwhelming majority of the Columbus NAACP's two thousand members. In the longer term, the actions of civilians on behalf of the military were even more significant. The Macon NAACP's angry protests over the assault on Private Alpha Josie, which culminated in a full-page advertisement in the local newspaper, marked an outspoken new departure for the local branch. Meanwhile, the Atlanta branch unsuccessfully requested the governor to allow all those in the armed services to vote.[67]

The integration of army militancy into civilian affairs intensified at the end of the war, when draftees returned to everyday life in Georgia. Almost without exception it was black veterans who were responsible for the most dramatic racial incidents on buses that were extensively reported in the black press. Highlighting the frequent, spontaneous battles for space on public transportation, Robin Kelley described buses during the war as moving "theaters in the sense of small war zones." Without the protection of their uniforms, veterans in Georgia risked their lives by defying Jim Crow. In two separate incidents in the spring of 1946, soldiers survived the war only to be shot by conductors in the front of the bus on a journey to their homes.[68]

The United Negro Veterans League channeled this defiance into organized protest. In Atlanta, one thousand veterans reformed ranks to wage a "war on the vote," proclaiming themselves foot soldiers in the campaign to register blacks for the 1946 primary. Often the veterans' methods outpaced those of the traditional black leadership. Martin Luther King Sr. admitted that because the returning veterans were "eager and unafraid" after World War II, "very severe differences of opinion split two generations of black Atlanta." When three hundred members of the women's auxiliary marched on the Atlanta City Hall demanding black policemen, the *Pittsburgh Courier* noted that "responsible Negro citizens did not condone the demonstration" and it was not endorsed by the local NAACP, which had chosen to petition the mayor.[69]

The war years in Georgia mirrored the black experience across the South, where the dominant attitude was summed up by the *Pittsburgh Courier*'s "Double-V" campaign for victory for democracy in Europe and at home. "The fight for democracy on two fronts," wrote Richard Dalfiume, "became the slogan of black America." The slogan "Back the attack on the home front by joining the Atlanta branch NAACP" helped attract a record forty-five hundred members in 1944. Georgia's black press adopted this rhetoric, equating previously commonplace white supremacist violence with the actions of America's avowed racist enemies abroad. "Hitlerism struck nearer home Friday night," the *Atlanta Daily World* reported in May 1940, "when 7 Dekalb County officers swooped down on the humble residence of Walter Preston, leaving a 24 year old son and his 57 year old mother near death with bullet wounds in their backs." One month later, the capitulation of France to the Nazis symbolically shared the headline with the Fulton County Court acquittal on technical grounds of W. F. Sutherland, the policeman responsible for the torture of Quinter South.[70]

The war also influenced white opinion in Georgia. More than three hundred thousand men and women served in the armed forces, mostly away from the Jim Crow South. Few proved so culturally adaptable as one amorous private, who wrote to the *Atlanta Constitution* that even Talmadge's "bigoted, prejudiced" antics would not prevent him bringing back to Georgia "the most wonderful girl in the world," whom he had married in Japan. White veterans took a lead in interracial postwar strikes. The deeper impact on some of those who remained at home, however, was that the war against a racist demagogue abroad challenged the white supremacist mind-set in Georgia. Although he still believed that blacks were ignorant, one writer to the conservative *Macon Telegraph* conceded the moral dilemma of the war: "We are fighting a Jew-baiter in Germany and I don't see how we can be consistent if we support a Negro-baiter in Georgia."[71]

Furthermore, the war years acted as an impetus for the growing number of whites actively seeking political reform, most of whom were concentrated in the cities. Both the Southern Regional Council (SRC) and the League of Women Voters were based in Atlanta, and the Southern Conference on Human Welfare (SCHW) had its Committee for Georgia headquarters there. As an explicitly interracial organization since its founding in 1938, the SCHW directly challenged southern racial mores. The SCHW actively supported the NAACP's legal campaigns for racial justice. Still, the cumulative effect of liberal groups on race relations in Georgia was minimal during the early 1940s. Even Clark Foreman, the chairman of the SCHW and one of the outstanding white activists of the period, felt that he was unable to make any progress, hampered both by the reluctance of Atlanta's white moderates to seek significant racial changes and by the rural domination of politics.[72]

White liberals often pushed less for racial integration than for more general political reform and an end to racial violence. The NAACP, for instance, reacted sharply to the meeting of one hundred southern white liberal leaders in Atlanta in April 1943 that preceded the founding of the Southern Regional Council. Although the resulting "Atlanta statement" on race relations showed "promise" and was "encouraging," the NAACP criticized the conference for ducking the question of the ballot by urging white people of goodwill "to do those things *for* Negroes which the Negroes could do for themselves if they had the ballot." "The policy of guardianship is thus once more enunciated," the *Crisis* concluded, "and it has been demonstrated again and again that guardianship is an unsatisfactory substitute for citizenship." Similarly, the League of Women Voters opposed the poll tax but not the white primary. Even the *Atlanta Constitution*'s famous liberal editor, Ralph McGill, insisted in 1942 that "anyone with an ounce of common sense must see . . . that separation of the two races must be maintained in the South." Reviewing the development of liberal organizations across the South, Patricia Sullivan concluded that "traditional white southern liberals had become apologists for the segregation system."[73]

If McGill and other southern liberals were cautious about the race issue, the Georgia author Lillian Smith became an outspoken critic of segregation and racial injustice. In 1944 Smith published *Strange Fruit,* which depicted an ill-fated love affair between a white man and a well-educated mulatto maid in the imaginary town of Maxwell, Georgia. Smith's intention was to help her readers to "think of our people, white and colored, as human beings, not as 'problems.'" In his history of mulattoes and miscegenation, Joel Williamson described *Strange Fruit* as "one of the most powerful assaults on the Southern racial establishment to occur during the first half of the twentieth century." *Strange Fruit* sold over three million copies. From her home in Clayton, in the north Georgia mountains, Smith edited the *North Georgia Review* (1937–41) and the *South Today* (1942–45), which examined southern culture and the effects of racial segregation on the region. In 1949 Smith published *Killers of the Dream,* a trenchant critique of the "distance and darkness" of the rural mind of the South. For such boldness Smith was often condemned by more moderate southerners. The *Atlanta Constitution* described *Killers of the Dream* as "very badly done claptrap" and did not even review *Strange Fruit.*[74] Defenders of white supremacy were even more direct. Eugene Talmadge described *Strange Fruit* as a "literary corncob," and in 1955 Smith's house was burned down by arsonists.[75]

The greatest contribution of white liberals to the black struggle for equality in Georgia would not be seen for at least a decade after the war years. But this growing moderate voice, particularly prominent in Atlanta's white press, proved a counterpoint to the excesses of white supremacists during the war years. The impact of the war on white opinion was demonstrated in concrete political terms too. A business-dominated independent movement overturned the infamous Cracker Party control of Augusta. At the state level, the more moderate candidate Ellis Arnall defeated Talmadge at the end of 1942 and introduced a series of electoral reforms, including the repeal of the poll tax. Arnall's victory and legislative program, his biographer concluded, "capitalized on idealistic and democratic sentiments of a nation at war with dictatorship." [76]

The war irreversibly changed Georgia's economy too. In many ways it merely accelerated the death of the already ailing cotton plantation system. Marginal workers flocked to the cities to find employment. And in a state where white supremacy was most virulently defended in the black belt, the transformation of Georgia's economy had profound consequences for Jim Crow too. Numan Bartley labeled World War II "Georgia one of the more heavily occupied political entities in the world." [77] The coastal cities of Savannah and Brunswick swelled with defense workers, while the central cities of Macon, Milledgeville, and Atlanta housed munitions factories.[78] Civilian employees at the mushrooming military bases settled in Columbus and Savannah. The new Bell Aircraft site of 1941 in Marietta, which built B-29 superfortresses, employed over twenty thousand workers and was the largest bomber and modification plant in the country.[79]

Although the transformation of Georgia's economy had major long-term implications for the state, the immediate racial impact of the wartime economy was to boost black employment.[80] Black Georgians gained a share of the one million new jobs created for blacks in the South between 1940 and 1944. The average family income in two black Atlanta housing projects increased by over 60 percent during those years. Two thousand black workers were employed at Bell Aircraft. Over half of the eight hundred newly employed laborers for South Eastern Shipyards in Savannah were black. Some five thousand black workers were hired in nontraditional textile jobs in fifteen mills in Georgia during the war years. The Southern Regional Council noted that at Bibb Mill No. 1 in Columbus, seven hundred black workers were hired in a department previously run by whites. The report concluded that there was a "Negro found in most every part of Mill working along with white." [81]

The impact of these economic changes on racial customs was partially indicated by the hostile white reaction to potential black employment in the federally funded military industry. At Bell Aircraft, black Atlantans were barred from training courses. Initially, Jake Henderson, head of the Atlanta Urban League's (AUL) Industrial Committee, William Bell Jr., the League's executive director, and A. T. Walden, the board chairman, attempted to influence Georgia school board officials and Atlanta's Labor Advisory Committee to change policy. With the support of the NUL, the Atlanta Urban League then took its complaints to the President's Committee on Fair Employment Practices. Training was not secured until four months later, when a school was established at Washington High School. [82] Similarly, the NAACP wired the War Manpower Commission to protest the layoff of five hundred black workers at the South Eastern Shipyard. [83] And the editorials in the *Macon Telegraph* blamed the employment of young black women at the nearby National Defense Authority for an increase in racial attacks in 1942. [84]

At the same time, the influence of the federal government presaged the end of Georgia's independence from the rest of the country. Executive Order 8802 insisted on nondiscrimination in military-related employment. Although the resulting commission was able to rectify less than a quarter of the 1,108 complaints it received, the very fact that the commission maintained a regional office in Atlanta represented a victory over those seeking to remove it. More often, federal interference was not racially specific. The Committee on Congested Production Areas, for example, chose Brunswick as one of its target cities, building an infrastructure to cope with the larger population and establishing the precedent of hourly wages and decent housing. Pete Daniel's conclusion in his survey of southern economic history was certainly applicable to Georgia when he wrote that by the end of the war "the federal government had become a familiar, and even expected participant in southern life." [85]

Unions also became a familiar part of Georgia life during the war years. Early in the century, W. E. B. Du Bois had written from Atlanta University (AU) that the major hope for dismantling Jim Crow was for "white and colored workers to unite," allowing shared class grievances to supersede racial differences. On the eve of World War II, however, such hopes for Georgia seemed ludicrous. The state leaders of the American Federation of Labor (AFL), the dominant force in the labor movement, supported the Talmadge machine. The oldest southern local of the

United Automobile Workers (UAW) at Atlanta's General Motors factory was typical of Georgia unions when it barred the eight black janitors in the plant from membership. Clark Foreman, who was based in Georgia, lamented that "unions were often the most vociferous force against the Negro." Meanwhile, union activity was limited in Georgia. Michael Honey noted that in Atlanta during the 1930s, "hired thugs and police arrested, beat and shot people for trying to picket, strike or assemble in demands for union rights."[86]

But in October 1941, a strike by black laborers in the Atlanta sanitary department gave credibility to Du Bois's prediction. The strikers refused to place their demands for a fifty-cent raise in the hands of the AFL. White truck drivers refused to move the city trucks when the mayor tried to break the strike by using prison labor. Works Progress Administration (WPA) employees also refused to breach the strike, and even when the mayor persuaded two strikebreakers to drive armed trucks they turned back at the picket line.[87]

The *Crisis* hailed this victory by "brothers in the union" as an illustration of a "new spirit of unity in the South" that was bound to shake the Georgia crackers. Talmadge was apparently unavailable to comment, reported the journalist Harold Preece, "but his remarks would have probably been unprintable." Talmadge soon produced antiunion, anti-Communist tirades when the Atlanta strike threatened to be a portent of further class action in Georgia. In 1943, for example, the Southern War Labor Conference meeting in Atlanta, with three thousand delegates from around the South, declared that "the labor movement should serve the workers without regard to race, creed or color."[88]

The Congress of Industrial Organizations (CIO) took the lead in interracial union activity in the South. Since its official founding convention in 1938, the CIO had distanced itself from the AFL, declaring an "uncompromising opposition to any form of discrimination, whether political or economic, based on race, color, creed or nationality." Both the economic and attitudinal changes engendered by the war seemed to provide an ideal opportunity for the CIO. By the end of World War II, southern membership in the CIO had risen to over four hundred thousand workers. The CIO also supported and partially funded the development of the Southern Conference on Human Welfare. In his overview of southern labor and black civil rights, Michael Honey concluded that at the end of the war, "biracial labor organizing more than ever seemed to provide a basis for union progress, democratization and liberalization." And in the spring of 1946, the CIO launched an organizing drive in the South dubbed "Operation Dixie," a self-proclaimed "civil rights crusade" aiming to extend unionism throughout the South.[89]

The overwhelming success of certain left-led unions in the South, notably in Winston-Salem, North Carolina, and Memphis, Tennessee, was so striking that the labor historians Robert Korstad and Nelson Lichtenstein concluded that the years of Operation Dixie were lost for a potential racial revolution. Barbara Griffith's assessment of Operation Dixie was far more appropriate for CIO activity in Georgia, however; she concluded that "black southerners got many different signals from the CIO." Despite the signals pointing strongly toward racial integration in Winston-Salem and Memphis, black Georgians more often received signals reinforcing Jim Crow. At the Atlantic Steel Plant to the north of Atlanta, for example, the local had separate meetings for black and white members. Lloyd Gussett, the organizer, admitted that some of the international representatives of the local were members of the Ku Klux Klan.[90]

In part, the limited impact of Operation Dixie stemmed from the tentative approach of CIO personnel in Georgia to racial segregation. Far from being a campaigning trailblazer, Charles Gillman, the Georgia director of Operation Dixie, was described by colleagues as an "unprepossessing and earnest man who had something of the solid citizen about him." This diffidence spread to the state headquarters in Atlanta, where staffers were lectured on the need to be circumspect on the race issue. Even when the Georgia Conference of CIO textile workers organized a labor stand against the "industrial dictators in the state" and against the Ku Klux Klan, there was no overall drive for an end to segregation.[91]

With the major left-led unions located in other southern states, the priorities of protest in Georgia unions were primarily industrial rather than racial. As one CIO official remarked, "Trade unions are less involved in community situations than in the area of organizing, internal union, and shop situations. Correspondingly unions, especially locals, are less likely to act on race relations issues in the community." A representative of the UAW concurred that "when we moved into the South, we agreed to abide by local custom and not hire Negroes for production work." Indeed, one Georgia CIO official who personally opposed discrimination admitted that "quite frankly, we aren't crusaders. We do our best to steer away from the race question whenever we can."[92] Thus the CIO in Georgia reflected the growing ascendancy of racial conservatives and anti-Communists in the national organization.

Even when blacks dominated the industrial workforce, the drive for improved conditions did not inevitably result in a demand for integration in the workplace or even in the union. In Savannah, for example, a survey in 1940 had recorded that "blacks maintained an overwhelming majority on the waterfront," after 1,308 black casual workers organized to form Local 1414 of the International Longshoremen's Association (ILA).[93] The smaller, all-white Local 1475 represented the more highly paid clerks and checkers. Integration of the skilled union would, however, have forced the black leadership to relinquish tight control over longshoremen's employment and admit whites to the industry. The "black leadership has been reluctant to change," the survey recorded, and thus eschewed the opportunity for economic advances. Instead, union activities focused on aggressive demands for higher wages and more courtesy for the longshoremen, continuing the tradition of black maritime union protest in Georgia.[94]

Above all, the realities of Georgia's white supremacy dictated that any CIO ideals of racial integration formulated at northern headquarters were likely to flounder at the local level. Sometimes the problem was the workers themselves, for as the Automobile Workers Local (CIO) president explained, "When the Atlanta G.M. plant was organized, the white workers not only refused to admit Negroes into the union but they attempted to secure their discharge. A compromise was effected," in violation of the CIO constitution, "wherein they were left in possession of their jobs but barred from the union." In the rural counties it was more often the local white elite who blocked integration. Sheriff Carlus Gay of Laurens County simply arrested the black and white laborers who had met with CIO organizers.[95]

But if Georgia's version of Operation Dixie fell far short of being a potential racial revolution, union activity still challenged some aspects of Jim Crow. Five years after the start of Operation Dixie, Atlanta civil rights leaders urged Scripto Ordinance employees to choose the CIO rather than the AFL. According to William Holmes Borders, the CIO "has done more for the working people than any other union, especially the colored people." In Savannah, local NAACP leaders supported the CIO's attempts to organize shipyard workers because the AFL, in contrast, followed discriminatory practices. Despite local resistance, the UAW eventually forced the Atlanta GM Local to admit black members during World War II, albeit with segregated seating during meetings. Equally, the attitude and example of officers from the North challenged the Jim Crow mind-set. The CIO head office in Atlanta treated black and white workers on the same basis. The Atlanta Meatcutters Local Committee noted that because black international representative Clarence Green gave a good talk on union laws and union work in 1945, "only a few members objected to him being there."[96]

Any interracial meetings also challenged the customs of Jim Crow. Whenever a regional or national conference was based in Atlanta, the social mixing often included interracial dancing, which was strictly taboo. And frequently, meetings challenged not just customs but individuals. One white organizer in Decatur, on the outskirts of Atlanta, called a meeting in his motel room until the manager insisted that "blacks don't come in this motel." So they went outside and met on the grass.[97]

Whereas the automobile union was tentative and the textile unions avoided the race issue altogether, the greatest impact on Georgia's racial segregation came from the big four packinghouse unions. As early as 1933, the Cudahy and Armour chains agreed to eliminate segregated facilities in all southern branches, including the four branches in Atlanta, and, more significantly, in the southwest Georgia towns of Albany, Tifton, and Moultrie. Initially, the usual story of local resistance blocked any attempts to integrate locker rooms or food facilities.[98] But the national directive provided the opportunity, and as often happened during the war years in Georgia, the emergence of a dynamic leader provided the catalyst for racial change.

A black fieldworker for the United Packinghouse Workers of America (UPWA), John Henry Hall, arrived in Georgia from Chicago in 1944 and organized workers in Moultrie, a town so aggressively segregated twenty years later that visiting civil rights workers despaired of finding any local black protesters, let alone any hope of dismantling white supremacy.[99] An accomplished organizer, Hall earned a reputation in the South as an entertaining speaker. Within two years Hall had organized a wages strike that brought Swift's Peanut Pork factory to a standstill. Attendant publicity revealed that black and white veterans stood under the same flag, united behind the placard proclaiming that "we whipped Tojo, Mussolini, Hitler. We'll whip Swift."[100]

With a zeal and organization that later made him the first black member of the union Hall of Fame, John Henry Hall struck at the foundations of Jim Crow. Class conflict replaced that of color, since Hall organized biracial strikes of all workers, not just veterans. Even concerned local white women were photographed applauding Hall's rally speeches from the platform.[101]

Union activity also reaped rewards in the fight against economic discrimination. The *Atlanta Daily World* found that "the racial sentiment of Albany is excellent. At the great Cuhady [*sic*] million dollar plant, colored men are employed in departments along with white workers and paid the same wages." After recent flooding in the city, "the racial cooperation shown in a condition in which over 99% of the deaths were colored is but a sample of the fine goodwill and interracial activities in existence in this fine Southwest Georgia city. Albany will come back."[102]

Considering the violent defense of segregation that became the hallmark of southwest Georgia during the 1960s, the challenge of the packinghouse locals to white mores produced a remarkable exception in the region's racial history. Though remarkable, it was not a revolution because even here integration was a by-product and not the primary goal of the union agenda. Hall's efforts failed to eliminate the more sensitive areas of social segregation in the factory food halls or water fountains or to alleviate the worst deprivations of Albany's notorious black ghetto.[103]

The radical and temporary impact of one union could not mask the fact that the contribution of unions to racial change in Georgia was typically halfhearted. But the activities of unions augmented the impact of the war in challenging Georgia's hitherto impregnable white supremacy.[104] Above all, these wartime changes provided the backdrop for the emergence of local black protest movements in communities across the state.

The growth of cities also set the scene for black protest movements. The Depression had forced many farmers off the land, and a booming wartime economy accelerated a more positive pull toward the cities. During the 1940s, more than one million black southerners moved from farms to cities in the South. According to census reports, the number of black Georgians in urban areas classified as professional workers, proprietors, or managers more than doubled during the two decades after 1930. Atlanta and Savannah were special cases, with over three hundred and one hundred black businesses respectively by 1946.[105] But across the state, a further fifteen towns had at least forty-five black professional workers and black proprietors during the war years.[106]

Urbanization and the growth of a black middle class did not lead inexorably to active black protest. In Augusta, for example, wealthy black community leaders Robert and Andrew Dent earned a reputation for conservatism and refused to speak out against the racial status quo. Most black farmers who owned their own land remained taciturn. But some black Georgians did take advantage of their relative economic strength to challenge white supremacy. As early as 1935, black Atlantans had launched an unofficial boycott of a grocery store where a black customer had been beaten for alleged thieving. In Dublin, increased wealth gave black business leaders the power to ameliorate racial conditions in the city's banks. During 1946, black account holders withheld their money until tellers addressed black customers with courtesy titles.[107]

Even in the rural black belt, some black Georgia landowners chose to challenge white supremacy. D. Ulysses Pullum's position as an independent landowner enabled him to form an NAACP branch in "Terrible" Terrell County during the early 1940s. By this time Pullum's farm produced cattle, peanuts, corn, cotton, hogs, and other crops. Born at the turn of the century, Pullum was described by a *Pittsburgh Courier* reporter as "so light he could pass for white if he wished to." His lightness convinced Pullum that racial segregation and discrimination was a false and invidious distinction. In the face of Klan reprisals and a fluctuating membership, Pullum assumed a vital role in maintaining NAACP activity in the county. NAACP officials often referred to the Terrell branch as a "one-man branch."[108]

The emergence of small pockets of relatively prosperous black Georgians in cities, therefore, provided the environment from which civil rights leadership could spring. Bill Randall, a young, prosperous building contractor in Macon and reputedly the wealthiest black building contractor in the Southeast, gathered together a group of fellow professionals during the early 1940s. These self-styled "Crusaders" met regularly to discuss various issues, including the vote and how to improve black employment. Randall continued to lead militant protest in Macon for the next thirty years. J. M. Atkinson in Brunswick, the Reverend Amos Holmes in Dublin, and Ralph Quarterman in Gainesville each led local protests for the vote and improved employment, using boycotts and mass meetings nearly two decades before the more celebrated protests of later years. In Albany, local businessman C. W. King, dentist Dr. Joseph Cheevers, and Presbyterian minister Rev. Millard F. Adams developed an NAACP branch founded in the 1920s, which increasingly focused on voter registration.[109]

Preeminent among this cadre of smaller city leaders was a medical doctor, Thomas Brewer, of Columbus in west Georgia. As early as 1929, he had founded the Social Civic 25 Club of leading professionals, most of whom were doctors and dentists from Columbus's unusually large black medical community, and he was reputedly the wealthiest of them all by far. There was no doubting Brewer's force of personality either, for black leaders in Columbus addressed him as "Chief." From this position of leadership during the 1930s, the *Columbus Ledger-Enquirer* later recorded, Brewer became "increasingly upset and irritated by the restrictions Jim Crowism placed upon blacks in the South at the time." Further afield, the *Pittsburgh*

Courier correspondent for Georgia, despite being based solely in Atlanta, acclaimed Brewer in his list of the top ten leaders in the state.[110]

In 1939, Brewer formed black professionals into a group directly opposed to white supremacy, when he organized twenty-one residents to apply for a local charter of the NAACP. Despite its urban location, the local branch had to meet secretly in basements, and Brewer was singled out for personal attacks by the Klan. Brewer's concern for the soldiers at nearby Fort Benning led the Columbus NAACP to challenge the legality of segregating soldiers on buses. Brewer's personal authority underwrote boycotts, which could be publicized only by word of mouth. But while boycotts remained unofficial, future mayor A. J. McClung recalled that shopkeepers coincidentally hired and upgraded black workers in a manner not repeated until the 1960s. Brewer used his own wealth to cover organizational and legal costs.[111]

Urban and industrial development also encouraged the emergence and strengthening of black business networks between various communities across the state, networks that could carry messages concerning the battle against Jim Crow. Of the twelve-member executive committee of the Georgia Negro Dental Society meeting in February 1941, for example, at least eight were prominent civil rights leaders in their hometowns. The black Masonic lodges provided one of the most extensive networks. W. L. Calloway, a realtor based on Atlanta's Auburn Avenue, believed that "everybody who was anybody was a mason." The Most Worshipful Highness of the Prince Hall Masonic Lodge (Ancient Free and Accepted Masons Jurisdiction of Georgia), John Wesley Dobbs, welcomed more than five thousand members from over 150 local lodges to the 1940 convention on Auburn Avenue. By this time Dobbs had retired from the postal service, having attained the position of a railway mail service clerk in charge. Dobbs's erstwhile rival in Atlanta, A. T. Walden, was the Grand Chancellor of the Georgia Grand Lodge of the Knights of Pythias.[112]

Communication across the state was further augmented by the development of black-controlled media. Founded as a weekly paper in 1928, the *Atlanta Daily World* became the nation's first black-owned daily newspaper in 1932. One decade later, the *World*'s circulation had soared to sixty thousand across the state. The *World* eclipsed the *Atlanta Journal* and *Atlanta Constitution,* which carried no news of black business or social affairs and had a combined circulation of less than forty thousand to black homes in Georgia during the 1940s. Consequently, the protests of individual communities that were reported became inextricably identified with a nascent statewide protest. Similarly, the South's leading black newspaper, the *Pittsburgh Courier,* carried a special Georgia section. Many of Georgia's black leaders of the 1940s later remembered both newspapers as tantamount to a protest update newsletter, while some of the leaders from the 1960s attributed their interest in civil rights to their youthful inquisitiveness during their newspaper delivery rounds.[113]

The late 1930s and 1940s also saw a rise in black-controlled radio stations. "The radio has been a . . . boon to our cause," trumpeted the *Atlanta Daily World* in 1940. "The radio has been made available and in every rural community there are those who can intelligently discuss the war, politics and economics." John Calhoun, who was one of Atlanta's leading civil rights activists during the 1950s, later recalled that "it was quite a thing. Quite a unique experience for Negroes to be able to hear about Negro news."[114] Radio WERD in Atlanta carried sermons by Rev. William Holmes Borders, a strong critic of Jim Crow. Benjamin E. Mays also broadcast regularly.[115] In Augusta, J. W. Brown, a history professor at Paine College, spoke on radio station WRDW on 1 December 1940 about Negro "accomplishment" and the need for "Negro opportunity." The show was hosted by Dr. T. E. Carter, who was publicized as Augusta's primary black dentist but was better known as one of the leading voices seeking racial change in the city.[116]

Together, the national changes sweeping the South and the emergence of an interlinked black leadership across the state provided a heightened challenge to white supremacy in Georgia. These developments also provided the opportunity for the growth of a more concerted protest. Building on these foundations, a state-wide protest movement emerged, based in Savannah and Atlanta, which threatened to overturn the worst excesses of white supremacy and even to challenge the very foundations of Jim Crow in Georgia.

2

The Upsurge of Black Protest across Georgia, 1943–1946

The increased black activism in Georgia mirrored a concomitant upsurge of protest across the South during the war years. In his study of Mississippi, Dittmer entitled his first chapter "Rising Expectations, 1946–54." Dittmer concluded that "the decade following World War II was one of intensifying black activism in Mississippi, beginning with modest voter registration efforts and culminating in an attack on the color line in the state's public schools." The upsurge of activism in Louisiana during the war years was even more pronounced. According to Fairclough, "blacks were speaking and acting in a way not seen since Reconstruction."[1]

In Georgia, however, the scale of black protest in the form of voter registration during the mid-1940s far exceeded that in the other southern states. By 1947, the Mississippi Progressive Voters' League had attracted 5,000 members, while between 1945 and 1947 the NAACP formed ten new branches in the state. At the same time, there were approximately 7,000 black registered voters in Louisiana and an increasingly active NAACP chapter in New Orleans. Black registration in Arkansas and

South Carolina had increased to 40,000 and 50,000 voters respectively by 1947.[2] By contrast, over 125,000 black Georgians had registered to vote for the gubernatorial election of 1946, representing approximately one-fifth of the adult black population, while fifty new branches of the NAACP had formed into a tightly knit state conference.[3]

A defining feature of this new wave of protest was that individual and sporadic acts of racial defiance were now channeled by statewide organizations into a concerted attack on Jim Crow. Not only did the major cities experience substantial racial change, but by 1946 the whole state of Georgia seemed poised to move away from violent white supremacy. Not surprisingly, in his study of Georgia during the 1940s, Clifford M. Kuhn concluded that "the question then is, why were black Georgians so comparatively successful in mobilizing politically, a question which, despite its seemingly evident importance, historians have only begun to answer?"[4]

Two political changes set the scene for the acceleration of a statewide voting registration campaign in Georgia. The first precondition was the outlawing of the Democratic white primary in each of the southern states. Initially, the system cracked on 3 April 1944, when the Supreme Court ruled in the Texas case *Smith v. Allwright* that "the right to vote in a primary for the nomination of candidates . . . like the right to vote in a general election, is a right secured by the Constitution." The *Smith v. Allwright* story, including the money raised by the NAACP branches in Texas to support the case, was extensively reported in the *Atlanta Daily World*.[5]

Immediately, A. T. Walden and black community leaders in Atlanta, working with national NAACP lawyer Thurgood Marshall, prepared to mount a similar challenge to Georgia's white primary. In open defiance of Atlanta's presumption of leadership and Marshall's directive, however, Dr. Thomas Brewer in Columbus both organized and funded Georgia's challenge to the white primary. At Brewer's behest, a local minister, Rev. Primus King, led a small delegation to vote, and it was this attempt that became the basis for the ultimate suit against the party. National NAACP lawyers did not become involved until the case had received wide publicity.[6]

On 12 October 1945, federal district judge Hoyt T. Davis decided in *King v. Chapman* that the Democratic white primary was "an integral part of the electoral process of this state. It may be fairly said that it is the hub of the process." Just as the *Brown* decision a decade later opened the way for the direct action campaigns of the King years, so the Primus King decision provided the opportunity for Georgia's voting campaigns of the 1940s. It was "the federal judiciary system," argued William Hamman in 1955, "rather than state or local pressure, which provided the wedge with which Georgia Negroes have received constitutional rights." The *New South* magazine in 1948 concluded that of all the factors leading to an increase in black voting, "none exerted a more powerful influence than the elimination of the white primary."[7]

The second essential political change was the surprise defeat of Governor Eugene Talmadge by Ellis Arnall in the gubernatorial election of December 1942. Ironically, the deciding issue was the so-called Regents' crisis of June 1941, in which Talmadge's purge of pro-integration educators had led to the removal of accreditation from Georgia's white colleges. In fact, the majority of the electorate was hostile not to Talmadge's racial politics but rather to his tyrannical attitude toward the revered university system as he rode roughshod over the protests of the Board of Regents. The Regents' crisis, John Egerton noted, was nothing more than a "clumsily attempted witch-hunt for liberals and other heretics at the University of Georgia."[8]

Before his inauguration, Arnall's rhetoric did little to engender hope among the black community. In his campaign speeches, Arnall insisted that his racial toleration extended only to those "Negroes who knew their place . . . at the back door." In response to Talmadge's taunts, Arnall publicly insisted in 1942 that "if a nigger ever tried to get into a white school in my part of the state the sun would never set on his head." At the end of his term, Arnall echoed the white supremacist argument that "the basic civil liberties of Negro citizens are respected thoroughly in Georgia."[9]

Contemporary black leaders in Georgia, however, unanimously believed the Arnall administration to be an important prerequisite for the development of a registration campaign. Benjamin E. Mays believed that Arnall's inauguration as governor on 12 January 1943 "marked a new era in Georgia politics." "While it must be admitted that the spirit of the New Deal as well as World War II had their impact," Mays continued, "Arnall's administration drew national attention for the many reforms introduced as well as the dignity with which he occupied the office."[10] Clarence Bacote, who helped to supervise voter education classes, was even more extravagant in his praise. Bacote concluded that Arnall's election was "one of the luckiest things that ever happened. In my opinion, Ellis Arnall was the best governor we ever had."[11]

The actions of Georgia's governor attracted national attention. The *New York Times* hailed Arnall as the governor who would lead Georgia away from the era of crackers and wool-hat politics, while the *Crisis* noted in 1945 that "Georgia's governor Ellis Arnall has taken the spotlight in the South and in the nation." It was a "refreshing sight," the *Crisis* stated a year later, "to see Georgia's governor fighting the revived Ku Klux Klan." This fight culminated in the prosecution of thirty-eight members of Atlanta's police force for membership in the Klan. Arnall removed the poll tax qualification for registration and lowered the minimum voting age from twenty-one to eighteen years. John Chamberlain wrote in *Life* in 1945 that Arnall has succeeded "in lifting his state from the benightedness of Tobacco Road to the position of runner-up to North Carolina for the title of 'most progressive southern state.'"[12]

In a national context, however, Arnall's racial outlook was far from progressive. In January 1944, for example, he vehemently condemned a call by the Atlanta NAACP to enfranchise Georgia's returning black veterans, asserting that "we in the South don't believe in social equality." Three months later, Arnall appointed a commission, funded by the state treasury, to try to find a legal means to circumvent the implications of the Primus King decision. In response to the publication in 1946 of Arnall's autobiography, *The Shore Dimly Seen,* one NAACP publicist, Ruth Wilson, reflected on his period as governor by asking, "How dimly does Ellis Arnall see?" While acknowledging that Arnall was "one of the best governors Georgia has ever had," Wilson lambasted his widely touted liberalism for stopping at the color line. "Is his sight so dim," Wilson continued, "that he has not seen the civil rights of Negroes customarily disregarded?" Fearing that Arnall was preparing to run for the Senate in 1948, the *Crisis* sought to expose him as a "phony liberal" based on his record in Georgia.[13]

But the national NAACP admitted to remaining taciturn during Arnall's period as governor because "all his running mates were worse, not even 'phony liberals.'" A. T. Walden commented that black Georgians felt that Arnall "is as liberal as it is possible for a white man to be and hold office in the South." In race relations, Arnall's significance while governor was, essentially, that he took the place of Talmadge. During his four years in office, only one lynching was recorded in Georgia, in contrast to eighteen in the previous decade and ten in the following decade. Numerous older black leaders later recalled a lull in white supremacist violence while Talmadge was out of office.[14]

Arnall's period as governor coincided with four years of fundamental social and legal challenges to Jim Crow. Although Arnall denounced the Primus King decision, he was not prepared to place his allegiance to white supremacy above the law. Clarence Bacote later remembered Arnall's assertion, "I will not be a party to any [illegal] effort designed to circumvent the decision. The Supreme Court has spoken," and he drew the obvious contrast, "now—if Talmadge had been in office...."

Talmadge himself reached a similar verdict, blaming Arnall for his connivance "with radicals outside the state to force the Democratic Party in Georgia to admit Negroes to its membership."[15]

The combination of the radical racial changes of the war years, the Primus King case, and the election of Ellis Arnall presented black Georgians with a window of opportunity unprecedented in Georgia's history since the establishment of Jim Crow. These changes alone, however, did not explain the comparative success of black Georgians. Rather, the outstanding feature of Georgia's history of black protest during the 1940s was the grasping of that opportunity by black leaders in the two major cities of Atlanta and, especially, Savannah. Both cities experienced black protest movements that resulted in far-reaching improvements in racial relations. The cities also became bases for a statewide movement that threatened to bring a permanent end to the excesses of white supremacy across the state as a whole.

Black Protest in Savannah

By 1940, the NAACP in Georgia had collapsed in all but name. The organization had dwindled to less than ten city chapters and was still decreasing. The Atlanta branch was in practice a talk-shop for a handful of individuals, while the charters at Rome and Athens were worth little more than the paper they were written on.[16] The charter of the Savannah branch was revoked in 1939 after a dramatic decline in membership. In New York, the national office made no significant attempt to rebuild the local organizations in the South, concentrating instead on northern membership to fund a legal offensive against Jim Crow. Meanwhile, the NAACP's Legal Defense Committee, founded in 1939 to spearhead grassroots activity, was concentrating its resources on the white primary campaign in Texas.

The impetus for renewed membership came from within Georgia itself, initially from Savannah. Rev. Ralph Mark Gilbert, the newly appointed pastor of Savannah's First African Baptist Church, applied for a charter on his arrival from Detroit in October 1942, only to discover that other black Savannahians had also made tentative inquiries. "I am very happy to know that someone else here was thinking in the same terms as myself," Gilbert replied to the head office. "The main idea is to get the job done. I am sure that we can collaborate with each other."[17]

NAACP officers were astonished by the ambition of the Savannah branch. NAACP national director of branches Ella Baker habitually urged conservative goals for branch membership campaigns. During its inaugural membership drive in

1942, the Savannah local committee insisted that the campaign goal be set at five thousand members, "which, strange as it may seem," Baker reported, "appears to be within the range of possibility." The following year, field representative Donald Jones was surprised when Gilbert and his team learned that Chicago was the largest branch in the country, with nine thousand members, and told Jones that the Savannahians would "strain might and main" to beat it. "Maybe if they don't realize that ten thousand is twenty per cent of their population," Jones concluded, "they might do it." [18]

Savannah's position as Georgia's second largest city and the relative prosperity of the black community provided the opportunity for a major movement in the city. A Morehouse College survey of southern black businesses included Savannah among the South's top twelve cities, recording that the local black community supported 177 businesses and 27 restaurants. Such enterprises, independent from the control of the white community, allowed the Savannah movement to expand beyond the traditional church leadership base. John McGlockton, for example, who became the president of the NAACP's Voting Registration Committee and the Citizens' Democratic Club, was a self-employed grocer. He was able to accommodate a busy speaking schedule and regular visits to the courthouse because his wife and two daughters could operate the store.[19]

The high profile enjoyed by the NAACP also reveals much about the relatively moderate race relations in Savannah. In contrast to rural communities in southwest Georgia, where clandestine meetings were held under the cover of darkness, the Savannah campaigns were both public and flamboyant. Window stickers proclaimed, "I am a member of the NAACP." The youth council performed New Year plays for the public, with *Little Women* attracting an audience of six hundred in 1945. The local branch joined in community-wide schemes such as Savannah's "go-to-school" drives and in April 1945 raised $170 for the city's Cancer Control Month Appeal.[20]

Savannah's relative racial liberality stemmed in part from its coastal location. As a major Atlantic seaport, the community was traditionally less introverted or closed than other towns, having long experienced a regular transient influx of people of different nationalities. Many of the senior NAACP leaders later attributed Savannah's less extreme outlook to its Atlantic trade. It was the first city to allow a black church when its free black community founded the First African Baptist Church in 1768.[21]

Savannah's long history of black activism and community involvement also laid the foundations for the movement. Ulysses Houston's local ordinance in 1870 requiring equal facilities for all races on public carriers was the only such bill to be passed in the state. Boycotts cost the Savannah Transit Company $50,000 in 1907 and briefly postponed attempts to introduce racial segregation on public transport. The *Savannah Herald* was the oldest continuously published black newspaper in the country. By the time of Gilbert's arrival, there were more than one hundred community organizations in Savannah, including the Longshoremen's Union, Masons and Elks, PTAs, and local social clubs.[22]

Yet while the unusual social mores of the city provided an opportunity for protest, the emergence of the local movement was far from inevitable. Savannah still retained the racial prejudices of the Old South. In a letter to the head office, Gilbert noted that "white supremacy forces . . . have even perfected an organization of over four hundred members in this city, which is the most liberal city in the state of Georgia." At the time of Gilbert's arrival, a white supremacist political machine, entrenched in power, governed the city by its manipulation of an illegal gambling racket. The majority of the white community supported Talmadge over Arnall. And at the street level, as in the rest of Georgia, white supremacist violence was endemic at the points of racial contact, particularly on buses and at the borders of racial districts. One of Gilbert's initial tasks after forming the NAACP was to investigate threats to the life of Joseph Wright, a black Savannahian who had moved into a predominantly white area, by Wright's new white neighbors.[23]

Nor did Savannah's tradition of black protest inexorably lead to the militancy of the 1940s. Probably the most effective opposition to the local movement came from within Savannah's black leadership, most notably from Rev. L. Scott, the head of the NAACP Legal Redress Committee and pastor of the Second African Baptist Church. Scott sought to undermine the local movement when he supported Mississippi senator Theodore "The Man" Bilbo's campaign to repatriate black Americans in Africa. In a letter to Bilbo, Scott agreed that it would be logical for American Negroes to return to Liberia and that the Negro "will forever be a menace until this is done." Bilbo subsequently used the letter during debates in the Senate as evidence of his desire to be "a real friend to the Negro." To sustain the momentum of the local movement, Gilbert immediately sacked Scott, angry that "we are not in reality dealing with another Negro but we are still dealing with those white interests and our avowed enemies."[24]

The lack of any parallel protest activity in either Charleston, South Carolina, or Brunswick, Georgia, both of which were similarly situated, further demonstrates that the movement in Savannah was not preordained. In trying to excuse what he presumed must be a sluggish membership drive, Gilbert lamented to the national office that "this is just a 'sleepy old town' and everything they accomplish has to be done with Herculean effort." Donald Jones described the priorities of Savannahians more cynically. "I'd be more optimistic," he reported of the 1943 membership drive, "if it were not so blamed cold (16 degrees)—you know these Savannah people. They won't be coming out in that kind of weather." [25]

Rather, the NAACP movement flourished because of Gilbert's leadership. Without doubt he was the catalyst for change; the frenzy of activity after Gilbert's arrival stands in stark contrast to the negligible black protest activity which Ralph Bunche recorded in 1939 and the apathy that had forced the national NAACP office to revoke the local charter in the same year. Savannah civil rights activists also pinpointed Gilbert's arrival as the starting point of the modern movement.[26]

Few records remain regarding Gilbert's personality and character. Published letters reveal an intelligent thinker, who was able to frustrate Senator Bilbo in what effectively became a public debate by letter in the black press over the question of resettlement in West Africa. "You make me sick and disquieted," Bilbo wrote to Gilbert in 1945, "when you try to argue that if it is best for the American Negro to move to the land of his fathers in West Africa, then the American white race should move to Europe and so forth ... God have mercy on your poor soul." Black leaders, in contrast, held Gilbert in high esteem. Field reports by NAACP officials visiting Savannah frequently remarked on his charisma, while the Georgia correspondent for the *Pittsburgh Courier* rated Gilbert among the top ten black leaders in the state.[27] Local oral recollections point to a gifted orator and dramatist who directed plays to teach black history and protest techniques. Gilbert also brought from Detroit the experience of living outside Jim Crow and personal assets more than able to fund his travels.

Gilbert's charisma was matched by a flair for organization. On her arrival in Savannah in November 1942, Ella Baker discovered that she was witnessing a thriving campaign rather than needing to organize a faltering drive, as was her custom. Five hundred block workers were already appointed, more than most towns aimed for in total membership during a drive, although the branch had been rechartered only in April with three hundred members. Such organization was facilitated by Gilbert's habit of delegating responsibility to black community organizations.[28]

Gilbert's personal authority kept the movement united. In the run-up to the election of July 1946, the *Savannah Herald* warned that the recent division and formation of breakaway clubs may "mislead and exploit these new voters to their own selfish ends." Gilbert responded to the danger through an open letter calling out "for serious efforts . . . to prevent serious division among our people during this time." Following his own advice, Gilbert chaired a crowded open meeting, in which all the various groups agreed to work together under an umbrella organization to be called "the Savannah Democratic Club," led by Gilbert's staunch ally John McGlockton, with Gilbert himself as vice-president.[29]

The major significance of Gilbert's leadership was that he inspired a movement that marked a radical departure from previous Georgia protest. In its emphasis on youth participation, mass community involvement, and the adoption of more confrontational forms of protest, the Savannah movement of the early 1940s presaged the city movements that were to sweep the South during the 1960s.

In contrast to the NAACP in Georgia's other major cities, the branch recruited members through Savannah's youth networks, such as the boys' clubs, scout troops, and especially the high school. The first youth council president, W. W. Law, recalled later that the NAACP became so popular that "membership of the youth council became a badge of honor and practically every student in the school joined." The delegation of responsibility in an active local branch attracted youth. In 1947, the youth council led a school boycott to protest against inadequate facilities, and Arnall's decision to reduce the registration age to eighteen years put the youth council in the forefront of registration campaigns. By 1943, according to a special feature in the *Crisis,* "the Savannah Youth Council is now the largest NAACP unit of its kind in the country." [30]

The 1940s protest further presaged those of the next generation because of the mass involvement of the community. Both the number of blacks per capita registered to vote and the proportion of the community who were members of the NAACP were the highest for any city in the South. Mass meetings justified their name; more than five hundred people were turned away from the First African Baptist Church when Walter White spoke there during the branch's first anniversary celebrations. Mass membership was secured as the NAACP recruited extensively through existing black organizations.[31]

The NAACP membership facilitated local action. Not only did the NAACP initiate a voting campaign, but a combination of meetings and marches, together with the work of youth volunteers outside the courthouse and adults in each residential block, resulted in the registration of some twenty-two thousand black voters. The success of the campaign reached the attention of the national media. In 1946, the *New York Times* noted that "practical politicians were impressed with the excellence of the organization of the Negro vote in the July primary," adding that the "black vote at the polls was higher in proportion than that of the local white community." [32]

Local action was not limited to voter registration, for Gilbert rejected negotiation in favor of more confrontational forms of protest. In a dispute with the local head of public housing over the all-white employment in the new black housing project in Savannah's Yamacraw district, Gilbert's thinly veiled threat of confrontational protest forced the hiring of black supervisors. Within six months of gaining the charter, the local branch organized a boycott of a store in which the white owner had beaten and then arranged the imprisonment of a black mother, whose only crime had been to complain about the incorrect change given to her daughter. Two years later, fifty Savannah State College students boarded a bus and refused to relinquish the front seats to white passengers until they were arrested. [33]

After the Primus King decision of 1944, however, the most potent weapon for black Savannahians was the vote. Within two years, almost half of Savannah's forty-five thousand eligible black voters had been registered. The protest movement of the 1940s and the black bloc vote transformed an already unusual city into one at odds with the violent white supremacy prevalent throughout Georgia. Savannah's perception of itself as a "semi-autonomous republic" in Georgia, the *New York Times* observed, "has extended to racial relations according to workers in the field." *New South* concluded in 1948 that "for the benefits received from participation in elections, the city of the South which leads all others is not Richmond, Va., or Nashville, Te., but Savannah, Ga." Among these benefits were a new high school, a swimming pool, a recreation center, street improvements, and two black jail matrons. *New South* noted that Savannah was the one city in which black citizens laid claim to diminishing police brutality by use of the ballot box. The allocation for black schooling of 50 percent of the 1946 bond issue was unprecedented in Georgia. [34]

The bloc vote provided practical gains, which changed relations between the black and white communities. The *New York Times* reported that the appointment of nine black policemen, the first ever in Georgia, was "proving so satisfactory that opponents now largely concede that they are here to stay." A Southern Regional Council investigation noted that Savannah's initial registration drive of 1942 secured the election of "a very liberal judge." As a consequence, local blacks "have been getting some very sound decisions from the court." Considering the context of Georgia's reputation for unequal racial justice, the report's conclusion was remarkable: "In the case that a dispute arises between whites and Negroes, if you are right, you are right." The appointment of black policemen, the report continued, meant that "white policemen seem to have stopped bothering people."[35]

Above all, the bloc vote redefined the racial balance of power in Savannah. Although at least five thousand black voters were effectively disfranchised in 1946 because of the deliberate tardiness of poll officials on election day, the nine thousand votes cast proved crucial for overthrowing the local conservative political machine. The city also returned three Progressive League representatives for the state legislature. Savannah became the first Georgia city to introduce a black advisory committee to the mayor, thereby establishing communication between the races, which was to prove vital during the ensuing racial struggles. "Savannah has become so liberal," NAACP official Gloster Current reported, "that Negroes humorously say that it has seceded from Georgia and is now in Chatham [County]."[36]

But because of the county-unit system and the importance of state politics during the 1940s, Savannah had not seceded from Georgia. Gilbert set his sights on expanding civil rights activity, and the logical next step was to foster a movement across the state. Initially, Gilbert established smaller branches in the local environs. It seemed only sensible to stay a few more days in Savannah, Donald Jones wrote to the New York office toward the end of 1943, to make a "flying trip to a half dozen or so branches in the vicinity. They are all under his wing, as you know."[37]

Within six months of receiving the Savannah charter, Gilbert had set his sights on creating an organization both involving and speaking for all black Georgians. After suggesting the idea to Roy Wilkins at the head office, Gilbert organized an inaugural state conference in 1943, expressly aimed at "making the NAACP articulate on matters affecting the Negroes of the State of Georgia." The conference concluded that the most effective tactic was to create numerous local branches, in addition to the six established branches. Thus Atlanta, Albany, La Grange, Columbus, Macon, and Savannah were each allocated target cities in their respective regions.[38] Gilbert was elected as the president of the state conference.

Gilbert approached his task with unbridled optimism and all the fervor normally associated with an evangelistic mission. He wrote to the New York office in 1944 that he was "convinced that the only people who will not join for the most part will be people who will not be approached." The following summer, this confidence had soared further. "Our movement is spreading like wildfire over Georgia," he exclaimed to Walter White. On their own initiative, four members of the newly founded Donaldsonville branch in central Georgia organized a branch in adjacent Miller County.[39]

Gilbert's success across the state justified his claims. Overriding the demarcation of area boundaries agreed on during the inaugural state conference, he established chartered branches in five towns in the Albany region and was confident of three more around Macon by the end of 1945. During the following summer, he had designs for 122 new chapters. Students responded to Gilbert's prompting at each of Georgia's six black colleges. "At the suggestion of Dr. Ralph Mark Gilbert," wrote Fort Valley State College senior William M. Boyd in 1944, later to become the state president, "I have organized a college chapter on our campus." By 1946, membership had risen from less than 1,000 to 13,595 in fifty-one branches across the state, many of which were in rural areas.[40]

As in Savannah, a crucial element in the development of the NAACP was Gilbert's organizational thoroughness. The establishment of a new branch was a well-prepared event. Before his planned excursion across Georgia during the autumn of 1946, Gilbert had written to all the principals of accredited Negro schools in towns where there was no branch. Receiving little response, he followed up by writing to the local ministers. Exchanging his role of evangelist for pastor, Gilbert visited every single branch except the more established branches in Atlanta and Augusta on what became an annual summer tour. Gilbert's dynamism became legendary in rural Georgia, as local leaders from the 1940s recalled visits from the "preacher" or the "dramatist."[41]

Clearly such a commitment required tremendous resources, namely, flexible and supportive employment, a safe haven as his hometown, financial security, and access to the network of Georgia's black leaders. The pastor of Savannah's First African Baptist Church held such a position rarely found in Georgia. Eloria Sherman Gilbert shared her husband's workload and established a reputation as an orator and organizer in her own right. On the three-week tour of summer 1946, Rev. Gilbert recorded that he "divided the territory between the wife and myself. . . . I took the new and weaker branches and got the Madam to take the strong and better establishments." She alone was responsible for the founding of the Hazelhurst chapter, for example, and gave a series of speeches in cities along the Atlantic coast on the way to joining her husband in New York.[42]

Of course, membership in the NAACP, as Aldon Morris has argued persuasively, did not necessarily involve active protest in the same way that being involved with SNCC or the Congress on Racial Equality (CORE) did in the 1960s. In certain branches, the local NAACP was merely a paper organization. "We had more when we had our picture taken to go in the Paineite than we had to meetings in a year," the frustrated president of Augusta's Paine College NAACP, Ruth Bacone, reported to New York in May 1945. "I was simply mad . . . we should give them some straight facts on how delinquent they are." Two months later, Bacone criticized Augusta's inactive adult branch, suggesting that "the young people catch the spirit of doing nothing from the adults."[43]

A high proportion of NAACP members were described in census records as professionals.[44] Two surviving branch membership lists that also note employment, from Cairo and Fitzgerald, reveal that over three-quarters of members had an income not directly dependent on a white employer.[45] Just because most NAACP members were relatively prosperous did not automatically mean they were acquiescent. While Augusta's branch was notoriously accommodationist, it was independently employed black Georgians who led the first wave of concerted protest in many areas of the state. D. U. Pullum was one of only a handful of black landholders in Terrell County. W. W. Law in Savannah and John Wesley Dobbs in Atlanta were both federal postal employees. William Randall, a building contractor, and Thomas Brewer, a medical doctor, were reputedly the richest black men in Macon and Columbus respectively.[46]

The stereotyping of the NAACP as conservative ignores the context of white supremacy during the 1940s. Even during the governorship of Ellis Arnall, becoming a member of the NAACP, in the smaller towns and countryside in particular, was tantamount to brazen protest, incurring the risk of a violent or even fatal white supremacist reprisal.

Such a stereotype also ignores the activities of many of the branches during the 1940s. Repeatedly across the state, local branches in the larger cities followed the example of Savannah and engaged in public protests against Jim Crow. In 1947, businessmen in Dublin forced one local bank to desist from its ruthless treatment of black laborers by withdrawing their accounts simultaneously. The La Grange branch, located near Fort Benning, organized a mass meeting protesting the treatment of blacks in the National Defense Program and followed up with a write-in campaign to Georgia senators in favor of the 1944 Soldier Vote Bill. In Macon, some local blacks refused to ride in the rear of the Georgia Power Company bus.[47]

The stigma that white supremacists attached to membership in the NAACP suggests that local chapters were neither dormant nor impotent. J. M. Atkinson, the driving force behind the Brunswick branch that was reorganized in 1942, refrained from being officially involved for fear of losing his job. The Macon NAACP was unsuccessfully ordered to disband by the local grand jury after a provocative newspaper advertisement to "Smash Racial Division! Join the NAACP today!" Such forthright talk confirmed in the minds of white Maconites that the alarming proliferation of racial incidents on the buses, together with black employment in the local defense industry, was linked with the organization of the branch. Indulging in supremacist rhetoric, the *Macon Telegraph* compared the local organization to carpetbaggers, a "smashing" group who "tore up the finest relationship and development the world ever saw—they set Negro against white and taught the art of rape, with what result?"[48]

The opposition of some conservative black Georgians also demonstrated the radical reputation of the NAACP under Gilbert. Several prominent business and community leaders joined the fracas in Macon by publishing a statement denouncing the recently formed local branch. In Savannah, the Second Baptist Church leaders spoke out against the drive for integration. Polk County in northwest Georgia and Camilla in the southwest were typical of many smaller branches across the state, where a faction of black community leaders set out to impede the activities of the local NAACP in order to preserve the status quo.[49]

In the rural areas of the state, the NAACP came to represent an almost mythical force fighting for the black community. Unsubstantiated rumors of small clandestine meetings of NAACP men circulated among the rural black community in Quitman County in south Georgia. One despairing scrawled letter smuggled out of a chain-gang prison camp reached New York, telling of a prisoner's sickness, extreme brutal treatment, and eventual incarceration in the dungeon after a request to see the prison board. The NAACP was the final hope. "Please sir if there is anything you can do in my case for me please please do so."[50]

The NAACP was also an outside supporter of black civil rights that could speak out when local leaders necessarily remained silent through fear of violent reprisal. As one branch leader explained to the head office, "If I tried to prosecute the case here in this county I would most likely be beaten with the same strap. For that reason I am obliged to get someone away from here to do it for me so that is why I am writing you. P.S.," he continued, "Do not put your name on the outside of the envelope." Another black man, shocked at the brutish purge of voters in Wilkes County, was even more explicit. "Now get me straight. I simply cannot be quoted. Don't by any means let me be brought into this. It will get me in trouble . . . don't mention my name. Don't even write back to me. That might be a give away." Local leader Dover Carter of Montgomery County wrote to the NAACP in desperation at the end of 1948, explaining that his white assailants "continued to beat me until my head was bloody. I don't know what to do now. I have no home anymore."[51]

Both the reputation of the NAACP and the fact that it was the only major organization of its kind meant that, in rural areas, an NAACP branch was often the rallying point for existing local radical leadership. Dover Carter, for example, formed a branch after hearing Ella Baker speak in Atlanta. "I can't forget those objects, they rested on my mind daily." Similarly, D. U. Pullum in Terrell County, whose militancy earned him numerous visits from the Klan, chose to speak out under the NAACP flag. By 1946, the NAACP in Georgia had become a symbol of black resistance. In many of the major towns, the local chapter had developed into an effective protest organization. Through annual state conferences, which included workshops on voter registration in rural areas and techniques of protest in the cities, the NAACP branches had become an increasingly intertwined and cohesive statewide organization. Few individual Georgians were to influence the state's civil rights protest as Gilbert did, and under his continued leadership the state NAACP appeared poised for further advances.[52]

Black Protest in Atlanta

The other major center of black protest in Georgia was Atlanta. By 1940, Atlanta was by far the dominant city in the state. The city also emerged as the industrial capital of the New South during World War II and increased in size fourfold through annexations. Numan Bartley concluded that Atlanta was "the banking, financial and administrative hub, not only of Georgia, but of the Southeast, and consequently captured a major share of the new jobs created by such rapidly expanding service occupations as government, finance, and insurance." Of America's 500 largest corporations, almost 350 had branches in Atlanta. With an average per capita income equal to that of the United States as a whole and almost double the rest of Georgia, Atlanta had, in a sense, broken free from the confines of the southern economy. Atlanta's importance was such that, according to Neal R. Pierce, "the real reason for Georgia's rise and regional pre-eminence . . . can be summed up in one word: Atlanta."[53]

Economic prosperity, however, did not engender racial liberality. "As I appraised bad human relations in the South," Benjamin E. Mays noted on his arrival in 1940, "I rated Birmingham number 1, Memphis number 2 and Atlanta number 3," although he conceded that Atlanta was "far ahead of the rest of the state in the area of race relations." In many ways, the story of race relations in Atlanta could have been the story of any Georgia city writ large. Jim Crow segregation had become even more explicitly entrenched after the adoption of a new series of racial ordinances during the war years. Frequent incidences of friction and violence at points where white Atlanta met black Atlanta, particularly on buses and the borders of racial neighborhoods, were exacerbated after the formation of the white supremacist Columbians in August 1946. To join the uniformed terror group, potential members simply had to pay three dollars and express their hatred of Jews and blacks.[54]

Ironically, it was Atlanta's rigid segregation laws, such as the 1925 ordinance proscribing white barbers from cutting black customers' hair, that forced the black community of 137,000 people to develop as an independent economic force.[55] In his autobiography, business entrepreneur T. M. Alexander remembered coming to Atlanta because of its reputation, by 1940, as the "mecca" of black business. Statistics bear out Atlanta's reputation. A survey of the twelve largest black communities of the South reported that Atlanta supported 641 black businesses and 225 restaurants—the highest numbers in the South.[56]

During the early part of the twentieth century, Hermon Perry had been the catalyst for the growth of black-owned big business in the Auburn Avenue district of Atlanta. Perry founded Standard Life Insurance, a large conglomerate providing both insurance and financial services. Although Perry overextended his business and suffered bankruptcy, spin-off companies swiftly filled the economic vacuum. Lorrimer D. Milton formed Citizen's Trust Company Bank, Jesse B. Blayton was president of Atlanta Mutual Federal Savings and Loan Association, and Eugene Martin helped to develop Atlanta Life Insurance.[57] By the end of World War II, the so-called Sweet Auburn district supported over half of the city's black businesses, including some of the wealthiest black firms in the nation. Citizen's Trust was the first black-owned bank to become a member of the Federal Reserve System. By 1944, Atlanta Life had developed into the largest black insurance company in the country, with over $100 million of insurance in force. During the postwar period, the value of black insurance in Atlanta equaled that in Chicago and was double that in New York, Los Angeles, and San Francisco.[58]

Atlanta's segregated black community constituted a reasonably independent and tightly compact city within a city. Atlanta's residential districts were the most segregated of Georgia's major cities because of a residential segregation ordinance adopted in 1913.[59] It was this unique situation and the nature of this relatively independent black community that defined the course of civil rights protest in Atlanta during the Arnall years. The high degree of political organization and activity that developed in Atlanta befitted the Auburn Avenue community's preeminence in black Georgia. But the cautious attitude of Atlanta's black community leaders also led to a protest that lacked the vibrancy and vision of the movement in Savannah.

By 1940, Atlanta had by far the most extensive and accomplished black community leadership in Georgia. In a survey of the "Negro upper class," August Meier and David Lewis observed that "economic leadership in the Atlanta Negro community has largely passed into the hands of a group of professional and businessmen who have come to Atlanta or risen to prominence in the past thirty-five years [since 1920]." Floyd Hunter, in his seminal study of community power, discovered that this black community leadership represented an unusually influential and tightly knit power structure that ran parallel to the power structure in the dominant white community. Meier and Lewis concluded that community leadership in general equated with business prowess in particular, "with the very highest social status being accorded to certain men prominent in business and professional life today." [60]

This black power structure centered on highly developed religious and educational institutions, as well as the business district based on Auburn Avenue. [61] Atlanta's leading three black churches, Big Bethel AME, Ebenezer Baptist, and Wheat Street Baptist, were situated on or adjacent to Auburn Avenue. With a membership of over three thousand by the middle of the 1940s, Wheat Street Baptist was reputed to be the largest black church in the South, ensuring the prominence of its pastor, Rev. William Holmes Borders. During World War II over fifteen thousand black Atlantans were full members of central churches. [62] Although black Atlantans represented only a third of Atlanta's population, they owned over half of the churches. [63] With regard to black political activism in Atlanta, Borders reflected, albeit from his perspective as a pastor, that the churches "furnished the people power of the whole thing." [64] Often fractious, church leaders met together as the ministerial alliance under the leadership of Martin Luther King Sr.

Further to the west of Atlanta lay the six black colleges that constituted the Atlanta University Center, with more than 2,700 enrolled students in 1940. During World War II, Atlanta was reputed to lead the country in the number of black educational establishments. David Garrow commented that Atlanta's "roster of important black-owned business and professional institutions—particularly the Atlanta University Colleges—was one that no other Southern town or city could match." The largest college, Morehouse, with 900 male students, was described by *Crisis* in 1940 as the "only institution of its magnitude in the Deep South devoted solely to the higher education of Negro men." The other colleges were Clark, Brown, Atlanta University, and Spelman (for female students) and the Gammon Theological School.[65] Largely because of Atlanta's colleges, 6,000 black Georgians had received B.A. degrees by 1947, in contrast to only 475 in 1917. Those with leading positions in the university often achieved community power. It was as president of Morehouse College, for example, that Benjamin Mays was asked to write regular editorials for the *Atlanta Daily World* and the *Pittsburgh Courier* and to speak on radio station WERD.

The strength of Atlanta's leading black institutions was mutually reinforcing and intertwined. As T. M. Alexander concluded, "A strong relationship developed between the educational institutions, the business community and the churches. All of these business leaders were church-going citizens, trustees, and were dependent upon each other in many ways." Borders reflected later that "the thrust of leadership in Atlanta was from the colleges and from the business and religious sectors of the city . . . it was shared." [66]

Pastors such as Borders and King were trustees of the Atlanta University complex while students taught Sunday school in the churches. Atlanta's business leadership mostly emanated from black colleges and retained close links: L. D. Milton and John Calhoun, a young accountant, both taught at Morehouse, while by the war years the student fraternal organization, Sigma Phi, was one of the leading business network clubs. The majority of employees at Atlanta Life were graduates of AU and many attended the First Congregational Church. Churches overlapped with businesses partly because churches were relatively large businesses in themselves. Under Borders's leadership, Wheat Street Baptist Church launched a housing project for the elderly, two shopping centers, and a credit union. Wheat Street Baptist's worship programs even listed the value of church real estate. Martin Luther King Sr., who was a trustee of Citizen's Trust Bank, sought to emulate his rival's building program. One well-known joke was that pastors met in the forecourt of Auburn Avenue banks on Monday mornings more often than at the ministerial alliance.[67]

This institutional development ran parallel with the unusually sophisticated social and political development of Atlanta's black community.[68] For example, L. D. Milton and Jesse Blayton built the Top Hat nightclub in 1938, which became Auburn Avenue's leading entertainment spot. The Top Hat hosted performers such as Ella Fitzgerald and Dizzy Gillespie. Little Richard, from Macon, also started his career there.[69] During the 1940s, Jesse Blayton headed Atlanta's Negro Chamber of Commerce, and Annie Mays was a leading speaker at the Atlanta Business and Professional Women's Club.[70] The 27 Club was a more exclusive forum for business leaders to discuss their concerns. The first black YMCA in the country, led by Warren Cochrane, was the venue for the Hungry Club, which met regularly to discuss social and political issues.[71]

At the opposite extreme, a proliferation of neighborhood and working-class organizations became established by the early 1940s. Lugenia Burns Hope, wife of John Hope (who was president of Morehouse College during the 1930s), was the driving force behind Atlanta's Neighborhood Union, a women's community action group that grew out of the settlement movement of the early twentieth century.[72] Leading social activist Ruby Blackburn's To Improve Conditions (TIC) Club, founded during the Depression years, incorporated a nationally renowned domestics' training school and a training center for the unemployed. Blackburn had herself been a domestic worker, then a beautician, and by the 1940s she was perhaps Atlanta's most influential black community organizer. Her TIC Club involved more people than any other black organization in Atlanta.[73] Such was Blackburn's renown that she was one of the regular keynote speakers at NAACP meetings. She was also able to attract white leaders such as Mayor William Hartsfield and the president of Georgia Power to speak at her programs.[74]

On occasion, such community activity was directly concerned with combating Jim Crow. In 1932, Lugenia Hope joined with A. T. Walden to organize a "citizenship school." Under the directorship of Clarence Bacote, over a thousand black Atlantans took a two-month course at the school on voter registration procedures and the structure of government. John Wesley Dobbs formed the Atlanta Civic and Political League in 1934 with the express purpose of attaining "political equality for Negroes." After inspecting city poll tax returns to find potential voters, Dobbs increased black registration from five hundred to three thousand within five years. A. T. Walden had also established a political discussion group of black supporters of the New Deal.[75]

In fact, the relative independence of black Atlanta determined that the greater part of black activism during the early 1940s was more concerned with social betterment than with challenging segregation. The Dixie Hills Political and Civic Club, for example, was founded in 1945 because of the "dire need of an improved community." To achieve this, the club prioritized the issues of garbage collection, water supply, school lights, and nine hundred new homes.[76] The TIC Club sponsored a beautification project known as the Tree Program.

In the context of 1940s Georgia, however, campaigns for community development often addressed the economic and social consequences of white supremacy.

Ruby Blackburn's organizations secured two new school buildings for black children, employment for black clerks in a handful of chain stores, and the relocation of garbage dumps away from exclusively black sections of the city. Atlanta's Urban League helped to secure two thousand jobs for black employees at Bell Aircraft Company in 1941.[77]

The key to the development of black protest in Atlanta during the Arnall years was that it was inextricably intertwined with the interests of the Auburn Avenue elite. The cadre of leaders who assumed control of civil rights protest owed their authority as racial spokesmen to their existing authority within the community, not necessarily because they had a specific or bold racial protest agenda. Although Walden and Dobbs were the most renowned, they were only two of perhaps twenty community leaders with similar, albeit fluctuating, influence. Walden's deputy leader of the Democratic Club, C. A. Scott, also edited the *Atlanta Daily World*. T. M. Alexander, who was president of the NAACP at the start of the 1940s, was also vice-president of the Atlanta Trade and Business Association and a leading member of Atlanta's black Democratic Club.[78] C. A. Harper, who succeeded Alexander as the head of Atlanta's NAACP, was headmaster of Booker T. Washington School. From the churches, Borders and King in particular helped to finance the work of the NAACP and supported the call to vote from the pulpit. E. M. Martin, who was brother-in-law of Walter White and on the national board of the NAACP, used his resources and position as an executive at Atlanta Life Insurance to support or protect particular individuals. One of Martin's most promising assistants, John Calhoun, was also Dobbs's right-hand man.[79] Grace Towns Hamilton, who became executive director of Atlanta's Urban League in 1943, was the most prominent female member of the elite. A graduate of Atlanta University and the daughter of an AU lecturer, Hamilton had previously worked for the national YWCA.[80]

Consequently, the development of organized black protest in Atlanta reflected the general outlook of the Auburn Avenue elite. In contrast to Savannah, the Atlanta leadership did not seek to create a mass movement. The Atlanta NAACP, for instance, was often a talk-shop for a privileged few, with a regular attendance of less than ten members at meetings. Thurgood Marshall's speech to the local branch in 1940 called for the involvement of the "little man around the corner." *Atlanta Daily World* columnist William A. Foulkes suggested that Marshall must have "heard things about Atlanta before coming here . . . there would be thousands [at meetings] if they were properly urged and made to feel welcome to the monthly and special meetings." Foulkes concluded poignantly that "this is no reflection on any NAACP leader, but a general Atlanta condition." One newly arrived Atlantan wrote to the New York head office in 1944 because he wanted to join the local NAACP but couldn't "find the branch in Atlanta." Ralph Bunche also reported that political protest in Atlanta was the preserve of the elite: "One hears from all sides the constant complaint that the college teachers and the college trained citizens offer the masses no assistance in their struggle." Bunche concluded "that more progress has not been made in bettering the social, economic and political life of the Negro is in large measure the fault of the ministers."[81]

The elitist outlook of the Auburn Avenue leadership was sharply criticized by members of Atlanta's wider black community. For example, in their biography of Grace Towns Hamilton, Lorraine Spritzer and Jean Bergmark concluded that "though the benefits of their status were circumscribed, the 'haves' among Atlanta Negroes were envied and resented by many among the masses of the 'have nots.'" One preacher, Benjamin Bickers, believed that some of the Atlanta elite patronized other black Atlantans on account of class and skin color. During his youth, Bickers worked for the Hamilton family and other members of the elite to fund his education. "I never had a word from Grace Hamilton, she looked down on me, on anybody who was poor, not as light as she was. She acted just like all the old Atlanta mulatto elite."[82]

Even Clarence Bacote conceded in his summary of black political protest before 1946 that when "the NAACP, the ACPL, the Alpha Phi fraternity, and other groups had conducted registration campaigns, they had failed to reach the masses." Despite the enormous potential of a highly politicized community and a large student body, black registration in Atlanta never exceeded three thousand before the white primary decision and had decreased to under two thousand by the beginning of the 1940s. It was Rev. Gilbert, when visiting from Savannah to speak at an ACPL meeting in February 1944, who first established NAACP chapters for students at the AU colleges.[83]

Membership in the NAACP increased rapidly during 1943 after Ruby Blackburn headed up a campaign. Attendance at meetings also increased as the local branch investigated incidents of white violence, particularly against black women. Blackburn spoke regularly at clubs and churches to raise money for a local NAACP Defense Fund. Ironically, far from securing her a place at the forefront of Atlanta's black protest leadership, Blackburn was sidelined by the local branch. One Blackburn supporter, Helen Randolph, was so incensed that she wrote to the national head office, noting the "jealousy of certain well known Negro women who are prominent in Atlanta." Angry that Blackburn's picture was never carried in any of the magazines, Randolph suggested that the NAACP nominate Blackburn for the prestigious Spingarn Award, the organization's highest accolade. "I know you wouldn't dare offer her as a candidate," Randolph concluded caustically, "because she is not an Opera singer or a movie star." [84]

Rather than seeking to organize a mass movement, some of the Auburn Avenue leaders sometimes seemed to focus their energies on assuming personal preeminence within the elite. Walden and Dobbs jealously guarded their own programs, while King's and Borders's rivalry escalated when Martin Luther King Jr. started to imitate Borders's superior oratorical style. Although most black leaders were content to have overlapping roles, the energies of the elite pulled in different, sometimes uncoordinated, directions. Atlanta provided a complete contrast to the clear channeling and direction of protest in Savannah. "It is not too much to re-echo the charge that we are over-organized," the *Atlanta Daily World* observed on 2 January 1946. Ruby Hurley wrote to Gloster Current that "our branch suffered from the influence of the Old Guard, the Negro power structure. There was a special, local committee set up for every problem that arose." [85]

The exception to such factionalism and diversity arose only in response to specific issues that threatened the well-being of the Auburn Avenue community. In a letter to Ruby Hurley, John Calhoun explained that "no matter in the history of Atlanta has so aroused and united Negroes as the suggestion [of the city government] to relocate the Auburn Avenue black business district to a designated area on the periphery of the city." More often, it was bond proposals that united the black leadership because the black vote had the potential to derail discriminatory spending. In 1940, for example, the Negro Chamber of Commerce joined with the local NAACP, the ACPL, and the TIC Club to organize the defeat of a $1.8 million bond issue that provided only $100,000 for Atlanta's black schools. [86]

Black Atlanta also contrasted with Savannah as members of the Auburn Avenue elite eschewed confrontational forms of protest in favor of negotiation or voting in bond issues. To a large extent, this reflected the inherent conservatism of an upper-class leadership. Such a tactic was more appropriate in Atlanta than perhaps any other southern city because the community leaders of both racial groups were well known to each other. In many ways, though, this left the black community at the mercy of white generosity. Clarence Bacote reminisced later that "before we had political clout how did we do it? Begging, almost hat in hand." After meeting with an eight-man delegation from Auburn Avenue at the start of the 1940s, for example,

Mayor William Hartsfield rejected the request for black policemen with the rebuff, "Come back with ten thousand votes." [87]

Before the Primus King decision, the only other method of seeking redress was through the courts. Since 1936, Rev. King had sought to challenge the legality of the practice that teachers' salaries were separate but not equal. On average, black teachers were paid two-thirds of the salary of their white counterparts. With Walden acting as the NAACP lawyer, in 1942 King persuaded high school teacher William Reeves to file suit. Within weeks, Reeves had been sacked for being morally unsuitable to be a teacher, and the case was subsequently dropped because he was no longer an employee of the school system.[88] At the behest of King, Atlanta Life had already agreed to underwrite Reeve's employment to insure against such an eventuality.

Considering the factionalism and conservatism of Atlanta's black political leadership, therefore, the ending of the white primary after *King* proved crucial to the development of Atlanta's black protest. The value of a black bloc vote to improve their own negotiating strength encouraged the black elite to seek more widespread voter registration throughout Atlanta's black community. The social and institutional development of black Atlanta proved to be a valuable conduit for registration campaigns. Furthermore, the candidature of Talmadge for the 1946 gubernatorial election provided an urgent issue that forced the cadre of leaders to unite.[89]

The power of the black ballot was unexpectedly and dramatically demonstrated before the primary. When Representative Robert Ramspeck of Georgia's fifth district in Atlanta vacated his seat at the start of 1946, a special election was called for 12 February to fill his unexpired term.[90] Immediately a widely publicized registration campaign was launched under the leadership of the NAACP. By the time of election, 6,876 blacks had registered. Of the nineteen candidates, the black leadership endorsed Helen Mankin, the only candidate who accepted the invitation to a clandestine meeting on Auburn Avenue. By the time the polls closed, all precincts had reported except for Precinct B, an exclusively black ward. At this point it was calculated that Mankin's chief rival, white supremacist Tom Camp, had a lead of 156 votes. But the overwhelming vote for Mankin in Precinct B secured her election by over 800 votes.[91]

Atlanta historians disagree over Mankin's precise relationship to the black voters.[92] Mankin herself claimed that the CIO played a far more important role than black Atlantans in her campaign. The *Pittsburgh Courier* also conceded in an editorial that "if that particular precinct box had reported earlier it is possible that some other precinct may now be claiming credit." But the black vote was widely perceived as deciding the election. Eugene Talmadge nicknamed Mankin "the belle of Ashby street," the major black residential road in the district. Both the *Atlanta Daily World* and the *Pittsburgh Courier* headlines proclaimed black victory. Even *Time* magazine covered the story under the title "The Negro Vote Did It," while *Newsweek* ran a story titled "Georgia's Black Ballots." Bacote reflected that Mankin's victory was a "red letter day" for black politics in Atlanta.[93]

While the Mankin election provided a blaze of publicity, the ultimate success of the registration campaign for the 1946 primary lay with the organizational structure of the campaign. At the suggestion of the leaders of Atlanta's Urban League, a broad cross section of Atlanta's organizational leaders united to form the All-Citizens' Registration Committee under the auspices of the NAACP. As a result, influential organizations that were previously outside the community power structure, such as Blackburn's TIC Club, were used to attract wider registration.[94]

Atlanta's highly developed institutional structure was a further reason for the successful campaign. The Auburn Avenue pastors exhorted their congregations to register. Atlanta Life Insurance and the Citizen's Trust Bank insisted that all their employees register. Atlanta Life also printed voter registration materials at minimal cost. Bacote supervised a survey of Atlanta's black wards before appointing 870 bloc leaders to canvass Atlanta blacks. The university provided numerous voting educa-tion workshops. As a result, some 18,000 Atlantans were registered in the month of May alone, and by the time of the primary, over 21,000 out of Atlanta's 70,000 registered voters were black. After the election, Harper and Bacote announced publicly that they were "grateful to religious, civic and political leaders for their support in assisting Negroes for the 5th district election."[95]

In her review of women's leadership in the Atlanta protest, Kathryn Nasstrom points out that the role of women's networks has been neglected from the narrative of Atlanta's early voting campaigns. According to Nasstrom, "The drive depended equally on women and men to succeed and employed women's and men's differing networks of work and leisure."[96] Blackburn's organization was merely the most widespread of many women's organizations that played an important role in the voting campaign. On 20 February 1946, for example, the *Atlanta Daily World* noted that the MRS Club, a social club of young working women, was the "first 100 per cent registered organization." If the churches and businesses provided the building blocks for the campaign, teachers also played a vital if less heralded role. Over three-quarters of Atlanta's black teachers were women. According to Nasstrom, "In this early mobilization for civil rights in the 1940s, female teachers were on a par with the ministers, the men who would come to be widely recognized for their leadership in the movement of the 1950s and 1960s."[97]

As in Savannah, the power of the black vote in Atlanta brought tangible racial changes. Faced with double his ten thousand votes, Mayor Hartsfield appointed six black policemen, although he refused to appoint black fire officers. The black vote also assumed the balance of power, as the black community allied with the wealthy, moderate white community in north Atlanta to form an unofficial majority coalition. Hartsfield was reelected in the three ensuing elections without winning a majority of votes cast by white Atlantans. At the neighborhood level, the increased political leverage of the Auburn Avenue elite led to a more responsive ear for calls for improvement schemes. Shortly after appointing the black policemen, Hartsfield responded to Harper's "quiet but insistent manner" by authorizing the New Anderson Park, complete with swimming pool and tennis courts.[98]

The other parallel with Savannah was that the Atlanta protest spilled over into the rest of Georgia. As the trend-setting city in the state, Atlanta's racial progress was important. News of Mankin's victory, for example, spread through the media and existing organizations. In his overview of black voting in Georgia, Hugh Carl Owen concluded that it was the "Atlanta election that turned the spotlight on Negro voting."[99]

Atlanta's influence on the state's emerging civil rights protest had already spread indirectly through the city's social and economic organizations. In his capacity as the Most Worshipful Grandmaster of the Prince Hall Masons, Dobbs urged Georgia Masons to register. The NAACP branches at Telfair County and La Grange used Atlanta Life Insurance Company paper when writing to the New York office, suggesting at least some connection between local leaders and the company. In 1945, the NAACP branch in Griffin, Spalding County, was organized in the local office of Atlanta Life by Alonzo C. Touchstone, the company's district manager.[100]

The Primus King decision presented Atlanta's leaders with an opportunity to become directly involved in civil rights activity throughout Georgia. Previously, the record of the Auburn Avenue elite's activity outside Atlanta had been somewhat checkered. The president of the newly formed Cairo NAACP branch in southwest Georgia complained to Thurgood Marshall in 1942 about Walden's paltry support of a local legal case: "So far as to his activities and interest toward conditions here . . . we would expect about as much from our present Governor Talmadge towards cooperation as from him." C. A. Scott had written a stinging attack against the Columbus branch in the *Atlanta Daily World,* concluding that "I was not cordially received and had to handle things rather tactfully." [101]

Within a month of the Texas primary decision, however, Walden called a meeting of black Democratic leaders in the central city of Macon, where the Association of Citizens' Democratic Clubs was formed. Representatives from the eleven participating counties agreed to urge black Georgians to vote. By the time of the Primus King decision, Dobbs's state Republican network had joined with the Democrats to form the bipartisan Georgia Voters' League (GVL).[102]

Although Walden and Dobbs held a few regional mass meetings to promote the registration drive, the main role of the Atlanta leadership was to coordinate and give technical advice, in contrast to Gilbert's more pioneering work.[103] Gilbert invited Dobbs to address a public meeting in Savannah in March 1946. According to the *Savannah Herald,* Dobbs's visit was one reason why "the people as a whole are becoming registration conscious." The success of the Georgia registration campaign, therefore, was entirely dependent on the groundswell of expectancy and on existing protest networks. City leaders such as Bill Randall of Macon and Dr. Brewer of Columbus had already initiated local registration campaigns. The Georgia State Conference of the NAACP had explicitly established registration as one of its inaugural aims. Indeed, the majority of Democratic Clubs developed in counties where there was an existing local NAACP branch, and voter registration workshops were conducted at the 1946 state NAACP conference.[104]

The groundswell of local protest, Gilbert's dynamism, and the expertise of the Atlanta elite proved to be a formidable combination. The *New South* concluded that "of all the Southern Voters' Leagues, the Georgia association has done perhaps the most effective job in establishing local branches." By the end of 1946, there were more than sixty affiliated clubs. Hugh Owen described the campaign as "phenomenal" in the context of the South, attributing the unique success of Georgia's Voters' League to an unusually high caliber of state leadership.[105]

The registration campaigns translated into tangible gains at the local level. In Brunswick, the black bloc vote assumed the balance of power. By 1946, black voters publicly endorsed and elected candidates who guaranteed black jurors and employment for black doctors in the city hospital. In the same year, archsegregationist leader Roy Harris of Augusta lost an election for the first time in twenty-four years. Although the black vote was barely greater than the margin of defeat, Harris and the black media both declared, though for different reasons, that the electoral result was primarily determined by the bloc vote.[106]

In the three months before the gubernatorial primary in June 1946, state black registration had increased from less than 30,000 to approximately 125,000, representing over one-fifth of the total state electorate. Forbidden by the state constitution to stand for reelection, Arnall supported the moderate candidate James V. Carmichael against Talmadge. Considering that Arnall had won the 1942 primary when it was exclusively white, the additional support of the black bloc vote seemed certain to guarantee another four years of moderate state leadership. The *Crisis* commented that the registration of black voters in Georgia "marks the beginning of a new day for the Negro, for the South and for the nation." [107]

The Gubernatorial Election of 1946

V. O. Key contended that the 1946 primary election was the "most important contest in a generation." Key observed that a second consecutive defeat for Eugene Talmadge would end his public career and jeopardize the future political career of his son Herman.[108] In the context of Georgia's race relations, the 1946 election assumed even greater importance. Not only had black Georgians secured major advances under Arnall, but Eugene Talmadge's racist rhetoric, bordering on hysteria, made the repeal of black enfranchisement the central issue of the campaign. Rather than equating the prospective black vote with a potential Republican or Communist conspiracy, Talmadge's most common theme was simply the danger of a "nigra takeover."

In the event, Eugene Talmadge defeated Carmichael by 242 to 146 county-unit votes. "Asking why Talmadge could win," the *Atlanta Constitution* concluded that "the people were made afraid of the Negro issue. That is 95% of the explanation." In fact, the technical reason for Talmadge's victory lay in Georgia's electoral system. Carmichael actually received a plurality of the popular vote and more votes than any previous gubernatorial candidate, defeating Talmadge by 314,000 to 297,000 votes.[109]

Talmadge's county-unit victory, moreover, was entirely dependent on a coordinated purge of black voters and fraudulent poll counts. FBI reports later revealed a sophisticated campaign through which Talmadge supporters across the state took advantage of a largely unknown constitutional provision allowing any citizen to challenge the right of another to vote. Most of the challenges were based on the issue of color, and some challengers simply asserted that they did not think "any nigger was qualified to vote." In the weeks before the 1946 primary, such challenges often led to the removal of an entire county's black electorate. Reinstatement in time for the primary ultimately depended on the opinion of the local registrar. In Schley County, for example, over half the voters were disqualified, thus reducing black voters to a minority of the electorate. C. A. Scott estimated that over twenty thousand voters were challenged in thirty-one counties. FBI records suggest that in approximately fifty counties where blacks were not permitted to vote, the racial purge decided the result. In his study of the 1946 election, Joseph L. Bernd concluded that "Talmadge would have lost without the benefits of the campaign against black voting."[110]

This campaign continued right up to election day. In Savannah, political boss Johnny Bouhan brought voting to a standstill by minimizing the number of polling booths. Consequently, thousands of black Savannahians were unable to vote, even though they had stood in line at the polls since dawn. In the black belt, violent intimidation of the remaining voters consolidated Talmadge's victory. None of the still-qualified hundred black voters in Schley County actually voted because the local state representative used the simple deterrent of standing outside the polling booth with a shotgun, exclaiming that "if a nigger votes in this election, he'll be a dead nigger." In Columbus, a local Klan member, Rev. E. G. "Parson Jack" Johnston, sent Dr. Brewer death threats. Eugene Talmadge warned that "wise Negroes will stay away from white folks' ballot boxes," and only three black voters had cast ballots in Talmadge's home county by the afternoon.[111]

In their overview of the civil rights movement, Reese Cleghorn and Pat Watters noted the black registration in Georgia and posed a counterfactual that is even more apposite in the light of the FBI reports: "We cannot know how history might have turned if Georgia had continued in that direction and if Negroes had begun to make a difference in state elections. Under those circumstances, Georgia might not have been fitted into the southern defiance of the 1950s." Evidence from oral interviews indicates that in all likelihood, four years under Carmichael's governorship would have allowed further advances for the black voting and protest network. "The Carmichael people wanted to get that black vote," recalled Osgood Williams, a member of Carmichael's inner circle, and so at the outset of the campaign they arranged a conference between Carmichael and Walden at the group's Atlanta Piedmont Hotel headquarters.[112]

The effect of Carmichael's defeat on Georgia's race relations was obvious to many observers. Harold Fleming, the future president of the SCHW, determined to leave Georgia in 1946, reflecting later that "a spirit of hope . . . went gurgling down the drain when Gene Talmadge was elected." Morton Sosna, in his study of southern liberals, noted that liberals in Georgia felt that any action during this "period of reaction" was "futile." The *Associated Press* reported that "after pioneering a new political way in the South that amazed the nation, Georgia has returned to rock-ribbed southern tradition."[113]

Black leaders in Georgia also feared the worst. Benjamin Mays recalled that "Mr. Talmadge's anti-Negro utterances were so vile and vicious that many of us were concerned about what might happen racially when the governor took office in January of 1947." Consequently, Mays drew up a resolution, which was adopted by the General Missionary Baptist Convention of Georgia, calling for a day of prayer on Talmadge's inauguration day. From Savannah, the convention called on members to "pray to the God of the universe for Eugene Talmadge" and to ask "God to make of him a good, just, democratic and Christian Governor . . . with malice toward none and with justice for all."[114]

White supremacist and other hate organizations also took their cue. One week after the primary, Georgia experienced its first lynchings in four years. Two couples were murdered for no apparent reason outside the town of Monroe, Walton County, fifty miles east of Atlanta. According to Guy Johnson, the executive director of the SRC, the lynchings were "the foulest crime that has been committed in many years." After hearing about the incident from friends in Walton County, Walter White commented that there were "several whites who were as appalled by the lynchings and condemnatory of the mob as were the Negroes." Three more lynchings were reported in the following two weeks. Such was the new atmosphere of terror that E. M. Martin warned Walter White not to come to the state because "you may rest assured that your life would not be safe in Georgia at the present time." Not even Atlanta was safe, Martin continued, because "Atlanta is truly the headquarters of intolerance and fascism and there are plenty of persons who would not mind attempting to assassinate the major leader among Negroes for crushing intolerance, segregation and the white primary."[115]

The precise extent of Talmadge's leadership of the supremacist backlash remains unknown, but contemporaries saw his election and the resultant violence as inextricably intertwined. After visiting Monroe, the investigative journalist Tom O'Connor reported in *P.M.* magazine that after Talmadge's primary victory, "the season on 'niggers' was automatically opened and every pinheaded Georgia cracker and bigoted Ku Kluxer figured he had a hunting license." It was "Gallus Gene Talmadge," O'Connor concluded, who was held "by every honest citizen of Georgia to be the real criminal in the present case." Aptly expressing the fears of black Georgians, the *New York Times* printed a cartoon depicting the Monroe lynch mob leaving the scene saying, "It's okay—Ol 'Gene will be back soon." [116]

In a letter to Walter White in August 1946, however, E. M. Martin made the point that Talmadge's victory was not simply a case of rural supremacists benefiting from the county-unit system. "The greatest enemy to the Negro is not the 'poor white trash' but the big moguls high up," Martin told his brother-in-law. "I think we all know that the powerful rich here and there were the backers of Talmadge, namely the first National Bank, the Candlers, the Mill owners and the Georgia Power Company officials." It was certainly true that Georgia's business community had reacted to the New Deal by supporting Talmadge. For example, Preston Arkwright, the president of Georgia Power, commented in a letter of 1935 that "he is perhaps lacking in the elegancies, politeness and very sensitive refinements, but . . . I am a great admirer of his and I am for him." [117]

In a symbolic sideshow to the governor's race, Mankin lost her seat during the 1946 primary, despite a comfortable popular majority of 53,611 to 42,482 votes. Under the county-unit system, Mankin's overwhelming victory in Fulton County, which contained over three-quarters of the electoral population in her district, was worth only six unit votes. These votes were offset by her narrow loss in DeKalb County and a heavy defeat in rural Rockdale County, worth six unit votes and a decisive two unit votes respectively.

Mankin's defeat was a microcosm of the statewide picture. Mankin's opponent, James C. Davis, was a close ally of Talmadge and a known former member of the Ku Klux Klan. The fifth district Democratic Executive Committee had exceeded its power in deciding by eight members to six to use the county-unit system of voting for the primary even though previous elections in the district had been decided by popular vote. Although the fourteen-man committee was allowed to choose the method of voting, in this instance the committee was one short and deliberately delayed appointing Mankin's nominee until after the decision. [118] The nonvoting chairman, who was an implacable Mankin opponent, illegally cast a vote to make up the numbers. When Mankin contested the general election as an independent candidate later in the year, observers accused poll workers of scandalously manipulating her write-in vote. [119] According to Mankin's biographer, "It was a day of confusion, collusion, misleading instructions, a breakdown of normal election procedures and miscounting—she called it stealing—of votes, with no investigative journalists in sight." [120]

In a final twist to a highly eventful political year, Eugene Talmadge died before he accepted office, to be temporarily replaced by his son Herman, who had not even stood in the election. After a series of bizarre events, which included a fistfight between Arnall and Herman and the armed occupation of the governor's mansion by Herman's supporters, the state legislature elected Herman on the strength of a handful of write-in votes.[121] Fifty-eight of these votes were found just before the final count in Talmadge's home county of Telfair. Many of the voters had, in fact, been dead for some years, and had conveniently cast their votes in alphabetical order.[122] Sixty-seven days later the Supreme Court overruled the legislature, appointing Eugene's running mate, M. E. Thompson, and setting a special gubernatorial election for the following year, which Herman won.[123] Even in his two months in office, however, Herman Talmadge initiated legislation allowing the Democratic Party to act as a private club that freed the primary from the Primus King decision.

The extent and violence of white supremacist forces in Georgia exceeded that in the rest of the South. Charles Payne noted that "racist violence across the South was less common than it had been. In Mississippi between 1946 and 1949, one observer found no evidence of significant Klan activity." "Inexplicably," commented John Egerton in his review of southern violence, "Georgia seemed in 1947, as in the preceding year, to have a worse case of racial bloodlust than most of the other southern states." All but one of the recorded lynchings in America in 1946 occurred in Georgia within days of the primary. The SCHW also noted the racial repression with alarm. Executive Secretary Robert Carr wrote in July 1947 that "there is no doubt that Georgia is passing through a veritable reign of terror and that shocking things are happening."[124]

In a review of the state, the SCHW recorded numerous incidents of these "shocking things." In Harris County, for example, police whipped the children of an escaped black suspect in front of their grandfather until he mentioned the name of the Gilbert family, who may have helped his son escape. Immediately the Gilberts, who were respected landowners in the community, were arrested and beaten. Peg Gilbert died shortly afterward, but, poignantly, Herman Talmadge refused to launch an investigation, insisting instead that "race relations were good in the state." The SCHW noted that "the local law is impotent to protect the rights of the Negro population in the face of rising public feeling." Little wonder, the SCHW concluded, that the "Negroes of Troup County and Harris County are living in a state of terror."[125]

In the context of Georgia's emerging black protest movement, the significance of this "terror" was the decimation of overt local protests, particularly away from the major cities. Elderly protest leaders later remembered the violent harassment in the rural counties of black leaders who had risked prominence before 1946. Black union leaders in southwest Georgia were hounded out of the region. In Taylor County, a young black veteran, Macio Snipes, who had voted in the 1946 primary, was murdered on his porch by ten white men just three days after the election. Ironically, Private Snipes had not planned to vote until he heard the Ku Klux Klan warning that the first black to vote in his county would be attacked. Membership in the NAACP had halved by the time of the membership review of 1947.[126]

In Atlanta, NAACP branch president C. A. Harper pondered an all-out drive for civil rights in Atlanta and Georgia in the wake of what he called "heinous lynchings" and the "diabolical Talmadge vote scheme." For Rev. Gilbert, the need to respond to the crisis was imperative. "We must do something in the face of the critical situation in Georgia," Gilbert urged the head office, "to justify the NAACP and the existence of the State Conference and to commend both to the masses of our people in Georgia." In an attempt to gather all the surviving active black leaders into a united force, Gilbert proposed an emergency conference of both heads of the Negro Baptist Convention, heads of all Grand Lodges, and heads of all insurance companies and independent black colleges. The crisis prompted the first and only attempt in Georgia to form a single, all-encompassing, and united state protest organization.[127]

Crucially, the New York office failed to support Gilbert's pleas for help. In his reply, Gloster Current, the NAACP's director of branches, argued that "the death of [Eugene] Talmadge obviates the necessity for calling the conference of top leadership." Current also ignored Gilbert's subsequent warning that "white supremacy is the main issue in Georgia and not Talmadge" and his repeated calls for a full-time state worker. Moreover, the New York office seemed to be either unable or unwilling to appreciate the imminent collapse of a statewide network. In a letter to the local branch president in 1946, National Membership Secretary Lucille Black naively concluded that "we feel certain that the recent violence at Monroe is going to stimulate the efforts of your workers in the membership drive." The subsequent reply from Monroe would have been appropriate for most branches across the state: "The political situation has been of such, that it has been very difficult for us to carry on in this branch." During the following year, every black church and school in nearby Loganville was put to the torch.[128]

It was probably no coincidence that Gilbert suffered a personal collapse within months of the resurgence of white supremacy. An apparent drift into despair and perhaps depression led to his resignation from all NAACP activities. His correspondence with the head office revealed an uncharacteristic pessimism: "It is very hard going, this keeping up of an active interest in the NAACP . . . it is next to impossible to get workers." The further decline of the organization, both in Savannah and the rest of the state, is perhaps the most telling evidence of the personal importance of Gilbert during the period 1942–48. Savannah's membership in 1949 was less than one-third of the total in the preceding year.[129]

Gilbert's resignation from NAACP leadership in 1949 sounded the final death knell for the protest that had emerged in Georgia during the Arnall years. Gilbert's final months were also shrouded in controversy. NAACP officials privately investigated a charge of financial misconduct. Whether true or not, one local NAACP official wrote to Roy Wilkins that the "prestige of the organization has been seriously damaged by the charges presently pending against Rev. Gilbert . . . of using the mails to defraud."[130] By the end of the decade, only eleven urban NAACP branches remained active, and membership had decreased to a mere quarter of the 1946 peak. Such a swift collapse was an indictment of the parlous foundations of many of the branches and Gilbert's failure to train and develop a broader leadership base. Voter registration also decreased by over fifty thousand, leaving the black bloc vote as the balance of power in less than 20 of Georgia's 156 counties.

In her study of black protest in the South after the New Deal, Patricia Sullivan concluded that during the late 1930s and 1940s, "hundreds of acts of coalition-building and consciousness-raising had transformed black expectations. Significant segments of the black community experienced a new sense of empowerment, which would be sustained in the face of increasing white resistance . . . the foundation for the civil rights movement was in place. It would be revitalized by the mass movement of the 1960s." In fact, the local leadership in the countryside was so decimated that any later signs of continuity were rare, albeit significant. When SNCC activists visited "Terrible Terrell" County in 1962, the only resident prepared to support them initially was D. U. Pullum, who had been inspired by Gilbert's leadership a generation previously.[131]

In some urban areas the threads of continuity were more readily discernible. After remaining relatively quiescent during the decade after 1946, Bill Randall of Macon responded to the direct action protests of the 1960s by leading a forthright and successful local campaign. But in most cities such links were dependent on individual leaders rather than the continued existence of organizations. Those cities without an outstanding leader often suffered a complete retrenchment in black protest. After visiting Brunswick in 1958, NAACP fieldworker Amos Holmes recalled, somewhat ruefully, the "luster of the forties," which contrasted with the "state of civic apathy" during the following decade.[132]

After the election of 1946, concerted black protest was mainly restricted to Atlanta and Savannah. Whereas these cities had been the bases for various statewide activities under the governorship of Arnall, for the ensuing decade they reverted to being islands of relative racial moderation in an otherwise ardently white supremacist state. After the resignation of Gilbert, the cadre of Atlanta leaders assumed the mantle of black leadership within the state. As a result of their leadership, the story of civil rights protest in the 1950s was limited to voter registration in the major cities and legal attacks on the foundations of Jim Crow.

Overall, although individual threads of continuity remained, the statewide network of local protests forged by Rev. Gilbert collapsed and was largely forgotten by the next generation of direct action protesters in Georgia during the 1960s. This discontinuity stands in contrast to the history of Louisiana and Mississippi, where the activities of the 1940s developed through the 1950s into the mass movement of the Martin Luther King years. Whereas Dittmer describes the 1940s as years of "rising expectations" in Mississippi and Fairclough concludes that activities in Louisiana were the "first act of a two-act play," the story of black protest in Georgia at this time could be better characterized as "great expectations partly fulfilled but then dashed" or "the first of two one-act plays."

3

The Effects of the White Supremacist Backlash on Black Protest, 1948–1960

The election of Eugene Talmadge in 1946 marked the end of the upsurge in black activism, but it was the election of Herman Talmadge as governor in the special election of 1948 that ushered in a further decade of aggressive white supremacy in the state. As *Harper's* magazine reporter Calvin Kytle predicted, the 1948 election represented a "long, dark night for Georgia." "Poor Ol' Georgia," one voter told a *Time* reporter, "first Sherman, then Herman."[1]

The Collapse of 1940s Protest

Far from being a linear escalation of black protest from World War II through to the time of Martin Luther King Jr., the 1950s in Georgia were years of retrenchment. The statewide NAACP network disintegrated. The number of branches fell from a peak of fifty-five in 1946 to under twenty by the early 1950s, many of which were inactive. NAACP membership, which had exceeded 11,000 during 1946–48, fell to

3,168 in 1949 and remained consistently below 4,500 thereafter.[2] Over two-thirds of this membership was in Atlanta and Savannah. When William Boyd succeeded Gilbert in 1949, he despaired that there were "so few chapters in Georgia" and decided to try to get members even where there were no chapters.[3]

The stagnation of black activism in Georgia after 1948 was in contrast to the situation in other southern states. Dittmer concluded that "although the early 1950s was certainly no golden age of race relations in Mississippi—Jim Crow and everything it stood for remained firmly in place—there were signs of gradual improvement in the racial climate." In Mississippi "the NAACP was experiencing slow but steady growth, with local branches becoming bolder in communicating their message to the general public." Raymond Gavins noted that in North Carolina, "the postwar decade saw a great increase in the number of branches and the scope of their location. The branch total increased to eighty-three, or by 60 percent, between 1946 and 1955." In Louisiana, black registration surpassed that of Georgia by 1956, increasing by over one-third during the four years after 1952. While noting the limits of politics as a means to racial progress, Fairclough recorded that "to be courted by white politicians was a novel and heady experience for black Louisianians." Fairclough concluded that "exhilarating, too, was the discovery that black votes, although still relatively few, could make and break politicians."[4]

In many ways the gubernatorial election of 1948 proved to be an accurate portent for the ensuing decade of white supremacist politics. First, the election demonstrated that under the county-unit system, the rural portion of the state retained political predominance. Georgia's governmental structure was "created in another era," the *New South* observed in 1949, and "bears little relation to the state's present-day economy and outlook." Therefore, the more moderate race relations in Atlanta and Savannah had no influence on statewide elections. Furthermore, over half of the black voters in the state were in the thirty-eight most populous counties, which were relatively underrepresented by the county-unit apportionment. And as V. O. Key noted, the legislature would never reform the county-unit system because the "legislators themselves are the beneficiaries of the malapportionment that would have to be altered."[5]

Defense of white supremacy and defense of the county-unit system, therefore, became synonymous during the 1950s. Charles Pyles noted that "if Georgia politics has been a history of rural-urban cleavage, it is the attitude toward the position of the Negro that explains the major peculiarities of the cleavage." Racial gains in the major cities fueled the campaigns of rural politicians. Herman Talmadge, for example, circulated over two million pieces of segregationist literature, including copies of a photograph of interracial dancing taken at an NAACP meeting in Atlanta. Certainly black activists saw the county-unit system as the major obstacle to black political progress. Bacote called it "the most invidious system that was ever invented." The *Pittsburgh Courier* saw the county-unit system as "the last stand of hate-inspired politics in Georgia."[6]

In every respect, Georgia's virulent white supremacist backlash was led from the highest official level. The *New York Times* labeled Herman Talmadge as the "all-time Georgia champion of white supremacy." By his own admission, Talmadge won the 1948 election on "as white a primary as possible" platform and introduced a four-point legislative program to secure white supremacy. Almost immediately, over twelve thousand black voters were purged and far more intimidated from exercising their vote in most counties across the state.[7]

Within a year, a new voter registration law reintroduced the poll tax and all voters were required to take a discriminatory test every two years in order to reregister. The fifty questions that could be asked in the test ranged in difficulty from "name the president of the United States" to "how many judges sit on the state court of Appeals?" While in no doubt that black Georgians would be asked the most difficult questions, a *New York Times* editorial thought the process particularly absurd because Talmadge and "the wool hat group" "could not answer over half a dozen of the fifty proposed questions." Such legislation gave free rein to local officials. In Savannah, five thousand black voters were sent cards requiring personal information and lost their registration if they did not reply promptly. In Johnson County, where black residents represented a third of the mostly rural population, prospective voters were required to sign a pledge in support of white supremacy.[8]

The voter exclusion bill was flanked by further minor pieces of legislation aimed at obstructing even the most tentative challenge to white supremacy. In the hospitals, all blood from black and white Georgians had to be marked separately. At the behest of Dr. Samuel Green, Georgia's Imperial Wizard of the Ku Klux Klan, Talmadge unsuccessfully sought to ban black baseball stars Jackie Robinson and Roy Campanella when the Dodgers played the Atlanta Crackers.[9]

Talmadge's supremacist stance presaged a decade of staunch defense of segregation by leading state politicians. In Washington, D.C., Georgia senator Richard Russell strongly opposed President Harry Truman's call for civil rights legislation. On 27 January 1949, Russell took the offensive against "northern hypocrites" when he introduced a bill in Congress to fund the relocation of black southerners to northern states. Minnesota senator Hubert H. Humphrey suggested that the $500 million scheme had been borrowed from the "Hitler-Stalin school of shifting [around] populations one doesn't want." [10] In July 1951, Talmadge asserted that "as long as I am governor in Georgia, Negroes will not be admitted to white schools." Shortly after his inauguration in 1955 as Talmadge's successor, Governor Marvin Griffin prohibited the University of Georgia from playing sports against any team that included a black player. At the end of September 1958, Governor Ernest Vandiver was elected on the same pledge that "no, not one" black student would ever enter a white public school. [11]

This blatant supremacist rhetoric was backed up by more sophisticated measures in defense of segregation. In 1951, Talmadge introduced a 3 percent sales tax to raise an extra $200 million for education in Georgia. Over half of the initial spending of $30 million was designated for black schools, even though black children represented only one-third of the total enrollment. The state administration also raised the budget to pay for out-of-state college education for black students by almost one-half. Under the heading "Georgia's Last Stand," a *Pittsburgh Courier* editorial jokingly asked, "Has Governor Talmadge sprouted wings and a halo?" Within three years, spending on education had soared from 2.6 to 53 percent of total state revenue. [12]

In reality, such generous spending was a vain attempt to justify the doctrine of separate but equal in advance of the *Brown* test case. [13] At the same time, Talmadge ushered in an appropriations bill that promised to withhold state funding from any white school in Georgia that admitted a single black child. Instead, the state would reimburse the parents of the schoolchildren concerned and lease the school buildings to a local resident who would then run an independent segregated school. Even leaving aside the other question of Talmadge's motives and moral principles, argued Benjamin Mays, Georgia's state administration needed to spend an exorbitant $175 million on black schools to equalize school standards. Georgia's Department of Education conceded that, if anything, Mays's estimate was slightly conservative. The *Pittsburgh Courier* was less sanguine about the political maneuverings. "The State of Georgia is demonstrating today how one evil man can set back the clock and lower the prestige of an important commonwealth." [14]

The Ku Klux Klan became inextricably linked with the Georgia administration under Talmadge. Gloster Current observed at the end of 1948 that the "election of Talmadge has apparently been a signal to these hooded devils to don their sheets." Grand Dragon Dr. Samuel Green and Talmadge shared the same racial outlook, both men asserting that "God himself segregated the races." In November 1948,

Talmadge officially designated Green a lieutenant colonel and his own aide-de-camp. Meanwhile, Green instructed all Georgia Klansmen that the most important task in 1948 was to elect Talmadge. In parallel with the renewed dominance of the Talmadge faction, the Associated Klans of Georgia reemerged from a wartime low of 12 Klaverns to over 110 Klaverns, with an estimated one hundred thousand members by the summer of 1949. At a time when Klan activity was decreasing across the South and even in Mississippi, Klan membership, therefore, almost equaled the number of black registered voters across the state. "The Ku Klux Klan is surging again in Georgia," the *New York Times* observed.[15]

The growth of the Klan translated into renewed racial violence. During the first six months of 1948, the Southern Regional Council documented an unprecedented dozen reported attacks in Georgia. The following year, Georgia led the South in extralegal racial violence. Typically, Klan activities were targeted at black advocates of racial change, beginning with the election of 1948. In one unusual instance, three investigative white reporters were beaten and stabbed with hypodermic needles for infiltrating an initiation ceremony outside Columbus. Cross-burnings were believed to have been the reason for the minimal turnout of black voters in the southeastern town of Valdosta. In Wrightsville, Johnson County, three hundred Klan members marched and then burned a fifteen-foot cross on the eve of the Democratic primary to remind residents of Dr. Green's warning that "blood will flow in the streets if the Negro votes." It proved to be no idle threat. A turpentine worker, Isaiah Nixon, in Montgomery County and Robert Mallard from Toombs County were both murdered for voting after having been specifically warned not to. Election managers across the state reported that "large numbers of Negroes have been too scared to vote." [16]

After 1948, racial violence was unrestrained and unchecked. After a lynching in Irwinton, Wilkinson County, the local jury deliberated for only twenty minutes before releasing the two local white defendants, not least because two of the jury had already served as character witnesses. Wilkinson County's solicitor expressed relief at the exoneration of the sheriff beyond "any question of doubt." "Most Georgia sheriffs," he explained to reporters, "would have shot the Negro instead of taking him to jail." Angry at the intrusion of the Georgia Bureau of Investigation and particularly the media, the *Wilkinson County News* expressed the hope that "maybe some of these Georgia editors will yet get the racial tar and rusty feathers they so much deserve for being traitors." White supremacist violence was not confined to the countryside. During 1951–52, Atlanta experienced almost monthly bombings of houses occupied by middle-class blacks that encroached on all-white residential areas. NAACP branch president C. A. Harper called an emergency meeting with Mayor Hartsfield to express the fears of black homeowners in the tension-filled areas.[17]

The white supremacist backlash succeeded in dismantling the nascent statewide civil rights movement. In 1951, leaders of the registration campaign in Savannah bemoaned the "loss of countless thousands of registered voters" in the southeast region of the state. In the same year, Hugh Owen concluded that "in state-wide elections Negro voting remains largely only an issue to be held up as a scare by the professional advocates of white supremacy." A 1956 Morehouse College survey found that "the pattern of excluding Negroes as registrants and voters" in the south-west Georgia counties "was virtually the same in each. There is the ever-present threat of racial violence which has erupted on occasions, especially following elections." Except for the atypically high black registration in Atlanta and Savannah, Georgia's proportion of black registered voters by 1952 lagged behind that of every southern state except for Mississippi and Alabama.[18]

Few local movements in Georgia were unaffected by the racial backlash of the Talmadge years. The lack of activity of the Georgia Voters' League mirrored the decline of the NAACP. In a detailed survey, the Southern Regional Council found negligible black political participation in Georgia during the early 1950s. In Early County in southwest Georgia, for example, the local unit of the Georgia Association of Citizens' Democratic Clubs had closed in 1948 because of a lack of leadership. Similarly, the local branch of the NAACP was dormant. One leader in Early County admitted that "we are taking it kind of easy now." The president of the Camden County branch laid the blame squarely on the racial terror when he concluded in a letter to Walter White in 1953 that "sometime ago a white man killed a Negro and some little threats was made and I never could get anything done since." The Camden branch had been founded only seven years previously.[19]

Across the state, white economic control buttressed the violent supremacist back-lash. "It is not so much the sheet wearing, cross burning, or casket placing activities of the Klan which is dangerous," reported William A. Foulkes in the *Atlanta Daily World* in October 1948. Of more importance "is the organization of prejudice and hatred and the use of systematized job and economic sanctions which mean stran-gulation and death for any Negro who dares compete with the supremacy system." In rural Georgia, individual examples of black economic independence or pros-perity were the exceptions that proved the rule. One black farmer, Dave Jackson, for example, owned over one thousand acres of land near Adel in south Georgia by the end of the 1940s. "Let's not get the idea that there's anything typical about the career of Dave Jackson," wrote Pulitzer Prize–winning reporter Ray Sprigle. "Why, clear across Mississippi I found that Negro leaders had heard of Dave." [20]

The lack of black political activity also reflected an overwhelming sense of the futility of voting. In Walton County, for example, the leadership of the Civic League lamented that even though black registration had increased by nearly one thousand during 1950, a common complaint was that "votes don't count," especially with the white man, "who is going to run things anyway." The story of Georgia, therefore, accorded with the observations of C. S. Johnson in the 1950s, when he wrote that, in general, "the southern Negro does not seriously expect very much change in his civil rights status through 'grassroots' conversion." Few black Georgians held out much hope of imminent change through federal influence either. In 1951, William Holmes Borders commented with typical vehemence that "the South gets only the butt-end of what the Democratic party has left, and the southern Negro gets only the butt of that butt." [21] Such a mood of endemic despondency stood in stark contrast with the hopefulness of the Arnall years.[22]

Pockets of Racial Protest

Within this general picture of retrenchment after 1948, however, there were still significant pockets of black activism. As in the years of World War II, Georgia's army camps were bases of racial moderation, enclaves of federal racial mores. At Fort Benning, over a thousand high school students were integrated in federally funded schools in 1953 after an NAACP campaign. A Georgia NAACP report concluded that "an observer would not have been able to tell the difference between this school and one like it in New York or Boston." The editor of the *Columbus Ledger-Enquirer* reported that it was the impact of Fort Benning's $9 million annual payroll that checked the resurgence of the local Ku Klux Klan during the early 1950s.[23]

In Camp Gordon, social integration among the races was commonplace and there was no discrimination in schools. Lieutenant Henry Wiggins of Arkansas was merely the most senior of several black officers. Integration at Camp Gordon, observed the *Pittsburgh Courier*, was "marred only by the way civilian prejudices of nearby Augusta slop over onto the post." Local agencies refused to send girls to the camp dance of April 1951 if black soldiers were going to be present. In fact, Augusta's segregationist stance provoked over one hundred white soldiers to boycott the dance after black soldiers were barred.[24]

As in previous years, such military activism spilled over into the civilian community. On 30 April 1951, black soldiers from Fort Benning were responsible for ambushing Columbus's white policemen and blowing up the city sheriff's car. In an anonymous letter, one veteran had warned that "soldiers are being beaten, their money taken ... we do not appreciate this after fighting in Korea." Two weeks later, eight soldiers were arrested after using hand grenades in the escalating feud between city police and federal black soldiers. The Columbus NAACP became involved, too, organizing a petition protesting the retaliation of the police, who, "motivated as if by basic mob instincts, roved through Negro sections of the city, indiscriminately beating, cursing, molesting ... and intimidating almost every Negro they saw."[25]

Nor did the white supremacist backlash affect the historically more moderate northern counties as completely as those in the black belt. "The predominantly white residents of the hill country were less immediately concerned with racial issues," concluded Numan Bartley, "and the north Georgia towns only occasionally demonstrated the same dedication to the social and ideological status quo that dominated the voting tendencies of south Georgia towns."[26] The main reason for this moderation was that blacks formed less than one-fifth of the total population in the northern upland region.

As the "capital of the north," Rome, Floyd County, exemplified this more moderate pattern of race relations. The *Pittsburgh Courier* asserted in 1951 that "Rome is one of the better cities in Georgia, where friction is at a minimum and where Negroes strive for the better things in community living." According to a survey carried out by Dean B. R. Brazeal of Morehouse College, by 1957 Rome was a "bristling, expanding city, with only a few vestiges of its former dominant agricultural background."[27]

In Rome, black political action continued to progress. Since the Primus King decision, city registrars had even encouraged blacks to vote by carrying the registration books to schools for convenience, appointing black poll workers, and ending the practice of counting votes according to race. The registration of over 45 percent of the potential black electorate led to change the city's racial mores. Police brutality had ceased to be a cause for complaint after the appointment of two black policemen shortly after 1946. M. D. Whatley, a black teacher, stood as a candidate for the school board in 1951 without suffering any recriminations.[28]

The sole reason Whatley received less than one-third of the registered black vote, the *Pittsburgh Courier* lamented, was voter apathy. According to Brazeal, such apathy stemmed from the widespread feeling that "the white folks are going to run things anyway." In fact, Whatley failed because of the outright opposition from the established leadership of the black Non-Partisan Voters' League, which felt that the time was not yet ripe for a black victory. With the support of a black bloc vote, Whatley would have won comfortably. The opposition to Whatley highlighted the major hindrance to black progress in Rome during the 1950s. The fact that the NAACP had been inactive for several years, Brazeal concluded, was "due more to a lack of leadership and interest than to any type of pressure."[29]

The six coastal counties also avoided the violent excesses of the white supremacist backlash. In contrast to northern Georgia, these coastal counties contained a large proportion of blacks, and in McIntosh, Liberty, and Camden Counties blacks formed the majority of the population. Black registration largely reflected the size of the black population, with black registered voters outnumbering whites in Liberty County and exceeding 35 percent of total registration in McIntosh and Camden Counties.[30]

Having a large bloc vote did not automatically engender racial moderation or black political activism during the early 1950s. In Liberty County, local sheriff Paul Sikes's economic power and the practice of racially segregated voting allowed him to control the black bloc vote. Sikes actually forced black sharecroppers, tenant farmers, and hired hands to register and vote. Brazeal concluded that in McIntosh County, "the prospects are somewhat bleak" because of a "lack of leadership ... lack of employment opportunities . . . and the lack of any type of voters' league." In *Praying for Sheetrock,* Melissa Fay Greene noted that there was no overt resistance to the often dictatorial rule of Sheriff Thomas Poppell in McIntosh County until the 1970s.[31]

Nonetheless, the size of the black vote did allow a modest amelioration of white supremacy compared with other rural areas in the state. In McIntosh County, local blacks asserted that the sheriff "won't squeeze Negroes too hard because back in his mind is the Negro vote." In Liberty County, Sikes employed a large number of black workers in county businesses to retain his economic control. In this way the black vote reinforced the historical tradition of relatively moderate race relations.[32] Contrasting the coastal region with the rest of the state during the 1940s, Hugh Owen pointed to a different "character and outlook of public officials."[33]

Above all, the cities that had experienced organized black protest during the

Arnall years continued to buck the trend of the supremacist backlash. The increasing rural-urban cleavage in Georgia, resulting from the rapid industrialization of the major cities after the war, was vividly demonstrated by the cleavage in racial mores. William Foulkes commented in the *Atlanta Daily World* in 1948 that "most Negroes in the cities do laugh at and ridicule the occasional Ku Klux Klan parades in the countryside, because they can see through the inferiority complexes of the wearers of sheets and hoods." [34]

In consequence, some black political activism initially continued in the cities after the return of the Talmadges. Numan Bartley noted that black Georgians in urban areas, "unlike their county relatives, voted on a substantial scale prior to the 1960s." Reviewing race relations in southern cities at the end of the 1940s, the social scientist Luther Jackson wrote that various amenities for blacks "have been secured in late years partly or wholly because of the demands made by Negroes as a price of their voting." Jackson concluded that "leading all States of the South in this regard is Georgia." In 1948, registered black voters provided the majority of the eighty thousand signatures that allowed the Progressive Party to get on the ballot for the presidential election in Georgia.[35] The Progressive Party's nominee for senator, Larkin Marshall, editor of the *Macon World,* was the first black Georgian to run for the Senate since Reconstruction. The city governments of Atlanta, Savannah, Columbus, and Macon also increased the number of black policemen in response to the black bloc vote in each city; by 1953 both Savannah and Atlanta had appointed ten officers. The Macon chief of police explained that "we hired two officers in 1951 as an experiment, but found them to be entirely satisfactory so we added two more in 1952." According to the *New York Times* in 1949, the black vote "was unquestionably a principal factor in electing a mayor in Macon." [36]

In Laurens County, in central Georgia, the black vote was purged from nearly 40 percent to 15 percent of the total electorate after 1948, but even this reduced bloc vote still represented the balance of power for the two antagonistic white factions seeking to control the county seat of Dublin. In an attempt to secure his position, Dublin's mayor instructed police not to strike anyone they arrested unless necessary and appointed the two prominent black leaders, funeral director H. H. Dudley and the Reverend C. H. Harris, to the county jury. By the middle of the 1950s, the county government had spent over $350,000 on basic amenities for black residents.[37]

Savannah also continued to experience relatively moderate race relations. By the end of the 1940s in Savannah, the *Pittsburgh Courier* reported, blacks were employed in many downtown stores, sometimes even as salesmen, "without the usual concerted driving of pressure groups." The movement under Gilbert had secured changes that ensured that Savannah would remain in the vanguard of black activism across the state. The NAACP's organizational structure remained intact, and an identical block-by-block registration system was used for the next twenty years. Continuity was also prevalent among the personnel, most notably when youth council president W. W. Law succeeded Gilbert as president of the branch and later the state chapter. "Race relations generally are good," the *Courier* reported in 1949, "very good for Georgia." [38]

Such race relations led both to tangible gains in black welfare and continued steps toward integration. Carver Village, the largest publicly financed black housing complex in the South, opened for 608 families in Savannah at the end of 1948. After touring the South at the end of the 1940s, Hodding Carter, the Mississippi editor, concluded that Savannah was "the ideal place in the South for the Negro and his attainments. Savannah is not paradise, but it offers proof that separation and subjugation need not go hand in hand." In 1948, Paul Robeson appeared at a campaign rally in Savannah in support of Henry Wallace's campaign as the Progressive Party candidate for president.[39] According to William Moody, the publicity director for Wallace's southern campaign, the meeting "turned out to be a sensational, nonsegregated meeting in the black section of town where no white policemen put in an appearance." In 1953, after Savannah's South Atlantic Baseball Club fielded a mixed-race team, the *Courier* trumpeted that "Savannah, long recognized as one of the most liberal spots in Georgia, has done it again." [40]

Race relations were considered liberal, however, only because they stood in contrast to the prevailing white supremacy in the rest of the state. The national NAACP denounced Carter's conclusion as complacent and paternalistic. One Savannahian, who replied anonymously to the *Courier,* insisted that "only a warped, prejudiced and blind person could believe that 'Savannah is an example of almost all that the Negro wants.'"[41] Compared instead with the rapid development of black protest during the Arnall years, the black activism in Savannah was little more than a consolidation of earlier progress.

In most other Georgia cities, the unwavering backlash that began under Talmadge quickly wore down local protest. The collapse of protest was perhaps most dramatic in Columbus. Despite the activity led by Brewer and the links with Fort Benning, the persistent violence by the White Citizens' Council eventually curtailed organized black protest. In 1956, Brewer was shot dead in a city street. Although the assailant was never caught, the murder was widely believed to have been orchestrated by local hate groups. In the face of unremitting pressure from the White Citizens' Council, Brewer's group retreated into permanent anonymity.[42]

The story of Brunswick by the middle of the decade was typical of many cities in Georgia. Local movement leader Rev. J. F. Mann bemoaned that "only about six people are trying to keep it alive. All enthusiasm seemed gone." Similarly in Augusta, NAACP fieldworker Amos Holmes recorded that "the Augusta situation is sad." Not only had the branch disbanded, but also "the city is a stronghold of the White Citizens Council, and Negro spies and informants have a demoralizing effect upon the mildly interested people."[43]

The Development of Black Protest in Atlanta

Protest in Atlanta differed from that in both the rural and urban areas of Georgia. While most rural movements disintegrated and urban protests struggled to survive, the movement for racial equality in Atlanta prospered during the 1950s. David Garrow wrote, "black Atlanta even in the early 1950s possessed a tradition of civic activism that only a few other southern black communities . . . could then equal." The Atlanta historian Annie McPheeters even argued that "perhaps at no time in the history of Atlanta's Negro community has there been such a tide of progress as was made in the areas of race relations . . . during the years 1950–60." Roy Harris, one of the leading members of the Talmadge machine, noted in the *Augusta Chronicle* that "Atlanta could be the Achilles heel in the fight to keep segregation in Georgia." This vulnerability, Harris continued, stemmed from the number of black colleges in Atlanta and the presence of "more leftist and left-wing groups in Atlanta than any other place in the state." Atlanta newspapers, Harris lamented, were only timidly in favor of segregation and, most dangerous of all, black voters held the balance of power in Atlanta politics.[44]

Harris's fears about Atlanta were realized through numerous examples of racial moderation. Much to Talmadge's disgust, over thirteen thousand black Atlantans watched an integrated Dodgers baseball team play the Atlanta Crackers on 10 April 1949 in front of a record twenty-five thousand fans, albeit from a section roped off from the rest of the crowd. When Jackie Robinson came to the plate, scattered boos were swiftly drowned out by cheers and applause. "The real story," the *Atlanta Constitution* noted with some prescience after the Crackers' victory, "is any time certain forms of Jim Crow are proven unprofitable the South finds a way to do away with them."[45]

Atlanta certainly avoided the worst excesses of white supremacy. "The Atlanta Negro population, as a whole," observed the *Pittsburgh Courier* in 1950, "live better than Negroes in Northern Communities with the exception of Cleveland, Detroit and Los Angeles." Under Chief of Police Herbert Jenkins, Ku Klux Klan members were purged from the city forces. Similarly, in 1949 the Atlanta City Council voted unanimously to ban the wearing of masks on any occasion except for Halloween, in contrast to the closely contested vote on the same issue in the Georgia legislature.[46]

Atlanta's moderate race relations resulted in increasing economic opportunities for black Atlantans. As in Savannah, such opportunities were impressive only in the context of the more extreme economic discrimination elsewhere. A Labor Market report in 1949 noted that even in Atlanta, "over a third of the total [job] openings for white workers were in clerical and sales occupations" while over half of black Atlantans were in service positions, especially domestic work, and the rest in semi-skilled and unskilled employment. Therefore, "this occupational analysis in a large measure accounts for the greater percentage increase of unemployment among the non-whites than among white workers." Nonetheless, by 1951, Atlanta's total of 768 black municipal workers was the second highest in the South after Houston, and the total of fifty-nine managerial positions was bettered only by the racially moderate cities of Norfolk and Louisville. Between 1945 and 1956, Atlanta's Urban League was responsible for the building of some five thousand homes and ensured that black developers, contractors, and financiers were involved in the construction process.[47]

Atlanta continued to be the home for racial moderates, too. Ralph McGill, the editor of the *Atlanta Constitution,* was widely acclaimed as a liberal voice and condemned many of the supremacist outrages.[48] Atlantan Frances Pauley headed several biracial and liberal white organizations, including the Georgia Council on Human Relations and the Georgia League of Women Voters. Morris Abrams, a Jewish lawyer and close friend of Hartsfield, emerged as one of the leading white legal advocates of racial equality in the South.[49]

The unique racial circumstances of Atlanta were demonstrated in the relationship between Mayor Hartsfield and black community leaders. Hartsfield began his career as a conventional segregationist, opposing the Fair Employment Practices Committee (FEPC) and even asking the House Un-American Activities Committee to investigate the NAACP in 1944. When Hartsfield first ran for mayor in 1941, he had rejected the demands of the Auburn Avenue leaders for black policemen. However, John Calhoun recorded that by 1946, Hartsfield had done a complete "flip-flop" in response to the registration of more than twenty thousand black voters.[50]

This flip-flop led to Atlanta's mayor acting completely out of step with Georgia's governor. Privately, Hartsfield kept in close communication with the Auburn Avenue leadership. In a letter in September 1949, for example, Hartsfield wrote to A. T. Walden, "Dear Cap, This is a very special letter of thanks to you for all that you did during the late campaign." Publicly, Hartsfield rejected a white supremacist stance. As early as 1947, Hartsfield opposed the segregation of visitors at the American Anniversary Freedom Train when it reached Atlanta. In direct contrast to the mayors of Birmingham and Memphis, Hartsfield declared that "I am willing to stand beside any American citizen, regardless of race or creed, in mutual admiration and respect for those great historical charters of American freedom." [51] Hartsfield even welcomed the National Negro Chamber of Commerce and the NAACP to their annual conventions in 1951. Although Hartsfield "was a segregationist and a racist," Warren Cochrane concluded, "he was also a man of integrity. And when he made a promise to you, he kept it." [52] While state politicians promised to defend Georgia's white supremacy at all costs, Hartsfield promoted Atlanta's reputation as a "city too busy to hate."

Atlanta's racial moderation gained wider recognition too, leading to a succession of black and interracial organizations choosing the city as a convention venue. The United Packinghouse Workers of America (UPWA) held both its 1952 and 1953 annual conventions in Atlanta.[53] In 1955, black and white delegates attended the South-wide Conference on Integration in Atlanta. On occasion such conventions broke sensitive social taboos. The UPWA hosted interracial banquets, while the NAACP convention featured interracial dancing.[54]

Whereas the state as a whole suffered restrictive voting legislation, black Atlantans gained new opportunities to vote. Before 1949, any person wishing to vote for the city executive committee had to pledge that "I am a white registered voter and have resided at my present residence a length of time sufficient to qualify me under law." After court action filed by A. T. Walden, based on the Primus King precedent, this pledge was dropped, heralding the enfranchisement of thousands of blacks for local elections. Luther Jackson concluded that black citizens of Atlanta, as in New Orleans and Memphis, "may qualify with as much ease as in any northern city." By the end of 1949, black registration had increased by almost 50 percent, from 17,000 in 1946 to 22,400. Local leaders boasted that the Atlanta black vote represented "the most powerful bloc south of Chicago." [55]

The high proportion of black registrants reflected the continued prosperity of Atlanta's black population. In 1956, *Fortune* magazine acclaimed Auburn Avenue as the "richest Negro street in the world." One detailed survey into black registration during the early 1950s revealed that whereas over 80 percent of all professionals surveyed had registered to vote, barely half of those who were unemployed had registered. This may also have been because the black community elite supervised the registration campaigns. Committee minutes of the Atlanta Civic and Political League revealed that over half of all leaders were actually centered on Auburn Avenue.[56]

The entrenched strength and independence of Atlanta's black community allowed the further development of black organizations. Neighborhood civic leagues proliferated throughout the Westside. The Royal Peacock Club opened on Auburn Avenue in 1949, hosting performers such as Nat "King" Cole and Cab Calloway. In the same year John Hope Elementary School was founded on Boulevard, which intersected Auburn Avenue. Community activist John Long was appointed as the first principal. Radio station WAOK signed on in Atlanta in 1954.[57]

Above all, Ruby Blackburn's various local improvement associations continued to prosper after 1948. Her TIC Club and Cultural League, for example, pressured the city government into building two new elementary schools and planting dogwood and crape myrtle on hitherto barren Westside sidewalks. As in the war years, Blackburn's social and women's improvement organizations dovetailed with registration campaigns. By 1956, the Atlanta League of Negro Women Voters, under Blackburn's presidency, grew to fifty district chapters, each with a membership of between fifty and six hundred voters. The league's motto was that "every woman and girl who becomes of age is registered." Ruby Blackburn also led the Georgia League of Negro Women Voters.[58]

Indeed, the key means for achieving racial progress in Atlanta was the development of the potential black vote after 1949 with the formation of the Atlanta Negro Voters League (ANVL). Previously, black Republicans and Democrats, led respectively by John Wesley Dobbs and A. T. Walden, had usually endorsed different tickets. In the election for solicitor of Fulton County in 1948, for example, Dobbs, C. A. Harper, and John Calhoun had successfully supported Republican Paul Webb against Democrat Dan Duke, who had been backed by Walden and Warren Cochrane.[59] Frustrated that neither candidate had addressed the black community, Grace Towns Hamilton joined with Morehouse lecturers Jake Henderson and C. A. Bacote in an attempt to unify registered black Atlantans for local elections.

According to John Calhoun, even though Henderson invited all black political activists to a special meeting at the Savoy Hotel to discuss strategy, Dobbs "came to the meeting to tear it up." Dobbs walked out of the Savoy Hotel insisting that the existing All-Citizens' Registration Committee, which was Republican-dominated, was more than adequate.[60] To circumvent any claims of partisanship, Henderson and Hamilton proposed that a Democrat and a Republican share each post in the ANVL. On this basis, Dobbs and Walden agreed to assume the roles of co-chairmen. Once established, the ANVL then screened candidates at special meetings at the Butler Street YMCA, one block away from Auburn Avenue, before endorsing a slate at a mass meeting on the eve of any election. It had, in fact, been the frequent intrusions at the YMCA by city police that had helped to unite the various black political groups in the first place.[61]

The ANVL enjoyed unprecedented success. After annual registration campaigns involving up to nine hundred volunteers, black registration increased to 27,432 by 1958. Two years later, it had soared to 34,642. In addition, citizenship schools based in the Auburn Avenue churches and led by Harper and Bacote helped to guarantee a bloc vote. Bacote observed that for the first time since Reconstruction, "no longer was it political suicide for a candidate for public office to openly seek the Negro vote."[62]

The black bloc vote represented only one-third of the overall total voting population in Atlanta. But it became effective because, as Bacote recalled later, "we would always unite and have an alliance with the Northside, with the upper middle class whites." David Goldfield commented that this "arrangement with the white economic elite who controlled the political system to deliver votes in exchange for black appointments and improved services" marked Atlanta out as the leading center of black protest before the King years.[63]

After 1949, every mayor in Atlanta and almost all other victorious candidates received the backing of the black bloc vote. In 1953, Hartsfield's opponent Charlie Brown even forged notice sheets in a vain attempt to pretend that the ANVL had declared for him. Atlanta also became the first city in Georgia where black candidates regularly won elections. In 1953, Walden and a pharmacist, Miles Amos, were elected from the predominantly black third ward as members of the City Democratic Executive Committee. In the same year Rufus E. Clement, president of Atlanta University, became the first black Atlantan to win a citywide primary when he was nominated for the Board of Education as the representative from the third ward. Clement's majority of over ten thousand votes reflected moderate white support too. In fact, the light color of his skin may have helped his cause. As Warren Cochrane admitted later, "a lot of people didn't know that Dr. Clement was black."[64]

Use of the ballot was augmented by legal action. Walden resumed court action to force the equalization of Atlanta teachers' salaries. At the beginning of 1949, U.S.

District Court judge E. Marvin Underwood gave the Atlanta Board of Education until 1 September to equalize teachers' pay. Walden also supervised a suit seeking equal facilities in Atlanta's schools. "The filing of the Atlanta school facilities equalization suit on September 19th," the *Pittsburgh Courier* concluded, "was the most important piece of news in 1950." [65]

The use of the ballot and piecemeal legal action, however, proved to be the extent of black protest tactics used by the Auburn Avenue leadership. In this way the Atlanta movement of the 1950s stood in contrast to the Savannah protest under Gilbert or the urban protests of the 1960s. In their biography of Grace Towns Hamilton, for example, Lorraine Spritzer and Jean Bergmark made the point that Hamilton "was not and never could be an abrasive and militant desegregationist." Instead, Hamilton followed the guiding principle of the YWCA, "to go as far as Negroes and whites are agreed to go together." Most legal cases did not directly challenge de jure segregation. In one annual report typical of the early 1950s, the Atlanta NAACP concluded that minor legal cases had been the story of the year. For the most part, "these were scores of small cases, which were resolved simply by letters, telephone calls, telegrams, conferences and/or investigations." Such cases included the trouble-free purchasing of homes in the previously all-white Mozeley Park area. [66]

Away from Atlanta, protest leaders regularly criticized the Auburn Avenue leadership. The *Pittsburgh Courier* lambasted the NAACP branch's 1951 campaign that realized only two thousand members. "Shame on Atlanta," wrote the *Courier*, "with upward of 150,000 Negroes in the metropolis and outlying area, from 10–20,000 of them ought to be members of the NAACP." Nor was the branch itself particularly supportive of NAACP activities outside the city. In February 1951, two black men were beaten and flogged in Douglas County but did not receive immediate assistance from Atlanta's NAACP. The *Pittsburgh Courier* pointed out that the Atlanta branch, "which has often needed such victims to stir up the support of the people, was embarrassingly slow in making a move to help." At the 1951 NAACP annual convention that was held in Atlanta, local leaders admitted that in comparison with the Carolinas, "we outdistance them in business accomplishments, but they are pushing farther along freedom road." [67]

Internal squabbling within Atlanta's black leadership partially explained the limits to local protest. Unbeknown to white supremacist leaders, Georgia's largest NAACP branch was actually turning fire in on itself. Shortly after becoming the branch's first executive secretary in 1949, John Calhoun was subjected to acerbic criticism. One anonymous letter to Roy Wilkins in New York called for Calhoun's dismissal, and Walter White's sister Madeleine sent him a highly confidential letter about the problem. Grace Towns Hamilton told one national official that "anti-Calhoun feeling is to the extreme of being psychotic." C. A. Harper, who had been president of the branch since 1942, was warned by a number of leaders that he would lose his own reputation if he stood by Calhoun. C. A. Scott, editor of *Atlanta Daily World,* used his paper to criticize the NAACP leadership and sought to persuade Walden and Hamilton to join his attempts to wrest control of the local branch. Meanwhile, Calhoun reacted angrily to criticism from Ruby Hurley in 1952, telling her to "keep your shirt on" and not to believe the reports in the newspaper.[68]

Ostensibly, the conflict centered on charges of financial misconduct. As executive secretary, Calhoun received a monthly salary of $300 plus expenses of more than $500. One Auburn Avenue publication, *Business Bulletin,* wrote that "many ask if the NAACP in Atlanta has become an agency to make a place of employment for someone at the expense of the masses." The *Bulletin* pointed out that the popular C. A. Harper had raised more money than Calhoun, without any salary or expenses. Rumors abounded that Calhoun's former wife had divorced him because he had stolen over $5,000 from her late father's business. The national NAACP was more concerned that only a fraction of the money raised by the Atlanta branch was directed toward legal expenses. After investigating the financial affairs, a head office report concluded that there were no financial irregularities but ruled that no branch with less than five thousand members should have an executive secretary.[69]

The fracas over finance also stemmed from Calhoun's activist leadership and the entrenched rivalry between Atlanta's NAACP and other black organizations in the city. Gloster Current noted that Grace Towns Hamilton and the "Urban League crowd was leading the opposition against Calhoun" because he was "too militant for her element." Georgia NAACP state president William Boyd threw his support behind Calhoun, angry with the "tactics of the Urban League in Atlanta of stealing credit for work done by the NAACP in educational and other cases." The national NAACP office sanctioned paid staff in an attempt to compete with Atlanta's Urban League. John Wesley Dobbs of the Masons and members of the Chamber of Commerce group criticized the NAACP as an outside organization interfering in local affairs. Such sniping, argued Gloster Current, was because "some of these people offer to compromise with Jim Crow and cannot do so as long as the NAACP is in existence."[70] In 1958, C. A. Scott opposed the Atlanta NAACP's suit for school integration.

The fracas was exacerbated by personality conflicts. One NAACP official sent to investigate the trouble concluded that Calhoun was "sincerely doing a good job" and was "making more noise and will probably try to accomplish more" than Grace Hamilton and Colonel Walden had in the past. The problem was simply that Calhoun "was not overly bright" and "lacked social graces" and therefore he was "very difficult for the elite in Atlanta to digest under any circumstances." Walden particularly resented Calhoun's reliance on younger lawyers, E. E. Robinson and Howard Moore, who in turn were openly contemptuous of Walden.[71] Personality feuds were compounded by fraternal rivalries. Calhoun and his leading supporters, branch president C. A. Harper and treasurer Jesse Blayton, were Omega men. The NAACP head office report concluded that, in part, the bad "feeling was a fraternity thing."[72]

Whatever the causes, the report noted that the situation was "depressing, highly complex and possibly explosive." In the face of unrelenting criticism, Calhoun resigned his position as executive secretary effective in March 1951. Even then he took a final swipe at the elite, insisting in his resignation letter that "the tragedy is that those who need it most can say the least, and those who can give the most, care the least; thus the cause is neglected."[73]

Although Calhoun was responding to his critics, the limited nature of Atlanta's black protest did indeed reflect both complacency and conservatism among the elite. R. R. Reed, secretary of Georgia's Negro Chamber of Commerce, wrote to the chairman of the Atlanta NAACP Executive Committee, conceding that "I doubt anyone could compile a finer list of citizens to serve the cause," but "the only criticism is that they hardly attend any meetings." At one Negro ministers' meeting every single member refused to support a proposed march to City Hall to protest segregated water fountains and elevators. A contemporary survey of registered voters in one black district discovered that when giving reasons for voting, the chance to help "advance the Negro race" was ranked third.[74]

Meanwhile, the Atlanta Business League, which included many of the Auburn Avenue leaders, eschewed a specifically antisegregation agenda. Dedicated to the "economic progress of Negroes in Atlanta," the league aimed primarily to attract one thousand members, keep Auburn Avenue out of debt, and name a man of the year. Similarly, the efforts of Atlanta's Urban League to improve black working conditions and job opportunities did not directly confront racial segregation. Hal Dumas, the president of Southern Bell, wrote to the AUL in 1949 that "it is our sincere hope that we can continue to increase Negro employment in our business within the framework of the customs of the communities in which we operate."[75]

The fact that the black vote formed only part of a coalition further engendered this conservative approach. "The terms of this alliance were quite simple," observed David Harmon. "The African American community would politically support the civic-business leadership ... in return the business-civic leadership promised a more congenial racial climate." Both sides agreed that behind-the-scenes negotiations to solve racial problems were preferable to open conflict.[76]

The very success of the alliance with the white business leadership entrenched a parallel leadership structure within the black community. Walden emerged as an unofficial black mayor because of his regular clandestine meetings with Hartsfield and white civic leaders. For example, Mills B. Lane, Atlanta's leading financier, invited select city leaders, including Walden, to a "dinner, 7 pm, August 22nd in private dining room at the top of the Atlanta Merchandise Mart to discuss a matter of vital importance."[77]

Nevertheless, it was an alliance in which the black voting bloc was very much the junior partner. T. M. Alexander believed that it allowed a "minority of the white voters to dictate to all of the black voters, a subtle kind of racial 'whitemail' that worked for more than 25 years." Alexander's verdict was demonstrated by the actions of Hartsfield himself, who insisted privately that "he knew how to 'use' the Negro, but was able successfully to avoid letting the Negro use him." After deciding to appoint black policemen, Hartsfield announced the measure in person to a mass meeting on Auburn Avenue and then presented the new recruits in full uniform to an almost hysterical reception. Dobbs admitted later that the introduction of the policemen was "akin to a circus." Hartsfield took a more incremental approach to the white community. To avoid controversy, Hartsfield eliminated the "white" and "colored" signs outside the rest rooms at Atlanta airport by gradually reducing them in size until they could hardly be seen before finally removing them.[78]

Hartsfield's airport desegregation policy proved to be the catalyst for a younger generation of black leaders to question the Auburn Avenue elite's gradualist approach. At a special meeting of Atlanta's 27 Club in 1957, Hartsfield was invited to field questions from club members and invited younger black leaders. One guest, Whitney Young of the Urban League, asked Hartsfield why he didn't just remove the airport signs. After noting Hartsfield's reluctance to act, Young assembled a small cadre of like-minded black Atlantans to reappraise the pace of racial change. The self-styled Atlanta's Committee for Cooperative Action (ACCA) was drawn from the same institutional base as the existing Atlanta elite. Young and Carl Holman, who later founded the outspoken *Atlanta Inquirer,* both lectured at the Atlanta University complex. From the business sector, Jesse Hill Jr. was an actuary at Atlanta Life, and Herman Russell was a successful contractor. Q. V. Williamson was a realtor, and Leroy Johnson was employed in legal affairs.[79]

The ACCA had no intention of supplanting the authority of the existing black community leadership. Instead, its chief aim was to expose as a myth Atlanta's reputation as the "city too busy to hate." Young's biographer, Nancy Weiss, concluded that the ACCA sought "to show that Atlanta's rhetorical commitment to opportunity and fair treatment diverged substantially from reality."[80] To this end, members of the ACCA embarked on one and a half years of research into the extent of racial segregation in Atlanta to be published under the title *A Second Look*.

After the launch of *A Second Look* in February 1960, Young told reporters that "Atlanta was comparing itself to Mississippi and saying how enlightened it was." In reality, "nothing was really integrated," Young concluded, "but the people were beginning to believe their own press clippings—even the Negroes." By way of introduction, the survey asked all "Atlantans to take a second look at Atlanta: specifically to take a long hard look at some of the problems which will not simply go away if we wink at them or ignore them long enough." Eliza Paschall, the leader of the Atlanta Council on Human Relations (ACHR), reflected later that "all of Atlanta, including the Council, was catapulted into a new awareness of what racial segregation was all about."[81]

The report passed a harsh judgment on race relations in Atlanta. White supremacy was clearly manifested in economic terms. For each black professional there were thirteen white professionals, and such a ratio increased to twenty to one for electricians and two hundred to one for bookkeepers. Although recognizing that housing conditions compared favorably with northern cities, *A Second Look* observed that black Atlantans occupied less than a sixth of the land while representing over one-third of the population. The death rate of 11.7 per 1,000 exceeded the white death rate of 8.3 by more than one-third.[82]

Racial discrimination was magnified in the realm of public services. Over one-half of black schools still taught double sessions, and the city provided no advanced training in medicine, dentistry, law, architecture, or engineering. Of 3,500 hospital beds in Atlanta only 589 were available for black patients, even though some of the segregated hospitals had been built with federal funds. Despite recent developments, the report noted that there remained very few black police and that black-on-black crimes generally received relatively light sentences. By 1959, there was still virtually no black representation among elected officials, city boards, and committees, and leading black Atlantans were frozen out of such agencies as the Chamber of Commerce.[83]

The survey unashamedly pointed the finger at the methods of the existing black leadership. To the surprise of the ACCA, the Auburn Avenue elite actually supported *A Second Look.* One senior leader paid for more copies to be printed, while the *Atlanta Daily World* reported that the report was "sober and factual," containing "no irresponsible rabble-rousing." Martin Luther King Sr. admitted later that the Auburn Avenue leadership had protested "very gently by any modern standard, most of us accepting the premise that half a loaf was better than one, so long as the division was temporary."[84]

The Atlanta elite accepted that many of the recent racial gains were limited in real terms. Black policemen were nicknamed "quasi-policemen," unauthorized to arrest white Atlantans. Although Bacote rightly contended that "the black vote has kept Atlanta free from demagogues, especially along racial lines," the black vote only forced candidates to give an ear, rather than full attention to black needs. The voting alliance between the black bloc vote and white north Atlanta was effectively "whitemail," Martin Luther King Sr. concluded. "No-one should be left with the impression that we controlled Atlanta politics, that just wasn't so."[85]

Other commentators put the point more strongly. In 1956, Representative William Dawson of Illinois told the ANVL to "snap out of their political lethargy." Visiting author James Baldwin observed that race relations were fair at the start of the 1950s, but they were "manipulated by the mayor and a fairly strong middle-class." Baldwin concluded that "this works mainly in the areas of compromise and concessions and has very little effect on the bulk of the Negro population and none whatever on the rest of the state." The desegregation of the city golf course in December 1955 and the removal of the "white" and "colored" signs outside airport rest rooms were cases in point. In 1959, even the *Atlanta Journal* recorded that in the area of race relations, "changes were more subtle than sensational."[86]

In the context of the South, the story of Atlanta was the classic case of minimal white concessions maintaining maximum racial segregation. As Whitney Young reflected later, it was as if "the old guard were brain washed into thinking that Atlanta was an oasis in the desert." Although Atlanta could have provided an ideal opportunity for a concerted challenge to segregation, the first citywide protest in the South took place in Montgomery, Alabama, in 1955. As in Atlanta, the Montgomery protest initially called only for better treatment of black residents in the context of segregation. Boycott leaders demanded the employment of black bus drivers on appropriate routes, more courteous behavior by white drivers, and a more flexible segregation line that would allow black passengers to sit further forward if empty seats were available. Ironically, it was the stubborn refusal of the Montgomery city government to allow even token changes that prompted the escalation of the boycott with the explicit aim of overturning segregation itself on the buses.[87]

The development of black activism in Atlanta was highly significant for the rest of the state. As the "city too busy to hate," Atlanta ostensibly stood out as the antithesis of the white supremacy prevalent in rural Georgia. Therefore, in the context of Georgia's resurgent supremacist violence, Atlanta became a safe haven of relative racial moderation. Rosa Lee Ingram, paroled after ten years' imprisonment for the murder of her white boss in self-defense, fled to Atlanta from her home in southwest Georgia. There she was housed and supported by the local NAACP. Dover Carter also headed to Atlanta from Montgomery County after suffering numerous assaults.[88]

Black activists in Atlanta assumed even more significance because the Savannah NAACP ceased to play a leading role across the state. Savannah too acted as a relative safe haven for the victims of hate groups. After the racially motivated murder of her husband in 1948, Amy Mallard moved from her home in Toombs County to Savannah.[89] But after Gilbert's personal breakdown, Savannah's broader influence across the state waned. Gilbert's successor, W. W. Law, initially concentrated on maintaining the local branch rather than supporting black activism elsewhere.

The conservative outlook of Atlanta's black leadership did, however, lead to a concomitantly cautious vision for black protest in the rest of the state. Atlanta Democrats did not seek to reactivate the Association of Democratic Clubs. Similarly, the Atlanta branch of the NAACP did not attempt to reestablish local chapters but maintained informal links until more suitable conditions arose. Such links included occasional speaking engagements, particularly on Emancipation Sundays in black Baptist churches in some of the larger towns. For example, John Wesley Dobbs, perhaps the most popular speaker, urged Griffin blacks to register in 1950. Often, such informal links stemmed from business connections. By the end of the 1950s, Atlanta Life employed over one thousand sales representatives. A. Clinton Brown, for example, one of two black members of the Gainesville School Board, was a local representative for Atlanta Life.[90]

The Atlanta NAACP had the potential to make an impact in the state through legal action. After the Ingram case, Atlanta NAACP lawyers filed a suit requiring black representation on Georgia's Supreme Court juries. In 1949, Walden supervised a suit in Irwin County seeking equal facilities in schools. Still, some branch leaders away from Atlanta criticized both the Atlanta NAACP and the wider organization for failing to provide legal support for local issues. For example, W. W. Law called on NAACP lawyers to defend Savannahian Ozzie Jones from the electric chair after Jones was convicted of rape. Law claimed NAACP intervention was justified because the original, white, defense lawyer had called no alibi or character witness and had to be reminded to represent Jones on the day of his trial. In an angry letter to Gloster Current in November 1950, Law made his frustrations clear: "God knows that we need your help but your brief letter gave me the impression that you did not care to come if it just did not fit your convenience." Walden and NAACP assistant counsel Jack Greenberg from New York subsequently agreed to handle the case after deciding that the evidence pointed to Jones's innocence.[91]

The lack of NAACP legal action in Georgia also reflected the dearth of black civil rights lawyers outside of Atlanta. From Savannah, state NAACP president W. W. Law complained to Jack Greenberg in 1955 that "the lawyer situation here is one of our grave problems in our sincere efforts to do a decent NAACP job in this section of the state." None of Savannah's three black lawyers were prepared to support the organization. When C. B. King, from Albany, acceded to the Georgia bar in 1953, he became the state's first black lawyer outside Atlanta to take civil rights cases. King had studied at Fisk University and at law school in Cleveland before being admitted to the Ohio bar. For King, whose father had been the leader of the Albany branch of the NAACP, practicing law was a way to assert black civil rights. Taylor Branch noted that King "wore a neatly trimmed beard and tailored suits, and he discussed all subjects in a melodious, polysyllabic stream . . . local white lawyers did not quite know what to make of him." His very act of qualifying challenged the racial mores of southwest Georgia, for as he himself reflected later, "after all, where else can you get twelve white men to listen to you even if they don't look at you?"[92]

The NAACP's legal impact was limited further by the dilatory efforts of Atlanta's established black lawyers. The Atlanta NAACP filed a suit in 1950 which charged that educational facilities for the races in the city were not equal. Two years later, a follow-up suit argued that segregated schools were inherently unequal. Because of the tardy handling of the case, however, the eleventh district court delayed a decision until the Supreme Court ruled on pending cases from other states. Walden's supervision of both cases was roundly criticized by Ruby Hurley, the NAACP's southeastern regional director. Writing to Gloster Current in 1951, Hurley recommended that Walden be removed from the case because his "inactivity is killing us in Georgia."[93]

The emergence of a new generation of black lawyers in Atlanta pointed to a future increase in legal activism.[94] In 1953, Donald Hollowell was accepted into the Georgia bar. A Californian by birth who had become engaged to a native Georgian when studying in Atlanta, Hollowell had forgone his career as an army dentist specifically to pursue racial justice. Although he trained under Walden, Hollowell associated particularly with the ACCA, and it was Hollowell and C. B. King who were to be Georgia's leading civil rights lawyers by the end of the decade. In her survey of school integration in Atlanta, Susan McGrath concluded that the legal situation improved after Don Hollowell and C. B. King assisted Walden.[95]

Overall, however, nearly a decade after the movement led by Rev. Gilbert, the prospects for racial protest had barely progressed within Georgia. Quite simply, massive resistance proved stronger than the civil rights protest that had emerged during the Arnall years. To be sure, organized black protest continued in Savannah and Atlanta in particular despite the supremacist backlash. The high level of voter registration and the consequent amelioration of the effects of white supremacy bore testament to the irreversible changes in both cities. But those protest organizations that did survive proved either unable or unwilling to mount a challenge to Jim Crow across Georgia as a whole.

The Effects of Brown *and the Montgomery Bus Boycott*

A renewed challenge to segregation came from outside the state, initially through a legal challenge supervised by the NAACP Legal Defense Fund.[96] In the *Brown v. Board of Education* decision of 1954, the Supreme Court ruled that segregated education was inherently unequal, thereby shaking the legal foundations of Jim Crow.[97] The following year, in a follow-up to the *Brown* decision, the Supreme Court ruled that desegregation should take place with all deliberate speed.

Michael Klarman has disputed the historiographical assumption that the *Brown* decision precipitated widespread black protest across the South. Klarman asserted instead that "political, economic, social, demographic and ideological forces, many of which coalesced during World War II, laid the groundwork for the civil rights movement and that *Brown* played a relatively minor role." According to Klarman, the ultimate importance of *Brown* was that it sparked massive resistance and "elicited for prominent display the full venom of southern Jim Crow." This segregationist intransigence in turn forced the federal government to intervene in the racial crises in cities such as Little Rock and Birmingham. The "backlash thesis" concludes that "while the civil rights movement did not require *Brown* as a catalyst, the massive resistance movement did."[98]

In Georgia, the *Brown* decision provoked an acerbic reaction from the state government. Governor Marvin Griffin responded to the "all deliberate speed ruling" by declaring "come hell or high-water, races will not be mixed in Georgia schools ... no matter how much the Supreme Court seeks to sugar-coat its bitter pill of tyranny, the people of Georgia and the South will not swallow it." House Speaker Marvin Moate vowed "to use all means possible to put it off in Georgia." On 24 January 1955, the Georgia General Assembly passed a bill that made it a felony, punishable by two years in prison, for any school official or system to spend money on a mixed-race school.[99] One year later, the legislature passed an interposition resolution declaring the U.S. Supreme Court's ruling "null and void and of no effect." Georgia's attorney general Eugene Cook admitted to reporters that "we might as well be candid" about the pro-segregation laws passed by the 1956 session of the state legislature. "Most of those laws will be stricken down by the courts in due course."[100]

For Georgia's government, like those in many southern states, the desegregation issue also provided an opportunity for a full-scale attack on the NAACP state conference. State revenue commissioner T. V. Williams sought access to the Atlanta branch files on the grounds that it had not filed state income taxes or applied for tax exemption. John Calhoun was sentenced to one year's imprisonment for denying access to Atlanta's membership records. Eugene Cook was even more direct, declaring that he intended to drive the organization out of the state. To justify his quest, Cook published what he called "the ugly truth about the NAACP." Indulging in the rhetoric of McCarthyism, Cook accused the "subversive" NAACP (as well as the SRC and Southern Conference Education Fund, SCEF) of "promoting Communist-inspired doctrine." Cook reclassified barratry as a felony and announced that any teacher linked with the NAACP would be permanently banned. Cook even called for a state law that would make it a capital offense for any state official or private citizen not in federal employment to assist in enforcing the Supreme Court decision.[101] At Cook's instigation, the state of Georgia introduced a test case at the end of 1955 enjoining the school board in Valdosta from "taking any steps leading to an elimination of segregation in the public schools under its jurisdiction."[102] The suit was dropped when the NAACP threatened to take the case to the federal courts.[103]

The cautious reaction of Georgia's black community to *Brown* also endorses Klarman's thesis. *Brown* was an important issue for the existing state NAACP, but it did not spark renewed widespread protest. The Georgia conference took no action until four days after the *Brown II* decision in 1955, when over fifty NAACP leaders from around the country met in Atlanta to discuss strategy. The resulting "Atlanta Declaration" called on local branches across the South to petition local school boards for compliance. W. W. Law called a meeting of Georgia branches in Macon on 13 August 1955. Branches were encouraged to file petitions, using samples provided by Atlantan C. E. Price. Litigants were also warned not to publish their addresses.[104] The weakness of the state NAACP was revealed when only eight branches in Georgia, seven of them in cities, actually did petition their local school boards.[105] Nor did the state conference follow up the head office suggestion that all teachers march to NAACP local offices to register. Meanwhile, the Georgia Teachers and Education Association, with a membership of almost nine thousand black teachers, merely passed a resolution hailing *Brown*. One critic commented that the resolution subsequently "got lost" amid other resolutions, one of which thanked state officials for "nice school buildings."[106]

The first Georgia integration suit after the *Brown* decision was not filed until 1958 in Atlanta.[107] In response to the first petition of 1955, the Atlanta Board of Education commissioned a detailed study of the effects of segregated education in the city. Far from unifying black protest, the response to *Brown* caused further division. In the first place, only a minority of the Atlanta elite, notably Calhoun, had supported it. Many members of the Auburn Avenue elite supported the board's proposal, believing that a study would dispel the myth of black intellectual inferiority. Calhoun, however, argued that such a study would cause unnecessary delay, especially because high school children already took annual tests.[108]

The decision to file a suit also brought opposition from the NAACP head office in New York. Mindful of Georgia's new law against barratry, the national NAACP quickly disclaimed any responsibility for the lawsuit. The New York office insisted that "the technical position is that these parents consulted an Atlanta attorney and that the attorney requested assistance of Thurgood Marshall and others in the NAACP's Legal Defense and Education Fund, Inc."[109]

Klarman's assertion that the *Brown* case was crucial only from the perspective of white resistance, however, does not corroborate with the story in Georgia. Klarman himself observed that "the first step in establishing this backlash thesis is to show that southern resistance to racial change was of a different order of magnitude before and after *Brown."* Across the South, *Brown* did indeed trigger a massive white backlash. "Overnight, the political climate darkened" in Louisiana, concluded Fairclough. "The segregationist onslaught stunned the NAACP." Dittmer recorded that "by the end of 1955 the black freedom movement in Mississippi was in disarray." [110]

In the case of Georgia, however, it was a reaction to black protest during the Arnall years and the election of 1946 that had precipitated violent white supremacy. Therefore, the acerbic reaction to *Brown* was a predictable continuation of an existing uncompromising stance on segregation. It was an increase in scale rather than "a different order of magnitude." For some Georgia cities, though, the *Brown* backlash did provide the final death knell for overt local protest. One anonymous black leader in Columbus told the *Pittsburgh Courier* in 1956 that "the white folks are desperate, there is a definite move on to remove all Negro leadership, by hook or crook." [111]

In addition, the actual consequence of *Brown* in Georgia was ultimately not to expedite set-piece confrontations between the federal government and southern white supremacists but to undermine the strength of Jim Crow in the state. Klarman is correct in tracing the origins of the Little Rock crisis back to the polarizing of opinion after *Brown.* In Georgia, however, the enforcement of school desegregation focused the spotlight on Atlanta and therefore challenged the supremacist stance of the state government at its weakest point. In the context of southern massive resistance after *Brown,* the city of Atlanta stood out for its moderate race relations. The southern regional office of the NAACP, for example, relocated to Atlanta after being outlawed in Alabama. [112]

In contrast to Atlanta's previously limited influence on race relations in Georgia, the outcome of Atlanta's school desegregation issue had vital ramifications for the state as a whole. In the first place, Governor Vandiver was not prepared to tolerate any exceptions to Georgia's segregated education, describing token integration as similar to a leaking sewer pipe. Promising to use all the resources of the state in the forthcoming showdown, Vandiver asserted in 1958 that "we can let the whole world know that Georgia is still safe, that her segregated schools, her county-unit system, her heritage and her sacred traditions are secure." Legislation enacted under Herman Talmadge's governorship ruled that the Georgia legislature would withdraw funding for any integrated public schools. After the closure of schools in parts of Virginia, Georgia's legislators appreciated that the closure of Atlanta's public schools might lead to the closure of the state public school system. [113]

The Atlanta case, therefore, assumed a fundamental significance as Georgia's test case. Claude Sitton reported in the *New York Times* that "the future of public education throughout the state is at stake to some extent." "It was a time," reflected the *Gainesville Daily Times*'s editor Sylvan Meyer, "when you could hear minds clicking all over Georgia." If anything, the focus on Atlanta widened Georgia's rural-urban racial cleavage. As the *Charleston News-Courier* observed, "Atlanta today is an island surrounded by more segregation feeling than exists anywhere else in the South. You are reminded of Berlin." The *Southern Patriot* was more succinct, describing the battle as "a case of Atlanta against rural Georgia."[114]

In this context, the atypical moderation of Atlanta proved to be of wider importance. "Atlanta Is Different," ran a *New Republic* headline, because of its "metropolitan values." "It is the first southern city to become greatly exercised about the possible loss of schools far ahead of the time it might occur." In November 1958, a widely publicized *Atlanta Manifesto* was issued by 311 ministers and rabbis calling for the schools to stay open. The following month, more than four hundred physicians echoed the manifesto. Ralph McGill argued in the *Atlanta Constitution* that "to speak the phrase 'close the schools' means a previous process of closing the mind has been completed." In a letter to McGill, Calhoun wrote that "for some time I have wanted to congratulate you upon the editorials contained in your column and the editorial pages of the *Atlanta Constitution*." Under the inspiration of Frances Pauley, white liberal groups joined together to form the Help Our Public Education (HOPE) campaign.[115]

HOPE was by far the most significant single contribution of white liberal organizations to Georgia's race relations in the history of the state.[116] In an attempt to circumvent his own ultimatum, Vandiver appointed a commission chaired by the prestigious banker John Sibley to ascertain whether public opinion in each congressional district favored a modification of school policies. In his survey of the commission, Jeff Roche noted that "the creation of the Sibley Commission represented a major shift away from Georgia's massive resistance program." Sibley admitted privately that HOPE had created a public climate that made the introduction of a commission politically feasible. Building on the League of Women Voters' network, which had only recently integrated, Pauley expanded HOPE to a membership of over twenty thousand across the state.[117] At the end of April 1960, the Sibley Commission recommended the discontinuation of school closing policies in favor of other legal means to maintain segregation.[118] Roche concluded that "the report was a bombshell in Georgia. For the first time, a government-sanctioned body advocated abandoning massive resistance and accepting the inevitability of integration."[119]

Faced by a federal ruling in favor of the integration of Atlanta's public schools,

Vandiver was under pressure to replace the school funding legislation.[120] In fact, Vandiver's dilemma was preempted and overshadowed by a second legal attack on education segregation when two students filed suit to integrate the University of Georgia (UGA). Whereas white liberals supported the high school case, litigation regarding the university developed under the inspiration and supervision of the ACCA. Jesse Hill had first planned the challenge to UGA as early as 1957, when he first started compiling a list of potential seniors. Although Walden initially filed the suit, by 1959 the legal case was supervised by Hollowell, who had succeeded Walden as Atlanta's leading civil rights lawyer.

In December 1960, when federal judge William Bootle ordered the university to admit a qualified male and female student, *Time* reporter Calvin Trillin pointed out that "their entry will crack the total segregation of all public education, from kindergarten through graduate school, in Georgia." Within a week, black students Charlayne Hunter and Hamilton Holmes were on the campus, facing death threats and a riot. Hill's logistical organization assured a safe entry for both students. Members of Athens's NAACP offered the students hospitality, and Hollowell was among those who escorted both students to the campus gates. Meanwhile, ACCA members maintained a nightly patrol of Hunter's home in Atlanta for the first weeks.[121]

Ironically, the riot actually benefited the desegregation case. Rather than having to decide between integration or closed public schools, Vandiver faced a choice between integration and the preservation of law and order. With the nation's media and the UGA faculty calling for an end to rioting, Vandiver guaranteed that peace would be maintained. Whitney Young was one of many who believed that the UGA crisis forced Georgians to consider the importance of segregation in terms of a revered institution rather than in terms of Atlanta's schools. "I think the governor might have closed the Atlanta high schools," Young concluded, but "he wouldn't dare close the University of Georgia." Vandiver himself admitted later that "had a case been filed against Georgia Tech, I think there would have probably been a difference because Tech . . . didn't have ties to every family the way the University of Georgia has. I mean, the University of Georgia is just part of the fabric of Georgia."[122]

Token integration in schools across the state followed in the wake of this first, single, breach of total segregation. In a leaked letter that became briefly famous, Jim Peters, the chairman of the State Board of Education and a close friend of Talmadge, admitted to Roy Harris that "some form of integration is inevitable." According to the *Southern Patriot*, one legislator conceded that "the second worst thing I can think of is integrated schools. The first worst thing is no schools at all." [123] After the riots at UGA, the integration of Atlanta's high schools by nine black students the following fall provoked little reaction. Typically, Hartsfield used the publicity to promote Atlanta's moderate image, providing a guided tour of the city and an information pack for all the visiting journalists.

Together, the education cases marked a watershed in Georgia's racial politics. The success of HOPE and the specter of racial crises elsewhere in the South actually prevented Georgia from following Virginia, Arkansas, and Mississippi into an official state education policy of uncompromising massive resistance. Meanwhile, the successful integration at Athens, backed by the ACCA, pointed the way to the more forthright challenge to Jim Crow backed by litigation that provided the hallmark of the city movements of the 1960s. As Hollowell concluded, the UGA case "turned the state around and allowed it to start, or at least to *see* what was in the other direction." [124]

The education cases were augmented by other legal cases at the end of the 1950s that demonstrated the limits to white supremacy. Preston Cobb, a fifteen-year-old mentally disabled black youth from Monticello in central Georgia, had been sentenced to death for the alleged murder of a white fish merchant. Cobb's mother contacted NAACP lawyers only five days before the planned date for the electrocution. From a legal civil rights perspective, the case set a precedent because defense lawyers overturned the case by showing the inadequacies at the original hearing, such as an all-white jury and confession under duress, rather than by calling for new evidence. The case also gained national attention when Eleanor Roosevelt mentioned it in her syndicated column. For black Georgians, the case was crucial because it demonstrated the power of urban civil rights lawyers to defend a black minor from the countryside against racial injustice. Reflecting on the key civil rights cases in Georgia, Hollowell considered the Cobb case to be as groundbreaking as the integration of the University of Georgia.[125]

While the NAACP supervised the education and justice cases, Atlanta's mayor filed a suit in 1958 challenging the county-unit system, which had further implications for Georgia's rurally dominated massive resistance. In response to the 1957 federal Civil Rights Act "forbidding any person in office to deprive others of civil rights," including voting, Morris Abram persuaded Hartsfield to put himself forward as plaintiff. The case lost narrowly by five to four in the Supreme Court, but with the appointment of two liberal justices the following year it was clear that the demise of the system was imminent. The county-unit system was finally dismantled in 1962.

Assessing the importance of the UGA case two years after the riots, Trillin reported that Georgia's "walk out of the Deep South mentality has been accelerated a good deal since then by a federal court ruling against the county-unit system." [126]

Renewed impetus for local urban protest also came from the example of black activism outside the state. During 1955–56, the black community in Montgomery, which had appointed Martin Luther King Jr. as its spokesman, successfully boycotted the city buses.[127] In the wake of Montgomery, two southern black communities launched bus boycotts and a dozen others filed suit. Atlanta followed the regional trend in March 1957, when William Holmes Borders persuaded prominent members of the Atlanta ministerial alliance to unite as the "Life, Love and Liberation Movement" and to sit at the front of city buses. One week later, ministers from around the South attended a meeting in Atlanta organized by the younger King which sought "to co-ordinate and spur the campaign for integrated transportation." [128]

Within Atlanta, however, the bus "Life, Love and Liberation" action did not mark a significant move toward confrontational protest. Before sitting at the front of the buses, the Triple L movement notified the mayor, the chief of police, and the president of the Atlanta Transit Authority. The movement remained the preserve of the elite too, involving only six ministers. The ministers dropped protests after one day after filing a desegregation suit. In many ways the protest saved the Atlanta Ministerial Alliance the potential embarrassment of hosting the regional meeting without having taken any local action itself. Moreover, the protest did not end bus segregation. In a separate action, Sam Williams, pastor of Friendship Baptist Church and a leading member of the NAACP, took the case of racial discrimination on Atlanta's buses to the federal court. Williams's case secured desegregation while the ministers' group's case was still in the courts.[129]

The Montgomery boycott did not provoke the leaders of the Atlanta black community into more vigorous protest against other areas of segregation. Dobbs criticized the bus boycott, insisting that "it's not the right way." Ruby Hurley was so frustrated by the "Negro old guard" that she recommended that the Atlanta branch of the NAACP relocate away from Auburn Avenue, "away from physical proximity to the power structure and attendant influences of those who do not want a vibrant branch." [130]

But if the Atlanta elite refrained from taking up the gauntlet of Montgomery, there were first stirrings of renewed protest in Georgia's other major cities. In Savannah, an NAACP-sponsored protest meeting in support of Martin Luther King Jr.

attracted over three hundred people. In Macon, a Citizens' Registration Committee formed within months of the *Brown* decision. In 1958, three black improvement associations formed in Columbus, concentrating on voting registration. In Dublin, the All Citizens' Voters League supervised the registration of nearly two thousand black voters during April 1956, which nearly doubled the total black vote. Indeed the *Dublin Courier-Herald* wondered, "why aren't the whites of the city and county equally as interested?" [131]

Despite these stirrings, black activism at the local level in Georgia at the end of the 1950s had not regained the impetus of the protest of the Arnall years. The Talmadge-led backlash, fueled further by the furor surrounding the *Brown* decision, proscribed the reemergence of local movements. But as an SRC reporter noted in 1958, "there are observable cracks in the segregation dam in Georgia. These cracks may lead to irreparable breaks as pressure behind the dam grows." [132] These cracks were caused primarily by the legal challenges to segregated education and were most obvious in Atlanta. During the 1960s, a fresh wave of expectant local protest movements across the state applied pressure behind Georgia's segregation dam.

Rev. Ralph Mark Gilbert and Eloria Sherman Gilbert (here pictured at their wedding on 22 October 1945) led the voter registration campaign in Savannah and across the state during the early 1940s. Rev. Gilbert was the president of the Savannah NAACP branch and the inaugural president of the Georgia NAACP state conference. (Courtesy of Willie Bryant)

In February 1942, the Savannah NAACP youth council was the largest NAACP youth council in the country. Included in this photo are Rev. Ralph Mark Gilbert and Ella Baker, the NAACP national director of branches and youthwork. Also included is a young W. W. Law, who later succeeded Gilbert as Savannah's NAACP branch president. (Courtesy of the Geneva W. Law Collection)

Col. A. T. Walden was one of the most renowned civil rights leaders in Atlanta during the 1940s and 1950s. He was also the first black lawyer to supervise civil rights cases in Georgia. (Auburn Avenue Research Library on African-American Culture and History)

John Wesley Dobbs, a federal railroad employee, founded the Atlanta Civic and Political League in 1934 and was one of the leading advocates of voter registration across the state. (Courtesy of Constance Carter)

Ruby Blackburn (*front*) was the foremost organizer of black neighborhood and civic leagues in Atlanta during the 1940s and 1950s. She also
founded the Atlanta League of Negro Women Voters. (Auburn Avenue
Research Library on African-American Culture and History)

Thomas Brewer, a dentist, was known as "the Chief" in Columbus during the 1940s because of his outspoken advocacy of black civil rights. (Courtesy of Billy Winn / *Columbus Ledger-Enquirer*)

William Randall Sr. was the leader of African American protest in Macon from the 1940s through the 1960s. (Courtesy of William Randall Jr.)

This strike at Swift's Peanut Pork factory in Moultrie was one of a number of postwar interracial strikes in Georgia. (Southern Labor Archives, Special Collections Department, Pullen Library, Georgia State University, Atlanta)

"It's Okay—Ol' Gene Will Be Back In Soon"

MURDER OF
TWO NEGROES
AND THEIR WIVES
IN GEORGIA

Herblock's cartoon of the lynching at Monroe in 1946 recognized the ominous significance of Gene Talmadge's gubernatorial victory.

Above: Thomas Brewer was murdered in 1956 in suspicious circumstances during a period of sustained supremacist violence in Columbus. His funeral attracted hundreds of mourners but also marked the end of overt protest in Columbus. (Courtesy of Billy Winn / *Columbus Ledger-Enquirer*)

Left: Clarence Jordan, a Baptist minister, founded the Koinonia community in 1942. The community, which pioneered new farming techniques, practiced racial integration. Despite violent reprisals from the Ku Klux Klan and the refusal of local businesses to trade with Koinonia, the community survived and provided a refuge for student protesters during the 1960s. (Copyright Koinonia)

Above: Calvin Craig, Imperial Wizard of Georgia's Ku Klux Klan, ordered Klan members to march in opposition to the protests of the 1960s. One of the unintended effects of Klan marches, such as this one in Atlanta, was to deter some shoppers from visiting downtown stores. (Courtesy of Calvin Craig)

Left: Martin Luther King Jr. preaching at Savannah's municipal auditorium on New Year's Day of 1964 called Savannah the most integrated city south of the Mason-Dixon Line. (Copyright Frederick Baldwin / Telfair Museum of Art)

Left: W. W. Law, speaking at the St. Philip AME church, led the direct action protests in Savannah which forced the desegregation of the city. (Courtesy of the Geneva W. Law Collection)

Below: Student demonstrators in Georgia used a wide variety of tactics during the early 1960s. These students were preparing to "swim-in" at Savannah's segregated Tybee Island. (Courtesy of the Geneva W. Law collection)

Mass meetings were a feature of urban protest movements during the early 1960s. In Savannah, mass meetings were held each Sunday at 4 P.M. for a period of ten years. By rotating the meetings between churches, the Savannah movement attracted increased support. (Courtesy of the Geneva W. Law Collection)

The Albany protest sustained national media attention from the beginning because of the masses of citizens arrested and, after his arrival, because of the involvement of Martin Luther King Jr. Although the movement was perceived as King's major setback, it was also notable for the great extent and longevity of community participation. (Copyright Albany Civil Rights Movement Museum)

Singing was an integral part of mass meetings across Georgia. SNCC's Albany Freedom Singers—Bernice Johnson, Charles Neblett, Bertha Gober, Cordell Reagon, and Rutha Harris—were famous across the nation. (Copyright Albany Civil Rights Movement Museum)

SNCC's Southwest Georgia Project attempted to register voters in the heart of Georgia's black belt. Charles Sherrod, who founded the project in 1962 and remains with its successor in 2001, is standing at the right. Randy Battle, who later would take a turn coordinating the project, is seated. (Copyright Danny Lyon / prints provided by Albany Civil Rights Movement Museum)

Protest in southwest Georgia met with fierce repression. These teenage girls were held in the Leesburg Stockade during the summer of 1963. They were given two cold hamburgers each day to eat, and the toilet was stopped up. (Copyright Danny Lyon / prints provided by Albany Civil Rights Movement Museum)

Warren Fortson, Sumter County's attorney, represented student protesters in Americus and tried to establish a biracial committee to address the protesters' demands. He was ostracized by most white residents, fired from his job, and left for Atlanta. (Courtesy of Warren Fortson)

Frances Pauley was the executive director of the Georgia Council on Human Relations during the 1960s and a leading voice calling for racial integration and social justice. (Special Collections Department, Robert W. Woodruff Library, Emory University)

Facing page: Sunday morning was often the most segregated time in Georgia. During the summer of 1965, Southwest Georgia Project activists tried to integrate the First Methodist Church in Americus. (John Pope, standing on the far left at the top of the stairs, later became a wealthy business-man and his philanthropy earned him—somewhat ironically—the Martin Luther King humanitarian award.) (Copyright the Associated Press)

Right: Herman Lodge was elected chairman of the Burke County Commission shortly after the U.S. Supreme Court ruled in *Rogers v. Lodge* (1982) that at-large systems in Burke County limited the voting power of black residents. He was also head of Burke County Improvement Association, one of numerous local organizations seeking the election of black officials and economic justice. (Courtesy of Herman Lodge)

John McCown (*right, front*) succeeded Frances Pauley as head of the GCHR. In 1968 he was elected to the Hancock County Commission, which was the first county government in Georgia to come under black political control since Reconstruction. An advocate of Black Power, McCown was responsible for the arms race which developed between some white and black residents. Georgia Governor Jimmy Carter visited Hancock in May of 1974 in an effort to defuse the violence. (George Clark / *Atlanta Journal-Constitution*)

4

Direct Action Protest in Georgia's Cities, 1960–1965

Legal action had chipped away at the foundations of segregation in Georgia during the 1950s, but after 1960 black protest in Georgia and across the South confronted Jim Crow head-on. On 1 February 1960, four students in Greensboro, North Carolina, refused to leave a local store when they were denied service at the lunch counter. Although such protests had occurred before, this particular sit-in inaugurated a new phase of confrontational civil rights protest throughout the South. By the end of the year, direct action protests had begun in over one hundred southern cities. This acceptance of a confrontational approach, four years after the bus boycott at Montgomery, marked the full flowering of what Aldon Morris describes as the "modern" phase of the civil rights movement.[1]

Martin Luther King Jr. was the most prominent leader of this phase of black protest, and King's southern Christian Leadership Conference was involved in the most well-known city protests in Albany, Birmingham, St. Augustine, and Selma. It was King who was recognized in the media as articulating most clearly the desire of black southerners for an end to segregation, most notably at the March on Washington of 1963. The Student Nonviolent Coordinating Committee, formed in response to the student protests, and the Congress on Racial Equality also supervised widely publicized direct action campaigns. In addition, local protest emerged in cities across the South, partly in response to the example of the more high-profile leaders and national protest organizations.

From a state of relative dormancy, a new phase of urban protest appeared in each city in Georgia too. The first sit-ins began in Atlanta and Savannah in mid-March 1960, but increasingly direct action protests spread to cities across the whole state. Jule Levine, a member of Rome's Human Relations Council, observed that "it was almost a contagion, one community to the next. And it came to Rome." Of all the Georgia protests, the Albany movement of 1961–62 received most of the national headlines, largely because of the involvement of Martin Luther King Jr. and the huge scale of protests. But even before the Albany movement, seven Georgia cities had experienced direct action protest. By September 1961, at least 7,000 Georgians had been involved in demonstrations and over 292 Georgians had been arrested.[2] The confrontational protests were paralleled by a rapid escalation in voting registration campaigns.[3] The *Atlanta Journal* noted on 8 April 1963 that "major spurts in Negro registration came chiefly in the larger cities such as Savannah, Albany, Columbus, Atlanta, Macon and Augusta." During the spring of 1964, over half of Georgia's counties witnessed voter registration campaigns.[4]

The increasing economic ascendancy of cities in Georgia gave these urban direct action protests even greater importance within the state. Whereas Georgia's rural population exceeded the urban population in 1950, by 1960 over 55 percent of Georgians lived in settlements of over 2,500 people. During the same decade, the population of metropolitan Atlanta alone grew from 726,989 to 1,017,188, an increase of almost 40 percent. By the middle of the 1950s, the annual payroll at Georgia's largest industrial plant, Lockheed, exceeded the total income from what was once King Cotton.[5]

Rural Georgia's political dominance also waned shortly after the Greensboro sit-in, following the dismantling of the county-unit system. As early as 1958, Atlanta's mayor William Hartsfield had challenged the system, albeit unsuccessfully. In 1960, however, the Supreme Court ruled in favor of "one man, one vote" in Tuskegee, Alabama. Within hours of the Alabama decision, Atlanta attorneys, led by Morris Abram, filed a successful challenge to Georgia's county-unit system. The eventual federal reapportionment of 1962 marked the final stage in the political ascendancy of urban Georgia over its rural hinterland.[6] Therefore, whereas Atlanta and Savannah (and to a lesser extent Macon) had been isolated examples of racial moderation during the 1950s, these cities now acted as trend-setters for the rest of the state.

If urban protest was a common phenomenon across the South, the experience of black protest was markedly different in each town. Robert Norrell concluded that "each community now has its own story to tell, and only when more of these stories are told will the southern civil rights movement be understood."[7] In Georgia, this diversity in protest was most clearly evident during the years of direct action. In towns such as Savannah, Macon, and Atlanta, the protests were exceptionally active. Protests in Columbus and Augusta, in contrast, were paltry and short-lived. Some local movements appeared to be self-contained, even at odds with the national leadership. Leaders in Savannah attempted to bar Martin Luther King Jr. from preaching there. In contrast, the Albany movement provided an example of urban protest in which both King and SNCC staffers played prominent roles.

This diversity stemmed, in part, from the dearth of statewide networks of protest. The white backlash of the 1950s had been so severe that the emerging statewide movement of the 1940s had all but disintegrated by the time of the Greensboro sit-in. There were, of course, informal networks. Donald Hollowell defended students in Augusta, Macon, and Atlanta, and Hollowell's assistant, Horace T. Ward, was a key supporter of student protest in Rome.[8] William Holmes Borders, who supported the student sit-ins, addressed a meeting of Georgia Baptists in Macon during April 1960. In the same town, over one thousand Masons met in September 1960 to hear John Wesley Dobbs and Thurgood Marshall. The NAACP and the Georgia Voters' League also had branches in over a dozen towns throughout the state.[9]

The state did provide an important context for local protests. After Governor Vandiver chose to follow the recommendation of the Sibley Commission, Georgia did not follow the path of massive resistance, in contrast to most Deep South states. But the state government still defended segregation. Shortly after the first sit-ins, the state General Assembly voted to label blood according to ethnic group. More significantly, the legislature showed its opposition to the new form of protests, ruling in February 1960 that it was a "misdemeanor to refuse to leave an establishment if ordered by the proprietor. Meanwhile, Charles Bloch, a Jewish lawyer and close friend of Richard Russell, drew over $300,000 from the state of Georgia to defend cases of constitutional law. Georgia also experienced continuing racial violence. At the end of 1961, the *Pittsburgh Courier* reported five unsolved murders of black Georgians for allegedly racial motives during the previous two years.[10]

But the state no longer provided the crucial context for black protest. Atlanta and Savannah had been major influences on state protest at various times since World War II. During the 1960s, however, it was highly publicized protests from outside Georgia and the leadership of Martin Luther King Jr. that provided the impetus and example for local protests. For example, James Brown, the Georgia NAACP youth secretary, observed in a mass meeting in October 1960 that youths in Georgia "could not see the struggle for freedom without participating themselves." Mass meetings in some of Georgia's larger towns featured speakers from around the South.[11]

At the same time, local protests varied because almost all of the urban movements in Georgia were dependent on local leaders rather than national organizations. Although Atlanta was the base for both SCLC and SNCC by the end of 1960, neither organization played a major role in Atlanta or any other Georgia city, with the notable exception of Albany. In November 1961, the state conference of the NAACP called on all of Georgia's NAACP units, youth and adults, to intensify their efforts toward opening all facilities. Two years previously, however, the national NAACP convention had decided against promoting direct action in favor of supporting local initiative, which gave the local Georgia branches independence of action under the umbrella of a national organization.[12]

The majority of detailed local studies concern communities that were either in the contemporary spotlight or illuminated the activities of a national organization or leader. Montgomery, Albany, Birmingham, St. Augustine, and Selma fit into both categories, Greensboro triggered the new wave of direct action of 1960, and Tuskegee was renowned for its institute.[13]

With the notable exceptions of Atlanta and Albany, however, the majority of Georgia's direct action protests were neither headline grabbing nor nationally significant for any reason save their cumulative impact. These movements provide a different set of individual stories; in a sense they constitute what remains a relatively hidden picture of the modern civil rights movement. Each of these histories demonstrates how particular aspects of the direct action protests worked at the local level, and together they provide a more informed and balanced picture of the national civil rights movement. Many of Georgia's urban protests are part of this picture—not influential on the national level but dynamic within their own respective communities. Taken together, they reveal a broader experience of direct action protest in a Deep South state.

Protest in Atlanta

As so often in Georgia's history, attention within the state focused on Atlanta. In part, this was because Atlanta students were the first in the state to respond to the sit-ins. As early as 5 February 1960, in a drugstore adjacent to Atlanta's Morehouse College campus, Lonnie King discussed with fellow undergraduate Julian Bond the possibility of replicating the Greensboro demonstrations. Lonnie King, who was already an active member of student government, became the driving force behind the nascent protest. Bond, whose father was a renowned black educator in the state, assumed the role of communications director. Within days Lonnie King had gathered a small cadre of like-minded students ready to lead downtown protest. After discussing plans with the six college presidents, the student leaders published an "Appeal for Human Rights" in the local press on 9 March. Six days later, Lonnie King initiated sit-ins, which involved over two hundred students in protests in municipal buildings across the city center.[14]

In Atlanta, the student movement began as a distinct break from traditional protest because the leaders of direct action came from outside the existing black power structure. Whereas the ACCA had reacted to the perceived failings of Atlanta's traditional leadership, student leaders took their inspiration from the new wave of direct action protest across the South. Students represented a new generation of leaders in Atlanta. Bond and fellow student leaders Ben Brown and Charles Black were born in the year that Daddy King had caused such furor by attending the premiere of *Gone with the Wind*. Student leaders were mostly from out of Atlanta. Lonnie King, for example, was from Arlington in south Georgia and had served with the navy for three years during the 1950s. Charles Black, who succeeded Lonnie King in the fall of 1961, came from Miami, Florida.[15]

The wider significance of the Atlanta protest lay in the prestige of the city. Atlanta was not only the capital of Georgia but was also far and away the leading city in the state. In 1961, the city boasted of having one million residents, over twice as many as the second city of Savannah and over five times the population of any other city in Georgia. This preeminence extended well beyond the state border; the *New York Times* described Atlanta as "the commercial, industrial and transportation capital of the Southeast."[16]

As was true of the issue of school desegregation, therefore, Atlanta's economic and political preeminence dictated that the city would also provide a wider example in terms of racial protest and progress. Once the sit-ins were under way, *Look* magazine predicted that "as goes Atlanta, so goes the South." Claude Sitton reported in the *New York Times* that the city's business leaders were a powerful influence in assisting "not only Atlanta but Georgia to escape from the trap of massive resistance." After attending the convention of American Chamber of Commerce Executives in New Orleans, Atlanta businessman Opie L. Shelton reported to the city's negotiating committee in March 1961 that "all southern cities were watching Atlanta closely." Atlanta's chief of police, Herbert Jenkins, was told by informers that the White Citizens' Council and the Ku Klux Klan "considered Atlanta the most important place to keep segregated" because the South would follow its example. Outside the South, the "Appeal for Human Rights" was reprinted in the *New York Times,* and all the major northern newspapers sent reporters to interview Atlanta students awaiting trial in Fulton County jail.[17]

The most striking feature of the Atlanta movement, however, was the failure of the student protesters to achieve a swift, comprehensive desegregation agreement. Ivan Allen commented that "Atlanta was still almost a totally segregated city when I became mayor in 1962. There had been some progress made in the two preceding years, but most of it was insignificant." In fact, more than 103 southern cities, including some in Georgia, had desegregated lunch counters by the time Atlanta stores desegregated in October 1961. Even then, further desegregation within the city was piecemeal and sporadic. In an open statement to the mayor on 14 March 1963, student leaders asserted that "the Appeal published in the Atlanta newspapers on March 9, 1960 has grown yellow. Three years have passed without our having realized the goals which we set down . . . expect more of the demonstrations which have revealed to the world that Atlanta does not measure up to her 'liberal' image." At the end of the same year, Martin Luther King Jr. warned that "time was running out for Atlanta" because it was "behind almost every major southern city in its progress toward desegregation." [18]

This failure was despite mass student participation, charismatic leadership, and the use of confrontational tactics. After the first sit-ins, the students formed the Committee on an Appeal for Human Rights (COAHR) under the joint leadership of Lonnie King and Herschelle Sullivan of the all-women Spelman College. At the urging of Atlanta's traditional black leaders, Lonnie King announced that no further public demonstrations were planned pending negotiations. But the outright antagonism of white businessmen toward COAHR in the first meeting shocked the students and forced them to abandon hopes of a swift negotiated settlement.[19]

Consequently, the leaders of COAHR sought the advice of the younger leadership of the ACCA with the intention of resuming direct action protest. Instead of continuing a citywide campaign, COAHR targeted individual stores. The first boycott and picketing of a single A&P supermarket on 22 May 1960 proved fruitless when the management resolved to close down or operate at a loss if necessary. To try to increase the momentum, COAHR called for a mass march to the state capitol to commemorate the sixth anniversary of the *Brown* decision. On the advice of Police Chief Herbert Jenkins, however, student leaders agreed to reroute the two thousand protesters to a rally at a nearby black church to avoid potential violence.[20]

By the time of the 1960 university summer vacation, which left the movement in temporary abeyance, COAHR had made little progress. By this time, approximately sixty cities in the Upper South and Southeast had already agreed to desegregate downtown lunch counters. During the summer, members of COAHR who lived in Atlanta continued to confront segregation, including conducting kneel-ins at central Baptist churches, in order to "place this problem squarely on the hearts and the moral consciences of the white Christians in our community."[21]

When the colleges reopened in September 1960, Lonnie King decided to relaunch a specific sit-in campaign focusing on Rich's, the largest department store in downtown Atlanta, and seven other stores. To ensure maximum publicity, COAHR delayed the protests to coincide with the presidential election and persuaded Martin Luther King Jr. to participate. The sit-ins resumed on 19 October, immediately after SNCC's regional conference in Atlanta. The SCLC president was one of over fifty protesters to be arrested that day.[22] In response, almost two thousand students closed down sixteen more lunch counters the following day. By Friday hundreds of students were picketing main downtown stores and Lonnie King called for an economic boycott to "bankrupt the economy of segregation." Meanwhile, some instructors tried to hold classes for students in jail, which by this stage included five student college presidents and two college beauty queens.[23]

With Atlanta increasingly under the national spotlight, Hartsfield arranged for the release of the protesters and a thirty-day truce to negotiate a settlement. COAHR and the Auburn Avenue elite negotiated together as the Student-Adult Liaison Committee. Once again such negotiations proved fruitless. Richard Rich, the owner of Rich's, steadfastly refused even to attend meetings, claiming disingenuously that he was unconcerned because black Atlantans provided a negligible amount of his business. Rich did agree to talks at the end of the truce period, during Thanksgiving. Even then, he merely insisted that public segregation should be dealt with first and that a single private institution should not be forced to become the "bellwether of change." The following day, student leaders announced that they were resuming their protests, and by the end of November, every downtown lunch counter in Atlanta had closed. On the advice of Georgia author Lillian Smith, students joined in the carols at Rich's department store's big tree-lighting ceremony to highlight the irony of singing "Joy to the World."[24]

The protests did make an impact in Atlanta. After hearing that downtown stores showed a 13 percent fall in sales compared with 1959, students announced a continuation of the boycott until Easter. Ironically, a counterpicket outside Rich's by the Klan had enhanced the boycott. One student leader recalled that "we were able to keep out those folk who were sympathetic to us and the Klan were able to keep out those people who couldn't identify or didn't want to be associated with the Klan."[25]

The Atlanta protests also affected national politics. Lonnie King and Herschelle Sullivan had hoped that the involvement of Martin Luther King Jr. in the run-up to the presidential election would secure maximum publicity for the movement.[26] In fact, the plan succeeded beyond expectations. Martin Luther King was arrested, and because he was already on probation for a minor traffic offense, he was transferred to a maximum-security prison at Reidsville in rural Georgia. The case became a cause célèbre when Robert Kennedy appealed to the DeKalb County judge for clemency and John Kennedy called Mrs. King to express his concern.

Nonetheless, segregation of downtown Atlanta remained intact at the end of 1960. After the desegregation of the University of Georgia in January (and after exams at the beginning of the second semester), the leadership of COAHR broadened the picketing to include all downtown department stores. COAHR also raised the stakes by following SNCC's new strategy of refusing bond so as to crowd the jails. By 10 February, more than eighty students were behind bars.[27] Two weeks later, in a copy of the first wave of sit-ins, the students posted bond on the assurance of renewed and more congenial negotiations.

The resulting negotiated compromise, however, provided for the desegregation of downtown department store lunch counters only after the integration of Atlanta's schools six months later in September. The compromise agreement, the *Atlanta Inquirer* reported, struck Atlanta's black community "like a bucket of cold water in the face." Misleading white press reports that downtown desegregation was dependent on successful school desegregation exacerbated this shock.[28] Lonnie King and Herschelle Sullivan admitted later that they had accepted the compromise under pressure from the more senior members of the Student-Adult Liaison Committee.

In the longer term, the student frustration over lunch counters was repeated on a broader scale as the protest enlarged its focus to include all segregated areas of the city. By the end of 1962, Atlanta had more desegregated movie theaters than any other southern city, and the swimming pools also desegregated without incident.[29] Even Atlanta's traditional black leadership admitted publicly, however, that any integration victories had been token victories at best. In December 1962, Mayor Allen erected a metal barricade at Peyton Road to maintain the separation of white and black neighborhoods in southwest Atlanta. Outraged black Atlantans referred to the barrier as Atlanta's "Berlin Wall" and started a boycott of Atlanta's West End. When UN undersecretary Ralph Bunche visited Atlanta for an NAACP convention in 1962, he was turned away from his hotel, just as he had been eleven years previously. After negotiations during the summer of 1963, only thirty of Atlanta's restaurants and less than twenty hotels agreed to serve black customers. To the extreme annoyance of student protesters, over half reneged on the agreement. In a survey during November 1963, the SRC reported that Atlanta lagged in the desegregation of public schools and public accommodations compared with eleven southern cities in Virginia, Tennessee, Louisiana, and Texas.[30]

In an attempt to make further progress, over two hundred leaders, representing over eighty organizations and all strands of the city's black leadership, joined together as the Atlanta Summit Leadership Conference in October 1963. The *Student Voice* commented that "the Summit Conference binds together, for the first time, widely divergent groups in the Negro community with some white support." Clarence Coleman of ACCA and A. T. Walden initially acted as the Summit's co-chairmen, and Wyatt T. Walker was called in as an adviser shortly afterward. At an outdoor rally in December 1963, Summit leaders outlined their plans to an audience of almost three thousand people. Taking the theme that Atlanta "is lagging behind other southern cities and even other Georgia cities," Summit leaders announced a drive for racial equality in all areas of city life.[31]

Various member groups of the Summit achieved successes. Shortly before Christmas, SNCC and COAHR launched demonstrations against the Toddle House restaurant chain. John Lewis and Lillian Gregory, wife of comedian Dick Gregory (and also a stockholder in the company), were among those to spend Christmas in jail before Toddle House agreed to desegregate. Meanwhile, Operation Breadbasket, representing hundreds of ministers, sought to persuade businesses to hire black employees. Using the threat of a boycott when necessary, Ralph Abernathy claimed that over 750 black Atlantans had gained employment during 1963, with a payroll worth over $2 million.[32]

Nonetheless, more active members of the Summit formed their own battle plan in early January. Frustrated at the slow pace of change, SNCC and COAHR launched an all-out drive for an open city. COAHR chairman Larry Fox explained that an open city meant "jobs, decent and integrated schools, and the right to eat or rent a room wherever we choose." With the support of SCLC, the local NAACP, and radio station WAOK, student activists decided to restart street demonstrations in an attempt to gain a public accommodations ordinance. Meanwhile, at the behest of SNCC, more than one hundred high school students boycotted school and sat in at Mayor Allen's office in an attempt to "play hookey for freedom." [33]

Demonstrations escalated dramatically at the end of January when a UN Sub-Commission on the Prevention of Discrimination and Protection of Minorities visited Atlanta to study race relations in the city. The commission, which included members from Sudan and Egypt, was met by a sign at the airport, "Welcome to Atlanta, a segregated city," and by students lying down outside their hotel. In response to KKK counterdemonstrations, some of the students donned bed sheets and struck up a new marching chant, "The old KKK she ain't what she used to be." Somewhat poignantly, protesters targeted Lebs, a segregated restaurant owned by a Russian-born Jew whose parents had fled to America after persecution. After fist-fights broke out between some of the protesters and Klan members, more than eighty students and Dick Gregory were arrested.[34] During the following week, over two hundred more students were arrested. Nonetheless, the commission members pronounced themselves "favorably impressed" before departing to visit northern cities.

The commission's view was not shared by the protesters. In an open letter to Ivan Allen at the end of January, SNCC member Prathia Hall insisted that "despite its liberal image Atlanta is still a segregated city." Julian Bond also pointed out that "Savannah has made greater strides in many fields." James Forman concurred, stating that "Negroes who live in Atlanta, work in Atlanta, die in Atlanta—know that the image is false." [35]

Allen claimed that voluntary desegregation would be possible if the demonstrations were called off. Following the interests of the more radical wing, Wyatt T. Walker rejected Allen's call, arguing that "if we waited for voluntary action, most of us would still be picking cotton." Angered at the resumption of confrontational tactics, Walden resigned his position as co-chairman and led the so-called dove faction out of the Summit. Although the remaining leaders of the Summit called for a "sacrificial Easter" boycott and supervised continued demonstrations, the protests failed to wring any further concessions from either public or private officials. By the time of the Civil Rights Act of 1964, Atlanta city officials had still not passed a public accommodations ordinance, and only twenty eating facilities were classified as desegregated.[36]

Both the development of protest and the limits to progress reflected Atlanta's unique circumstances. In the first place, it was Atlanta's relative moderation that provided the opportunity for the emergence of a large-scale local protest. As a reporter, Robert Nelson, observed, "Georgia is a high ground of the South. 'Atlanta,' says a native Georgian looking north toward the mountains, 'is the tail of the Blue Ridge spine.'" Within Georgia too, Atlanta was increasingly seen as a city out of character with the traditions of the state. Lawrence Hanks concluded that "people in south Georgia think of Atlanta as a foreign country in the state of Georgia." [37]

Local black leaders also acknowledged that Atlanta was different. Benjamin Mays contended at the end of the 1960s that "I have never been able to sing Dixie" but continued that "if Dixie were Atlanta and Atlanta were Dixie, I could sing Dixie." Even the jails were considered superior by student protesters. In a diary she wrote during her imprisonment, Adelaide Taitt of Spelman College described the city jail as the "Hilton Bars ... like a penthouse compared to some of the jails." [38]

The attitude of Atlanta's white political leadership was out of step with the ardent white supremacy of Georgia's state government. Chief of Police Herbert Jenkins told his officers that "personally I favor the status quo. But ... I am prepared to yield to the judgement of the Supreme Court. Why? As law-enforcement officers, there is no other position we can honestly take." Hartsfield announced shortly before the end of his term as mayor in 1962 that "regardless of our personal feelings or past habits, we are living in a changing world. To progress, Atlanta must be part of that world." Ivan Allen, who succeeded Hartsfield, continued this moderate approach. The *Atlanta Journal* commented that Allen "could remember most of Hartsfield's speeches even if he couldn't remember all of his own." Some black leaders judged Allen more kindly. Shortly after Allen retired in 1969, Rev. William Holmes Borders described him as "Atlanta's best mayor." In 1963, Allen testified at President Lyndon Johnson's Commission on Civil Rights in Washington despite the opposition of leading city businessmen. When Martin Luther King Jr. won the Nobel Peace Prize in 1964, Allen supported a biracial banquet in King's honor. [39]

Atlanta's preoccupation with its national image and business also proscribed a violent white response. In a meeting with businessmen in 1961, Hartsfield asked, "What do you plan to do with the Brazilian millionaire who flies in with some money to invest but happens to be black? Send him to the Negro YMCA? Think about it friends." Certainly the attempt to justify Hartsfield's slogan of being a "city too busy to hate" reaped financial dividends. In August 1961, the *Wall Street Journal* reported that Atlanta snatched a $7 million plant from Birmingham because the northern industrialist who built the plant believed that "in Alabama they're fanatics on segregation." [40] By 1960 Atlanta had the nation's third largest airport, and many of America's largest businesses were based there.

Without doubt, Atlanta's concern for its reputation had a moderating effect on race relations in the city. After conducting a survey of influential black Atlantans, Benjamin Mays concluded that because "the economic growth of Atlanta has been phenomenal," the city had developed a "cosmopolitan atmosphere shared by no other comparable cities in the South."[41] The city golf course and library had been desegregated before COAHR began to demonstrate. The Freedom Riders passed through the city without incident en route to a riotous reception in Alabama. By the end of 1960, the headquarters of SNCC and SCLC and the regional office of the NAACP were based in Atlanta.

The economic and institutional development of the city's black community also provided the opportunity for the sheer scale of the student movement. David Garrow commented that Atlanta's "roster of important black owned business and professional institutions—particularly the Atlanta University Colleges—was one that no other Southern town or city could match." At the beginning of the 1960s, Atlanta had a larger and more concentrated black college population than any other city in the South, with almost eight thousand students in the six colleges that made up the Atlanta University complex. Columbus in southwest Georgia, by contrast, experienced minimal direct action protest, primarily because it had no black college. "In really analyzing it," said Lonnie King, "the only people in the black community at that time who were free to take on the Establishment were college kids."[42]

It was little surprise that a cadre of talented and dynamic leaders emerged from such a large student population. Herschelle Sullivan already had experience of leading the Spelman student body, while Ben Brown was the student president of Clark College. Lonnie King, who was a leading member of the college football team, was widely recognized as the charismatic inspiration behind student activism. Charles Black described King as "the key to Atlanta protest," while Bond concluded that "the success of the movement here is owed, I think, entirely to him."[43]

The extensive development of Atlanta's student community was further reflected in the sophisticated nature of the direct action movement. COAHR was the best financed student sit-in protest in the South. In his review of student protest, Howard Zinn described the Atlanta movement as "one of the largest and best organized sit-in demonstrations of all." Bond and King counted the number of seats at every single lunch counter before the initial sit-ins. After the summer vacation, Lonnie King used his military experience by targeting Atlanta's largest department store, Rich's, in a version of the domino theory. King believed that "if we could break Rich's the rest of them would just run in line." All the initial protests were organized by

Morehouse student Fred Bennett, a former sergeant in the army, who was known as La Commandante. Bennett appointed group captains who used a two-way radio system and returned regular action reports.[44]

Atlanta students had participated in organized protest against segregation before 1960. Under the tutelage of Howard Zinn, students of Spelman College formed a Social Science Club dedicated to the achievement of civil rights. In January 1957, club members tried for the first time to sit in the white-only section of the gallery in the state capitol. Two years later, groups of female students paid regular visits to the city's Carnegie Library to highlight the fact that only three of Atlanta's libraries served black citizens. Under the threat of legal action brought by Zinn and Whitney Young, the library agreed to desegregate.[45]

The student community was also able to build on the foundations of existing protest groups. Adelaide Taitt believed that because of the booklet *A Second Look,* "the Atlanta movement was spurred on, and out of that came the appeal for Human Rights."[46] ACCA's Carl Holman, who lectured at Atlanta University, became the unofficial adviser of COAHR. The student movement also got airtime and support from radio station WAOK.

While the context of Atlanta and the presence of organizations within the black community provided an opportunity for widespread black protest, it did not make success inevitable. In the first place, Atlanta's reputation for racial moderation masked the reality of resistance to racial change. Samuel Du Bois Cook, a lecturer at Atlanta University, lambasted black community leaders for deluding themselves into thinking that Atlanta had good race relations. Margaret Long, editor of the *New South,* observed in February 1964, "There's not much hatred here to be sure ... but there's not much integration or equality for Atlanta Negroes either." Although he praised Atlanta's moderation at the Atlanta Summit Leadership Conference rally of December 1963, Martin Luther King Jr. blamed the city's image for becoming "a tranquilizing drug to lull us to sleep, and dull our sensitivity to the continued existence of segregation." It may have been a city "too busy hustling a buck to hate," Hunter James reported, but "Georgia was always out there to remind it of what it was and where it had come from."[47]

Behind the official public pronouncements, there was no coordinated drive to promote integration, merely a concerted effort to avoid publicity from racial incidents. When Spelman's Social Science Club attended *My Fair Lady* at the Fox Theater in 1959, Hartsfield told a worried manager simply to "ignore them and turn the lights off." Even Mays accepted that lunch counter desegregation "died hard."

"How can I sing Atlanta," Mays admitted, "when it took the white power structure more than twelve months to agree to desegregate the city and allowed eighteen months to pass before the students actually achieved their objectives?"[48]

Similarly, white businessmen resisted racial change, despite the fall in retail sales. The negotiated agreement to desegregate the lunch counters was worded carefully to safeguard the signatory white merchants from charges of capitulation. Reflecting on his first years as mayor, Allen observed in 1963, "The battle line had been drawn quite clearly at the restaurants and hotels. Everything I had tried in those areas had failed." Allen was particularly frustrated that the "hotel and restaurant associations would not even respond to the pragmatic argument that unless they opened their doors to everyone, Atlanta's convention and tourist business—not to mention its favorable image—would plummet."[49]

Nor did the liberal voice within the city engender a decisive move for desegregation in the face of direct action protest. Eliza Paschall, who headed Atlanta's most outspoken liberal organization, the Atlanta Council on Human Relations, lamented later that "we were long on ideal but short on power." The role of white liberals in the city reminded Paschall of an ostensibly committed lover who told his beloved that "I will climb the highest mountain and swim the widest ocean for you, and I will be round tomorrow . . . unless it is raining." In Paschall's candid opinion, "it must have rained" in Atlanta, as far as white liberals were concerned.[50]

The Atlanta movement failed, however, because it was unable to mount an effective challenge to this nonconfrontational white resistance. The student movement in the similarly progressive city of Nashville, by contrast, had secured the desegregation of lunch counters over a year before the Atlanta movement.[51] Even in Atlanta local politicians revealed that, under extreme pressure, positive progress could be made. When faced by the furor over the arrest of Martin Luther King Jr., Hartsfield revealed his flair for political manipulation by arranging the release of all protesters. Initially, the mayor gained the support of the Student-Adult Liaison Committee by falsely invoking the name of John Kennedy as the prime mover behind Hartsfield's own truce conditions. Then Hartsfield visited the state prosecutor and Richard Rich separately, assuring each that the other had already agreed to drop all charges.[52]

The weakness of the Atlanta movement lay primarily in the fact that it was divided between the student advocates of direct action and the established leaders, who favored persuasion and political pressure.[53] The *Atlanta Daily World*, for example, published the "Appeal for Human Rights" at the full advertising rate and editorially opposed the sit-ins. John Mack, a vice-president of COAHR, told a mass meeting that "we need the press, but there is one newspaper—the *Atlanta Daily World*—that is fighting us." In response, students wrote their own newsletter, the *Student Movement and You,* which developed into the *Atlanta Inquirer* in July 1960. Edited by Carl Holman, the newspaper advocated direct action rather than gradualism, pointedly declaring that it was founded by people who "felt a void existed in the reporting of the news." Approximately twelve thousand copies of the first issue were printed, denouncing the "public pronunciations from so-called leaders, advocating a doctrine of stop, wait and see . . . and do nothing." [54]

For the students, this division was often expressed as outright antipathy toward the Auburn Avenue leadership. Lonnie King believed that Martin Luther King Sr. was "sometimes with us and sometimes against us, depending on, seemingly, which side of the bed he got up on." In his first time before the court, Bond was incredulous that his defense lawyer, A. T. Walden, had fallen asleep. "I'm looking at Walden and I said, this guy's my lawyer and he's asleep." [55] Some of the leaders of COAHR later believed that the college presidents' suggestion of publishing an "appeal for human rights" was a delaying tactic. [56] Carl Holman did not reveal his age to the students because he observed that the leaders of COAHR trusted only those under thirty years old. [57]

Ostensibly, the division within the black leadership centered on tactics and the pace of protest. But the students themselves thought that the divisions were over goals too. Summing up the students' perspective, Carl Holman asked, what is best, "Cadillacs, split-level houses or freedom? To the students, freedom is the highest goal." In fact, divisions were also fueled by the battle for control and finance. Bond sharply criticized the "adult" half of the Student-Adult Liaison Committee for controlling protest finances and diverting money to the NAACP, "much against our will." [58]

Undoubtedly there were exceptions to such division. Students conducted voting registration campaigns under the direction of the All-Citizens' Registration Committee. Students also appreciated legal and logistical support. In 1963, Ralph Moore of COAHR wrote a letter of thanks to A. T. Walden: "This is not the only time that you have come to bat for the students and we want you to know that we appreciate the many acts you have done." Rev. Sam Williams, the activist president of the local NAACP in 1960, pledged the organization's support for the students and raised money for those arrested. At a mass meeting in June 1960, Williams promised the students that "we shall do our part to help you achieve your goals." Williams was arrested in the courtroom during the trials of the students after the Rich's campaign.

But even Williams had initially refrained from pledging legal support for the first sit-ins and, in any case, the NAACP remained subsidiary to the Auburn Avenue elite. Within the elite, differing attitudes to the students also reflected internal wrangling between leaders. Rev. Borders stood out as the most vocal advocate of COAHR, but some students believed that this was primarily an extension of his rivalry with Martin Luther King Sr.[59]

The younger generation of ACCA provided a bridge between the students and the traditional leadership. ACCA supported the student protests. Charles Black remembered that the financial and moral support came from mostly younger professionals, who "tended to be a bit more militant." John Calhoun met with Lonnie King for breakfast during each day of the sit-ins. Q. V. Williamson took advertisements away from the *Atlanta Daily World* to help finance the *Inquirer,* and Jesse Hill incorporated the *Inquirer* to put it on sound financial footing. ACCA also sought to defuse the students' impatience with the traditional leadership. The *Inquirer* pointed out in January 1961 that "it might lend some perspective on the very real risks and the very great courage involved in the early career of A. T. Walden to consider how much harsher then was the opposition to the NAACP than today's daring young sit-in pioneers are faced with."[60]

At times, the intransigence of the white community briefly united Atlanta's black leadership. After its formation on 2 June 1960, the Student-Adult Liaison Committee endorsed the objectives stated in the "Appeal for Human Rights" and declared that "we also endorse efforts of the student movement to secure increased employment opportunities for qualified Negroes." Such intergenerational unity peaked after the failure of negotiations during the truce after the arrest of the younger King during the fall of 1960. Even Daddy King donned a sandwich board with the slogan "Jim Crow must go" while marching, somewhat incongruously, alongside rock 'n' roll musician Clyde McPhatter. After Allen erected "Atlanta Wall," COAHR and SNCC joined with ACCA and the Negro Voters League to form a planning committee and all groups refused to negotiate until the wall was removed.[61]

More often than not, however, the generational division resembled internecine warfare rather than mere tactical disagreement about the type of protest. Charles Black recalled that "the structured and established businessmen, for the most part, were resentful of the movement and actually made efforts to defeat any further progress." The criticism from the traditional leadership reached a peak during the sit-ins that targeted Rich's during the fall of 1960. Richard Rich, who was Jewish, had been renowned for his moderate racial outlook. Rich's had also been the favorite store for black Atlantans for a generation, the first to extend credit to all races by 1944, and subsequently the first to have desegregated water fountains. Warren Cochrane, a fierce critic of the renewed sit-ins, argued that instead of pinpointing Rich's, "the race must keep all of the friends it has in the dominant white world and work unceasingly to multiply them." The *Atlanta Daily World* attacked the students' adult advisers as well as the students themselves. "In the present controversy," the *World* argued, "there is serious question as to whether these adult advisors cautioned or urged the proper exhaustion of other remedies before resorting to picketing." The opposition of the traditional leadership undermined the effectiveness of student protest as black shoppers reneged on the downtown city boycott until it was less than 50 percent effective.[62]

Such mounting criticism from the traditional leadership also focused on the involvement of Martin Luther King Jr. Holman reflected later that "the leadership group in Atlanta, many of them, didn't want King there." When King returned to Atlanta on 7 February 1960 to co-pastor Ebenezer Baptist Church, the understanding was that he would use Atlanta only as a base for his national activities. The *Pittsburgh Courier* commented, "That's very wise, for Atlanta leaders are very, very jealous about that leadership. . . . Yep, there's some really heavy artillery lined up along Sweet Auburn Avenue." King's own father had advised him not to participate in the Atlanta demonstrations.[63] The furor and swift reaction of Hartsfield on the one occasion when Martin Luther King Jr. did join the students revealed the potential impact King could have made.

The parlous alliance between the traditional leadership and the students was openly sundered at a mass meeting to explain the desegregation agreement in March 1961. Walden insisted to the two thousand members of the audience that "we've been fighting this thing for one hundred years; now we have it within our grasp." After hecklers openly called Walden an "Uncle Tom," laughter erupted when he urged that "you'll have to take my word for it." Shortly afterward, when Daddy King justified himself by saying, "I've been around this thing for thirty years," one heckler called out, "That's what's wrong," prompting further laughter and boos. Lonnie King reflected later that "they really brutalized King up there." One speaker from the floor received a standing ovation when he insisted that the desegregation of lunch counters must happen quickly, arguing that it "may not be an if, but it certainly is a when situation."[64]

Chaos was averted only after the late arrival of Martin Luther King Jr., who had been urgently roused from his bed. Carl Holman, who chaired the meeting, believed that the younger King was incredulous that his father had signed an agreement that allowed temporary segregation but thought his speech had circumvented the "lynch mood which was pervasive that night." In response to his father's humiliation, King lamented that a struggling people had surrendered to the "cancerous disease of disunity." Instead, his typically passionate address culminated in an appeal that "if anyone breaks this contract, let it be the white man." Taylor Branch recorded that after finishing what many observers believed to be his most powerful speech ever, "he vanished from the hushed church, leaving Daddy King rescued, Lonnie King relieved, Ivan Allen in awe, and the settlement effectively ratified." [65]

The creation of coalition protest groups could not paper over the cracks of disunity. The Student-Adult Liaison Committee, in reality, had been established by the Auburn Avenue leadership to try to influence student activities. As a result, student leaders felt under no obligation to follow its advice once negotiations had broken down. Similarly, it was partly because of internal disunity that the Summit conference called in Wyatt Walker. Within weeks, Walden resigned as co-chairman of the Summit conference in anger at SNCC's unilateral decision to resume direct action.

The significance of the public division lay in its debilitating effect on the attempts to secure desegregation. In some respects, this division in leadership benefited the Atlanta protest. Faced with the belligerence of a student protest, the city leadership both sought out and accepted the more moderate demands of the Auburn Avenue elite. After studying the Atlanta protest, Jack Walker suggested further that "it would seem that a Negro community in a southern city is likely to be more effective in eliminating the institutions of segregation if it has both conservative and protest elements within its leadership." [66]

The clear division in tactics, however, primarily hindered student attempts for a full-scale downtown integration agreement. Rather than acting for the students, the Auburn Avenue leadership held secret negotiations with the representatives of Rich's during November 1960 until one black leader leaked news of the meetings to the press. During the eventual negotiated settlement, Herschelle Sullivan and Lonnie King accepted the delayed desegregation agreement only after what Jack Walker described as "considerable persuasion" from the senior black leadership. Later, both Sullivan and King proffered their resignations as chairmen because they felt that they had betrayed the COAHR, although the student body refused to accept. Bond concluded later that, with hindsight, "we would have been much better off if we had maintained much more independence than we did." [67]

The city's white leadership successfully exploited the division. The Chamber of Commerce clearly identified the importance of students, refusing to start negotiations with the Student-Adult Liaison Committee until King and Sullivan were present. Once the meeting started, however, Commerce representatives purposefully addressed the adults only. In fact, the merchants had already secured a deal with the established black power structure. Charles Black concluded that the upper Negro business class "considered themselves on the 'in' with other businessmen in town" but "considered the students upstarts." [68]

Julian Bond believed that a series of clandestine meetings between Hartsfield and the Auburn Avenue elite seriously undermined the student leadership. In fact, such meetings were often conducted openly. After the first sit-ins, Hartsfield appeared before the Hungry Club warning the adult leadership of potential violence. After Hartsfield claimed to have secured a truce in November 1960, a student spokesman had to issue an immediate denial, insisting that "the mayor has talked to no student leaders. He cannot speak for us." After the formation of the Summit, Allen appointed Walden as a standby judge for the municipal courts but complained of the new organizations, "whose actions are alien to Atlanta's tradition of co-operation and understanding." [69]

City businesses also avoided outright intransigence after the use of strong-arm tactics had briefly united the movement in late 1960. In response to the Summit's threat of an economic boycott in November 1963, the Chamber of Commerce publicly urged downtown businesses to desegregate. In his review of the Atlanta movement, David Harmon concluded that "one reason for the passage of these resolutions was to create dissension between conservative and more militant African-American leaders." [70] Certainly COAHR and SNCC ignored the Summit's call for a postponement of the boycott, choosing instead to demonstrate at Rich's for fair employment.

The ending of the Summit's drive for an open city proved to be an apposite epitaph for the direct action movement in Atlanta as a whole. Martin Luther King Sr. followed Walden out of the Summit because he believed that the battle plan would provoke violence. Meanwhile, Walden and Allen met separately to call a truce that the Summit subsequently turned down. The Summit in turn proposed its own terms for a truce, which were rejected by Allen. Wyatt Walker remembered later, "That's the one time I went to jail that I felt was useless." In his history of SCLC, Fairclough noted that Walker's "battle plan" could have succeeded if the "older leaders had not scuttled it." Fairclough's conclusion about the open city plan would be equally appropriate for the direct action protest in Atlanta as a whole. "The demonstrations attracted little active support from Atlanta's black population and petered out inconclusively." [71]

Overall, the history of Atlanta's civil rights protest during the early 1960s sheds light on the widespread contemporary assumption that the protest movement there was successful. *Newsweek* acclaimed Atlanta as "a proud city" after the school desegregation, and President Kennedy personally congratulated Atlanta leaders. This presumption of success has been reflected in many historical surveys. Alton Hornsby, for example, wrote that "in order to understand how Atlantans succeeded when so many other cities had failed, one must begin with the six institutions of black higher education." [72]

The years of protest can be described as successful, however, only from the perspective of the white power structure or in that violence was avoided. Members of the black power structure also retained their influence, albeit publicly criticized, at the head of the community. Atlanta's direct action protest achieved numerous victories but ultimately did not secure a citywide agreement, an even greater failure considering the opportunity for protest and the potential economic and political strength of the black community.

Just as the very success of the Auburn Avenue elite had militated against more belligerent protest during the 1940s and 1950s, the strength of the traditional black power structure undermined the direct action protests of the student movement. This opposition denied the students the complete community support that could have reinforced their protest against Jim Crow. It was a division cleverly exploited by the city's political and business leadership.

In 1968, Julian Bond argued that the student demonstrations should not be remembered for specific victories, nor could students be credited with sparking an effective protest movement. Bond concluded, instead, that the major achievement of the years of direct action was their legacy to Atlanta's black community. Student protest "created a climate in which the much maligned masses of people, mostly Negro and mostly poor, felt that in them, and them alone, rests a chance for changing their own lives." It was groups from the black "maligned masses" who subsequently took the initiative in the struggle for black equality in Atlanta after the passage of the Civil Rights Act in 1964. [73]

The Atlanta protest did not act as the vanguard for urban protest in the state. Protest leaders from Georgia's other cities remembered later that Montgomery,

Alabama, and Greensboro, North Carolina, rather than Atlanta, provided the primary examples for their own local movements.

Protest in Savannah

In contrast to Atlanta, the Savannah movement stood out among the various local civil rights protests in both Georgia and across the South primarily for its success.[74] In his 1964 New Year address, Martin Luther King Jr. described Savannah "as the most desegregated city south of the Mason-Dixon Line." Such plaudits were, above all, owing to the comprehensive racial desegregation of public and private facilities from 1 October 1963, eight months ahead of the national Civil Rights Act. This concession, with the support of the city government, was agreed by a committee of leading white business, church, and social leaders who further fulfilled their promise by accompanying black Savannahians to the newly desegregated areas.[75]

The movement also brought other important, if less dramatic, achievements. An economic boycott that extended from March 1960 to October 1961 resulted in Savannah becoming the first city in the state with desegregated lunch counters.[76] Despite forming only one-third of the total city population, the registration of 57 percent of eligible voters (a higher proportion than that of the white community) coupled with a 95 percent bloc vote enabled the black community to play the crucial role in electing a moderate city government in 1960. Hosea Williams, the head of the political arm of Savannah's NAACP, triumphantly annotated a pun on a copy of the 1962 local election results: "It used to be said 'so the fourth (district) *goes* so the election goes.' Now they are saying 'so the Ne*groes,* so the election goes." This voting power forced white candidates to address black concerns. Malcolm Maclean, for example, after becoming mayor in 1960, fulfilled his promise to appoint one black member to each council board.[77]

Furthermore, this success was achieved without outside leadership or significant outside help. Only during the climax of protests in the summer of 1963 did some of Williams's future SCLC colleagues come to participate, but they reinforced rather than directed the protests. Indeed, Williams himself stated that "we want to keep this thing among Savannahians, we don't want to have to bring Martin Luther King here." Savannahians took on leadership roles in other local protests. Judson Ford, an active protester who later went to Americus, Georgia, believed that "this was a breeding ground for civil rights workers." On 8 July 1961, for example, the Savannah student James Alexander announced a special Georgian NAACP youth task force to stimulate protest in quiescent Georgia cities. Most of the members of this task force were Savannahians.[78] Local NAACP leader W. W. Law had been president of the statewide NAACP since 1955 and was a director of the national board. Law's vice-president, Hosea Williams, subsequently became a colleague of Martin Luther King. Willie Bolden, Benjamin Van Clark, and James Brown, who later became fieldworkers for SCLC, also saw their first action in Savannah.

The other outstanding feature of the Savannah movement was its completeness in every sense of the word. The local protest often engulfed the entire city. Maclean, who was mayor from 1960 to 1966, recalled later that "it was like 95% of everything anybody thought about." The movement was continuous and durable rather than spasmodic. The economic boycott of 1960 continued for eighteen months before the downtown shop owners agreed to integrate their lunch counters. This contrasts with what the *Savannah Herald* called the "weird compromise" agreed by Atlanta's black leadership as the commitment to their concurrent boycott began to wane.[79]

Although the outcome of the Savannah protest was different, the local movement followed a chronology similar to that in Atlanta. Students in both cities responded swiftly to the Greensboro sit-ins. On 16 March 1960, small groups of students sat in at the lunch counters of eight large downtown stores, refusing to leave until they were served. By October there were "kneel-ins" in the segregated churches, "wade-ins" at the beach, and "ride-ins" on the buses. After being arrested for (unintentionally) using a segregated rest room, Judson Ford claimed the first unofficial "piss-in." After the arrests of the first sit-in students, the black leadership called for a total economic boycott of the downtown area until the charges against the students were dropped. In addition, they demanded the desegregation of lunch counters, higher-ranking jobs for black workers in these stores, and the use of courtesy titles for black customers.[80]

After its success in October 1961, the boycott was subsequently used in other areas of the city and its suburbs. During 1961–63, targeted campaigns won the integration of the city buses, golf course, parks, library, and the airport and bus cafes, as well as the hiring of black firemen. But when the cinemas reneged on their agreement to integrate from 4 June 1963, Savannah suffered a hot summer of confrontational protest, as in Albany and Birmingham, though significantly in this case with negligible violence.[81]

Over the whole period, the Chatham County Crusade for Voters (CCCV), the political arm of the NAACP, led voter registration campaigns, held meetings for white candidates to decide on endorsements, and produced a sample ballot for bloc voting. The voter registration rebuilt the Negro vote to over seventeen thousand by 1962, despite a county ordinance of 1948 that had cleared the register and subsequently imposed a highly subjective literacy test. From October 1962, however, the leader of the CCCV, Hosea Williams, at odds with the NAACP board, declared that the CCCV was "independent and responsible to no other organization." A charismatic crowd gatherer, Williams inspired the night street marches of the summer of 1963. The resultant rivalry between the NAACP and the breakaway Crusade spurred both groups to more aggressive protests than had been seen in Savannah previously. After 1963, the strength of the NAACP was such that Williams left for Atlanta and joined the SCLC.[82]

As in Atlanta, Savannah's moderate racial mores provided the opportunity for the emergence of a large-scale local protest.[83] A reporter, Douglas Kiker, remarked in the *Atlanta Journal* in June 1960 that "Savannah society is traditionally self-contained and aloof from the rest of Johnny-come-lately Georgia. Savannah aristocrats nod coolly to Atlanta, smile at Charleston, but bow only to London and Florence."[84] Most important among Kiker's many pertinent insights was his observation that the situation of Savannah was not typical of Georgia, let alone the South as a whole. Overall, Savannah displayed the racial discrimination and supremacist mores characteristic of the Old South without the overwhelming bitterness and proclivity to violence associated with the Deep South.

By 1960, Savannah had slightly under 150,000 inhabitants, 36 percent of whom were classified "Negro." A comparison of the bare statistics concerning the relative prosperity of the black and white communities reveals an economic gulf typical of the South. As a proportion of the employed in their racial community, over three times as many whites were skilled workers while nearly 40 percent of blacks were employed as laborers. The black unemployment rate of nearly 10 percent was double that of their white counterparts. As a result, the median black individual income was only about one-third of the white income.[85] Housing conditions also reflected a massive racial divide. Only half of the housing units in the black community were classified as sound, and nearly one in five were dilapidated. In the white community, by contrast, more than four in five houses were sound and a mere one in every twenty-five was dilapidated.

Nonetheless, this racial barrier was not accompanied by the vindictive race relations found in the Deep South. As a major Atlantic seaport, the community was traditionally less introverted and closed than inland towns, experiencing a regular transient influx of different nationalities. Certainly W. W. Law, lawyer Eugene Gadsden, and Dr. Jamerson, all senior leaders in the NAACP, later attributed Savannah's more liberal outlook and openness to its Atlantic trade.[86]

Savannah was also widely regarded as a liberal city by the 1960s. Along with rival Charleston it was one of the two banner cities of the old Confederacy. The two cities also experienced similar race relations. For example, Maclean later recalled "calling up Palmer, mayor of Charleston, and asking him" what he had done about library segregation. The conclusion of the Charleston historian William Smyth applies equally to Savannah when he wrote that "most white Charlestonians never wanted their community to be known as a backwards, racist, segregated society. Charlestonians had panache. Traditions of gentility were important for both blacks and whites to uphold." Whereas Atlanta publicized the slogan a "city too busy to hate," Savannah could be described as "too dignified to hate." After the hot summer of protest in 1963, the *New York Times* accurately concluded that "the decision of the business community to end the blight of racial conflict through negotiations was the act of a community conscious of its place in American history."[87]

This liberalism seems to have been acutely self-conscious during the 1960s. Partly because of pride and partly because of the importance of tourism to the economy, many white Savannahians later remembered that they did not want to be in the national press because of racial violence. In this respect, Savannah was very similar to Greensboro. There, argued Chafe, the desire by the majority of whites to retain their national reputation for "civility" ultimately outweighed their desire to defend white hegemony. This does not mean that white community leaders took the lead in desegregation, as in Charlotte and Durham. But it does suggest that Savannah was unlikely to produce an Orval Faubus or Bull Connor figure, defiantly shaking his fist at the outside world in defense of segregation. Malcolm Maclean's view was typical of the city's white consensus—his primary aim was "to preserve Savannah's good name."[88]

By 1960, Savannah had built up what Eugene Gadsden described as "a tradition of non-violence between the races." This tradition had a vital bearing on the peaceful outcome of a protest against nearly all areas of discrimination, contrasting with the situation in southwest Georgia, where even attempting to register to vote risked a violent backlash. It also influenced the strategy of the black protest, which aimed to coerce local whites into integrating, rather than provoking violence in an effort to secure federal help. Henry Brownlee, a well-traveled protester, summed up the racial situation: "I never felt the same fear here . . . in Mississippi, Alabama and

Louisville, Kentucky I thought I was going to die. Here I was just looking to go to jail." Savannah, therefore, seems to support the conclusion of Elisabeth Jacoway and David Colburn, who argued that "those cities that experienced comparatively mild racial disturbances during this period . . . tended to have historically good race relations prior to 1954." [89]

Although the economic situation was patently unequal, the overall welfare of the black community was less bleak than in much of the Deep South. In part, this was because of what the *Atlanta Journal* described as the "fairly prosperous" nature of Savannah as a whole.[90] Within the parameters of an unjust society, the position of Savannah blacks was better than that of their counterparts in rural southwest Georgia. Sitton reported in the *New York Times* that "on balance, the Negro sections of Savannah do not produce the impression of utter gloom and hopelessness found in other southern cities and in northern urban centers." [91]

The final major influence on the Savannah movement was the history of black protest and community involvement. This tradition had been galvanized into a strident, organized movement under the leadership of Rev. Gilbert. After Gilbert's demise, the drive for racial change had diminished. Nonetheless, Gilbert's legacy continued both through individuals and through the NAACP's deep penetration of Savannah's black community.

As in Atlanta, however, the opportunity for the emergence of a protest movement in the city did not predetermine a successful outcome. The more moderate attitude of whites did not preclude racism. "This community has a very sophisticated form of racism," wrote Otis Johnson, a prominent student activist, although "it is not nigger-nigger racism like in Alabama or Mississippi." For Benjamin Van Clark, this racism was a "tokenism and do-nothingism of white people when confronted." Certainly racism seemed prevalent despite the supposed liberal nature of Savannah; movement leader W. W. Law was sacked from his post office job in 1961 because of his leadership in the NAACP, and many of the protesters later recalled personal incidents of abuse.[92]

Until the end of 1960, the city government was intensely hostile to protests. In April 1960, for example, the city council passed a new ordinance outlawing the picketing of "two or more persons" to prevent the operation of business. According to an *Atlanta Journal* report, Mayor Lee Mingledorff defiantly asserted that "I don't especially care whether it's constitutional or not." [93] The subsequent more moderate government still took advantage of the precedents of the Mingledorff era.

The distinguishing feature of the white business reaction was not compromise but intransigence. Downtown business leaders held out against the black boycott for eighteen months until their economic prospects became increasingly bleak as the boycott gave no hint of crumbling. Indeed, five central stores went bankrupt rather than desegregate their lunch counters or promote eligible black staff. Savannah also lacked a moderate press counterpart to the *Atlanta Constitution.* According to the *Pittsburgh Courier,* it was "the policy of the white press to distort the facts." [94] In the end, it took the fear of potentially explosive conflicts in the summer of 1963 as a climax to the three years of protest to force white community leaders to the negotiating table.

The success of the direct action protest, therefore, lay in the ability of the protesters to exploit the opportunities of the 1960s. In many ways, the strengths of the movement stood in counterpoint to the weaknesses of the Atlanta protest. For in Savannah, the movement was characterized by a united confrontational approach, community-wide support, and an unrelenting momentum of protest.

Both the belligerence and the unity of the Savannah movement resulted primarily from the local preeminence of W. W. Law. At the onset of militant protest in 1960, Law stood out as the black community leader; as head of the NAACP he inherited the mantle of Gilbert and the authority of the preeminent black organization. His acceptability within the community was further enhanced by his involvement with the scouts and the YMCA and his work as a postman. His undoubted charisma and ability, recalled without exception by Savannahians of both races, led to his appointment as the youngest director to the NAACP national board in 1952 and his eight successive reelections as state NAACP president. According to the *South Carolina Times,* "Law was considered as one of the heroes in the civil rights struggle in the South." [95]

Law's victimization in what *Jet* magazine called "the year's worst scandal" broadened and underlined his prestige. On 11 July 1961, Law was dismissed from his post office job, ostensibly for code violations such as urinating in public. The NAACP claimed the dismissal was "on trumped up charges." Law admitted to urinating behind trees in the park during the previous sixteen years because there were no black rest rooms available on his delivery route. Roy Wilkins pointed out that although Law had been a postman for sixteen years, the code violation had come to light only during the economic boycott. The dismissal became a scandal when it emerged that Michael Monroney, the top aide to Postmaster General Edward Day and son of a senator, had promised Georgia congressman C. Elliot Hagan that Law would be fired, an action that "violated every federal regulation." Therefore, Day reinstated Law, but with a scathing attack, saying, "I wouldn't want a person of Law's record delivering mail to my family home." This bungle outraged both races; to blacks it was a slur on their leader and for whites it implied that Day was more interested in his own home than theirs. As a consequence of the affair, President Kennedy replaced Day as the keynote speaker at that week's party Philadelphia convention, forced him to retract his statement, and relieved him of his job the following year.[96]

The main repercussion, however, was that Law, who remained quiet throughout the whole affair, emerged with enhanced authority and for a time celebrity status in Savannah. As the *Pittsburgh Courier* remarked in March 1961, "In Savannah circles Mr. Law's word is the law."[97] His very presence as a leader attracted people to the protest, and his own credibility and prestige reflected on the local branch of the NAACP.

Whereas the Atlanta elite sought to negotiate on behalf of the students, under Law's guidance the traditional Savannah leadership actually adopted direct action tactics. The board treasurer, Dr. Rankin Jaudon, challenged Law for the presidency, calling for a moderate separatist approach that would involve the establishment of black business and capital. Whereas in other communities such a divergence of views could lead to the formation of two movements, the vote in favor of Law ended the public debate, as the directors accepted the majority decision in favor of direct action.[98]

The key to the breadth of the Savannah movement and in further contrast to Atlanta was the incorporation of youth. First, the students protested under the leadership of the NAACP. Inspired by the Greensboro sit-ins, local students approached Law, eager to join in the new wave of protest. At this vital stage, the NAACP leadership supported direct action wholeheartedly. Local board member Mercedes Wright orchestrated what may have been the first successful wade-in by students in the country. Hosea Williams led the training in nonviolent resistance. This full preparation also contributed to the peaceful nature of the demonstrations. Neither Ben West nor James McMillan, for example, retaliated after suffering broken jaws in separate incidents.

The swift incorporation of the students was partly because of the emphasis on youth before 1960. Savannah claimed to have the largest NAACP youth council in 1961, with over 650 paid-up members.[99] The local branch had also anticipated the national directive of 1961 to create subchapters in the schools and colleges. Edmund Josey, for instance, organized an NAACP youth chapter at Savannah State College. When the direct action of 1960 started, the loyalty of the students was already established and the local NAACP was in a position to respond.

It did so primarily because of the attitude of the major leaders. Williams, as his subsequent confrontational marches of 1963 and later role in SCLC were to prove, had the dynamic approach that appealed to would-be protesters. Law was only twenty-seven years old and the youngest branch president in the country when he was appointed in 1950. Older, more cautious leaders, such as Dr. J. W. Jamerson Jr. remember being swayed by the attitude of Law and Williams. Youth were regularly placed in positions of responsibility and often led mass meetings. This early responsibility was a major reason why the Savannah branch produced such an extraordinary crop of young leaders in the early 1960s: James Brown and Bobby Hill both became national NAACP youth secretaries and Amos Brown became the national youth work committee chairman.[100]

The initial preeminence of the NAACP also allowed the development of a diverse and paced strategy, in contrast to the somewhat stop-start events in Atlanta. This process was furthered by the delegation of responsibility within the NAACP. Rev. Louis Stell was assigned to lead the fight for integrated education. Mercedes Wright chaired the Boycott Committee, assisted by NAACP youth council president Curtis Cooper. A student, Carolyn Quilloin, led the ride-ins, and Deacon Winters led the membership drives. This delegation also heightened the success of the movement, for different members were responsible for particular protests. The achievements in voter registration, for example, stemmed from the undivided attention of Williams and, later, Eugene Gadsen.

The Savannah protest was also distinguished by its durability: the fervor of March 1960 was sustained and accelerated right through to the desegregation agreements of October 1963. Remarkably, the Savannah boycott continued for eighteen months until lunch counter desegregation was finally won. Savannah businessmen lost over $1 million during the first month of the boycotts and reported reductions in sales of up to 50 percent during 1961.[101] This culmination of three years of successful direct action provided the 1963 upsurge in protest with credentials that underwrote the decision of white leaders to desegregate. Atlanta's Summit Conference of 1963, by contrast, was in part an attempt to overcome previous failings of black protest.

Finally, the eventual division in the Savannah movement reflected a personality clash rather than the fundamental tactical disagreements that characterized protest in Atlanta. Despite the consensus among the major leaders in support of direct action protest, Williams announced that the Crusade was an independent protest organization in the fall of 1962. Williams was a colorful and aggressive character. Howell Raines aptly remarked on "the barely contained rage, the roaring voice and the prize-fighter build which served [Williams] so well against the cracker sheriffs." Williams attributed his commitment to civil rights to a life-changing experience in the trenches of World War II, when an exploding shell killed all his colleagues and ripped open his stomach. After this fortuitous escape, as Andrew Young later recalled, "Hosea decided that the Lord saved him to fight segregation." [102]

The genesis of the division lay in Williams's ambition clashing with Law's own stubborn determination to retain a firm grip on the leadership. By 1961, Law was the incumbent state and branch president, so firmly entrenched after the post office scandal that Williams decided not to run against him at that year's state conference of 1961. Instead, Williams sought to be elected to the national executive at the annual convention of 1962. Law, however, derailed Williams's bid by backing the Florida candidate for the southeast nomination. Vernon Jordan, field secretary for the NAACP Southeast Region, believed that Law had opposed his deputy "because he felt that Williams had not been faithful at the state level." Whatever the cause of Law's action, Williams felt that "this was kinda' like telling a man . . . your family won't vote for you." Fairclough concluded that, "frustrated by his failure to receive promotion within the NAACP, he turned the crusade [CCCV] into his own, autonomous power base." [103]

The division led to a bitter rivalry. Mercedes Wright told Vernon Jordan that she was "soundly convinced that Law and Williams have a personal feud, that both have psychiatric problems and that the wounds will never be healed." Jordan tried to reconcile the two combatants during his visit to Savannah in December 1963. Much to his dismay, Jordan reported that "they forgot their differences and I was the target . . . [there is] no experience like having the joint venom of Law and Williams spewed on you, especially when you are trying to help." Some local activists feared that the split between them would derail the movement. During a visit from Jordan, Phillip W. Cooper, a dentist, spent half an hour expressing his fears that Law and Williams spent too much time fighting each other. This was much "to the detriment of his patient," Jordan reported, "who, I'm sure by that time, needed more novocaine." [104]

In fact, the split between the organizations furthered the enthusiasm for the climax to the protests. Fairclough noted that the "rivalry, far from hampering the attack on white supremacy, had given it added momentum." To the press, Law and Williams retained a united front, as did the rank and file; many faithful NAACP members marched alongside Williams. Equally, when one of the CCCV night marches threatened to dissipate into violent anarchy, the protesters responded to

Law's appeal for order. The goal of desegregation was kept in perspective ahead of internal squabbles. Henry Brownlee, who joined with Williams, remembered that "after all, we knew who the Devil was." But the perceived threat to their dominance forced NAACP leaders to step up their protests. More than seven hundred people were arrested when police feared the marches would lead to violence.[105] In short, a long, hot summer ensued, one that would not have reached such a crescendo without Williams's unilateral action.

The aggressive protest resulting from the rivalry between the two organizations undoubtedly accelerated the time scale of the desegregation settlement. Therefore, Savannah, rather than Atlanta, supports Jack Walker's thesis that disunity may prove beneficial to a local movement. But this impetus was effective only because it came at an opportune time for the movement. The hot summer of 1963 heightened the protest of an active NAACP, a protest that was wide-ranging and sustained precisely because the NAACP had previously been the unchallenged leader.

Similarly, the fierce crescendo of protest forced the white community to seek an accommodation with the protesters. Feay Shellman, a local historian, concluded that "the initiation of night marches created alarm. A new urgency fostered serious negotiations and the search for compromise." The *New York Times* rightly noted that the "white community" was not a homogenous group. "Old families, who were aware of the history of Savannah," feared for internal order and the city's reputation. For the "new aggressive businessmen, who only see things in terms of economics," the decision to negotiate was necessitated by the loss of up to 30 percent of trade during the unrest. The Chamber of Commerce called for the desegregation of public facilities.[106]

The black protest, therefore, created a climate for negotiation, but this alone did not ensure a settlement. As the *Atlanta Constitution* commented, "Even the most moderate is likely to contemplate desegregation with real uneasiness. The fears, sound or baseless, of segregationist reprisal and economic failure run strong. When the chips are down, it is a clutching pit-of-the-stomach sort of thing." In part, these fears diminished through the diplomacy of key individuals. Later interviews confirmed the conclusion of the *New York Times* that in 1963, "Monsignor John D. Toomey is the unsung hero of the interracial truce signed Thursday night by white and Negro negotiators.... Mgr. Toomey's faith and energy brought action."[107]

Above all, though, white fears were sidelined by the longevity and effectiveness of the black protests. Arthur Gordon, founder of the biracial Savannah Greys, later believed that his most powerful argument was, "Listen! The tide's coming in and you might as well be ready for it." The backdrop of controlled, sustained protest also helps explain the completeness of the success of the black negotiators, in contrast to Atlanta or Dallas, for example, where "whites accepted limited change and blacks accepted change that was limited." [108] In the face of unremitting black pressure, the establishment concluded that social stability required social change.

Protest in Other Cities

Although Atlanta and Savannah led the way for black Georgians, almost every major town in Georgia experienced some form of renewed protest during the early 1960s.[109] Preeminent among the successful city movements in Georgia was that in Brunswick, Glynn County, a city on the southeast coast with a population of twenty-seven thousand people, including nearly ten thousand black citizens. After negotiations during the summer and fall of 1962, all lunch counters and city-owned facilities were desegregated by the start of the following year. The *New York Times* reported that "Brunswick has the special distinction in the Deep South of seeking an accommodation with the Negro population without pressure of court actions or demonstrations." In a wide-ranging local survey, Pat Watters concurred that "Brunswick achieved its racial rapprochement before the summer of 1964 without a single street demonstration or boycott, and without a law suit instigated by Negroes." [110]

As in Georgia's other major coastal city of Savannah, the local NAACP chapter led the movement. Branch president Rev. Julius Caesar Hope admitted to reporters that he had "successfully opposed the penetration of Brunswick by the younger direct action groups such as CORE and the SNCC." As was the case with W. W. Law, Hope's youthful belligerence, rather than stubborn conservatism, kept the town exclusively the preserve of the NAACP. Hope was only thirty years old when he arrived in Brunswick from Montgomery, Alabama, in 1962, with leadership experience of direct action protest honed during the bus boycott there. As late as November 1961, Vernon Jordan observed that the Brunswick branch was dormant and had "a dire need of leadership." Less than a year later, Jordan noted that the branch "began to take on a new life" and "such new life is attributed to a young minister there." By the end of 1962 and after a series of mass meetings, the branch had 777 members, including an active youth council, and over one thousand black voters had been registered.[111]

Brunswick also shared Savannah's relatively moderate racial mores. In part this stemmed from Brunswick's prosperity. According to a 1962 urban renewal publication, Brunswick's mean family income for black families of $2,744, while only half that of their white counterparts, was higher than in all other cities in Georgia, with the exception of the Atlanta area and the Warner Robins military complex. Local NAACP leaders reported that very few blacks had difficulty finding work, even if most jobs were menial.[112]

Brunswick's relative prosperity was allied to a cosmopolitan outlook common to the coastal cities. It was "a sizeable Jewish population; a colony of Portuguese people, descendants of fishermen attracted to the shrimp-rich south Georgia shores; a Catholic influence," the city manager Bruce Lovvern suggested, that gave the people of Brunswick "experience in tolerance toward those different from themselves." According to J. M. Atkinson, Hope's predecessor as NAACP president, such toler-ance manifested itself in the fact that "Negroes and whites lived side by side in some parts of the city."[113]

This moderate outlook had a direct bearing on the outcome of the local move-ment. An *Atlanta Journal* reporter, Fred Powledge, commented in February 1963 that "observers note that this element of good faith between whites and Negroes was lacking in other southern towns, such as Albany." The observer was Vernon Jordan, who had been so impressed during a visit to Brunswick that he subsequently con-tacted the *Atlanta Journal, New York Times,* and *Newsweek.* Jordan was particularly pleased that the local Council on Human Relations was exerting a strong influence on the negotiations and that there were white members of the NAACP.[114]

Brunswick's moderate response to the civil rights era was also informed by the example of the futility of white resistance in other Georgia towns. In this context, Lovvern's study of the turmoil in Albany in 1961–62 was instrumental in Brunswick's decision to acquiesce to the demands for desegregation. "In this country, Albany can't win." Closer to home, the collapse of downtown stores in Savannah demon-strated the dangers of resisting calls for change. In a city that was 40 percent black, Brunswick's merchants "aren't fools," Watters concluded, "they had read and heard about boycotts."[115]

Such economic pragmatism was reinforced by Brunswick's economic history. During the boom years of the war the city's population had swelled to seventy-five thousand because of shipbuilding contracts. Shortly afterward, the shipyards closed, making Brunswick a ghost town. It was "the necessity of reactivating the economic life of the city," J. M. Atkinson believed, that caused the city to place a premium on good order to attract out-of-state capital. The adjoining federal Glynco Naval Base, for example, exerted pressure during the 1962 lunch counter negotiations. Similarly,

Thiokol, the city's major corporation with three hundred employees, was seeking a federal contract at the time of the school desegregation negotiations and could not afford adverse publicity.[116]

In this context, Hope's tactics to seek negotiated change under the threat of direct action, rather than launching a Montgomery-style campaign, were vindicated. Hope himself concluded in 1963, "I don't think Brunswick's so much different. I think it's the strategy that has been used. I think likewise Albany, Little Rock, Mississippi, and all those places have helped here. In order for it not to happen here, we sit down and try to work it out." Using the precedents of other Georgia cities and the threat of direct action protest if necessary, the Brunswick movement took advantage of the local racial moderation and economic pragmatism to engineer a swift and comprehensive desegregation. In turn, movement leaders agreed to integrate facilities in a nonprovocative fashion, with only two to four volunteers using facilities each day for the first two weeks.[117]

Rome rivaled Brunswick as the city that made the smoothest transition to downtown desegregation in Georgia, shortly after the first demonstrations during the summer of 1963. With a population comparable to Brunswick's, although less than half the proportion of blacks, Rome shared Brunswick's relative racial moderation. At the end of the 1950s, a Southern Regional Council report observed that "Rome is a rapidly developing industrial center; with Negroes voting to a reasonable extent some wedges are being driven into the stereotype pattern of race relations—though slowly."[118]

What distinguished Rome was the powerful activity of a determined biracial council. As early as 1956, B. R. Brazeal of Morehouse College had observed an interracial ministers' discussion in Rome. Brazeal concluded that "this meeting together by Negro and white ministers in Rome, Georgia, has created friendships and a reasonable degree of communication between these groups and this extends to several areas of activity beyond the field of religion." By 1963, Rome's Council on Human Relations had swelled to over 180 members, incorporating a wide spectrum of professionals.[119]

Whereas most local Councils on Human Relations sought to moderate the response to black protest, Rome's council actually initiated steps to desegregate the city. John Bertrand of Berry College encouraged his students to correspond by tape with black college students in Montgomery, Alabama, during the bus boycott there. Berry College accepted black students one year ahead of the rest of Georgia's colleges, despite the opposition of the local Ku Klux Klan. In a similar vein, academic pressure influenced Rome's Carnegie Library to integrate in March 1963. In her history of the library, Helen Hutzler recorded that "it is the opinion of many community leaders that the integration of the library, achieved only a few weeks before the sit-in demonstration, served as a valuable showcase."[120]

Uniquely in Georgia, the local chapter of the Council on Human Relations played an active role in direct action protest. During the spring and summer of 1963, more than one hundred high school students staged Rome's first sit-ins, the first such activity in northwest Georgia. Jule Levine, a leading member of the Rome Council on Human Relations, was also on the board of the Chamber of Commerce. Levine relayed the daily plans of the Chamber and local police to his wife by coded telephone messages. In turn, Rose Levine drove over across town to the dance studio of Fransiska Boas, daughter of the renowned anthropologist Franz Boas, who acted as liaison with the high school student protest group. Through the consequent effectiveness of protest strategy and the mediating influence of the Rome Council on Human Relations, those students involved in the sit-ins avoided lengthy arrest and completed attempts to desegregate public amenities by the end of the year.[121]

Georgia's third city, Macon, situated in the heart of the state, experienced one of the most belligerent and effective protests in the state. *New South* suggested in April 1963 that "probably no other community in the state has moved further than Macon to grant its Negro citizens free use of both public and privately operated facilities and equality of opportunity." Trezzant Anderson, who covered Georgia for the *Pittsburgh Courier,* wrote that "looking back upon the past year, 1962—one must choose as the most outstanding accomplishment of the year, the masterful and brainy successes of the Negro leaders in Macon." Writing from Savannah, W. W. Law told Anderson in March 1962 that "we here are proud of Macon's success. My hat is off to Paschal, Randall, Malone, Davies etc. Tell them to keep it up."[122]

Downtown stores had responded to sit-ins and a threatened economic boycott by desegregating most lunch counters in November 1961.[123] After a three-week bus boycott during the following spring, Bibb County Transit Company dropped segregated transport.[124] By the summer, Macon's city government had desegregated the libraries, golf course, and airport terminal as well as voluntarily passing a new city code against discrimination in elections. In October 1962 a black youth, A. C. Hall, was killed after being shot in the back by two policemen. After their subsequent acquittal, a comprehensive downtown economic boycott between Thanksgiving and Christmas 1962 forced merchants to accede to demands for improved black employment. Following the example of the local Piggly Wiggly supermarket, more than sixty downtown stores employed over 150 black clerks by the spring of 1963. According to the *Baltimore Afro-American,* it was "the most spectacular and successful selective buying campaign in the history of the employment gain drive in the South." [125]

Unlike Brunswick and Rome, the comprehensive desegregation in Macon stemmed primarily from the belligerence of a direct action local movement in the face of the city's white supremacist mores. As in Savannah, the traditional leaders, particularly William Randall, welcomed the more radical student protest. Although more than three hundred high school children joined the NAACP youth group, it was Randall's own five children and ten of their friends who were the first to board the front of the buses. Rev. E. B. Paschal, a longtime leader in the NAACP, was also one of the first to be arrested on the buses. In many ways, the movement at Macon mirrored the scale and belligerence of its Savannah counterpart. Mass meetings numbered over one thousand people during the bus boycott, and the concomitant voter registration campaign doubled the number of black registered voters by May 1962. [126]

The belligerence of the movement united Macon's black community. Under the continued authority of William Randall, the Bibb County Coordinating Committee (BCCC) incorporated most local black organizations with the existing NAACP and later affiliated with the SCLC. During the bus boycott, Randall undermined black critics of his tactics by telling a mass meeting, "If I had a preacher who couldn't support the effort of his people for freedom, I wouldn't put anything in the collection plate but a button." According to Randall, offerings in some churches dropped by 90 percent, while the number of buttons put in the collection plate increased in inverse proportion. [127] Both the intransigence of the transit company and the murder of A. C. Hall provided crucial momentum in stimulating community-wide support for the local movement. At least fifteen hundred Maconites marched on City Hall after Hall's murder, and at subsequent mass meetings movement leaders read out the names of target businesses. [128]

Such united militancy overcame white resistance and set the agenda for swift racial change. When Governor Marvin Griffin's appointee to the Bibb Transit Company, Linton Baggs, refused to follow the local pattern of negotiation, the BCCC backed up a threat to "let her rip" with a nearly 100 percent effective bus boycott the following day. Within a week of picketing outside downtown stores before Christmas 1962, merchants agreed to negotiate a racially just employment policy. [129]

The success of the BCCC, as in Georgia's other successful local protests, was also dependent on the response of the city government and business leaders. Macon, however, was far from being a haven of racial moderation akin to Rome or the coastal cities. The BCCC chose to boycott the buses only after the Bibb Transit Company refused to negotiate. Ku Klux Klan night riders riddled Randall's home with bullets, although Randall's family had been tipped off and was fortuitously absent. Local NAACP members protected Randall's home with an assortment of weapons, including an army issue submachine gun. Violence broke out too during February 1962, when black protesters tried to board the front of city buses. When Macon's parks were first integrated in April 1963, one black youth was stabbed. After Mayor Ed Wilson refused to close the parks, his mailbox was bombed.[130]

The key to Macon's acquiescence to the demands of the local movement was the presence of strong advocates in favor of accommodation who were able to outflank the proponents of massive resistance. The leaders of both racial communities had a tradition of effective communication. Macon's mayor during the 1950s appointed black policemen while his successor after 1961, Ed Wilson, was described by Randall as "a man we could work with." Mercer University professor Joe Hendricks was one of those who observed that such communication was underwritten by regular payments from mayoral candidates in return for the black bloc vote.[131]

Hendricks, who was on the executive committee of the Georgia Council on Human Relations, also believed that the presence of a college significantly increased the likelihood of racial cooperation in towns across Georgia. Mercer University faculty provided the vast majority of the white members of the active Macon Council on Human Relations. In Macon, Mercer certainly led the way toward desegregation. In his history of the desegregation of Mercer University, Will D. Campbell recorded that under the influence of Joe Hendricks and president Rufus Harris, "for a time, with no court order, there were three times as many black students registered at Mercer than at the University of Georgia, and Georgia had five times the total enrollment of Mercer and was desegregated by mandate of Judge Bootle's Court."[132] Under Hendricks's initiative, Mercer faculty had even begun a clandestine tutorial scheme for black students.

Campbell concluded that, if anything, "Mercer was changing too fast for Macon, Georgia. Sometimes the changes were anticipated and, in part, orchestrated by Mercer." Certainly changes in Mercer affected the rest of the city. Mercer accepted a Ghanaian student, Sam Oni, in 1963, three years before the congregation of the city's leading Baptist church at Tatnall Square denied him entry and ejected the minister for supporting Oni's attempted visit. The irony of Oni's exclusion, after he

had been converted by missionaries commissioned by Tatnall Baptist, gained international prominence and was even recorded in Ghana, Nigeria, and the *Nairobi Daily
Nation* in Kenya. The college newspaper, the *Mercer Cluster*, reflected the more
radical outlook of the students, arguing that "if God is dead, it's churches like Tatnall
that killed him." Students were suspected, too, for placing a poster on the bulletin
board outside the church advertising "Pastor wanted: he need not be a Christian." [133]

Members of Mercer, under the auspices of the Macon Council on Human Relations (MCHR), also provided practical assistance to the local civil rights movement.
Although Human Relations Councils were often only local talk shops, Hendricks
led a group of Mercer students who accompanied the sit-in demonstrators and
ordered food for them. The Macon council also articulated a response to black
protest based on pragmatism rather than capitulation or resistance. The question
facing Macon "is no longer can we continue in the past?" argued one published
MCHR statement. "It is whether change will come under community planning and
control, or whether it will come under the explicit direction of a federal court." [134]

Despite the advances in Macon, Rome, Atlanta, and the coastal cities, urban
protest in Georgia was far from a catalog of success.[135] In Columbus, direct action
protest was sporadic and relatively ineffective during the early 1960s. As in other
Georgia cities, students sparked initial protests. In Columbus, however, the NAACP
did not initially support the first six students arrested on the city buses in July 1961.
During 1962, a student-adult liaison committee discussed the desegregation of some
downtown lunch counters and the gradual desegregation of the buses. Protests began in earnest when seven black teenagers were denied borrowing rights at the
Columbus library during July 1963. The subsequent read-in led to seven arrests and
an escalation of protests, including further read-ins and renewed ride-ins on the
buses.[136] Concerned at the weakness of the local leadership, NAACP national youth
secretary Bobby Hill arrived from Savannah to foment demonstrations. Some 150
high school students attended a rally calling for the integration of downtown movie
theaters.

The high school student protests were undermined by a lack of support from the
wider black community. In fact, Columbus gained a reputation in Georgia for a lack
of adult leadership. During the summer of 1963, *Pittsburgh Courier* correspondent
Trezzant Anderson filed a report concerning the "criticisms leveled at local ministers for failing to show leadership or concrete interest in the events of the past seven
weeks." Anderson showed his exasperation by urging the *Courier* editor, "Please run
this. These jerks must stand up." The Southern Regional Council recorded that

during July 1963, three separate groups of black community leaders expressed opposition to student protests.[137]

In contrast to Savannah and Macon, the local NAACP did not actively support more belligerent forms of protest. Randolph Blackwell, a visiting VEP fieldworker, reported that the local branch of the NAACP had lost prestige when it tried to rein in the demonstrations of an active youth council during the summer of 1963. George Ford, the branch president, did not attend the trial of NAACP youth council leader Colfus Tyson. Meanwhile, A. J. McClung, head of the student liaison committee, believed that no additional demonstrations were needed. Jean Benton, a local realtor, complained to Blackwell that "they treated the youth dirty . . . they closed the churches to them . . . the national youth secretary couldn't even get a room at the YMCA."[138] According to Benton, McClung was angered at Bobby Hill's visit to Columbus. In this context, the lack of a college in Columbus proved decisive because college students spearheaded protests in other Georgia communities where the traditional leadership had been slow to act.

The lack of support for the student protests pointed to more general problems in Columbus. By the 1960s, there was little legacy left of Brewer's leadership and the activism of the 1940s. In fact, leading black activists recalled later that Brewer's murder left the greater legacy, and it was the fear of economic or violent retribution that prevented them from initiating local protest. Randolph Blackwell noted that although the Non-Partisan Voters' League still existed, "most of what the organization stood for died with Dr. Brewer. And yet the organization still lives." Although the league organized regular get out the vote campaigns, critics pointed to a tape-recording of a deal between county commissioners and one of the league leaders. "One does not have to search very hard," Blackwell concluded, "to find persons that will, in vile language, accuse the members of the League of selling the Negro vote to the highest bidder."[139]

In contrast to the protests under Brewer, the community leadership of the direct action years was characterized by endemic disunity. Katie Wootten, who directed voter registration campaigns, complained that "much enthusiasm and dedication was missing, and this was due to the local community. There were people who decided that if they couldn't pilot the plane, they would rather see it crash." Lillie Brown, who was married to a soldier at Fort Benning, attempted to start citizenship schools on the base. But she admitted to VEP representative John Calhoun that she was very discouraged by Columbus people and that citizenship schools seemed to be opposed as much by the black community as by the white. Consequently, when

Septima Clark traveled to Columbus to lead workshops on citizenship schools, only two counties were represented. After visiting registration projects across Georgia, VEP workers concluded that Columbus was the only community where the "existing leadership . . . is not equipped at this time to conduct the type of intensive drive that should be carried on." In fact, much of the most effective registration work was conducted unheralded by women at the grassroots level.[140]

The ineffectiveness of protest in Columbus was highlighted by the paltry progress made during the 1960s. In July 1963, the city council appointed a biracial advisory committee. By October the main library and movie theater had integrated. But such moves represented the limits of change. In July 1963, the city closed two swimming pools rather than allow integration. During the same month, students were attacked when trying to use nearby national parks, then the parks were also closed. Moreover, fourteen of the twenty members of the biracial committee were white, and the committee was sharply criticized by some local leaders. Jean Benton, for example, "got off the biracial committee because all the Negroes seem to have turned white."[141]

Protests in Augusta, too, met with limited success. In contrast to events in Brunswick and Rome, the salient feature of the early 1960s in Augusta was the intransigence of local white supremacists. "Racism in Augusta," observed an SRC report, "is as much a part of the local ambience as the oppressive heat and the wisteria." The resistance of the white majority to racial change demonstrated the extent of this racism. Students from Paine College had organized sit-ins and ride-ins during March 1960, one of the first three student demonstrations in the state. Three of the students were seriously injured when fights broke out at the lunch counters. In a portent of future white high-handedness, the white negotiating committee subsequently reneged on an agreement to desegregate all lunch counters.[142]

In an attempt to heighten pressure, some sixty students picketed Augusta's golf course when President Dwight Eisenhower was playing there during December 1960.[143] During the following months, students picketed downtown stores in an attempt to force the creation of a biracial committee and persuaded Ray Charles to cancel an appearance at the segregated Bell Auditorium. Charles told reporters, "I feel that it is the least I can do to stand behind my principles and help the students." But without active support from existing civil rights groups in the city, the student protests were unable to force change.[144] Two years after the first sit-ins, Augusta languished as the only city in Georgia to have experienced direct action protest and retained full segregation.[145]

In contrast to events in Savannah and Rome, when protests reached a peak they met with fierce resistance. After the NAACP youth council attempted to play-in at May Park on 16 March 1962, various youths were beaten and C. S. Hamilton, the branch president, had his windscreen smashed. Segregationist resistance took a variety of forms. Two reporters for the *Augusta Chronicle* were fired after sending articles about protests in Augusta to the Associated Press. Meanwhile, Sallie Hamilton, wife of the branch president, was summoned to face charges of assault and battery after allegedly spanking one of her students. An NAACP report noted that "white persons encouraged the student's mother to file charges so as to intimidate the Hamilton family." [146]

Toward the end of March, college students called on Mayor Millard A. Beckum to reopen negotiations on lunch counter desegregation. In the event, only the threat of widespread demonstrations overshadowing the opening of the world-famous U.S. Masters Golf Tournament in April 1962 forced downtown merchants to agree to negotiate in an attempt to avoid adverse publicity. [147] Frustrated at the slow pace of negotiations, college students desegregated a handful of stores before the conclusion of negotiations.

This first desegregation merely served to heighten segregationist resistance. On 7 April, Hamilton warned Beckum that gangs of white youths were threatening black customers at the recently desegregated H. L. Green store. That very evening, a Paine College student, William Didley, was stabbed before being arrested by police for disorderly conduct and carrying a weapon. In fact, Didley was injured while trying to protect a white student friend from attack, and he had no weapon. When college students started to picket Augusta's Varsity Club Markets on Monday, 16 April, local white youths pelted them with rocks and bottles and one car tried to run picketers down. Although the picketing was called off late on Wednesday, the eighteenth, during the following evening the police stopped cars of white youths carrying lethal weapons, including guns and iron pipes. [148]

In the face of such intransigent and often violent resistance, the local branch of the NAACP lost control of the movement. On Wednesday, the third night of rock throwing, black youths retaliated in kind. Fearing an escalation of violence, the local NAACP asked Vernon Jordan to visit Augusta. The following afternoon, Jordan met with local gangs. According to Jordan, the leader of the rock throwers "promised to get the word around that rocks are not helpful to the integration cause." Late that evening, however, a white teenager, Leslie Lee Luttes, was murdered some twenty blocks away from the Varsity Market in an alleged revenge killing. [149]

The murder of Luttes undermined the campaign and further intensified resistance to black protest. Although the Varsity Market Club agreed to hire a black cashier, little progress was made in the rest of the city. May Park remained segregated until the end of June 1963, and Mayor Beckum appointed a biracial committee shortly afterward to consider desegregation and a controversial urban renewal scheme. Both the failure to achieve racial progress and the proclivity toward violence foreshadowed the racial riot in Augusta that followed at the end of the decade. Mayor Beckum himself admitted that "Augusta was sitting on a powder keg." [150]

In many ways, the movement in Albany, in southwest Georgia, during 1961–62, was the exception to the urban protests in Georgia. Albany, a commercial city of fifty-six thousand people with a 40 percent black population, bore a close economic and demographic resemblance to the state's other second rank of cities. [151] The Albany movement, however, was the only Georgia protest to be joined by national organizations. With the involvement of SNCC and Martin Luther King Jr., Albany witnessed demonstrations on a massive scale.

Still, the movement failed to wring any concessions from the city government and was widely recognized as a major setback for the national civil rights movement. At the March 1963 Conference on Civil Disobedience in New York, Wyatt T. Walker, who helped supervise the Albany demonstrations, concluded that "here, one of the largest of the desegregation struggles was effectively broken and the entire desegregation movement faltered." David Chappell put it even more bluntly: "Here they had lost a big one to the segregationists." [152]

In many ways, the demonstrations in Albany also had a negative effect on the aims of local protesters. In March 1963, Trezzant Anderson reported in the *Pittsburgh Courier* from Albany that "this is the most messed-up, most fouled-up, most confused, most complicated place in the U.S.A." Slater King, vice-president of the Albany movement, estimated that 20 percent of the maids and cooks lost jobs permanently because of animosity raised by the protests. Whereas most Georgia cities made at least some moves toward desegregation, Chief of Police Laurie Pritchett told reporters at the end of 1963 that "Albany is as segregated as ever." Outside observers also commented on the breakdown of communication between the city government and local black leaders, as both sides lost trust. The *New York Times* commented in 1962 that "there is no fund of trust between the dominant leaders of both races that would allow them readily to bridge their differences." [153]

The Albany demonstrations failed despite the presence of far more outside support than any other movement in Georgia. In October 1961, SNCC fieldworkers

Charles Sherrod and Cordell Reagon arrived in Albany to set up a voter registration office with a view to initiating registration projects throughout the southwest region. On 10 December, eight SNCC freedom riders from Atlanta were arrested when they entered the local train terminal. Five days later, Martin Luther King Jr., invited by the executive committee of the Albany movement, addressed a rally and was arrested the following night. Both SNCC and King promised to "turn Albany upside down" at mass meetings. During its subsequent involvement, SCLC also contributed over half of the $20,000 costs of the protest.[154] The presence of such high-profile, charismatic leaders did motivate a protest on an unprecedented scale in Georgia, with regular mass meetings of over a thousand people, and more than twelve hundred people were jailed during the course of the campaign.

The failure at Albany seemed more acute because of the hubris of expectation. Initially, this expectation was fueled by the rapid escalation of local participation. The Albany movement proper, under the leadership of local osteopath William Anderson, formed on 17 November 1961. One week later the movement called its first mass meeting in response to the arrest of five local black students at the Trailways bus station. Albany's mass meetings were later remembered by civil rights activists for their extraordinary intensity and fervor. SNCC member Bernice Reagon, who later became one of the Freedom Singers, recalled that "when I opened my mouth and began to sing, there was a force and power within myself I had never heard before." [155] After the arrest of the SNCC freedom riders in December, the movement launched a series of marches, and more than five hundred demonstrators were arrested during the first week alone.

The expectation of the movement spiraled higher after 15 December, when Anderson invited King to lead the demonstrations. The following day more than 250 marchers were arrested, including King and his lieutenant, Ralph Abernathy, who vowed to spend Christmas in jail. King, however, accepted release on bail after city officials agreed to a truce with other local leaders. In fact, the city government had merely promised to consider a petition of grievances in January and made no written promises about desegregation. As King himself admitted later, "We thought that the victory had been won. When we got out, we discovered it was all a hoax." [156]

The truce swiftly collapsed because the city council made no attempt to negotiate further. On 12 January 1962, a teenage girl, Ola Mae Quarterman, refused to move from the front of a bus, telling the driver that "I paid my damn twenty cents and I can sit where I want." Her subsequent arrest, for using obscene language, prompted a bus boycott. After movement leaders refused to accept another truce, city officials discontinued the bus service at the end of January.[157] Sporadic sit-ins and demonstrations continued through the spring, especially after Albany policemen killed a black man for allegedly resisting arrest. A selective boycott of the downtown stores proved ineffectual because Albany's black population lacked sufficient buying power.

When King and Abernathy returned for sentencing on 10 July 1962, it was clear that the local momentum had been lost. King hoped that his incarceration would provide a rallying point for renewed demonstrations. But the following day, against his wishes, King was released on bond paid by an anonymous "well-dressed" Negro. Unbeknown to King, the payment of the bond had been authorized by Pritchett and Mayor Asa Kelley. In a famous comment, Abernathy told a mass meeting, "I've been thrown out of lots of places in my day, but I've never been thrown out of jail before."

Dismayed at the uncompromising stance of the city government, King sought to relaunch a mass campaign, promising to establish an SCLC office in the city. But the movement lost even more momentum when King accepted a federal court injunction on 20 July proscribing demonstrations. Although King resumed marching when the injunction was lifted four days later, he had clearly lost his authority over the protests. A violent mob of black youths provided the city government with sufficient propaganda to undermine King's leadership. "Did you see them non-violent rocks?" Chief of Police Laurie Pritchett asked reporters. In fact, such violence had always been simmering alongside the peaceful protests. Howard Zinn observed that "on the first day that Dr. King led his hymn-singing marchers toward City Hall, two well-established Negro teenage gangs lined the streets with concealed knives and other weapons, ready to move on if the nonviolent Negroes were attacked. That is a fact that television cameras, Dr. King and perhaps Chief Pritchett missed."[158]

In a final attempt to regain the initiative over the protests, King toured the back streets of Albany and proclaimed a day of penance on 24 July. After local lawyers overturned the injunction, King sought to restore momentum by being arrested once more on 27 July and refusing bail. At a mass meeting that night, only fifteen people volunteered to go to jail with him. Charles Sherrod remonstrated with the congregation to no avail, saying, "You ought to be ashamed of yourself for sitting on your chairs while our leaders are sitting in a filthy jail." The city commission remained intransigent, insisting pointedly that it would meet with law-abiding Negroes only. In his history of the Albany movement, Richard Moberley noted that "it was painstakingly clear that the whites used King's presence as an excuse not to meet with local leaders." After he received a suspended sentence on 10 August, King left Albany in the hope that negotiations might resume. But the city commission refused to talk to leaders of the Albany movement, insisting that they were hoping for a "new and responsible voice for the colored citizenry of Albany." King himself conceded that, despite nearly a year of demonstrations and incarcerations, this attitude remained one of "utter contempt." [159]

The failure at Albany precipitated a plethora of postmortems. Andrew Young, one of King's colleagues on the staff of SCLC, later concluded that "the weakness of the Albany movement was that it was totally unplanned and [SCLC] were totally unprepared. It was a miscalculation on the part of a number of people that a spontaneous appearance by Martin Luther King could bring change." Lack of preparation led to tactical mistakes. Coretta Scott King believed that her husband's acceptance of the injunction against demonstrating was "the factor that broke the backbone of the movement." The tactic of filling the jails proved to be equally ineffective. As Reese Cleghorn concluded, "Albany City jail . . . proved a bottomless pit." More caustically, Ruby Hurley, the NAACP regional director for the Southeast, concluded that "Albany was successful only if the goal was to go to jail." [160]

Such bad planning also meant that the SCLC had initially sought a single, comprehensive desegregation settlement. In this sense, the movement handed Mayor Asa Kelley an ultimatum requiring complete and public capitulation, which proved untenable. Although Kelley and some businessmen were prepared to negotiate, the city commission remained steadfast. As the *New York Times* observed, "Albany is governed by a group of urbane segregationists who have left the city's white racial moderates no middle ground." King himself admitted in 1963 that "I think it would have been better to concentrate on one area." [161]

Part of this lack of foresight meant that King joined a protest beset by local factions. Sherrod and Reagon had ousted the incumbent NAACP leader by calling a meeting in October 1961 without his knowledge. At the same time, Sherrod and Reagon had usurped the NAACP's youth affiliate by setting up a rival group. Far from being a united protest, the Albany movement was partly an attempt to paper over divisions. The president of the movement, William Anderson, was a compromise candidate. The vice-president, a real estate broker, Slater King, represented the local NAACP, and Marion Page, a retired railroad man, was appointed secretary.[162]

With hindsight, too, the presence of SCLC, and, more specifically, Wyatt T. Walker, who tried to assume day-to-day control, exacerbated divisions within the local movement. SNCC workers, in particular, resented the idea of bringing in King, who they nicknamed "De Lawd," in order to turn Albany into a national battleground. After SNCC was excluded from one press conference with King, Cordell Reagon commented that nobody "appreciates going to jail, getting their balls busted day in and day out, and then you don't even get to speak on it." After arguing publicly with Walker outside Albany's jail in December 1961, Marion Page allegedly shared ideas with Laurie Pritchett on ways to remove King from the protest. John A. Ricks III was one of many who argued that "Martin Luther King's participation in the Albany movement seems to have been an unfortunate decision which delayed desegregation in that city for several years."[163]

As in other Georgia cities, the racial mores of the region also affected the outcome of the campaign. Whereas the coastal cities and Rome were havens of racial moderation and Atlanta and Macon sought to avoid notoriety, Albany was chosen by SNCC precisely because it represented the South's slave plantation country. "When we first came to Albany," Charles Sherrod reported, "the people were afraid, really afraid." Although Albany was a fast-growing commercial center, it was also the capital of Georgia's black belt, a region recognized as a bastion of white supremacy.[164] In July 1962, William Hansen, a twenty-year-old white SNCC worker, was beaten up so severely in prison that his ribs and jaw were broken. Shortly afterward, movement lawyer C. B. King was hit on the head with a cane by the Dougherty County sheriff and taken to the hospital.

In contrast to Macon and Atlanta, the city government actually championed, rather than circumvented, the calls for massive resistance. Even before King's arrival, Pritchett insisted to reporters that "we can't tolerate the NAACP, or SNCC or any other nigger organization to take over the town with mass demonstrations." In a bid to coordinate opposition to the Albany movement, the city commission granted the police chief extraordinary powers to act on behalf of the white community. At the same time, segregationist judge Robert Elliott, an appointee of President Kennedy, passed the injunction banning King from further protest. James Gray, who owned the *Albany Herald* and Albany's only television station, took a firm segregationist stance.[165]

Crucially, Pritchett shrewdly outmaneuvered the local campaign. By exercising restraint in public against the protesters and on several occasions arranging for the release of King from jail, Pritchett denied the protest the type of outrage needed to attract sympathetic publicity. Pritchett had even investigated Gandhian nonviolent philosophy and read King's *Stride Toward Freedom* to prepare for the arrival of SNCC and SCLC. His avowed aim was to "meet violence with nonviolence." As David Lewis commented, "In Laurie Pritchett, King met a travestied image of himself—a non-violent segregationist law officer." Pritchett certainly earned a grudging respect from King, who canceled one demonstration when he discovered that it was Pritchett's wedding anniversary.[166]

In reality, Pritchett was far from being a disciple of Gandhi. Slater King resented the adulation given to Pritchett by the national press. John Lewis believed that "Pritchett was a cunning man, as deceitful as he had to be." Marion Page later recalled Pritchett turning a black delegation away from City Hall, saying, "It's all a question of mind over matter: I don't mind and you don't matter." At times, Pritchett indulged in more brutal tactics, but only away from the attention of national reporters. Pritchett incarcerated local protesters in squalid conditions, but only in jails in the rural hinterland. At rural Camilla jail in July 1962, Marion King, the wife of Slater King, was so severely beaten by guards that she had a miscarriage.[167] It was this beating that provoked the outbreak of violence in Albany.

In the context of local supremacist intransigence, the lack of federal involvement proved telling. Demonstrators were particularly frustrated by the lack of protection given by the FBI, even after they had presented FBI agents with clear evidence. Howard Zinn remarked on the popular perception of the FBI as "a bunch of racists . . . whether true or not, this is the feeling of many Negroes who have had contact with the FBI." King himself publicly accused FBI agents in Albany of favoring the segregationists. David Garrow confirmed that Marion Cheeks, the head of the Albany division of the FBI, "hated black people with a passion."[168]

Although the demonstrations in Albany failed to achieve any of their immediate goals, the campaign did have some positive repercussions. At a national level, the lessons of Albany forced SCLC to launch a better-prepared, clearly focused, and therefore successful campaign in Birmingham two years later. After leaving Albany, King reviewed the campaign in order "to see where mistakes were made [and] determine what could be done in Birmingham to offset them."[169]

At the municipal level, the withdrawal of the SCLC did not mark an end to black activism either. Indeed, SNCC's Charles Sherrod had originally envisaged a longer-term protest based on community organization. In his review of the Albany movement, Michael Chalfen noted that protest continued "long after Augtust 1962, when its historiographical grave is traditionally marked." Initially, both the local NAACP and SNCC supervised piecemeal boycotts and picketing. During the first quarter of 1963, Dougherty County was the only one of Georgia's larger counties not to show gains in retail sales because of boycotts and demonstrations. In the longer term, Albany leaders filed suits to desegregate local schools and emphasized voter registration, especially when C. B. King ran for Congress during the summer of 1964. In a single week in July, over one thousand black voters were registered in southwest Georgia, and over five thousand black Albanians were registered by the end of 1965.[170]

Theories in Urban Protest

Not only was black protest in Georgia diverse during the years of nonviolent direct action, but also there were no hard or fast rules that determined the nature and outcome of local movements. The BCCC in Macon overcame violent white supremacy, while protest in Columbus and Augusta floundered in the face of such racial resistance. More moderate environments did allow the emergence of black protest but did not make the success of such protest inevitable. Protest in Atlanta failed to achieve its ultimate goals, partly because the relative racial moderation of the city undermined the unity of the local movement. In contrast, a durable, belligerent protest in Savannah and a brief series of sit-ins in Rome forced local desegregation. In Albany, protest failed not just because of entrenched white supremacy but because the movement was divided and unable to provoke a violent reaction for the watching media.

Nor did the history of earlier protest in Georgia's cities always leave a direct legacy for the direct action movements of the modern civil rights era. The dearth of protest in Columbus during the 1960s contrasted with the earlier activism of Dr. Brewer, whereas in Brunswick concerted protest first emerged during the 1960s after the arrival of Rev. Hope. Where there was a tangible legacy of black protest, however, it clearly influenced the course of the modern movement. In Macon, Randall adapted his forthright stance to include direct action and Savannahians continued the belligerent approach first begun under Gilbert. In Atlanta, the Auburn Avenue elite's inherent conservatism spilled over into the 1960s.

The success of local protests was primarily dependent on the ability to exploit the opportunity of the 1960s rather than because of any particular tactic. In Brunswick, Hope used the threat of racial crisis to preempt the resistance of the city government. In Savannah and Macon, it was the unrelenting pressure of direct action protest that forced change. The direct action movement in Atlanta, by contrast, was consistently undercut by the entrenched influence and gradualist approach of the Auburn Avenue elite. Without doubt, those cities that were home to more strident defenders of white supremacy provided less opportunity for local protest. It was primarily the arrival of SNCC and SCLC that led to the emergence of black protest in Albany.

For all their diversity, local protests in Georgia did influence each other. The moves to desegregation in Savannah and Atlanta, not to say Montgomery and Nashville, gave weight to the sense of inevitability. Conversely, the racial turmoil in Albany influenced white negotiators in Savannah, Brunswick, and Rome into seeking a peaceful settlement. The history of direct action protest in Georgia confirms Slater King's assessment of the Albany campaign in August 1962, when he accepted that there were "hardly any visible rewards that one can see ... but the largest gain has been this: that in the surrounding cities they are determined that they do not want the confusion to come to their cities that has come to Albany." [171]

If Georgia urban protest lacked a single uniting theme, it had some common features. For example, the present orthodoxy among sociologists, as propounded by David Garrow in *Protest at Selma,* suggests that the resource mobilization theory explains the creation and sustaining of social movements. "One version of this theory," according to Aldon Morris, "says that dominated groups rarely possess the skills and resources needed for social protest and are unable to organize and sustain movements by themselves unless they receive assistance from outside elites." [172] In fact, the history of direct action protest in Georgia confirms Morris's own view that this theory assigns undue weight to the role of outside elites. The movements in Savannah, Macon, Rome, and Brunswick were organized and sustained using local resources. Outside elites were necessary only in the most hostile white supremacist environments, as demonstrated by the protest in Albany and negligible activity in Augusta and Columbus.

The activities of local branches of the NAACP were among the more striking features of Georgia protest. Often civil rights historiography has stereotyped the NAACP as aloof from confrontational protest. John White noted that "during the 1960s ... civil rights strategy shifted from the legalism and pressure group tactics of the NAACP ... to the direct actions of CORE, SCLC and SNCC." Recent historiography, particularly the state studies of Mississippi and Louisiana, has revised this conservative picture of the NAACP. In the context of postwar Jim Crow, the legal and voting activities of the NAACP have been recognized as a direct challenge to southern racial mores. As Fairclough concluded for Louisiana, "the habit of ignoring the NAACP and highlighting the 1960s, has resulted in a kind of historical amnesia" that ignored the impact of the NAACP before *Brown.* [173]

In Georgia, however, to ignore the NAACP movements when highlighting the

1960s would also be to ignore some of the more active, confrontational, and certainly successful urban protests in the state. From his experience as a reporter in Georgia, Trezzant Anderson commented in April 1960 that "up to now, actually, the NAACP has laid it on the line. . . . Don't disregard the NAACP, whatever happens." In Savannah, Macon, and Brunswick, the decisive break in the civil rights movement from legalism to activism and the involvement of the youth came under the auspices of the local NAACP branches. From the perspective of Georgia during the years of direct action, August Meier was correct when he concluded in 1963 that "it is impossible to generalize about the NAACP . . . some branches have embraced direct action whole-heartedly." [174]

The stereotype of the NAACP as moderate and legalistic during the 1960s was certainly fulfilled by the national board. James Lawson, the hero of the Nashville movement, lambasted the NAACP for its lack of aggressiveness during his speech at the inaugural SNCC conference in Atlanta in 1960.[175] But after 1959, the national board had devolved responsibility to local initiatives and NAACP activities in Georgia were very much locally based. In practice, the distinction between the New York head office and local branches may not have been as clear-cut. Board members Ruby Hurley and Gloster Current praised the Savannah protests as a model for local branches, while Law, Randall, and Hope remained loyal to the national board.[176]

The case of Macon blurred the differences between the major civil rights organizations still further. By the end of 1960, the Bibb County Co-ordinating Committee was affiliated with both SCLC and the local NAACP. In practice, all local Macon organizations were a vehicle for Randall's leadership. Similarly, Hosea Williams worked in the Savannah NAACP until his personal clash with W. W. Law, before moving to work with SCLC in Atlanta. Unless national leaders were involved, as in Albany, it was the outlook of local activists, rather than the emphasis of the major organizations, that determined the nature of local protest.

Across Georgia, youth provided the impetus for protest. Students initiated a new era of confrontation in Atlanta, approached W. W. Law in Savannah, and the *Pittsburgh Courier* reported in June 1961 that "the Augustans are relying on their students to fight their battles." Students led the way in some of the smaller towns too. For example, the VEP noted that students at Fort Valley State College were "99% responsible for the success of the campaign," which registered over two thousand voters in six weeks during the summer of 1964.[177] Conversely, the lack of a college hindered protest in Columbus. But if youth provided the impetus for direct action, adults (albeit youthful adults) often provided the leadership and the personnel. Law and Williams incorporated students into existing NAACP strategy. In Macon, Randall actually urged the youth to act. And in Brunswick, Hope used the prospect of youth direct action movements to threaten the city government.

The outcome of black protest in Georgia's cities was also dependent on the reaction of the local white leadership. Jacoway and Colburn have argued that the "response of the southern leadership to the desegregation challenge was an accommodation to what was perceived as inevitable change—an accommodation based on a conscious choice between the past and the future." In so doing, they revise the traditional view, expressed by Numan Bartley, that the response of white southerners was merely a "conservative reaction in defense of southern continuity and represented no real break with the past."[178]

The city governments of Brunswick and Rome certainly chose to accept inevitable change. Yet the experience of most of Georgia's cities does not accord with Jacoway and Colburn's optimism. Atlanta may have styled itself "a city too busy to hate," but it could also have been described as a city seeking to avoid racial trouble and racial change. Atlanta's white political and business community negotiated token integration to debilitate the emerging student protest. Even in Savannah, renowned for its liberality, the most striking feature of the white response was just how long the establishment retained segregation. In Albany and Augusta, the city governments resisted the desegregation challenge altogether, thus highlighting the need for the Civil Rights Act of 1964.

The advent of the direct action phase of protest precipitated an often strident dialogue within both the black and white communities in Georgia's cities. In Atlanta, students and the adult leadership disagreed over tactics. In other cities, divisions within the black community were even greater. William Randall reflected later that "some of our greatest opposition was from within the race." At a mass meeting of over two thousand people in Savannah, W. W. Law denounced James McMillan, pastor of Emmanuel Baptist Church, as "a new Judas" for publicly opposing the sit-ins. Similarly, in some white communities, defenders of segregation argued with moderates and advocates of integration in response to the demands of black protesters.[179]

Consequently, direct action was not simply a confrontation between black activists and a resistant white leadership. David Chappell explained that the starting point for his research into white liberals was "a startling observation: there were white southerners who supported the civil rights movement."[180] Of course, the applicability of this statement varied between communities. While Atlanta was home for a number of liberal voices, Columbus, Augusta, and Albany were more renowned for entrenched white supremacy.

Chappell concluded that "the lesson of greatest consequence for black leaders, however, was that they could not rely on white dissenters."[181] Certainly this was true in Atlanta, where Paschall lamented that "it must have rained" as far as white liberals were concerned. But other Georgia cities revealed a more positive role for white dissenters than Chappell allows. In Macon, an active human rights council facilitated interracial dialogue, while the Savannah Greys helped to put integration into practice. In Rome, white dissenters were actually the first in the city to respond to the challenge of Montgomery.

Albany proved to be the major exception, with near ubiquitous support for Jim Crow from the white community. As Chappell himself admitted, Pritchett was a police chief "at the apex of this amazingly cohesive white community." After the successes of many urban protests, Georgia's last bastion of intransigent white supremacy was to be found in the small towns and rural areas surrounding Albany. In this context, the significance of Albany was that the local protest provided the first incursion of the civil rights movement into Georgia's black belt. Local leaders hoped, therefore, that the Albany movement marked a beginning rather than an end of protest in the southwest region. Such a view was expressed most poignantly by Marion King after her miscarriage, when she asserted that "I would thank you young people of SNCC for starting something that will not die and cannot be stopped."[182]

It was from Albany that SNCC workers attempted to organize protest throughout the southwest Georgia black belt. But Albany's intense segregationist resistance, even under the spotlight of the national media, provided a harbinger of even greater problems to come in the surrounding rural areas. For SNCC staffers, the Albany movement had also answered a vital question: Which side is the federal government on? The students believed that the lack of federal intervention meant that the government was on the side of the segregationists. Nevertheless, after the experience of Albany, SNCC workers became increasingly determined to take the struggle for black equality from the city into the heart of Georgia's black belt. Subsequently, SNCC's Southwest Georgia Project became the primary attempt to effect racial change in the most white supremacist rural areas of the state.

5

Protest in Rural Georgia: SNCC's Southwest Georgia Project, 1962–1967

While protest flourished in Savannah, prospered in Rome, and escalated across most of Georgia's major cities, the civil rights movement initially bypassed the countryside. "Years after the movement had begun to transform the rest of the South, news of it had barely filtered through to McIntosh County," concluded Melissa Fay Greene. Interviews with rural black teenagers during the 1960s revealed that many young Georgians lacked even a cursory knowledge of Martin Luther King, let alone what he stood for or the aims of the movement. In general, where rural protest did occur, it was merely as the spillover from urban protests into their respective metropolitan counties. In middle Georgia, protesters joked ruefully that the civil rights movement finished at Perry, a small town one hundred miles south of Atlanta.[1]

The exception was in the southwest Georgia black belt. In 1962, SNCC launched a major project that sought to bring the civil rights movement to southwest Georgia. By 1965, SNCC had employed staff workers in the twenty-three counties surrounding the cities of Americus and Albany, which formed the second and third congressional districts. Most of these twenty-three counties were overwhelmingly rural, with a population divided approximately equally between black and white, and only five counties contained a settlement with a population of over five thousand people.[2]

The region represented a complete contrast to Georgia's urban counties. For civil rights reporter Anne Braden, southwest Georgia most vividly conjured up Lillian Smith's evocative phrase the "distance and darkness of the Deep South." Economically, southwest Georgia formed a cohesive region, both in terms of the basic crops of cotton, peanuts, corn, and small grains and because of the extent of rural poverty. The region contained by far the largest concentration of Area Redevelopment Act–designated counties in the state, meaning that the median average income was under $1,560 for all families and under $1,170 for farm families, in contrast with a state average of over $3,000 for each family. One of the consequences of this economic stagnation was that the region's population decreased from 1950 to 1960, a time when the population of Georgia as a whole was on the increase.[3]

Politically too, the region was both isolated and cohesive. Under Georgia's county-unit system, the rural counties dominated the state politically during the 1950s. The overturning of the county-unit system in 1962 dramatically shifted the balance of power toward the metropolitan counties. Such political isolation and economic impotence, wrote SNCC worker John Perdew after spending two years in the southwest black belt, meant that "the region's backwardness is usually ignored by the ascendant 'moderates' in state and national affairs."[4] Perdew described southwest Georgia as a "tragic area, the stepchild of the New South."

The struggle of SNCC in southwest Georgia assumed greater significance because the region was the most strident defender of white supremacy in the state. The racial mores of the region were most forcibly expressed through official white violence. Whereas Atlanta's police had been purged of the Ku Klux Klan during the 1950s, and most of Georgia's major cities had hired black policemen by 1960, the local authorities in southwest Georgia were invariably the leading perpetrators of racial violence. Within the region Baker County had the worst reputation for unfettered official violence. A Southern Regional Council report in 1959 recorded that "Albany Negroes characterize Baker County as being 'one step down from hell.'"[5]

After a front-page story in the *Washington Post* in June 1958, "Terrible" Terrell County had gained national notoriety for racial violence. The *Post*'s simple headline ran, "The Negroes of This South Georgia Town Are Scared." During the course of a single week, three black men had been shot and killed by the police while numerous other black men and women were beaten. One of the men, James Brazier, had merely tried to stop police from beating his father, who had been arrested for drunk driving. Brazier was then beaten in front of his young son, suffered a skull fracture, and never regained full consciousness. Brazier was even dragged into court before receiving medical treatment. It was the resulting atmosphere of despair and terror, the *Post* concluded, that drove one Terrell resident to contact and meet with reporters. Although the witness remained anonymous, local suspicion fell on Rev. Hollis Hooks, the outstanding minister in the county seat of Dawson. Within six weeks, Hooks had been hounded out of the region and moved to Washington, D.C. During the next two years, another three men were killed by police because of allegedly racist motives. Meanwhile, the undertaker who handled Brazier's body was forced to close his establishment.[6]

The regional cohesiveness and strength of white supremacy in the midst of a majority black area attracted the attention of SNCC. At their third general conference, held during 27–29 April 1962, staff members finalized plans to initiate two community-organizing projects based in the black belts of Mississippi and Georgia. In fact, project leader Charles Sherrod had first visited the area during the summer of 1961, after doing careful research into concentrations of black adults not registered to vote.[7] In many ways, community organizing marked the transition within SNCC from campus-based direct action protest to a fundamental reappraisal of American society as a whole. What was new in 1962 was the determination of a major civil rights organization to take the movement into hitherto untouched areas of the rural Deep South.

Civil rights historiography has largely focused on black protest in an urban context. The Southwest Georgia Project, therefore, represents an ideal case study for an insight into rural protest. In the first place, it stands alongside Mississippi as one of the two classic set-piece confrontations between a major civil rights organization and massive resistance in the rural black belt. One SNCC fieldworker, Charles Black, felt that "Southwest Georgia was far worse than Mississippi."[8] Moreover, the problems faced by civil rights activists in southwest Georgia shed light on the reasons why protest was so slow in forthcoming in the other rural areas in Georgia and across the South.

Whereas the Mississippi Freedom Summer has been extensively researched, the story of southwest Georgia has largely escaped the scrutiny of historians.[9] Undoubtedly, Sherrod did not possess the charisma of Bob Moses, the leader of the Mississippi Project. In contrast to the Freedom Summer, the Southwest Georgia Project became increasingly marginalized both from the SNCC head office and national attention. Above all, the Georgia project never escalated to the scale of the Mississippi Freedom Summer, when some 650 students worked in the Magnolia State.[10] As a result, the works of SNCC historians Howard Zinn, Emily Stoper, and James Forman reflect the head office's preoccupation with Selma and Mississippi.[11] Clayborne Carson notes in his definitive study of SNCC that "the two most important testing grounds for SNCC's community organization approaches were southwest Georgia and Mississippi." Carson, however, merely mentions the formation of the project and then, five years later, its official disbanding.[12]

The project also provides an ideal case study because the staff workers were required by SNCC to file regular field reports, particularly when the project received funding from the VEP intermittently during 1962–66. Pat Watters and Reese Cleghorn concluded that SNCC reporting "constitutes a unique contribution to the literature of American history." In part, this was because the writers were both literate and often highly articulate. James Forman, SNCC executive secretary, thought that field reports had an almost "Proustian influence." SNCC communications secretary Julian Bond wrote to Bob Moses that "Sherrod is writing like a drunk Jack Kerouac and [fieldworkers] O'Neal and Chatfield write like drunk Sherrods." Taken together, the uncensored reports provide a unique insight into the realities of rural protest and the experiences of the students involved.[13]

Within Georgia, though, the project's significance lay in its attempt to confront white supremacy in the southwest black belt. During the early 1960s, it was clear that Georgia's major cities were moving toward some form of desegregation, however reluctantly. In the eyes of the first students to enter southwest Georgia, the transformation of the black belt represented the key to unlock the remaining rural areas of Georgia.

When Charles Sherrod first arrived in Albany in 1961, he was only twenty-two years old but already a veteran of civil rights protest. Sherrod had led sit-in protests in Richmond and had worked in SNCC's McComb Project in Mississippi. Clayborne Carson aptly remarked that Sherrod "infused his work with the religious zeal of a southern black preacher and with the idealism of SNCC's early years." In part, Carson concluded, this idealism stemmed from Sherrod's own personal triumph over adversity. Having grown up as the eldest of eight children in a fatherless home in the slums of Petersburg, Virginia, Sherrod studied religion at Virginia Union University while working "as hard as two men to get through school." He became a highly articulate preacher. Sherrod's theological training encouraged him to investigate the radical implications of the Christian faith.[14]

Using contacts made in Albany, Sherrod aimed to transform the region through community organizing rather than direct action, although even at the outset Sherrod recognized that direct action could act as a catalyst for voter registration. Ostensibly, the transformation of southwest Georgia was to be effected by mobilizing the majority black vote through canvassing and citizenship education. In reality, Sherrod explained to the Voter Education Project, "Our criterion for success is not how many people we register, but how many people we can get to begin initiating decisions solely on the basis of their personal opinion." Above all, Sherrod continued, "we feel that we are in a psychological battle for the minds of the enslaved." [15]

Sherrod's long-term aim was to place two fieldworkers in each of the twenty-three counties, with Albany receiving no preferential treatment. To counter the cohesive oppression of white supremacy in the region, Sherrod hoped to bring the disparate local black protest groups together as an intercounty movement far more powerful than the sum of the individual counties. Sherrod's ultimate objective was to create a self-sustaining regional network of local leaders. As the largest town in the region, Albany was the obvious base for the project. In a report in October 1962, Sherrod explained that Albany acted "as the 'Crossroads of Civilization' in South West Georgia. All that happens in Albany is new and house gossip in the surrounding counties." [16] Sherrod's "intention was to charge the leadership in Albany with the responsibility of aiding in the struggle in the counties, the fight being 'one.'" But the mass movement in Albany, and particularly the involvement of King and the SCLC, had not been part of Sherrod's original strategy. The subsequent failure of the Albany movement slowed the momentum of the wider project.

The SNCC team was to include black, white, male, and female members to act as an example of how an integrated society could flourish, as well as directly to challenge the racial customs of the region. From the outset, Sherrod stamped his personal authority on the project, attracting like-minded idealists to his team. "Southwest Georgia," noted Emily Stoper, "was where those committed to non-violence and white participation tended to cluster." By the spring of 1963, the project consisted of eleven students, including five northern white students and three women. Don Harris, a charismatic twenty-two-year-old black student from Rutgers University in New Jersey, had already been involved in fund-raising activities and local civil rights efforts before joining SNCC. Ralph Allen, who became Harris's co-worker, was a white student activist from Trinity College in Connecticut. Not all of the team, however, had thought through SNCC's goals. Jack Chatfield, for example, joined SNCC because of the example of his college roommate, Ralph Allen. John Perdew, the son of a college professor and a junior at Harvard in 1963, admitted later that he joined the project because he "wanted to do something adventurous and different." Acutely conscious of being a white outsider in southwest Georgia, Perdew undertook many of the more logistical tasks. Perdew said he joined SNCC with "no idea at all of any kind of violence and daily oppression that millions of people went through ... but then I got my ass kicked." After his first arrest, Perdew decided to join the field staff rather than return to Harvard.[17]

First Forays into Southwest Georgia: Lee and Terrell Counties

Although the ultimate goal was to transform the region as a whole, Lee and Terrell Counties were designated as the pioneering projects because they appeared to be two of the most impenetrable counties in the region. If SNCC could progress there, staff workers reasoned, the way should be clear in almost all the other counties in the region, with the exception of Baker County. Both counties were overwhelmingly rural and neither possessed a settlement of over five hundred inhabitants. Although black residents formed over 60 percent of the population of both counties, never more than fifty registered during the 1950s. Lee and Terrell also had particularly notorious reputations for entrenched white supremacy backed up by violence. As the *Southern Patriot* noted in 1962, Lee and Terrell Counties represented "a part of the country where it is still literally true that Negroes have no rights which the white man has to respect."[18]

Terrell County's racial mores had also withstood federal intervention. In 1957, Congress passed the first civil rights bill since Reconstruction, which empowered the attorney general to act against any person who infringed voting rights. During the following April, four Dawson teachers and an employee of a Marine Corps supply center in Albany tried to register to vote, only to be denied. All five were college graduates and three held master's degrees. One of the teachers was failed because she mispronounced the word "equity" while another teacher, Edna Mae Lowe, was subsequently fired from her job on the grounds of being illiterate. Superior court judge Walter Geer threatened to put FBI staff in jail if they seized voter records. Ignoring the threats, the Justice Department tried to bring an injunction against the local registrar, only for the district court to reject the 1957 act as unconstitutional. It was not until September 1960 that the Supreme Court upheld the civil rights act. Federal district judge William Bootle issued an injunction against Terrell County registrars to prevent them from denying black voting rights. Nevertheless, by 1961, there were only fifty-three registered black voters in Terrell County. Meanwhile, Jim Gibson, the father of one of the teachers, was arrested for receiving stolen goods in what was widely perceived as a frame-up. Gibson, who ran a barbershop, had merely agreed to accept an overcoat as a deposit when a customer had been unable to pay for a haircut.[19]

Although SNCC workers intended to develop a new strategy for rural community organizing, the first incursions into the counties resulted from student protest more akin to the direct action protests in the cities. Soon after a press release in Atlanta announcing that SNCC would move into the counties, local students had initiated boycotts of both Lee and Terrell high schools to protest the expulsions of two local students. On 17 January 1962, Charles Wingfield had been expelled after asking for improved school equipment at Leesburg High School. The following day, Roychester Patterson was expelled from Dawson High School in Terrell County. Patterson, who had been arrested during the Albany campaign the previous year, was expelled for holding lunchtime civil rights discussions.[20]

Just as the first sit-ins had sparked wider youth protest in Georgia's cities, the high school expulsions galvanized Lee and Terrell's student bodies. For many students, the expectations raised by the nearby Albany movement outweighed any fears of white supremacist reprisals in their own counties. As in similar youth protests across Georgia, the activism of students provoked the adult black communities into action. Four hundred parents supported the Lee County school PTA resolution to keep the students out until the principal resigned and Wingfield was allowed back. By 19 January, only 132 of the 1,300 students attended Lee County Training School. The following day, the boycott was almost complete.[21]

Within days, however, the enduring strength of white supremacy in rural southwest Georgia became clear. The boycotts were crushed through firm repression. Neither Wingfield nor Patterson was reinstated. SNCC workers were barred from both schools, and no gatherings of four or more were permitted within school premises. Dawson High School principal E. F. Sykes even restricted the school's government class to only one semester because, as he told one parent, "all kinds of embarrassing questions about citizenship came up."[22] One year later, SNCC field staff reported that high school students were still "slow in moving" because of the restrictions.

The Problems of Rural Organizing

If the school boycott proved to be a fleeting digression for SNCC workers, the swift backlash was an accurate precursor of the vehement supremacist reaction to black community organization. Rather than recording any positive progress, the first project field reports mostly summarized the attempts of fieldworkers to survive a violent onslaught. Jack Chatfield may have been unique when he was shot in the arm within forty-five minutes of his arrival in Terrell County, but each staff worker suffered injury or physical threat and admitted to fear.[23]

For Charles Sherrod, however, simply withstanding the worst excesses of racial violence constituted progress because such steadfastness dovetailed with his goal of transforming the fearful attitude of local blacks. From the outset, Sherrod determined that fieldworkers would live in the counties. At the first open meeting in Terrell County in February 1962, Sherrod promised that "when you suffer, we will suffer." Sherrod's focus on the importance of withstanding violence proved to be prescient. After each violent outrage, noted the *Southern Patriot,* the "attendance at weekly mass meetings fell off sharply, and many have never come back."[24]

Consequently, much of Sherrod's early planning focused on strategies for staff survival. All project workers spent an orientation week at Dorchester Academy in east Georgia and some time in Albany before they moved into the rural counties. Supremacist violence also influenced his determination to have an interracial team, even when other SNCC project leaders in the South increasingly favored all-black teams. In a report to the VEP in early 1963, Sherrod wrote that "I knew the Justice Department and the media and the country would not consciously let anything happen to them white kids."[25]

To make sure, the project issued a regular stream of press releases detailing the full extent of rural violence. Sherrod also invited journalists from Atlanta, Washington, and New York to the region. It was a tip-off by Sherrod that ensured newsmen were present when an angry group of white men, led by Terrell sheriff Zeke Matthews, invaded an early registration meeting at Mount Olive Church in Terrell County. That a church was violated (not to mention the fact that the gas tanks of the reporters' cars were filled with sand) provoked outraged newspaper headlines. Claude Sitton's article in the *New York Times* read more like a drama exposing the racial hostilities of the South than a conventional news report. Sitton included an interview with Matthews, who confided, "You know cap, there's nothing like fear to keep niggers in line." Taylor Branch suggested that the story was "perhaps the most remarkable news dispatch of the entire civil rights generation." It certainly affected President Kennedy, who ordered the Justice Department to issue a voting rights complaint against the white intruders. Mary King of SNCC's communications office believed that after the incident, Sitton's "coverage lost the distant, flat quality of most news reportage of the time and leaped to life."[26]

White supremacists attracted even greater national exposure without any further help from Sherrod. During August 1962, Mount Olive and two other churches associated with movement meetings were burned to the ground. If the violation of the churches had provoked widespread shock, the burning of the churches aroused ubiquitous condemnation. President Kennedy called the burnings "cowardly as well as outrageous." The media spotlight continued to focus on Lee and Terrell Counties when Martin Luther King Jr. spoke at a memorial service shortly after the conflagration. King told local blacks that "the tragedy should make us go out with more determination than ever before to achieve our rights" and announced the creation of a national fund to rebuild the churches under the chairmanship of Georgia baseball star Jackie Robinson.[27]

Without doubt, the media spotlight, combined with the tenacity of the project workers, modified the pattern of racial violence in Lee and Terrell. Jack Chatfield believed that the summer outrages had secured "enough publicity to choke a hog" and that without the mob attacks and public violence the counties "appear to be an acquiescent, outwardly peaceful stretch of acreage." In a review in 1963, Ralph Allen concluded that the major success of the project was that local people held SNCC responsible for the decrease in harassment. Such moderation of supremacist behavior was personified in the unlikely figure of Sheriff Zeke Matthews. Matthews avoided controversy after what he later admitted to be the unsettling experience of being portrayed across the nation as both an Uncle Remus figure and the county czar. Jack Chatfield concluded that Matthews had been "backed off by the fatal combination of press and federal action."[28]

Sherrod himself was the first to admit, however, that the outward peace was a mere facade masking continued entrenched white supremacy. As Chatfield ruefully concluded in January 1963, "I think to myself that when you have conquered the mobs and the violence you have only pinched a sand grain from your eye."[29] The project may have removed the excesses of unrestrained violence, but staff workers quickly discovered that white supremacists in southwest Georgia had more potent means to protect rural racial mores.

If violence temporarily abated, fear among the local black population still remained. By the end of 1963, Terrell County worker Carver Neblett still bemoaned the "blanket of fear which is wrapped around the people of Bronwood and Terrell County." Local support was not forthcoming, argued Chatfield, because white supremacists had got the "Negroes of Terrell County . . . like a hacked dog. A hacked dog won't eat meat until the master leaves, for fear of being hacked again." After the church burnings, black ministers in Lee and Terrell refused to allow registration meetings in their churches.[30]

Successive staff workers in both counties concurred with Ralph Allen when he argued in early 1963 that "the main factor working against us in Terrell seems to be the organized economic tyranny of whites." Another white fieldworker, Larry Rubin, noted that "Lee County, like all the other counties around here, seems to be controlled by just a few of the families who live in it." Robert Lee, the largest landowner, was also the mayor of the county seat and president of the county's only bank, while the Forrester family held offices of sheriff, state senator, and secretary to the tax collector and registrar.[31]

This economic control often translated into economic oppression. "The main thing holding Terrell back," Allen observed, was that "the people *do* have something to lose." In some cases, intimidation was such that local residents who had started to help the movement turned away from SNCC. In one instance, Wilbert Henderson of Bronwood, Terrell County, initially welcomed staff workers in November 1962. Within days, local white traders had refused to weigh his corn and became tardy in providing fuel. Bronwood mayor A. B. Henry ordered his hired hands not to help at Henderson's farm. As if in sinister warning, a black man was found castrated and dead from bullet wounds; no arrest was made. When staff workers returned in December, Henderson refused even to see them.[32]

As in other areas of the state, teachers also refrained from openly supporting the local movement. In southwest Georgia, simply registering to vote was an overt defiance of white supremacy. Only one teacher in either county, Mildred Beasley, dared to challenge the threat made by the school supervisor of redundancy for any teacher who registered. In every way Beasley was the exception that proved the rule. SNCC workers described her as the "unteacherlike schoolteacher." Other teachers refused to associate with her, and the five teachers who wanted to talk about citizenship dared meet her only on the pretext of playing bridge.[33]

In southwest Georgia, even high school students were cowed by their dependence on white authorities. As student leader Clovis Jones confided to staff workers, the threat of poor references and immediate expulsion precluded his involvement in a county with high black unemployment and where only five black students had graduated from college during the previous decade. At Carver High School in Dawson, the first eight students to associate with voter registration were all put on probation.[34]

If the handful of potential local black leaders were bullied and threatened into inactivity, then the vast majority of blacks in Terrell and Lee Counties were under the complete economic control of the white minority. Time and again, SNCC reports pointed to myriad examples of economic pressure. Chatfield sympathized with one woman in Bronwood who was warned that if she registered to vote, her husband would lose his job as a farm hand. "Then where will she be? One day of the year she will be at the polls. The other 364 are not accounted for . . . she is openly and concretely scared."[35]

Each example of economic tyranny told a different story, but each had the common aim of preventing any organized racial protest. The observations of visiting Negro county agent Alfred Mackenzie concurred with those of staff workers. During 1963, Mackenzie noted the fear of "tenants and sharecroppers, who as a group, will not talk to the movement." Allen recorded that it was "understood that anyone who works for a white man in Terrell County and is registered to vote can expect to lose their job." Local sharecropper Charlie Sheard prohibited his daughter from attending a meeting when he heard of plans to remove any "out-of-line Negro" from their land. The four hundred black workers at Dawson Cotton Oil Company, the largest employer in either county, became afraid to register once it became known that registered voters were automatically fired.[36]

The ability of SNCC workers to resist violence stood in stark contrast to their impotence in the face of this white economic stranglehold. This form of racial domination did not attract publicity and remained unchallenged by the continued presence of a few students. Bemoaning what they saw as the movement's failure in Terrell after two years of organizing, SNCC workers Wendy Mann and Bob Cover conceded in early 1964 that "only the people who are in some way economically independent have registered to vote. The vast majority of people dependent upon whites for their livelihood have not been touched by the voter registration program."[37]

Alongside the twin obstacles of racial violence and economic control, SNCC workers also faced the inherent problems of community organizing in a rural area characterized by poverty. Don Harris, a project worker for four years, noted that "the biggest difficulty in the counties was that both Lee and Terrell Counties are just completely rural, not even a hint of a town." Perhaps it was because they had been so well prepared for racial violence that visiting fieldworkers were most shocked by the reality of rural poverty. "When I compare it with the slums of the cities," Terrell County worker Prathia Hall reported in 1963, "it seems that here, even the poverty seems primitive. The shacks are low, the food simple, the work back-breaking, the poverty degrading."[38]

Economic statistics confirmed Hall's observations. In Terrell County, the median income for white families was $4,300 but less than $1,300 for black families. The

median income for the United States as a whole, by contrast, was $5,600. Less than
1 percent of blacks in either county were employed in any management, clerical, or
overseer capacity. Of those who farmed in Lee County, only thirty retained the
relative independence of sharecropping by 1960; all other farmers had been reduced
to the position of temporary laborer after the consolidation of local farms during the
previous two decades.[39]

The harsh realities of life under rural poverty restricted SNCC's community
organizing. Staff worker Penny Patch conceded that "when you work in the cotton
fields all day and come home to nothing but pork and beans and get ready for another
day—it's hard even to think about registering." Even the white farmers who didn't
run SNCC workers off their fields released workers to register only on rainy days.
And at Sasser, Terrell County, citizenship meetings were postponed during the
planting and harvest seasons.[40]

Furthermore, educating the few who did want to register required tremendous
effort and resources beyond the capability of a handful of visiting students. "Illit-
eracy," noted Lee County staff worker Ernest McMillan, "was a problem exclusive
to the rural counties" and proved to be insurmountable. In both counties, adult
blacks had completed on average less than five grades of education, in contrast to an
average of ten grades for whites. Over three-quarters of black students had not
completed the seventh grade. When fourteen people in Terrell County agreed to
attend citizenship classes at the end of 1962, they needed three months to become
prepared to attempt to register.[41]

The widespread extent of rural poverty also hindered the project's attempts to
develop a self-sustaining local leadership. In contrast to urban areas, the counties
provided a mere handful of leaders independent of white economic control. Dolly
Raines, who became known as Mama Dolly, mother of the movement in Lee County,
owned substantial property in Albany. Carolyn Daniels, who played a similar role in
Terrell, maintained a successful beauty parlor. In Terrell County, B. W. Cooper
owned an independent black morticians company, while two of the mainstays of the
Lee County movement, Agnew James and Tea Kunney, owned well-established
farms. In some communities, the initial hope of project workers to network and train
existing leadership quickly degenerated into despondency at the dearth of any
leaders at all. After repeated visits to Bronwood, for example, Chatfield reported
that "we failed to find the leader that I expected we might find."[42] Similarly, field
staffers were frustrated that the two main black community organizations, the
church and the schools, provided little support for the movement.

An irony that was not immediately apparent to the fieldworkers was that many of the core leaders in both counties had already been established before the Southwest Georgia Project began. D. Ulysses Pullum, described by Sherrod as the first person openly to welcome the students to Dawson, had been at the forefront of civil rights protests as early as the 1940s and was honored by the Georgia Voters' League at a ceremony in Macon in 1960. Because of his unwavering leadership of what NAACP officials described as a "one-man branch," Pullum had been pistol-whipped as recently as 1961, and gasoline dealers had refused to sell him fuel.[43] Agnew James and Carolyn Daniels had been involved in the local adult leadership in Albany before SNCC arrived there.

Many of the handful of local leaders who did support the movement found the cost of active involvement too high to sustain in the face of supremacist pressure. Agnew James, president of the Lee County movement, was barred from using local supply stores and was threatened with the removal of his telephone when he housed SNCC workers in the summer of 1963. Similarly, Carolyn Daniels suffered bombings at her house at the end of 1963, which hampered her work as a home beautician, briefly forcing her reluctantly to play a less prominent role.[44]

The problems of the rural environment were exacerbated by the project's own lack of resources. Frequently, staff workers were forced to earn a living in the field that kept them away from their intended work of community organization. Although the Voter Education Project did provide some funding during 1963–66, the maximum allowance was only $10 weekly and even this money arrived sporadically. When money was not forthcoming, Sherrod explained to civil rights reporters, they would have to "go back to hustling, washing floors, windows, cutting lawns and somebody may have to get an eight hour job."[45]

Canvassing across the rural counties was particularly hampered by the project's lack of transport. Although staff workers showed initiative in using the existing network of school buses to spread information using students as messengers, Sherrod concluded that the lack of mobility was "our most deadly handicap." Acquiring a car was considered an essential prerequisite to progress. But the long-awaited freedom bus could not be bought until the end of 1962 and was largely based in Albany.[46] Meanwhile, staff workers had to manage with one car bought with a VEP grant during November 1962.

Staff workers were also honest enough to concede that the movement had been weakened by their own mistakes. Although it was a criticism more commonly leveled at the SCLC and Martin Luther King Jr., fieldworker Bob Cover bemoaned that the "off and on, in and out, aspect of SNCC has been a serious problem in Lee and Terrell Counties."[47] Without a self-sufficient local leadership, the movement had ebbed and flowed with the departure and arrival of various staff members.

Equally, the project failed to encourage more than a token amount of intercounty unity to support the movement. In an evaluation at the end of 1963, staff workers admitted that "we have been very negligent in bringing the few active people from this county in to contact with movement people from other places." Initially, Sherrod had hoped that activists from Albany would reach out into the surrounding rural counties, but the visits of Albany movement leaders Slater King and William Anderson to mass meetings in Terrell and Lee became increasingly infrequent after the churches were burned. The comments of one female leader in Albany were more typical. She admitted, "I know I ought to, but everyone has something they can't do, and going out to Terrell is mine."[48]

Indeed, the majority of intercounty activism proved to be counterproductive. Sherrod himself noted despondently that by the end of 1962, the only Albany students willing to be involved were those who thought that SNCC was a "great way to meet girls." All too often it was the prospect of kissing on the back seats rather than being able to canvass rural blacks that inspired such students to ride in the voter registration bus. The question students were asking was not "how can I help the movement?" project worker John Churchville concluded, "but how can I hit on one of those fair broads?" Such questions suggested that SNCC's strict rule proscribing volunteers from forming relationships was regularly flouted. As Sherrod admitted in response to a question from Wiley Branton of the VEP, "Yea, sexual relations. This is a hell of a problem."[49]

Fieldworkers had caught a glimpse of the potential impact of an intercounty movement when an all-female group of nineteen student canvassers visited Terrell County using the Albany bus. It is "the greatest thing, perhaps, that has happened in Terrell County thus far," Randolph Battle wrote during the summer of 1963, resulting in four new applications to register in one week. It also proved to be the final visit of a group from Albany.[50]

The project also failed to harness the full potential contribution of women. Individuals such as Mama Dolly and Carolyn Daniels were the greatly admired mothers of the movement. Sherrod commented that "there is always a 'mama.' She is usually a militant woman in the community, outspoken, understanding and willing to catch hell, having already caught her share." Daniels was also the mother of Roychester Patterson and encouraged him in his protests at Dawson High School. Prathia Hall concluded that "Mrs. Daniels is the symbol of resistance in the area. People in the Negro community have regarded her with an awesome respect coupled with fear that association with her will bring danger and reprisal to them and their families." Sherrod described Dolly Raines as "a gray-haired old lady of about seventy who can pick cotton, 'slop more pigs,' plow more ground, chop more wood and do a hundred things better than the best farmer in the area." [51]

The project did not initially canvass local women as a distinct group. Only at the end of 1962, Daniels and Prathia Hall visited Terrell County "to provide the punch that Bronwood had not seen: women." Even then the punch proved to be a one-day experiment. The relative success of Daniels's own citizenship classes, with forty-five newly registered voters by the end of 1963, exposed SNCC's mistake of initially using local women only for support and hospitality rather than as canvassing activists. By the beginning of 1965, Prathia Hall noted that "more people frequent her beauty shop and talk openly with her about voting and about matters of civil rights." [52]

The frustration of project workers was often vented in personality clashes. John O'Neal and Larry Rubin refused to work together, Mama Dolly did not allow white students on to her farm, and Carolyn Daniels welcomed only favored students to her house. Fundamentally divergent views on protest ideology separated the Terrell County team of John Churchville, an early advocate of black nationalism, and Jack Chatfield, a white student with interracial ideals. After his experience in southwest Georgia, Churchville concluded that "all white people are racists; that is, no white person (when you get down to the nitty-gritty) can stand to deal with black people as humans, as men, as equals, not to mention superiors." Personal tensions were manifested in the increasing antipathy of black team members to some of their short-term white counterparts. "It makes you cringe to see them trying to catch the rhythm," Churchville confided to the head office. [53]

Judged in the context of rural southwest Georgia, the project had made a discernible difference. The number of registered black voters in Terrell County more than doubled to 128 by April 1963. This increase even caught the attention of the *Atlanta Constitution*, which noted that the chief impetus had been from SNCC. By November 1964, when the first VEP funding ended, the registration figure had more than doubled again to 340, and Lee County had 167 black voters. "When you consider the past year of harassment and intimidation," Daniels explained to the VEP, "I know we have accomplished much." [54]

But the project did not achieve a widespread breakthrough. Although both counties had majority black populations, the proportion of black voters remained negligible.[55] Successful canvassing was both piecemeal and sporadic. The hubris of expectation that typified early field reports was quickly replaced by a sober realism that judged a single positive conversation to be a significant success. For example, Terrell County staff workers recorded that a meeting with Les Holly, a seventy-year-old blind man who was keen to register, was the canvassing highlight of December 1962. "It is my opinion," the report concluded, "that this blind man can see a lot more than most of the people with two eyes." Somewhat poignantly, two months later Holly offered numerous excuses to avoid the trip to the courthouse to register.[56]

Even judged by Sherrod's basic criterion for success, to win the psychological battle for the hearts and minds of local black residents, the pioneering movement in Lee and Terrell clearly failed. Indeed, fieldworkers reported that even by the end of 1964, whenever they seemed to be making progress, "every time some violent reaction from the white community unfurls to slow down our activity."[57]

The fragile foundation of the movement was exposed in December 1963, when no local blacks attended mass meetings after Daniels's house was bombed. "In other words," three fieldworkers concluded after one year of canvassing, "the new incident of violence has left us with the same really committed people who have been with us consistently from the beginning. It has retrenched the idea that there is nothing the Negro can do against the power of the white man."[58] As early as the summer of 1963, staff workers admitted that they had made little impression on rural southwest Georgia and decided to undertake a fundamental review of their approach to Lee and Terrell Counties.

The Development of Protest in Americus

Instead, the project's major breakthrough occurred in Sumter County, which had never been one of the initial target areas. When Ralph Allen, Don Harris, and John Perdew arrived in Sumter in February 1963, it was with the primary intention of community organizing and voter registration. The fieldworkers initially spoke at local churches and befriended high school students at Weston's Soda Shop in Americus, the county seat. By July, however, SNCC workers spearheaded a direct action protest. Hundreds of marchers, mostly students, demonstrated at the reneged promise of the local movie theater to desegregate. The resulting arrests sparked a school boycott by over two thousand black teenagers. One week after the boycott, SNCC workers found their names on the front pages of the *Washington Post* and *New York Times* and themselves in jail on the charge of insurrection, a charge that carried the death penalty under Georgia's 1871 Anti-Treason Act.[59]

This media attention was heightened because the students were from so-called respectable northern universities. The three SNCC workers were joined in jail by local CORE agricultural worker Zev Aeloney.[60] Students from Harris's home university of Rutgers raised over $1,000 for the NAACP Legal Defense Fund which was supporting the so-called Americus Four. Congressmen from a host of northern states, and even Mississippi, asked the Justice Department to investigate the insurrection charges.[61]

As in Lee and Terrell, the direct action protests quickly collapsed in the face of firm repression. The Americus Four were held until November, and even after their release Allen was charged with assault with intent to murder a policeman. The *New York Times* reported that the first marches of 1963 were "all but crushed by the use of the law." Harris, Perdew, and Allen were not replaced for three weeks. During that time, demonstrations had dissipated after several violent beatings and the lengthy imprisonment of persistent marchers. "As a result," fieldworkers concluded in September 1963, "the many big and little pieces of the movement drifted apart and a lot was lost in the immediate effect of the August demonstrations and in the long-range strength of the movement in Americus."[62]

SNCC workers also acknowledged that they were ill prepared for the arrests of the Americus Four. The charismatic leadership of Don Harris was not matched by a concomitant broad organizational base, so the incarceration of the Americus Four dealt a shattering blow to the local movement. Harris's successors in Americus reluctantly, but unanimously, criticized him when they evaluated the state of the project. We "feel that the responsibility for the present situation lies partly if not wholly in Don's negligence," wrote David Bell and Bob Mants in September 1963. "In allowing the Sumter County movement to depend on him, he allowed the potential leadership within the community to remain dormant. . . . Now with Don removed from the scene, the leaders are running around like chickens with their heads cut off wondering what to do next."[63]

The collapse of the demonstrations also exposed conflicts within the project. Even before the summer marches, Americus fieldworkers had privately expressed annoyance when Sherrod had recalled them to protest in Albany, where they were consequently held in jail, when "we had begun to think about organizing demonstrations here." After the arrest of the Americus Four, Mants and Bell sought to organize a rally at nearby Andersonville to maintain the momentum, but they found that most of the Albany staff were unconcerned, "busy doing nothing," and claimed to have no time to help. "After listening to that crap," recorded Mants, both he and Bell "walked out, disgusted, disappointed and angry." Although the existence of internal project divisions could be masked, the effects of the lack of support could not as the rally had to be canceled. "The thing that bothered me most," Mants concluded, was, "what do we tell the people of Americus?" In the event, Bell's attempts to explain the cancellation at a mass meeting met with "sh's and boos."[64]

Nonetheless, whereas involvement in the Lee and Terrell movements virtually disintegrated in reaction to white violence, both students and adults in Americus continued to participate in voter registration and education campaigns. Mass meetings justified their name as up to five hundred people met monthly. Bloc canvassing and regular citizenship schools led to the registration of over two thousand black voters by the end of 1965.[65] During the summer of 1965, demonstrations resumed on a larger scale than in 1963.

In many ways, the emergence of an active movement in Sumter County rather than Lee or Terrell showed that SNCC was still struggling to adapt to a rural environment. Whereas Terrell and Lee Counties were principally rural, over half of Sumter County's population was concentrated in the county seat of Americus. With over thirteen thousand inhabitants, the majority of whom were black, Americus's population alone outnumbered the total population of either Lee or Terrell County.[66] In many ways, the Americus movement followed the pattern of direct action typical of other urban areas in the South, rather than forming a prototype for rural protest. The field reports of SNCC workers who did venture into Americus's rural hinterland voiced the same frustrations as those from Lee and Terrell.

Therefore, the Sumter County movement, based in Americus, became crucial to the wider Southwest Georgia Project. In his overview of the various county projects during the summer of 1963, Ralph Allen noted that "Sumter County has a little story to it that sets it off from all the others." "These are the most amazing people we deal with," Charles Sherrod concurred. "Nothing can defeat them ... they turn out every week in large numbers. This week we had an overflow crowd and we were late. They were there as always." The Sumter movement provided a second, and final, opportunity for a successful urban bridgehead into the region after the demonstrations in Albany failed to force concessions from the city. After the frustration in Lee and Terrell Counties, the Sumter movement also became the flagship protest for the whole project. John Churchville, who was based in Lee County, conceded that "the people in Sumter are putting us folks in the other counties to shame."[67] Although fieldworkers visited twelve counties during 1963 and 1964, it was Americus that formed the vanguard behind which the wider project hoped to follow.

The fact that the county contained a city was unusual for the region. *Newsweek* reporter Marshall Frady remarked that "Americus had the appearance of having been abruptly plopped down intact, out of nowhere, into the negligibly inhabited spaces of south Georgia." Simply because it was a sizable town, though, did not make Americus atypically progressive. Frady thought that the city had a depressed air, reflected in the fact that "the number of suicides in Americus had always been extravagantly disproportionate to the population." For Don Harris, Americus was "a shitty, terrible little town out in the middle of the country."[68]

The urbanized nature of Sumter County did not engender a more moderate racial climate than that found elsewhere in the region. Claude Sitton reported that local sheriff Fred Chappell "was beyond all question the worst southern sheriff I have seen in my life." John Barnum reflected that "anything you can think of that has been done to the Negro anywhere—murder, rape, exploitation—it's been done here in Sumter County." In fact, the county seat of Americus proved to be the linchpin of Sumter's racial mores. Frady concluded that "intimidation pervades every corner of the community." Frady noted that white landlords dealt with nonpayment of rent in converted chicken-shed apartments by "removing the front door from the delin-quents' quarters; one winter a child was found in these dwellings frozen to death." Reflecting on business communities in Georgia, Frances Pauley concluded that in Americus, "they would rather have had their banks and businesses fail than to deseg-regate their town." Whereas business leaders in most Georgia cities sought to mollify protesters at the very least, the 1963 president of Americus's Chamber of Commerce rebuffed calls for a biracial committee with a bemused "what the hell for?"[69]

Organized racial brutality in Americus was on a par with the worst in the Deep South. *Newsweek* recorded that "in the South's gazetteer of racial crucibles, the name Americus has a special viciousness of its own." Police Chief Ross Chambliss's special corps of "blue angels" was widely feared within Americus's black community. Bar-num complained to reporters that during the 1963 marches "officers started blud-geoning groups of boys and girls with clubs and cattle prodders." Ralph Allen and John Perdew were beaten over the head and had their hair shaved, local activist James Brown was fatally shot in the back of the neck, and an innocent bystander, James Williams, had both legs deliberately broken. After the marches, students were held in jails described by SNCC activists as animal cages. In one of the worst cases, twenty preteenage girls were held for six weeks in a cell the size of a classroom during the sweltering heat of the summer. Both toilets were stopped up and food consisted of four cold hamburgers a day for each girl.[70]

Indeed, SNCC activists had arrived at a town that had already demonstrated its bellicose attitude to any form of racial change. In 1942, Baptist minister Clarence Jordan had founded Koinonia, a Christian interracial farming community eight miles east of the city.[71] A Ku Klux Klan terror campaign of bombing and sabotage, starting in the summer of 1956, attracted so much attention that clergymen from across the country volunteered to patrol Koinonia's grounds.[72] In July, a dynamite attack destroyed Koinonia's roadside market. Six months later, vandals chopped down over three hundred fruit trees. The Jordans sent their fourteen-year-old son, Jim, to friends in North Dakota after he was attacked in school. Meanwhile, Americus's business elite closed down Koinonia's credit and trading contacts with the city. One company that initially continued to trade with Koinonia was bombed.[73] A committee of ten leading citizens reinforced the message to Jordan in person. Claiming that Koinonia had "created hatred, bitterness and every emotion that is contrary to my concept of Christianity," the committee spokesman expressed the "hope [that] the Lord will tell you that maybe you can do him more good . . . in some other place than here." The stubborn survival of Koinonia was a continued irritant to the city. As the *Greensboro Daily News* perceptively noted, the survival of Koinonia represented "a thorn of bitterness which had never been plucked."[74]

Although Americus was a town firmly rooted in the customs of its region, the relative size of the city had subtle yet important implications for the development of the project. Staff workers reported that blacks could register in Americus, albeit with some difficulties, which allowed SNCC campaigns to retain some momentum. The contrast with Terrell County was displayed most vividly at Americus High School, where the principal held voter registration meetings with the full backing of the mayor. The principal told SNCC workers that the mayor "sees need of colored citizens." Similarly, the segregationist attitude of the Chamber of Commerce stopped short of racial vindictiveness. For example, the Chamber supported the creation of an industrial corporation headed by blacks to alleviate unemployment.[75]

The size of Americus relative to the region allowed the emergence of an indigenous group of black leaders independent from white economic control. These included the major church leaders, such as Rev. R. L. Freeman and Rev. J. R. Campbell, who were free from the overwhelming pressure faced by their counterparts in Lee and Terrell. Above all, leadership lay with a handful of concerned black business-men. John Barnum, a funeral director, was reputed to be the richest black man in the region. According to one SNCC worker, Barnum also owned "the most fabulous house [I have seen] since I came to Georgia." His wife, Mabel, was widely regarded as the mother of the movement in Americus, their home was open to the SNCC workers, and both Barnum and his children suffered arrest.[76]

The presence of Koinonia also benefited staff workers because it provided a base that was a relatively safe haven and a center for staff training. In June 1963, for example, Koinonia hosted the orientation of twenty project workers. At a less quan-tifiable level, the survival of Koinonia in the face of the 1957 terror provided an inspiration for blacks just as much as it was an irritant to white supremacists. "When people saw that little group wasn't going to let the Klan run them off, they knew from that time on that you don't have to be scared of the Klan," Mabel Barnum told reporters. Sherrod concurred, noting that "much of the spade work has already been done by the Koinonia farm people . . . this is a good start even if it is emblazoned with bullet fringes."[77]

Above all, it was the presence and attitude of local high school students that fueled the movement. The *Southern Patriot* noted that in Americus "local teenagers were the first to respond and in the early demonstrations carried it almost alone." Students at Americus High School later recalled that the demonstrations in Greensboro, Atlanta, and Savannah had inspired their own involvement. This impetus had been harnessed when a core group of a dozen students, including future local leader Sammy Mahone, had participated in the Albany movement.[78]

The students provided all the initial manpower. The marches of 1963 consisted almost entirely of school members, and over two thousand students participated in the school boycott. Local students Sammy Mahone and Collins Maghee established a monthly newsletter, the *Voice of Americus,* which included news from across the country as well as the southwest Georgia region.[79] Students also accompanied staff workers in the less glamorous tasks of rural networking and organizing throughout Sumter County. Typically, five students would join two SNCC members in the shanties along the roads leading out of town.[80]

Students remained the driving force behind continued protest. Don Harris re-ported in early 1964 that student restlessness meant that direct action protest was once again imminent. The typical complaint, Harris concluded, was, "When can we start demonstrations again? I'm sick of this damn place." Such tension inevitably escalated at the beginning of each summer break. "It's summer again," commented a

Voice of Americus editorial in 1964, "students are out of school, the weather's hot and everyone is expecting something to happen in our civil rights movement." The demonstrations of 1963 and 1965 erupted within weeks after the beginning of the summer vacation.[81]

While Americus provided a more fertile context for protest than Lee and Terrell, the SNCC workers in Americus also proved to be an unusually gifted team. Later fieldworkers in Americus agreed that Don Harris in particular "developed a tremendous fellowship and is thought of as a quasi-saint."[82] Ralph Allen became such a favorite son of Carolyn Daniels that his successors resented the comparison, while John Perdew's commitment to integrating into the community was sealed with his marriage to student protester Amanda Bowens.

The Americus team also used the chastening experiences of 1963 to conduct a valuable reassessment of the strategy of community organizing. "Americus has not yet reached its potential," Allen and Harris suggested after their release. "There are many resources we are just beginning to tap . . . some still untouched." Primarily, these untapped resources included specific groups within the adult community. During the fall of 1963, SNCC workers persuaded the existing black ministerial alliance to support the movement more directly. Fieldworkers began dialogue with existing community groups, noting that "there are a few local Negro organizations in Americus whose leaders . . . will at least talk to some people about going to register."[83]

SNCC workers in Americus developed a broader attack on the problem of economic discrimination. Unlike their counterparts in Savannah and Atlanta, blacks in Americus lacked the financial muscle to bring concerted pressure against the white community. Attempts at a downtown boycott proved to be ineffectual, not least because the economic power in Americus was concentrated in the hands of the committed segregationist and businessman Charles Wheatley. Described by SNCC as a "true monopolist," Wheatley owned the city hospital, bus station, largest factory, and four of the five supermarkets, and his wealth extended into enterprises not dependent on downtown sales.[84]

Nevertheless, attempts to address specific economic issues did bring tangible, albeit piecemeal, economic gains. John Perdew arranged a meeting in Washington between the vice-presidents of Americus's largest employer, the Manhattan Shirt Company, and representatives of the Amalgamated Clothing workers. With SNCC observers present, the Manhattan Shirt Company finalized plans to contract and train black female workers as seamstresses. Similarly, SNCC successfully used economic concerns to draw female domestic workers into the movement. Initially, project workers circulated over six hundred leaflets emblazoned with the promise that "together Maids in Americus WILL WIN the battle for decent wages." By rotating those on strike so that their fellow maids could support them financially, domestic workers reportedly received their hoped-for pay increase.[85]

Although the movement in Americus developed a broader base of support within the local black community, it was still far from universal by 1965. Field reports divided the black leaders in Americus almost equally into movement sympathizers and "Uncle Toms," "Aunt Nellies," and "Rev." or "Dr. Thomases." Allen noted with frustration that "one Negro businessman, owner of several 'colored' establishments, refuses to allow members to patronize his restaurant, pool hall or liquor store, insisting that 'I don't want no stinking niggers.'" The majority of the ministerial alliance, including the pastor of the largest church in Americus, refused to host mass meetings. Other, seemingly more maverick personalities refused to take any side. One woman not only refused police calls to shut her restaurant by pointing a gun at the marshal and "gave them hell, lip for lip," one report noted, "but she refuses to serve movement faithfuls" because she would lose her beer license.[86]

Even so, by the time direct action protest again engulfed Americus in 1965, the local movement had clearly emerged as by far the most deep-rooted community protest within the Southwest Georgia Project. As the *Southern Patriot* suggested at the end of 1964, "the continuing militancy of the Americus movement may reflect what it has already 'overcome.'" In many ways, the movement was far more comparable to some of Georgia's urban protests, with its broad base of support and diverse range of tactics. It seemed that if the project was to establish a beachhead in the region, Americus presented the ideal opportunity.[87]

The Collapse of Protest in Americus

The community organizing during 1963–64 laid the platform for a long, hot summer of confrontational demonstrations during 1965. As in 1963, the citywide protest of 1965 was not planned but provoked by unforeseen racial incidents. On 9 March, John Barnum, the local movement treasurer, was imprisoned on the charge of drunk driving. To protest his innocence, Barnum burned his mattress, only to be convicted of arson, leading to a four-month sentence and the threat of the notorious chain gang. Exactly one month later, outspoken high school student leaders Alex Brown and Robertina Freeman were arrested on a charge of fornication in a public park in a gesture widely interpreted as an attempt to exclude them from the movement.[88] Because both students were among the many on probation for their 1963 arrests, Brown and Freeman were sent away to the Georgia Reform School for five and three years respectively.[89]

The catalyst that finally set off the summer demonstrations was the arrest of four local women, including a Spelman graduate, Mary Bell, for refusing to stand in a segregated line during the election for justice of the peace on Tuesday, 20 June. Mary Bell was also one of the six candidates. The women refused to post $1,000 bond until all the charges against them were dropped and would not compromise with the "same men who in the summer of 1963 participated in brutalizing heads and bodies of black brothers and sisters."[90] The following day, twenty-five people marched in protest. Demonstrations escalated when a team of SCLC staff led by Hosea Williams arrived in Americus to fan the flames of confrontation in order to pressure Congress to pass the Voting Rights Bill.[91] By the weekend, the marches had swelled to almost eight hundred people. Protesters called for the release of the women, police protection, a rerun of the election, Saturday opening for registration, and a biracial committee to solve the impending racial crisis.[92]

The summer movement of 1965 was qualitatively different from its predecessor in 1963. Despite all the staff changes, SNCC project workers had developed a local leadership able to continue the protest after the first round of arrests. SNCC leaders had also developed the infrastructure to harness the new enthusiasm, as more than fifteen hundred new voters were registered during the summer of 1965 after the passage of the Voting Rights Act on 7 August. Dick Gregory, a high-profile SNCC supporter who flew in to help the voting drive, told local activists, "Let's get every-one registered. If your grandma won't come, hide her snuff and tear up her pension."[93] The project had learned from 1963, too, immediately sending in staff workers to support the Sumter County team.

The summer demonstrations failed, however, because the white establishment still refused to accept the most minimal changes to supremacist customs, even in the face of local pressure and national attention. Mayor T. Griffin Walker insisted that he would allow a biracial committee only if he appointed all the members. "The chasm between the races was more obvious in Americus than other southern towns," Frady reported, "because the failure of the white community has been greater."[94] If the development of the movement had owed much to the exceptional urban context of Americus, the eventual failure to force concessions from the city government owed everything to the prevalence of the region's white supremacy.

As in Lee and Terrell Counties, the durability of the local protest had lessened the extent of officially sanctioned racial violence. As the *Southern Patriot* noted, "Police who cracked heads during 1963 demonstrations were much more restrained in 1965." As in Albany, however, the subsequent nonviolent but intransigent official resistance proved to be an even more formidable obstacle to effective protest. Perdew believed that "the struggle in Americus does not involve complete resistance to Negro voter registration, lynchings, constant bombings and harassment of civil rights workers, rabid legislatures or nigger-hating" governors, as in Alabama or Mississippi, "but otherwise it is hard to see the difference." Perdew continued that "the more moderate the front presented . . . the more bitter the struggle." [95]

The exception to such intransigent resistance was personified in the story of Warren Fortson, the county attorney. Marshall Frady described Fortson as a "heavy bearish man, usually a bit tousled and crinkled in the heat, with a bland full-moon face, a perfectly circular retreating hairline and eyes narrowed to a thin squint behind black framed glasses. But more than anything else, there was about him an essential quality of mildness." Fortson represented Robertina Freeman and Alex Brown and became the leading voice seeking to accommodate with black protesters. In many ways, Fortson was an unlikely advocate of racial change. Having grown up in the rural black belt, Fortson later remembered that he shared the region's view of white supremacy. He was a member of the local country club, Rotary Club, and school board. His brother Ben Fortson was secretary of state during the supremacist state governments of the 1950s and supported moves to restrict black voting. For Warren Fortson, however, a dilemma arose when he realized that white supremacy impinged on basic human and legal rights. After he saw the local prison and the treatment of the teenage girls in 1963, Fortson's commitment to white supremacy at all costs wavered. "The idea that something like this could go on, not way out in the woods somewhere, but actually right here in the stark middle of the town . . . that's when I decided that nothing like that was ever going to happen again in Americus if I could help it." [96]

As a result, Fortson organized a tour by a busload of the town's civic leaders through the black neighborhood, during which "a burly businessman suddenly bolted out of one hovel, snatched his collar open, and vomited in the front yard." Initially, Fortson's moderating influence reaped dividends. At his urging, the school board faced up to the inevitability of federal insistence on integration and proposed a twelve-grade desegregation of the local schools, one of the rare instances of immediate full integration in the whole of Georgia. Sumter County also established an

Economic Opportunity Authority in February 1964, with a steering committee divided equally between eleven black members and eleven white members.[97]

By 1965, Fortson's goal of circumventing the crucible of bitter racial division seemed attainable. Even though he represented the students charged with fornication, Fortson retained sufficient credibility among the white city fathers to try to effect a moderate response. A former neighbor, who was also a leader of the John Birch Society, telephoned the Fortsons with a somewhat drunken message of support: "We might disagree, but we've known each other six years. Why, yawl's dogs used to bite my children." One city councillor even admitted privately that a "lot of times he'd gotten the feeling himself deep down that nigras weren't really being treated fair at all."[98]

As the racial crisis intensified, Fortson, with the help of Rev. Campbell, led a secret delegation of twenty-five leading businessmen to a mass meeting. Although Fortson overstated the fact when he claimed later that the remarkable meeting represented "something absolutely unheard of in the South," it certainly was true that such a meeting was unique in Americus or southwest Georgia. In response to the demands of the black leadership, the delegation offered to put up bond money for every demonstrator who had been arrested and to form an informal biracial committee. After the meeting, Fortson was convinced that his gambit had successfully divided the moderate and extreme sections of the black community. "We had them licked," he noted privately.[99]

If it is possible to say that the failure of the Americus movement turned on a single event, it was at the collapse of the dialogue between racial leaders. Crucially, the white community did get to hear of the meeting, and the city was in an uproar. A combination of delays in the agreed press release and, ironically, the betrayal of the meeting by the visiting SCLC activist Ben Van Clark to the local media, led to a public meeting where the vociferous conservatives took over. "Then we'd lost everything," Fortson concluded, "and the demonstrations really began."[100]

For Fortson himself, the ensuing drama proved to be a personal tragedy. Within days, he was relieved of his position as county attorney. His proposals for a biracial committee were rejected by both sides. At the same time, Fortson found himself isolated from all local institutions, including the school board and his church. Within weeks, he fled with his family to Atlanta. "It was as if we didn't exist any more," Mrs. Fortson explained to reporters later. Ralph McGill reported that the hounding out of a previously respected white official was unique in the South: "The Devil has just made Jesus look bad in Americus. The Devil won hands down. Here's a story that hurts more than violence. Murder, beatings, shootings—all these come and go." [101]

However, it was precisely the murder, beatings, and shootings rather than Fortson's exile that left the biggest scar in the city. When the local protest failed to wring sufficient concessions from the city government, the demonstrations moved beyond nonviolence. In part, this was because SCLC workers tried to intensify demonstrations. In a copycat of protest in Savannah, SCLC staffers led nighttime rallies and marches. At one mass meeting, Willie Ricks, who later coined the slogan "Black Power," told the crowd to "go out and get yourselves some guns." The tactics and the perceived arrogance of the visiting activists alienated both the southwest Georgia team and many of the local black community leaders. The *Wall Street Journal* quoted Hosea Williams as saying, "They need us more than we need them. We can bring the press with us and they can't." [102]

As in 1963, the national media spotlight fell on the demonstrations in Americus. But in 1965, media attention focused on the murder of a young white man, a story in contradistinction to the usual white supremacist violence in southern towns. During the early evening of 28 July, a gang of white youths threw rocks at passing cars a few hundred yards away from a demonstration. Shortly afterward, shots were fired from a passing car in retaliation. Andrew Whatley, a twenty-one-year-old marine recruit, was killed by two bullets that hit him "right between the eyes." Witnesses insisted that Whatley was an innocent bystander, returning from his job as a projectionist at a drive-in movie theater. [103]

In some ways, the Americus movement provided a case study in the argument raging within SNCC by 1965 over the efficacy of nonviolence. Although nonviolence had failed to force significant progress, racial violence culminating in the murder of Andrew Whatley provoked a reaction unprecedented even in southwest Georgia, which presaged the destruction of the local movement. The *Wall Street Journal* recorded that in the aftermath of the murder, pistols were selling like "hot cakes" among the white community. Incidents of racial violence by roving gangs of white hoodlums proliferated and went unpunished. In the week after the murder, more than six hundred members of the Klan and hundreds more sympathizers marched in the streets surrounding the county courthouse. During the same week, a former Georgia legislator, J. W. Sewell, was charged with attacking six voter registration workers with a cement block and a stick. On 31 July, county welfare officials announced that they were going to halt work in "tense areas." The officials insisted that "it just so happens that right now the tense areas of the city are Negro areas." [104]

Meanwhile, the degeneration of protest into violence undercut the project's authority. Local SNCC leaders lost control of the demonstrations and despaired of the racial violence. Randy Battle actually tried to stop night marches by sitting down in the street. Dick Gregory reminded crowds that "we got this bill through by throwing bricks—but it stands for one man one vote—not one man one brick." SCLC staffers admitted to Hosea Williams that "SNCC has completely pulled out . . . they will fight us all the way in Americus." Even Williams, who had earned a reputation as the most bellicose member of the SCLC staff, conceded that Americus had turned into a "helluva mess." [105]

The demonstrations dissipated in the face of retaliatory violence and the uncompromising stance of the city government. Locally, the momentum for mass demonstrations was lost for good. "Americus is the same as it was last summer," Rev. Campbell told reporters in 1966. One year after the long, hot summer, no biracial committee had been established and Saturday registration was still not forthcoming. Although two black policemen were appointed, they were chosen by the city government. The policemen's subsequent rough behavior outraged Americus's black community.[106]

The lack of concessions from the city government meant that some local students were determined to resume protest in 1966. But the summer of 1965 had rendered any new sustained protest untenable. "We aren't satisfied now but we got to rest. I'm so tired of it," Campbell concluded. "The majority of the adults—the old people—is very tired." After 1965, most of the SNCC staff members left Americus. Local student leaders were forced to leave the city when they left school because black unemployment had risen to 20 percent by 1965. As Sammy Mahone noted in the *Voice of Americus*, "It's hardly worth looking for a job when all you can find is work for long hours and $24 a week." [107]

SCLC workers believed that, at a national level, the struggle in Americus, coupled with the media coverage of the death of Andrew Whatley, had some bearing on the passage of the Voting Rights Act of 1965. But the failure of the movement to effect significant racial change in Americus had direct, catastrophic consequences for the wider movement in southwest Georgia. The initial hope had been to establish Americus as the beachhead into the region and to set Sumter as an example for southwest Georgia in community organizing and voter registration. SNCC activism in Americus had escalated beyond voter registration into a community-wide confrontation. Yet the only example it gave in 1963, and again in 1965, was that the regional racial mores could withstand the concerted efforts of an outside organization even in the glare of national publicity. As Perdew had predicted in 1963, "if we fail the movement can degenerate, feeding upon itself and doing more harm than good for the goals of SNCC."[108]

The Southwest Georgia Project Plods On

After SNCC failed to make a breakthrough in Americus, it was little surprise that the project made no impression when it moved into Baker County in 1965. Back in 1963, Sherrod had explained to the head office that "we feel Baker should be given more time . . . it is the real symbol of resistance to voter registration in S. W. Ga., more so than Terrell." When project workers entered Baker County in July 1965, they admitted that previously "fear had kept the movement out of this county."[109]

Baker County's sheriff L. Warren "Gator" Johnson, who succeeded Claude Screws, was exceptional even among the sheriffs of rural southwest Georgia for his acts of racial violence. James Forman observed that "Baker is said to be worse in police brutality and judicial injustice than the well-known Terrell County." By 1965, Johnson had allegedly been responsible for at least four murders, while each of his three assistants, all of whom were related to Johnson, had killed at least one black man.[110] Since the rise to prominence of Martin Luther King Jr., Johnson's energies had been concentrated on rooting out any hint of protest locally.

Baker County also provided the most extreme example of rural poverty and white economic control in the region. According to federal government statistics, Baker was one of the two poorest counties in Georgia and the twenty-seventh poorest county in the whole of America. "On the surface," a project review concluded, "Baker County appears isolated from the modern world." In fact, economic control was more akin to economic imperialism because the majority of land, and consequently labor, was under the control of four major plantations owned by absentee landlords. The major landholder was Robert Woodruff of Atlanta, who delegated the workings of the plantation to county managers well versed in Baker's racial mores.[111]

Furthermore, Baker County officials pioneered legal attempts to resist racial change. During the summer of 1965, the Board of Education accepted only 7 of 165 applicants under a freedom of choice plan designed to minimize the effects of school desegregation. Under the plan, all students were allowed to choose which school they wanted to attend, but the local board decided which candidates were suitable to transfer. The plan had been initiated to circumvent the possibility of the U.S.

Department of Health, Education and Welfare (HEW) withholding a prospective federal grant of $70,000. And as the *New York Times* perceptively noted, "white residents of Baker County consider it a major concession that seven Negroes were accepted into a heretofore white school." [112]

As often happened in Baker County, however, violence reinforced white supremacy. Within a week, four of the first group of black children to transfer schools suffered knife attacks and returned to their all-black schools, too terrified even to notify the SNCC workers. Their withdrawal, according to Rev. Sam Wells of Albany, put a "black mask upon the community." Two weeks later, a mob of twenty local whites built a fire near SNCC's new so-called Freedom Center, "yelling about barbecuing niggers." One incredulous SNCC worker reported that the mob was "even saying that Johnson was letting Negroes take over Baker County." In fact, the county police had started to use unmarked patrol cars in an attempt to harass SNCC workers to leave the county. [113]

Within months, project staff unanimously admitted defeat. Before entering the county, Sherrod believed that the battle for people's minds was ultimately more important than the battle for the vote. In Baker County, however, the battle for the vote was inextricably linked with the psychological battle. As staff members conceded in 1967, "Everyone feels that until you get Sheriff Johnson out of office, you haven't done a damned thing." [114]

Far from overturning the reputation of Baker County, therefore, the project's failure to make an impact merely served to confirm that the county was the symbol of white resistance to the racial changes sweeping the rest of the state and the South. But if Baker County stood out, it was merely the most extreme example of the entrenched white supremacy prevalent across the region. The project expanded into each of the twenty-three counties in southwest Georgia, but the subsequent struggles in each county demonstrated that the original problems facing staff workers in Lee and Terrell remained intractable.

To a large extent, the field reports from this expansion across the region resembled a catalog of violent attacks as SNCC workers entered each county. In Crisp County in 1966, for example, a white mob attacked a group of black teenagers as they swam in the state park while state troopers looked on. Three years later, the movement reached Sylvester, Worth County. Local blacks marched with Ralph Abernathy, Martin Luther King's successor, in response to the imprisonment for delinquency of two of the first girls to transfer schools. The elder girl, aged fourteen, was accused of using the words "damn" and "godamn." As the *Atlanta Inquirer* commented, "Few youngsters go to jail for that." In this instance, white supremacists refrained from physically assaulting the marchers. Instead, they placed numerous beehives along the route, each one stirred up by fire as marchers passed by. The attendant state and local policemen, newspapers reported, did not see the incident.[115]

Each county had its own story to tell, but each was simply a variation on the regional theme. In general, schools consistently provided the first toehold for SNCC workers. In many counties, project workers provoked school boycotts. But often, as in the case of Moultrie, Colquitt County, school boycotts represented the culmination rather than the beginning of local protest. Moreover, school boycotts were increasingly in protest at the poor equipment in the overwhelmingly black schools rather than a push for full integration.[116]

As in Lee and Terrell, voting registration remained piecemeal and sporadic. In the months leading up to the congressional elections of 1964, Albany lawyer C. B. King's candidacy in Georgia's third congressional district sparked the largest canvassing campaign yet seen in the region, adding over two and a half thousand registered black voters from twenty counties. Still, this remained less than 20 percent of the potential black vote and represented the apogee of registration rather than the springboard for future campaigns.[117]

Sherrod regularly insisted that statistics told only part of the story. "We count success," he reminded staff members, "by the number of minds freed to think as they will and act in proportion to their willingness to suffer." But even using these criteria, there was little success to count. As staff worker Robert McClary noted in Warwick, Cuthbert County, at the end of 1967, "What is so striking is the great number of Negroes who simply do not believe they can do anything other than what the white man wants them to do."[118]

Actually, active local movements after 1965, such as they were, often developed independently of SNCC's project. "The strongest leadership of any black-belt county was in Worth County," fieldworkers concluded in 1965, where thirty farmers got together on their own and formed a local improvement league and then invited SNCC to join them. In Thomas County, staff workers encountered a long-established NAACP, which had helped influence the county seat of Thomasville to become the most liberal town in southwest Georgia. The local NAACP certainly "didn't want visiting students to rock the boat or hinder the biracial action on poverty." Meanwhile, the Nation of Islam bought fifteen hundred acres of farmland in southwest Georgia to ship vegetables, melons, and canned fruit to its members in Chicago and Detroit.[119]

The problems encountered by SNCC across the counties of southwest Georgia were the same as in Lee, Terrell, and rural Sumter writ large. SNCC workers continued to find it difficult to network with existing leadership. "There is no true leadership here" in Colquitt County, wrote Herman Kitchens in 1964. The county seat of Moultrie, Kitchens concluded, "is filled with toms and it is hard to get any kind of leadership going." Kitchens claimed that the local Voters League was paid for by white officials.[120] Staff still faced the problem of inadequate transport, having access to a maximum of two cars and occasionally the Albany freedom bus.

As in the cases of Lee, Terrell, and Sumter, the failure of the wider project led to regular reassessments. Increasingly, however, specific suggestions had developed into a flood of criticism about the very goals of the project. In February 1965, Kitchens argued that SNCC had done "more harm than good . . . only trying to meet immediate needs and not taking time out to evaluate the kinds of programs that can solve our problem." Randy Battle, who coordinated the project during 1967, believed that "no longer can it be a group of kids doing things because they are not going to put up with the kind of life they are living." Less reliance on students was especially important "as so many of those kids took the first opportunity to leave the region," Battle continued. "Now it has to be a group of people doing things because of their need to live."[121]

Staff members agreed that poverty was the root of the problem. In a widely circulated research pamphlet, Perdew concluded that "if you want to change things you have to look at who owns what, for businessmen are the ones who really swing the billyclubs." Staff members agreed that a full-scale attack on white economic supremacy was doomed to failure and that piecemeal attempts at improving black welfare provided the stepping-stones for community organizing. What was clear, however, was that the initial idea of an intercounty project, based on voter registration, simply did not work in practice. "We should get off this little wagon," wrote Perdew at the end of 1963, because the project is "simply too big for Sherrod to keep in his head."[122]

Meanwhile, the project gradually became estranged from SNCC leaders in the Atlanta office. The project had already asserted its independence when it had agreed to rescind its contract with the Voter Education Project in favor of initiating direct action protest. But it was the lack of support during the imprisonment of the Americus Four that had particularly exacerbated tensions with SNCC. From Americus, Mants and Bell fumed that "Atlanta had shown that they were not concerned about the [Andersonville] rally and for that matter, the Southwest Georgia Project." Americus staff workers felt that the Atlanta head office insisted that "you do it. We don't have time. Selma is our pet now." In his autobiography, James Forman argued that the pressure of Selma prevented him from visiting Americus but conceded it was a tactical mistake.[123]

To try to maintain the momentum begun in the summer of 1963, project staff had decided to return to their northern home cities to attract media attention about the plight of the Americus Four. After a meeting in Atlanta, however, the SNCC head office rejected the plan. "Atlanta doesn't care anymore," complained an increasingly exasperated Bob Mants. "The Southwest Georgia Project is a has-been project. A casket that carries around the living bodies of eight or nine people." Within a week of the Atlanta meeting, two of the field staff had resigned their positions.[124]

Project workers were also annoyed at some of the white northern students who were sent to southwest Georgia. This antipathy fueled a barely concealed loathing toward one female student sent to the project to file press reports to the Atlanta head office. In a passage burgeoning with expletives, one unnamed staff worker told the Atlanta office that "if you want a vague presence just to be there, to float around experiencing, then you can have her."[125]

The rift with the head office undermined the development of the wider project. Perdew reported the sense of isolation by the end of 1963. "We are unclear as to what the relationship between Atlanta and the various field projects is and what it should be," although he warned team members that "there's no sense at the same time in building up resentment toward Atlanta." For Perdew, this sense of isolation was all the more frustrating because "we could learn from swapping ideas and experiences ... what is happening in Savannah, Selma, Pine Bluff?" Even Don Harris, who remained committed to SNCC's authority, vented his anger after the supposedly brief transfer of Georgia fieldworkers to Selma in 1964. "Of course they got arrested," he wrote, "and the subsequent trials delayed their return." After SNCC moved its headquarters to Mississippi at the end of 1964, a full separation became inevitable.[126]

The separation was hastened as SNCC leadership adopted the ideology of Black Power under Stokeley Carmichael and voted to exclude all white students from the organization. Sherrod resigned from SNCC in 1966 after the central committee unanimously rejected his plan to bring more northern white students to the region. The Southwest Georgia Project disbanded to be replaced ostensibly by the Southwest Georgia Independent Voters Project, which still received intermittent grants from the Voter Education Project. Meanwhile, Sherrod and the remaining staff also channeled their energies into the New Communities Corporation that sought to address economic issues.[127]

In practice, the corporation lacked a coherent theme. Each county had its own particular preoccupation. Baker County workers concentrated on gaining support from the Ford Foundation. Lee and Terrell leaders hoped to develop a farming cooperative and a quilting and gardening program, not unlike other communities affiliated with the Federation of Southern Cooperatives, a poor people's technical assistance organization that Sherrod had cofounded. Sherrod himself proposed a lay training service center in Cordele to overcome what he described as the "embittered powerlessness of the Negro community." But workers in each county reached similar conclusions to the Baker County Committee, which noted in 1966 that, despite the best efforts of SNCC, "there is much to be done in Baker County." [128]

Some plans by their very nature linked particular groups across the counties. Frances Pauley helped to develop local branches of the federally funded Operation Headstart program, and Agnew James of Lee County acted as regional representative for the National Sharecroppers Organization. The project held meetings each Saturday in Albany, where local leaders across the region could discuss practical matters such as sharing fertilizer and learn about issues such as welfare and Medicare. Again Sherrod suggested innovative initiatives, particularly when he sought funding from various foundations for an "indigenous theater in the rural and semi-urban Negro communities of southwest Georgia." [129]

If the plans were initially incoherent, it was clear that black activism in southwest Georgia had developed into a new phase of the struggle for black equality. In 1968, the *Southwest Georgia Newsletter,* an outgrowth of the *Voice of Americus,* appositely summed up the aims of the new project in its first major editorial: "How the Southwest Georgia Project will transform 'Black Power' from a slogan into a program and from a program into some reality remains to be seen. The key to this puzzle lies in 'Community,' but the power to turn this key lies in many communities. We are now only learning the relevant questions to ask." [130]

In 1962, the Southwest Georgia Project had initiated a unique experiment in rural protest in Georgia but one that had failed to transform the region. Five years later, the twenty-three counties followed the pattern of rural and urban communities across the state, where black activists struggled with the puzzle of obtaining tangible benefits for their own community. The well-publicized direct action phase of the civil rights movement in Georgia came to an end with the collapse of the Southwest Georgia Project. For most communities in Georgia, however, as in the southwest black belt, the puzzle of how to achieve racial equality in practice was only just beginning.

6

Black Protest after the Federal Civil Rights Legislation of 1964–1965

A southern journalist, Hunter James, wrote in 1966 that in terms of race relations, "nobody could recognize Georgia as the state I had first known six years earlier."[1] Although James was based primarily in Atlanta, it was certainly true that the Federal Civil Rights Act of 1964 and Voting Rights Act of 1965 radically and irreversibly overturned Jim Crow across the whole of the state, not to say the South. The Civil Rights Act empowered the attorney general to ensure the end of discrimination in all places of public accommodation. Title VI of the Civil Rights Act authorized the Department of Health, Education and Welfare to withhold federal funds from any school districts that refused to integrate. The Voting Rights Act outlawed any attempts to restrict black voting, and crucially it empowered the attorney general to send federal voter registrars to areas covered by the legislation.[2]

In the political arena, the Voting Rights Act seemed to signal the end of "the rule of the rustics." By 1966, Georgia had seven black state senators, including Leroy Johnson, a founding member of Atlanta's Committee for Co-operative Action.

Across the nation, only Michigan and Illinois had more black senators. Grace Towns Hamilton became the first black woman to serve in a legislature in the Deep South.[3] In 1972, Andrew Young of the SCLC became the first elected black congressman from a southern state covered by the Voting Rights Act since Reconstruction. A year later, Maynard Jackson, the grandson of John Wesley Dobbs, was elected mayor of Atlanta.

The end of the rule of the rustics was most vividly exemplified in the unlikely visit of Herman Talmadge to the Atlanta Hungry Club on 5 January 1966. Twenty years previously, Talmadge had been the featured speaker at the celebration birth-day barbecue for Dr. Samuel Green, the Georgia Grand Dragon of the Ku Klux Klan. In 1949, Talmadge had implied in a radio broadcast that A. T. Walden was a Communist sympathizer after Walden supervised a suit to equalize school facilities in Irwin County. In 1955, Talmadge had launched his senatorial campaign with the publication of his book *You and Segregation,* which justified racial segregation as an act of obedience to God as well as on genetic, historical, and cultural grounds.[4]

At the Hungry Club, Talmadge publicly lauded his old-time enemy, the late A. T. Walden.[5] Offering himself as a candidate who sought "to represent all the people of Georgia," Talmadge expressed the hope that the era of race-baiting was over. If he was elected, Talmadge insisted that he would "appoint Negroes to high office" because "there are, in my judgement, outstanding Negroes qualified for appoint-ment now." The poignancy of the remarks was not lost on the chairman, who asked why the so-called integrationist Talmadge had not visited the Hungry Club previ-ously. "Because you never invited me," Talmadge replied to polite laughter. "Ne-groes did not forget the past," one reporter concluded, but the applauding audience of 250 "liked what he is saying now."[6] True to his word, during the ensuing decade as a senator, Talmadge appointed a black administrative assistant and approved grants for legal cases against discrimination. He was even photographed kissing black babies on the campaign trail.[7]

If some politicians were mouthing conciliatory platitudes, however, the federal acts did not swiftly usher in a complete revolution in race relations in Georgia. Although black voter registration increased, disproportionately few black Georgians were elected as public officials. If there was some grudging token integration in schools, the vast majority of children remained in segregated schools during the 1960s. And of course, the federal acts did not directly address issues such as poverty, unemployment, and discrimination in housing.

Meanwhile, opponents of integration retained their power, if not their unfettered supremacy. Within Georgia, the election of arch-segregationist Lester Maddox as governor in 1966, with only 4 percent of the black vote, highlighted the continued strength of resistance to racial equality.[8] During the early 1960s, Maddox had secured his segregationist reputation by refusing to allow any black customers to eat at his Pickrick restaurant in Atlanta. To make sure, Maddox kept an ax handle behind the counter in his shop. After the Civil Rights Act, Maddox chose to close his restaurant, and he sold his supply of ax handles to souvenir hunters. He was to sell over one hundred thousand in total. Maddox also organized Georgians Unwilling to Surrender to boycott any store that desegregated in response to a black boycott.[9] Such was Maddox's reputation that in an unprecedented move one Democratic state congressman, Charles Weltner, resigned from office in protest. According to Weltner, Maddox was "the one man in our state who exists as the very symbol of violence and oppression."[10]

For black Georgians, Maddox's election was another reminder that the struggle for equality was far from over. Alderman Q. V. Williamson, a member of ACCA, believed that "the election of Maddox gave the knuckle-headed white people of Georgia the license to do anything they wanted to Negroes." Although this was something of an exaggeration after 1965, Williamson's fear of continued racial violence certainly seemed to be borne out in rural Georgia. In Griffin, Spalding County, the *Atlanta Inquirer* noted a rise in violent crimes against black residents. Alonzo C. Touchstone, who had first founded Griffin's NAACP chapter in 1945, observed that the situation had deteriorated markedly since Maddox's success at the polls.[11]

If the Civil Rights Acts did not end racial discrimination, however, they did mark the end of high-profile direct action campaigns against Jim Crow in the South. With the passage of federal legislation, the focus of the major civil rights organizations shifted from the battle against legal segregation to the wider issue of discrimination in practice. As William Chafe concluded, the federal acts marked "the end of one struggle, the beginning of another."[12]

For Martin Luther King Jr., this shift was reflected by a change from protests confronting segregation to organized strikes and demonstrations highlighting economic discrimination and deprivation.[13] In January 1965, for example, King picketed with strikers at the Scripto Plant in Atlanta in an ultimately successful demand for an equal pay raise for both the skilled and the predominantly black unskilled workforce.[14] King's concern with de facto discrimination also led to a changing geographical focus to the problems of the North. "Chicago is on fire with a nonviolent movement," King told an emergency meeting of SCLC's executive staff in August 1965. "They want us to come in September. We must not ignore their call."[15]

By contrast, SNCC and CORE adopted Black Power. The slogan was ambiguous, ranging from an emphasis on black community institutions to black nationalism and violence. For SNCC and CORE, Black Power meant the abandonment of the central tenets of the civil rights movement, the rejection of the philosophy of nonviolence and the goal of integration. In 1966, for example, in the wake of the riots in Los Angeles and Chicago, SNCC chairman Stokeley Carmichael addressed a cheering crowd from a parking lot at Morehouse College, denouncing the college's white trustees as thieves and urging students to relate to the ghettos.[16] Under the influence of SNCC workers in Atlanta, who developed more extreme ideas about racial separatism, the organization also voted in 1966 to expel white members from the ranks. In fact, by the end of 1966 both SNCC and CORE were heading into terminal decline, a process hastened by SNCC's brief alliance with the Black Panthers in early 1968.

For many commentators, the termination of SCLC's southern campaign and the rise of Black Power signaled the collapse of the national civil rights coalition. In a review of the civil rights movement at the end of 1966, a reporter for the *Los Angeles Times* argued that the movement in the South "was winding up this year in disarray." Certainly there was no repeat of the major set-piece confrontations in the South led by major protest organizations that had characterized the decade after Montgomery. Former SNCC president Atlantan John Lewis lamented in 1967 that "people just seem to have lost the desire and drive to demonstrate . . . they are tired and weary, weary of getting jailed and beaten when they protest and demonstrate." "Confused, divided and weary from battle fatigue," Fairclough observed in his history of SCLC, "the black movement in the South ground to a halt."[17]

State and local studies have demonstrated, however, that the South still witnessed active racial protest after 1965, even if it was rarely in the spotlight of media attention. Fairclough concluded that "the evidence of Louisiana contradicts the notion that the civil rights movement suddenly collapsed after Black Power supposedly split it asunder." As Steven Lawson commented, the civil rights movement evolved from seeking equality of opportunity to achieving equality of results.[18] John Dittmer observed that in Mississippi the movement continued in a new political form focusing on Lyndon Johnson's War on Poverty. Fairclough noted that in Louisiana, "if the civil rights movement disintegrated as a coherent national force, it survived, albeit in an attenuated form, in the states, cities and rural areas where blacks continued to struggle for jobs, integrated schools and political representation."[19]

In many ways, the civil rights movement in Georgia followed this pattern, with continuity of protest at the local level as much as change. In part, this was because

Black Power did not split the movement in Georgia asunder. SNCC's direct influence there was limited to Atlanta and the southwest region, and Sherrod distanced himself from SNCC after its adoption of Black Power. Undoubtedly there was support for Black Power in some of the urban slums. In 1967, one report on urban violence in Georgia concluded that there was "a hate-whitey condition prevalent." Carmichael's rhetoric also struck a chord on campuses. In 1968, Willie Ricks demanded that white students leave the hall at a lecture sponsored by Mercer's black student association, even though the meeting was funded by the university. Ricks, a close ally of Carmichael, told the audience that "the sisters haven't come all the way down here to entertain the white folks."[20] During the following year, a group of Morehouse students stormed a trustees' meeting and held the trustees hostage until the white trustees resigned and the remainder agreed to rename the university after Martin Luther King Jr. But even in this case the Student Government Association disassociated itself from the militant action "because it is false and not on our behalf," and a student vote rejected the concessions.[21]

There was also continuity of protest because local people, rather than major organizations, led protest in most communities across Georgia. After 1965, many of the leading activists in Georgia included luminaries of earlier local protests, including Carolyn Daniels in Terrell County, Leroy Johnson and Julian Bond in Atlanta, W. W. Law in Savannah, Bill Randall in Macon, and Julius Hope in Brunswick. For local leaders, most of whom had been active in civil rights protest for several years, the emphasis after 1965 was not to repudiate previous goals and tactics but to try to make rights real at the local level. Similarly, numerous SNCC workers continued to be active at the local level, even though they left the organization after SNCC adopted an extreme Black Power position. Prathia Hall, who had been involved in the Southwest Georgia Project, worked in the area of school integration. Lonnie King worked for the Department of Health, Education and Welfare in the area of school integration. After a hotly contested election, King subsequently became the president of the Atlanta branch of the NAACP in 1969.[22] Julian Bond and John Lewis, who had been president of SNCC, became involved in Atlanta politics.

The development of black protest in Georgia was certainly a case of evolution rather than revolution. Before the passage of the Voting Rights Act, the *Atlanta Inquirer* commented that "the civil rights struggle is now on a new level. Leading civil rights leaders realize that they are not now leading a protest movement but a political, social and economic movement."[23] In fact, community protest in Georgia had long included political, social, and economic issues. In southwest Georgia, Sherrod had sought to build black community institutions and local leadership networks. Across the state, voting registration had been an important part of the struggle for equality from the 1940s onward and had continued to be so during the early 1960s. In many towns, direct action protests had not simply focused on integration but had encompassed a range of economic issues. In Savannah, for example, downtown sit-ins had secured improved conditions of black hiring.

Continuation of Direct Action Protest

In many ways, the history of Georgia during the Black Power era suggests that local protest not only continued in an attenuated form but actually strengthened in the form more commonly associated with the early 1960s. The issues of voting, education, and integration remained salient in the years after the Civil Rights Acts. Moreover, local protest continued to take the form of community-wide, direct action campaigns. Rather than simply being the beginning of another struggle, it was also a continuation of the same struggle that had first flowered in Georgia at the start of the 1960s.

Immediately after the passage of the Civil Rights Act on 2 July 1964, existing urban movements in Georgia used the legislation to conclude their direct action campaigns to desegregate public facilities. In Albany, only two hours after President Johnson signed the bill, Nathaniel "Sprayman" Beech entered the Holiday Inn and sat down at the first table he saw. In Savannah, a number of biracial groups, drawn from the local NAACP and Human Relations Council, tested the compliance of motels and restaurants. In Rome, the local NAACP chose volunteers to integrate restaurants, movie theaters, and drive-in eating places.[24]

In Macon, two uniformed servicemen were among ten blacks arrested for trespassing after they attempted to wash their clothes at a segregated suburban Laundromat. Under the leadership of William Randall, and with some support from the business community to finance bond payments, the protests continued until the "white-only" signs were removed. Direct action protest against segregation continued even in Atlanta, Georgia's "city too busy to hate." The Civil Rights Act provided the basis for picketing and sit-ins in June 1967 at the Wren's Nest, a privately owned high-class restaurant. The protest was so overtly belligerent that one of the pickets, Eliza Paschall, was forced to resign from her post as chairperson of the recently formed Atlanta Community Relations Committee.[25]

Occasionally, such direct action protests encountered fierce resistance. Americus reaffirmed its white supremacist tradition when gangs of white youths attacked integrators testing recreational facilities. In 1968, Macon's Mayor "Machine Gun" Ronnie Thompson caused disbelief and consternation when he blocked a Memorial march after Martin Luther King's death with a tank across the main downtown street.[26] On the whole, however, cities that had experienced major movements before 1965 witnessed a relatively rapid transition away from segregation. Even Albany experienced minimal overt resistance to desegregation during 1964, as the mayor told reporters that he was powerless to resist in the face of federal law. Laurie Pritchett insisted that "we obey the laws but we would never have bowed to trouble-makers." Albany restored its bus service, which had been halted three years previously. Two weeks after the passage of the Civil Rights Act, Slater King announced the end of the boycotts in Albany.[27]

In Albany black activists were not the only ones who desegregated facilities. For the first few weeks after passage of the Civil Rights Act, white youths visited black pool halls in the Harlem district and laid bets on matches. Also in Harlem, a white drunk interrupted a meeting where a black leader was playing the guitar and singing freedom ballads. Seizing the microphone, the drunk told the crowd, "The bill a rights done been pass! We got a right. We gonna stay and we're gonna ask this kin' lady to sing 'This lil' light of mine' fo' the white folks of Albany, Georgia, who need it, God knows."[28]

In many of the smaller urban areas of the state, the federal acts of 1964 and 1965 actually provided the impulse for a first wave of direct action protests. For those towns and cities that had not experienced any active protest during the King years, the federal acts prompted a local beginning rather than an end to the struggle against segregation.

Although the NAACP had dwindled to only sixteen branches in Georgia by 1965, the active coastal branches of Savannah and Brunswick inspired and organized protests in the surrounding counties. In Effingham County, for example, Savannah leaders supervised a local protest for countywide desegregation. In Monroe, five members of the local youth council were arrested at Bolton's Restaurant on 3 August 1964. Savannah's Bobby Hill wired the U.S. Justice Department. Nearer Atlanta, the active NAACP chapter in Griffin, Spalding County, supervised demonstrations in June 1965, including over one hundred pickets and marchers at Pomora Products Plant, the city's major employer. By July 1965, all lunch counters in the town were desegregated despite the segregationist attitudes of local officials. Four years later, Griffin's NAACP chapter launched a movement "employing every honorable and legal method" to obtain the goals of desegregated recreational facilities, integrated government employment, and the use of courtesy titles in all official business.[29]

In southwest Georgia, SNCC expanded its protest into a further ten counties, even though each march or boycott was curtailed by violence. During the summer of 1967 in Sylvester, a group of young black men were threatened by local police when trying to buy tickets at the "whites only" window of the Capri Theatre and seeking to eat at Mammie's Kitchen. The ensuing desegregation suit, filed by eight local businessmen, successfully forced an end to segregation.[30]

The SCLC, however, became the driving force in the development of small town protests across Georgia after the Civil Rights Act. In many ways this was surprising, not least because King's own attention had become firmly fixed on economic issues, particularly in the slums of northern cities. Moreover, immediately after the Voting Rights Act, SCLC decided to concentrate its remaining southern staff on Alabama's "campaign for equal justice."[31] The only SCLC directive concerning Georgia was for its inclusion in the southwide 1965 Summer Community Organizing Project (SCOPE). Under the leadership of Hosea Williams, SCOPE was intended to repli- cate the Mississippi Freedom Summer by bringing northern white students to coun- ties in those southern states (particularly Georgia and Alabama) with the greatest levels of black disfranchisement.

Billed as "the most comprehensive voter registration project ever attempted in the South," SCOPE promised to "promote direct action as a means to political power."[32] In practice, SCOPE's impact on voter registration was negligible. Even the program's own claim (which was greatly inflated) to have registered twenty-six thousand new voters in Georgia represented only a modest increase.[33] Some of the SCOPE students even admitted to feeling that they were merely pawns between SCLC and local leaders. SCLC executive members Bayard Rustin and Stanley Levison agreed with Rev. F. R. Rowe of Fitzgerald when he described SCOPE as "the worst run program I have ever seen." Even the *Atlanta Inquirer* editorialized in October 1965 that "Hosea may need a rest—what about several weeks' rest in the Caribbean?"[34]

The public failure of SCOPE, however, obscured the unheralded and low-key work of the remaining staff members in Atlanta. As protests flared up across the state in the wake of the Civil Rights Act, local leaders often called in the remaining staff members in Atlanta to act as "hit and run" supervisors in precisely the same manner for which SCLC had previously been criticized. During the first years after the Civil Rights Act, SCLC fieldworkers became the spokesmen for a series of direct action local protests across the state.[35] In effect, Atlanta office staff members such as Willie Bolden, James Orange, Tyrone Brooks, Richard Boone, and Charlie Brown became a mobile cadre of protest leaders available for hire.

In Twiggs County in 1968, for example, black community leaders called for an end to educational and employment segregation. When Twiggs County officials refused to negotiate, local leaders invited SCLC workers to build a movement of mass marches. After ten days of demonstrations, the county commission agreed to hire a black deputy sheriff, relieve overcrowding on black bus services, and provide equal medical facilities. One black community leader told reporters from the *Atlanta Inquirer* that "the movement could not have succeeded without the help of the SCLC."[36]

One decade after the Civil Rights Act, direct action local campaigns were still emerging, for a variety of reasons, in increasingly smaller communities across the state. In Talbot County, east Georgia, in 1974, demonstrations began after a local policeman shot a black resident in the back. Georgia Council on Human Relations member Joe Hendricks called up his friend Will D. Campbell, a staff person of the Fellowship of Southern Churchmen, with the news that "the movement has finally made its way to Talbot County, Georgia." Campbell replied with some prescience, "Come to die?" After visiting Talbot County, Campbell recorded that "the movement had in fact arrived and in the same form as it had gone to Montgomery, Albany, St. Augustine, Birmingham and scores of other towns, cities and counties." With the support of SCLC, black community leaders led a direct action protest, which forced a biracial agreement providing for improved black hiring and a more progressive attitude toward voting registration and school integration.[37]

Like every community in Georgia, Talbot County had its own individual history of race relations. In 1974, local blacks still remembered that a partially blind, nameless preacher had visited the county in 1909 and had called on the sharecroppers to "declare their independence and be free, as he was free." In response, local whites formed a "committee of the people" instructed to flog the preacher. His host, one Carreker, shot a member of the committee before the preacher was bound and thrown off Talbotton bridge. Meanwhile, Carreker was taken from jail and lynched in the town square. "When the doors were opened it was the work of but a few minutes to get the Negro," the *Atlanta Constitution* recorded. "It was all done quietly and in perfect order." It was Carreker's grandson who was shot in the back in 1974. The subsequent demonstrations and negotiated agreement represented a second attempt to "declare their independence and be free" in Talbot County.[38]

In the state context, the noteworthy feature of the Talbot County campaign was that the demonstrations marked perhaps the final outpost of the civil rights movement in Georgia in its classic community-wide direct action form.[39] But by 1974 it was clearly out of date. The media ignored the protests. "A white officer shooting a black man is not news," one NBC producer told movement leaders. "It has lost its sexiness." The marching song of "No more Sheriff Hendricks over me" rang hollow, protesters admitted later, because Jeff Hendricks had never directly violated the Civil Rights Act of 1964. Above all, a direct action campaign against the local authorities seemed inappropriate. "I knew, and am certain that they knew," Campbell concluded later, "that a greater enemy is the corporate structures. And agribusiness, with its callous disregard for their lives or needs. But try substituting 'military-industrial complex,' 'corporate structure' or 'agribusiness' for 'Sheriff Hendricks' in the lyrics of the freedom song."[40]

Education

As with public accommodations, the struggle to secure full integration in education became a salient issue throughout Georgia after the Civil Rights Act. During the decade after *Brown*, less than one-third of 1 percent of Georgia's black children were educated in schools with white children. Across the state, desegregation was restricted to Georgia's largest towns. Only ten of Georgia's school systems, out of a total of nearly two hundred, had begun to desegregate.[41] And over 90 percent of all transferred school children were in Atlanta and Savannah.[42] After the Civil Rights Act, however, each school district had to face the issue of integration.

In theory, Title VI of the Civil Rights Act authorized the Department of Health, Education and Welfare to cut off federal funds for segregated schools and authorized the attorney general to act against systems unwilling to desegregate. Initially, the legislation seemed to have a decisive effect. The Georgia Board of Education signed a desegregation pledge in January 1965 to secure HEW funds worth $55 million. The board then urged all local school systems to submit desegregation plans by 15 May to prevent the federal government from cutting off funds. Only Taylor, Lincoln, and Sumter Counties refused to comply, Dawson and Forsyth Counties had no black schoolchildren, but fifteen counties did submit plans immediately and the remaining 170 school boards assured compliance.[43]

As was also the case with public accommodations, however, the federal legislation did not end the struggle for racial equality in education. Quite simply, Title VI did not lead to a swift desegregation of Georgia's public schools, let alone integration. If anything, the Civil Rights Act heightened opposition to school desegregation. Despite assurances of compliance, more than one hundred of Georgia's school districts remained completely segregated by the spring of 1967, and in at least fifty other districts over 98 percent of black children attended segregated schools. The *New South* pointed out in December 1966 that although Georgia had been "one of the most vocal states complaining about the over zealousness of the Federal Government, still over 95% [of black children] were in segregated schools." In 1966 a statewide committee was formed to fight the federal guidelines. In February 1967 the assistant U.S. commissioner of education, David Seeley, accused Georgia educators of "doing more to arouse hostility to federal school desegregation guidelines than those of any Southern state."[44]

Few counties in Georgia openly refused to desegregate. Perhaps not surprisingly, Baker County was an exception. In fact, Baker County was the first school district in the South to face penalties for violating its desegregation plan. In the fall of 1965, the local school board accepted only seven transfer students, and these students returned to their original school after being beaten and attacked with knives. Prompted by complaints from local SNCC workers, the Office of Education sent investigators to Baker County. Their report concluded that Baker County was the "hardest nut in Georgia to crack" and recommended that the school board should be cited under Title VI. In practice, the citation did not lead to the immediate ending of funds but initiated a lengthy procedure that began with notification of a formal hearing. At a press conference in Atlanta during 1967, black pupils spoke of being beaten by white classmates. Consequently, the black students boycotted the school and the county lost federal funds. In response, Baker County school superintendent Eugene Hall went so far as to appoint one white female teacher as a librarian at the all-black schools. Shortly afterward, Hall was assaulted in his office by the teacher's father.[45]

Opponents of desegregation did not generally indulge in the overt supremacist rhetoric of previous generations, but covert resistance to desegregation proved to be just as effective. An interracial liberal group, the Georgia Leadership Conference on Education, sponsored a Ten Communities Project during 1965 to investigate school desegregation in the state.[46] Constance Curry, who spearheaded the initiative, learned of a telephone conversation between Georgia school superintendent Claude Purcell and presumably a local education official.[47] In a memo to her co-worker Jean Fairfax, Curry wrote that "it was very obvious that Dr. Purcell was suggesting strategy to be used to keep desegregation to a minimum. He suggested that a plan be submitted to HEW accompanied by a letter explaining the plan which appears to be a 'freedom of choice.'" In reality, this "freedom of choice" would extend only to the first and twelfth grades, and Purcell suggested that a minimum of published details would encourage a minimum of students to request transfer. If students did request transfers, then "it might be necessary to let a few in—preferably girls first." [48]

Purcell recommended further ways of avoiding controversy. By appointing a token biracial committee, the local school board could give the impression of acting without prejudice. By insisting to HEW that teachers' salaries were fixed yearly, any preassignment targets were rendered impossible. Any local initiatives should be made "retroactive to desired date." And by rehiring the buses in advance, any problems of busing into new areas could be stalled each year. "The interesting thing about this," Curry concluded, "is that we have found elements of all of the above in several of the plans that have been submitted." [49]

Certainly local officials used ingenious tactics to satisfy HEW without committing themselves to anything more than token desegregation. In Houston County, the desegregation plan drawn up in September 1964 allowed for only twelfth grade students to transfer for their final semester. Not surprisingly, no students applied. The following April, sixteen families filed suit concerning the poor conditions of the black high schools and the inadequacy of the desegregation plan. David Purdue, Houston County school superintendent, told representatives from the Ten Communities Project that Perry was not ready for school desegregation. He even admitted that he intended to play "cat and mouse" with the federal government and do everything possible to have the least amount of desegregation and that he would not do anything until the court decision. [50]

While most local officials played cat and mouse with HEW, they were able to circumvent desegregation locally. In many counties, the prospect of an interview with the school superintendent deterred students from applying for a transfer. Even when students did apply, these interviews were rarely objective. The rejection of all but seven candidates in Baker County may have been an extreme case, but there were complaints about the subjective nature of testing in supposedly more liberal environments. Reviewing what she described as Atlanta's "tokenist" integration by 1965, Margaret Long of the Southern Regional Council lambasted the interview process. School superintendent John Letson screened applicants, and according to Long, successful applicants needed to be a "blend of Joan of Arc and Albert Einstein." One NAACP official commented, "We've got a saying around here that it's easier to go to Yale than to transfer from one public school to another in Atlanta." In

Athens, Clarke County, the school board claimed to have introduced an eight-grade desegregation plan. Ten Communities Project workers, however, asserted that the situation was in fact "frozen." Transfer applicants were required to answer nineteen questions, which allowed the school superintendent to reject the vast majority of applicants. Project workers concluded that "the power structure's hope is to postpone any real integration other than token as long as possible by whatever means." [51]

In many counties, school boards released as little information as possible about transferring. Details were invariably advertised only in the local newspaper and the application period often lasted for only two weeks during the summer. In some counties the local school board actively spread misinformation. Prathia Hall, who worked for the Ten Communities Project, recorded that in Alamo, Wheeler County, the school superintendent told a group of black citizens that if any black students transferred, the white students would leave the school system. His disingenuous conclusion was that the system would lose the funds allotted for these children and this would lead to the eventual closing of the county's public schools. Although two schools in Augusta, Richmond County, allowed some racial desegregation in 1965, they were also segregated by sex for the first time. County officials denied that the segregation was intended to separate black male teenagers from white teenage women. [52]

At times local officials resorted to more blatant intimidatory tactics, reminiscent of the backlash of the early 1940s. In Claxton, Evans County, project worker Joe Tucker reported that black residents were made to sign statements saying that they would not try to send children to the white school. Prathia Hall, who had served on SNCC's Southwest Georgia Project, commented that "once more the Negro citizen of Georgia wonders when his rights will be protected by the Federal Government." [53]

In the face of such resistance to school integration, protesters initially drew on long-held direct action tactics. In the most extreme effort in Georgia to preserve educational segregation, the Taliaferro County school board had agreed to integrate its white high school in Crawfordville but had bused all white students to segregated schools in the surrounding counties of Wilkes, Washington, and Lincoln. "If Taliaferro County used as much ingenuity in educating children as in evading the civil rights law," Frances Pauley told the Hungry Club in the fall of 1965, "it would have the greatest school system in the state." Under the leadership of Calvin Turner, who had already been fired from his teaching post because of his leadership of the local voters' league, Taliaferro's black students boycotted their own schools in October 1965. [54]

Within days, the boycott escalated into widespread confrontational protest. Turner called in SCLC to orchestrate protests, which centered on trying to get black children to board the buses. At the same time, SCLC opened a freedom school for three hundred of the boycotting children. In response, the Taliaferro school board fired the black principal and five teachers, as well as two bus drivers, two cooks, and two custodians. In addition, twenty parents were fired from their jobs, while six families were evicted from their homes and four suffered foreclosures.[55]

Within the county, the school protest became the focus for a wide range of issues. After visiting the county, Senator Leroy Johnson concluded that the busing had been merely the most pressing of many racial grievances: others were the loss of jobs by black leaders associated with the local movement, all-white policy boards, and the failure of county officials to introduce a food stamp plan and antipoverty measures.[56] Calvin Turner asserted that "these issues were at stake long before the school question."[57] In Lincolnton, Lincoln County, SCLC's Rev. Charlie Brown urged those attending the courthouse rally to register to vote and to desegregate the town's only cafe. Taliaferro County briefly gained a notoriety beyond its immediate environs in northeast Georgia. Hosea Williams told a local rally that SCLC leaders hoped that "Crawfordville could become the symbol of token school integration for the nation, just as Selma became the symbol for voting registration difficulties." Within a week, boycotts and marches of hundreds of local protesters spread to neighboring Lincoln and Wilkes Counties when SCLC targeted a seven-county integration drive based on the school issue. Martin Luther King Jr. promised the Taliaferro Improvement League that SCLC "are not here on a dash-in, dash-out basis. We are here to stand by your side until freedom is yours." In response, Georgia's Grand Dragon, Calvin Craig, assembled nearly two hundred members of the Ku Klux Klan and urged white Georgians to stand up in the fight against integration. "Crawfordville, Georgia," wrote Ralph McGill in the *Atlanta Constitution,* are "two words now being printed around the world . . . the latest in a long procession of names—Little Rock, Oxford, New Orleans, Selma, Americus, Watts." Such journalistic coverage escalated after CBS reporter Laurens Pierce had part of his nose bitten off by two segregationist vigilantes.[58]

In fact, the momentum at Taliaferro dissipated after Governor Carl Sanders entered into the negotiations and called for a truce. Acting quickly to avoid a potentially embarrassing showdown, Sanders sent a delegation of notable black Georgians, led by Leroy Johnson, on a fact-finding mission. King returned to Chicago immediately afterward. The introduction of the fact-finding mission divided the protesters and exposed the different factions within Georgia's black leadership. SCLC's Andrew Young angrily announced that "the time is past when a governor can pick Negroes he wants to negotiate with and ignore those who have done the suffering." Leroy Johnson, on the other hand, claimed that "we represent the Negro leadership in Georgia, and it is determined to see first class citizenship come to Georgia." [59] Within Taliaferro County, disagreements surfaced over whether to continue the marches during the negotiations and whether keeping children away from schools was of long-term benefit to the black community.

The federal court resolved the issue, ostensibly in favor of the protesters. In a temporary injunction, federal judges declared the Taliaferro County school system bankrupt and named Georgia school superintendent Claude Purcell as receiver. In response, King immediately called off further demonstrations. Tensions defused further after court cases were dropped against all black protesters, and seven members of the Ku Klux Klan were indicted for violence. [60]

In practice, the Taliaferro protest achieved an unsatisfactory compromise. At the local level, King himself admitted that "there is still the issue of five teachers and a principal fired for participating in a voting drive," not to mention the issues of economic reprisals against other participating protesters. Nor did Taliaferro County act as the vanguard for school desegregation protests across Georgia or the South. Alexander Stephens School was reopened but became exclusively black. Meanwhile, only forty-two black students joined their white peers in busing out of the county to superior schools. [61] Rather than acting as "another Selma," Crawfordville merely represented one of the most nationally prominent of a host of small town direct action protests in Georgia focusing on education.

Direct action tactics, however, were superseded by less headline-grabbing methods to secure the desegregation of schools. The work of the Ten Communities Project was a case in point. Simply getting students to apply to transfer was part of the problem. In Perry, project workers had to visit families in their homes to persuade students to transfer, and Joe Hendricks offered to tutor potential transfer students. According to Constance Curry, "They really responded when they were told they would have an opportunity to go to Macon twice a week for six weeks . . . in several of the families the news about the tutoring was the deciding factor in the student's transfer." [62]

At the local level, the ease of desegregation differed across the state. In some counties, the process of transferring was relatively easy. In April 1965, Bill Randall told project workers that he hoped that Macon would become a "model community that could set an example of extensive school desegregation in the Deep South." Two months later, Jean Fairfax reported that Macon's Freedom of Choice for the first and ninth to twelfth grades had attracted over two hundred transfer requests and sixty first graders had registered. "Actually," Fairfax concluded, "we were elated." In other counties, there was minimal progress. Rev. Charles Hamilton, the head of Augusta's NAACP, noted that in Dublin, Laurens County, "there is tension building up here because the people have been frustrated in their every effort toward breaking down the barriers." The Ten Communities Project gave up on Dublin because the local leadership was weak and divided. "Things in Dublin look pretty dismal," Hamilton concluded, "and with the tight, close schedule that we have I would suggest ruling out further follow-up in Dublin for the time being." [63]

Even when schools did desegregate, the actual transition was fraught with difficulty. For many of the families and students involved, desegregation was a long-term sacrifice rather than a single act of courage. [64] Many of the families of the first transfer students in each school system risked reprisal. In 1965, seven first grade students transferred at Perry, Houston County. Within days, the mother of one of the children, Mrs. Carlton Carrington, lost her job as a domestic. Her boss, Maude Du Bois, claimed that she had received a telephone call instructing her to dismiss the "black brazen bitch." Du Bois urged Carrington not to transfer her daughter because the teacher would ignore her, the cafeteria would not serve her, and it would not be in the best interests of the child to suffer. When Carrington refused, she was fired from her job. In nearby Johnson County, the uncle of one transfer student was taken to jail by the local sheriff and persuaded to withdraw his niece. [65] In Terrell County, Prathia Hall noted that "the fear of loss of jobs is a real one and I hope we can work out something with other federal agencies on this problem." [66]

For the students themselves, transferring often meant facing unremitting hostility. In Baker County, the first seven transfer students were beaten so badly that they returned to their previous schools. In Waycross, one child transferred back. In Americus, one of the initial three transfer students was struck by a bottle on both of his first two days at school. Even in Savannah, with its reputation for more moderate race relations, two fights broke out at Groves High School, causing W. W. Law to wire the Department of Justice and call for a temporary boycott by the twenty students. [67]

The reminiscences of Ulysses Bryan, one of Savannah's first transfer students, highlighted the difficulties of transferring even in one of the more moderate areas of the state. After preparatory academic coaching by members of the Council on

Human Relations and more practical training in nonretaliation by leaders of the local NAACP, Bryan remembered feeling that "we were ready for anything ... but then we didn't know what was to come." Once inside the school gates he found himself the spokesman in front of the television cameras while angry shouts of "here come those niggers" and the chant "two four six eight we don't want to integrate" rang in his ears. Each of the twelve transfer students was placed in a different homeroom class, minimizing the support they could give each other. Bryan remembered suffering "so many little incidents" from "butts on my arm, spitting in my dinner," and "having my books thrown on the floor" to after-school harassment such as damage to his car and anonymous telephone calls threatening a lynching. Normally he took the precaution of leaving his workshop class last so he could keep his classmates in view. One October day, however, "someone got behind me, and the next thing I knew was when I woke up in the nurse's office with an egg lump on my head and a couple of stitches."[68]

Ulysses Bryan persevered to graduation, winning the prestigious cadet award at Savannah High School. Although he didn't make any new true friends, he recalled that the "last months were easier than the first" and that he even received some warm, if rather shy, messages of good luck on graduation day.[69] Some of the Savannah students later admitted that they might have refused to transfer if they had known what to expect. In other counties, some of the first transfer students later resented being the guinea pigs, believing that their grades and subsequent careers had suffered as a result.[70]

But for all the efforts to end school segregation, the transition to desegregation was extremely slow after the Civil Rights Act. In 1967, only 8.8 percent of black children in Georgia attended desegregated schools. By July 1969, this figure had risen to only 15 percent. Across the state, 112 school districts, some 60 percent of the state, were not in compliance with HEW guidelines by 1969. Because of the slow process of prosecuting intransigent school boards, only 36 school districts had actually lost their share of HEW's $30 million for Georgia schools. In Taliaferro County, there was still no desegregation whatsoever, as all the white students continued to be bused to adjacent counties. Even in Atlanta, the first school system to desegregate, over 80 percent of public school students still attended segregated schools by 1969. Ten years later, John Letson admitted that "resistance was part of the statewide political position . . . the board felt it had no alternative but to resist if it was to express the will of the people." If anything, such resistance had increased during and after Richard Nixon's successful campaign for president. "Throughout Georgia," the *Atlanta Inquirer* commented in December 1968, "an increasing number of local authorities are defying school guidelines . . . because of their belief that the Nixon administration is going to look the other way." The Worth County school board, for example, withdrew its desegregation plan after interpreting Nixon's campaign rhetoric as opposed to enforced integration.[71]

Ironically, it was during the first year of the Nixon presidency that federal rulings made a decisive impact on school integration in Georgia and across the South. In September 1969, the Supreme Court ruled in a Mississippi case, *Alexander v. Holmes,* that there was to be no further delay in school desegregation.[72] One month later, as part of a new Nixon policy to substitute legal action for cutting off federal school aid funds, the government sought a federal court order to desegregate every public school in Georgia by September 1970. It was the first statewide case of its kind. In December 1969 a three-judge panel in the U.S. District Court ruled to cut off state funding for any Georgia district not in compliance by 1 September 1970. State funds represented some 75 percent of local school budgets. At the time of the ruling, 81 of Georgia's 192 school districts were not in compliance. The panel also specified for the first time exactly what Title VI meant in practice. In each school district, three-quarters of all pupils in the minority race had to be enrolled in integrated facilities, where the numbers of both faculty and students were within 50 to 150 percent of their proportionate number in the district.[73]

Almost inevitably state politicians opposed what they called federal interference. In February 1969, Lester Maddox urged the Georgia legislature, albeit unsuccessfully, to replace any federal funds that Georgia might lose with state funds. After the government had sought a court order against the state in October 1969, Maddox charged that Georgia was singled out simply because Nixon didn't like him. Maddox concluded that "when the President singles out one state and four and a half million people and threatens them because he doesn't like the Governor of the state, it's a sad day for all of America." After the court order, Maddox sought to abolish the state's compulsory school attendance law. Maddox told reporters that "so far as I'm concerned, they can take their ultimatum and ram it in their satchels or their suitcases. Phooey on that crowd."[74]

As had previous federal involvement, the enforced changes provoked resistance at the local level. In January 1970, 1,500 white students walked out of Atlanta schools and marched in freezing conditions to the Federal Building to protest the transfer of 1,800 teachers. Chanting, "Hell, no, we won't go," the students also made clear their opposition to the plans for pupil integration. Three months later, over 350 white parents were arrested in Athens after protesting against integration. The following February, less than a year after the riot, over half of Augusta's thirty thousand white students boycotted the city's busing plan.[75]

Opponents of integration also responded in less confrontational ways. In Atlanta, twenty-three desegregated schools had resegregated by the summer of 1969 because white families had moved out of the school districts. The *Alexander v. Holmes* decision also prompted a surge in the number of all-white private schools. During the summer of 1969, more than six hundred white residents in Washington County went to the local courthouse to support plans for a private school. During the decade after 1969, the number of private schools more than doubled to 366, representing almost one-tenth of Georgia's school-age population. In Sumter County, for example, the exclusively white Southland Academy opened in 1970, enrolling over one thousand children. The exodus to the academy left the public schools 80 percent black. At the same time, county property taxes were dropped from nearly 20 percent to 7 percent, leaving Sumter's public schools in a state of severe disrepair. By 1983, some 40 percent of students in Sumter's public schools dropped out and a further 30 percent did not pass requirements for graduation.[76]

Although the federal directives ended school segregation once and for all in public schools, the logistics of integrating schools presented further challenges for local black leaders. When school boards did integrate hitherto segregated schools, invariably it was the principal of the white school who was automatically appointed as the new overall high school principal, regardless of experience. The Georgia Teachers and Education Association (GTEA) president, H. E. Tate, publicly deplored the displacement of black principals throughout the Georgia school system. In what he described as "the most flagrant misuse of justice," Tate pinpointed the demotion of a black principal in Carlton, Madison County, even though she had been employed for the previous thirty-nine years.[77]

The widespread demotion of black teachers became a salient issue in many localities. For example, in the summer of 1969, 360 black pupils in Pike County walked out after the displacement of the principal, D. F. Glover. The situation was more poignant than many others were, the GTEA noted, because the local school superintendent, Harold T. Daniel, himself acknowledged that Glover had the second highest academic credentials in the state school system. In 1967, Glover had been a delegate at the first interracial meeting of school principals in Georgia to discuss the issue of desegregation. Ironically, Glover had warned the meeting that "the problem faced by the Negro principal is equal to, if not greater than, the problem faced by the white principal."[78] Within days of his dismissal, Glover visited the SCLC office in Atlanta.

Threatening to "turn this place into another Charleston, S.C.," SCLC staffer Willie Bolden orchestrated daily marches of up to one hundred students from the black school at Concord to the all-white school in the county seat of Zebulon six miles away. True to the pattern of SCLC's successful campaigns, the protest provoked violent responses as two teenage girls were bludgeoned by night watchmen. Meanwhile, Daniel appointed ten truant officers, empowering them with the right to enter homes and arrest miscreants. As black outrage escalated after the firing of a further twenty-three teachers, SCLC sent in Ralph Abernathy to oversee daily marches of over a thousand students and adults. Simultaneously, SCLC challenged Danields's legal tactics in the courts. The resulting compromise, negotiated by SCLC, provided for the rehiring of all teachers and a broader role for Glover.[79]

Across Georgia, the impact of the federal enforcement after 1969 varied among localities. In some cases, desegregation proceeded relatively smoothly. In Clarke County, the school board completely integrated its system within two years. Previously the school board had stalled on the issue of desegregation, introducing a Freedom of Choice plan in 1965 and then suggesting a neighborhood plan in 1969, both of which were rejected by HEW. What was unique was that in October 1970 school board lawyers went to the Supreme Court to defend busing against a charge of "unconstitutionality" which had been brought by some parents and subsequently supported by Georgia's state supreme court. As Clarke County superintendent Charles P. McDaniel pointed out, busing was not a new phenomenon. McDaniel commented wryly, "For half a century we've been busing ... to maintain segregation, now we are busing to eliminate segregation."[80] In a small district like Clarke County, busing made practical sense, for the majority of bus rides were under twenty-five minutes. Despite initial protests, only 130 of 11,500 children left the public school system. Meanwhile, faculty from the University of Georgia, who had supported integration, gave extra tuition to biracial teams of students.

Even in Clarke County, however, the seemingly smooth process of integration did not prevent racial tensions in the classroom. In one Athens high school, black students voiced grievances, particularly that the white football coach was discriminating against black players. More broadly, the successful integration of the schools could not obscure wider issues within the community. Edward Turner, the first black councilman in Clarke County since Reconstruction, argued that the bigger problem was "raising immediately the socio-economic status of most of the students' parents." By 1970, only 7 percent of black workers in Athens had white-collar jobs while over 50 percent were in service jobs, almost the exact reverse of the white population. Turner argued further that despite a monthly biracial meeting, "the black people have not been heard. There's a terrible lack of communications. The city seems blind to poverty."[81]

In Atlanta, the complex negotiations over the process of school desegregation highlighted the fact that there was no easy formula to resolve the issue of fair schooling. Initially, desegregation in Atlanta passed smoothly, partly because of the influence of black educators. By 1970, three of the ten members of the Board of Education were black, including the president, Benjamin E. Mays. A biracial committee for desegregation advised the school board. The desegregation proposals allowed students to transfer from a school where they were in a racial majority to one where they would be in a minority. Nevertheless, only 2,800 black students and no white students took advantage of the opportunity to transfer. By 1972, 106 of Atlanta's 153 schools were almost totally segregated.[82]

The local branch of the NAACP, led by Lonnie King, negotiated an agreement in 1973 that did not include widespread busing to secure racial integration. Given that city schools were already 83 percent black, King believed that busing would disrupt neighborhood schools and might further increase the white flight from the city school system. Instead, King accepted a settlement providing that no school in the system would have less than 30 percent black pupils. At the same time, the majority of black children would remain in segregated schools. The central features of the agreement were that there would be a black superintendent for Atlanta public schools and that black Atlantans should fill at least half of all administrative posts. Alonzo Crim, a black Harvard graduate, replaced John Letson as school superintendent in July 1973.[83]

The resulting controversy highlighted the conflicting views within the black community about the paramount importance of integration. Roy Wilkins, head of the national NAACP, lambasted the agreement as the second "Atlanta Compromise." Wilkins suspended the local chapter for abandoning the goal of full integration. Lonnie King, no stranger to controversy, argued instead that the compromise allowed black protest to "get out of court and move on to the more important issue of educating kids."[84] At a meeting with NAACP leaders in New York, King argued that Atlanta had a uniquely positive racial situation and so it was a local issue rather than a national precedent. Somewhat ironically, Lonnie King was using the very same rhetoric that he had deplored during the negotiations to resolve the sit-in crisis a decade previously.

Surveying the history of black protest against discriminatory education, David Plank and Marcia Turner noted that good education rather than integration had, in fact, always been the motivating force for black protest leaders. During the middle of the twentieth century, "the goal of integration was pursued by local black leaders as the most effective strategy for bringing about improvement in the educational opportunities available to blacks." In this sense, Plank and Turner argued that the second Atlanta Compromise was an extension rather than a betrayal of previous protest for integrated schools. "When this strategy was no longer effective ... and when a more attractive alternative strategy became available ... the goal of integration was abandoned."[85]

In contrast, in Fort Valley, the local school board sued for the complete integration of Fort Valley State College, one of the few predominantly black colleges in the state. Far from being a move to promote racial harmony, however, the suit was intended to weaken black political power. During the city elections of 1972, five victorious black candidates in the Republican primaries all had links to the college. The *Macon Telegraph* concluded that "it was obvious college students ... turned the trick for the black candidates." The suit called for the proportion of black students at the college to be reduced to 15 percent to put it on a par with the state average (although the state average was only as high as 15 percent because of the existence of a handful of predominantly black colleges in Georgia, including Fort Valley). A follow-up suit claimed that the college's principal, Jack Hunniwit, kept the college substandard to deter white applicants. By the school year of 1976–77, however, white student enrollment had only risen to 13 percent, leaving the way clear for the future elections of black officials. Fort Valley's first black mayor, Rudolph Carson, was elected in 1980.[86]

Voting

In theory, the Voting Rights Act provided the means for black Georgians to achieve political power at the local level and assume greater influence in statewide elections. Despite gradual out-migration during the century, blacks constituted almost a third of the total state population by 1965. Thirty-four of Georgia's 159 counties had a majority black population, and 21 of these had a majority black voting-age population. The act abolished Georgia's literacy test for voting registration and a 1964 law that required poll workers to be "judicious, intelligent and upright." Unlike previous voting legislation, the act provided for the direct interference of the federal government to secure voting rights for black southerners. Section 5 of the Voting Rights

Act also required local jurisdictions to prove, before introducing new voting practices, that they were not discriminatory.[87]

As in public accommodations and education, however, the Voting Rights Act did not end the struggle for equality in the political arena. In the short term, the act did not even expedite the expected mass registration of black voters in Georgia. As Vernon Jordan, Georgia's VEP director, lamented to Atlanta's Hungry Club in the summer of 1966, "we have cut the orange and failed to squeeze it."[88]

Significantly, in the context of the South, only sixteen thousand black Georgians registered to vote in the first six months after passage of the Voting Rights Act, compared with seventy-six thousand in Mississippi and one hundred thousand in Alabama. By the end of 1966, Georgia had more unregistered black voters than any other state in the South except for Mississippi. This disparity, however, was not caused by relatively poor organization or the influence of Richard Russell but was primarily explained by the failure of federal registrars to visit Georgia before the spring of 1967. "Georgia counties are small," chief federal examiner John Doar explained to the U.S. Commission on Civil Rights in 1968. "It takes a lot of shoe leather to cross and re-cross the state. Georgia has suffered from neglect of the enforcement program."[89]

The increase in registration in the three Georgia counties that were visited by federal registrars underlined the importance of federal intervention. By the spring of 1967, 11.1 percent of Terrell County blacks, 30.7 percent of Screven County blacks, and 9.9 percent of Lee County blacks were registered to vote with the help of Sherrod's New Communities Project.[90] This registration represented the first significant percentage of voters since the arrival of SNCC and the first increase since the Voting Rights Act, including over three hundred registered voters in the first week alone.[91]

More generally, the limited initial increase in registration immediately after the Voting Rights Act also reflected the fact that a large number of black Georgians in urban areas had actually registered before 1965.[92] In Mississippi, by contrast, only 6 percent of potential black voters had registered by 1965 and so gains were more spectacular. In Savannah, the NAACP voting registration director, Curtis Cooper, complained in 1966 that "it is nearly impossible to devise new techniques that have not been used." In a complaint typical of many city movements, Cooper reported that "one of our main problems has been apathy among our people."[93]

In the longer term, the Voting Rights Act did make a significant impact on black voter registration across the state. A U.S. Commission on Civil Rights report of 1968 recorded that the number of black Georgians registered to vote had risen to 334,000, almost double the pre-act estimate. This figure represented just over half of Georgia's black voting-age population and 18.4 percent of the total electorate. By 1972, an additional 100,000 black Georgians had registered, increasing the proportion of eligible black Georgians who were registered to vote to 67.8 percent. This proportion was ten points higher than that of Alabama, Louisiana, or the Carolinas and was only 3 percent less than the registration rate for white Georgians.[94]

As with public accommodations and education, however, the benefits of the Voting Rights Act had to be fought for at the local level. Although the act closed King's headline-grabbing campaigns, it opened a new chapter in the struggle for political equality at the local level. Despite the Voting Rights Act, or perhaps even because of it, black Georgians continued to face obstacles to voting in many areas of the state and particularly in the rural black belt.

In the first place, local officials regularly refused to designate additional registration sites in the black community or canceled previously authorized neighborhood registration drives. The director of Georgia's Voter Education Project described the relationship between black leaders and election officials as "adversarial." In Columbus, local leaders failed in their efforts to have new registration sites located in black areas of Muscogee County.[95] In DeKalb County, only legal action in 1980 under Section 5 forced the reintroduction of neighborhood drives. By this point, only 24 percent of eligible black voters were registered, in contrast to 81 percent of eligible white voters.

Local officials often used aggressive tactics to restrict black voter registration. A U.S. Commission on Civil Rights report of 1975 discovered numerous incidences of fraud during the preceding decade. In Sandersville, Washington County, in north Georgia, after blacks won three of five seats up for election in December 1971, a Committee of Four was established to purge voters for nonresidency in the town. The purge, based solely on the discretion of the committee, was allegedly "instituted for the purpose of removing black voters from the list of electors in order to insure that black candidates for office would be defeated in the December 5, 1973, General Election." More fundamentally, as an SRC survey observed in 1969, there were "still fears about voting among Negroes in rural Georgia." A federal survey concluded that "blacks in an economically dependent position in rural Georgia are reluctant to vote or to vote the way they want." In Taliaferro County, local movement leader Calvin Turner believed that blacks were reluctant to vote for fear of losing their welfare benefits. In neighboring Sandersville, in June 1973, Julian Davis was fired from his job as principal of the elementary school, and Eloise Turner was fired as a teacher. Both had actively campaigned for a black candidate the previous year with the support of the NAACP.[96] In Talbot County, J. B. King, who had been a high school principal for seventeen years, ran unsuccessfully for Talbot County school superintendent in June 1973. The following March his contract was not renewed. Such incidents, the federal survey concluded, "whether claims of discrimination are ultimately upheld or not—deter blacks from active participation in the political process."[97] Pat Watters reported that in southwest Georgia at the end of the 1960s, to "try to register to vote is still to take your life in your own hands if you are black."[98]

Such fears were exacerbated by the machinations of rural registration officials. In Macon County, for example, which had a 61 percent black population, only three of the thirty election workers were black in September 1974, and those were only minor staff members. In Fitzgerald in south Georgia, no bank would take money from the local affiliate of the NAACP that sought to supervise a local registration campaign. In a letter to Vernon Jordan, Curtis Thomas, the leader of the Thomasville NAACP and voters' league, complained that in Thomasville in 1966, approximately one thousand "unproperly marked" ballots were thrown out. In neighboring Grady County, Alley Ben Prince told black voters that "if you DON'T want Maddox, mark an X by his name." "For this reason," Thomas concluded, "we feel that there is great need for the Voter Education Project."[99]

In fact, it was the SRC's Voter Education Project, based in Atlanta, that took the lead in trying to ensure that the Voting Rights Act resulted in increased voter registration throughout Georgia. The VEP financed hundreds of local movements to organize voter registration drives across the state. In 1971, for example, the VEP reported an expenditure of $96,897, amounting to virtually one dollar for each new registered black voter that year. Even in the relative prosperity of Atlanta, the local All-Citizens Registration Committee (ACRC) reported that "it would have been impossible for us to conduct our campaign without the $3,600 grant we received from the VEP." Concerned at the lack of statewide progress by 1970, the VEP switched all its resources to rural registration programs. By this time, Georgia's VEP was issuing grants with increasing discernment. Vernon Jordan refused a further grant to the Fort Valley registration drive in 1966, for example, after the initial campaign had floundered because it coincided with the peach harvest.[100]

The VEP provided funds regardless of the affiliation of the local movement. In Savannah, funds were entrusted to the dominant local NAACP, while SNCC received $3,700 in 1966 for voter registration in southwest Georgia. When the VEP supported a combined SCLC-NAACP voter registration drive in Macon, the money was given to Bill Randall, who was the de facto head of both local organizations. In Terrell County, the VEP awarded a grant to the independent Terrell County Voters' League in April 1967 to fund salaries for a director and four transport workers. D. U. Pullum, who was the director of the league, was also the longest serving president of an NAACP branch in Georgia. As a result of internecine bitterness in Columbus between the traditional NAACP and a new SCLC affiliate, VEP fieldworkers were regularly sent to Muscogee County in an attempt to discern where funding should be directed.[101]

Through a combination of local activism and the VEP, the Voting Rights Act did indeed lead to the most dramatic increase in black voter registration across the state since Reconstruction. But increased registration did not translate into black political power. The initial slow pace of registration of black voters in Georgia after the Voting Rights Act meant that Georgia had a dearth of black officials even in comparison with other Deep South states. Whereas Georgia had only 29 black elected officials by 1969, Mississippi had 51, Louisiana had 53, and Alabama had 69. As voter registration increased in Georgia, the number of black elected officials increased too, rising to 80 by the beginning of 1970 and to 137 during 1972.[102] Even so, 137 black elected officials represented less than 2 percent of the total in 1972 and were vastly disproportionate to 25.9 percent proportion of registered black voters in Georgia.

Moreover, as a federal investigation in 1975 concluded, "most offices held by blacks are relatively minor and located in small municipalities." Although black politicians included Congressman Andrew Young, across the state as a whole only twenty-two black officials had been elected to legislative seats by November 1974, representing a mere 9.3 percent of the total. Consequently, black politicians served only as a token lobbying voice, although Senator Leroy Johnson's bill in 1964 to outlaw the thirty questions rule for registration aided the work of the VEP.[103]

The ineffectiveness of the black vote was partly owing to poor organization. In the senatorial race of 1968, Maynard Jackson lost heavily to Herman Talmadge, winning only 22.9 percent of the vote. Although Jackson carried Atlanta and did well in Savannah, in many urban areas, Jackson's vote was hampered by a low turnout. Only a third of black voters turned out in Macon, Columbus, and Augusta. In rural areas, the turnout was similarly poor. In Thomas County, for example, only 35 percent of registered black voters cast a ballot, and 10 percent of those voted for Talmadge. In a story typical of many rural counties, some black voters thought that Jackson was white and did not realize that both candidates were Democrats. In one precinct, which was 80 percent black, 407 votes were cast for Jackson and 390 for Talmadge.[104]

The primary reason for the lack of electoral success, however, lay in the nature of the electoral system at the local level. In 1964, the state of Georgia inserted a majority-voting clause into its election code. According to J. Morgan Kousser, this "majority-voting requirement was passed . . . to preserve the rule of the white majority against the growing bloc vote." Representative Denmark Groover Jr. of Bibb County, who introduced the bill, admitted that "bloc vote" was a "euphemism" for "blacks voting in a bloc, that's what it meant."[105] By 1965, the overwhelming majority of Georgia's counties and cities also had at-large elections. Given the racially polarized nature of voting, at-large systems rendered the black vote impotent in all counties where white voters held a majority. Indeed, thirteen counties with a large black population that had single-member districts in 1965 switched to at-large systems immediately after the Voting Rights Act, without submitting the election changes for preclearance by the Justice Department. ACLU lawyer Laughlin McDonald believed that under a single-member system, each of these thirteen counties "almost certainly would have had one or more majority-black districts as a result of increasing black registration."[106] By 1980, almost all the at-large systems in the state remained intact.

Where single-member district elections remained, the apportionment of districts often diluted the black vote. In Seminole County, for example, the local apportionment plan had been enacted in 1933. The vast majority of local black voters lived in the most populous district, which was some ten times larger than the smallest one.[107] It was not until local blacks filed a lawsuit in 1980, which forced the adoption of a new apportionment plan, that the first black county commissioner was elected.

The election of Andrew Young from Georgia's fifth district highlighted the determination of Georgia officials, even in the state legislature, to dilute the black vote.[108] By 1970, Georgia's fifth district exceeded the limit for a congressional district by thirty-eight thousand and was more than three times the size of the smallest district. Most of the fifth district was based in Atlanta, which had a majority black population in 1970. Under the reapportionment plan, however, Atlanta's black population was split into three separate congressional districts (4, 5, and 6) with only 38.3 percent black population in the fifth. Under Section 5 of the Voting Rights Act, the attorney general rejected the plan because it sought to dilute the black vote. The attorney general pointed out that the plan "cut likely black congressional candidates, including Andrew Young (who ran a solid race against an incumbent white in 1970) and Maynard Jackson (popular vice-mayor of Atlanta) out of the Fifth District by a few blocks." [109] Consequently, the General Assembly proposed a revised increase to 43.8 percent and, despite objections, it was accepted by the attorney general. In November 1972, with crossover support from progressive white neighborhoods, Andrew Young became the first black congressman since Reconstruction from a southern state covered by the Voting Rights Act.

The prevalence of at-large elections and white majority districts also brought into sharp relief the failure of biracial politics after the Voting Rights Act. Andrew Young proved to be one of the very few black candidates able to win with significant support from white voters. When Robert Benham was elected to the court of appeals in a statewide election in 1984, Tyrone Brooks commented that in the white community "nobody knew he was black." To ensure that race did not become an issue, "Benham's picture could only appear on brochures distributed in the black community," and all civil rights leaders refrained from endorsing him. [110]

Indeed, after the Voting Rights Act, it was not simply that black registration did not translate into black political power but that black voters were unable to influence the election of moderate candidates. In statewide elections, the black minority vote was clearly unable to secure the election of politicians sympathetic to racial equality. Two years after electing Maddox as governor, Georgians gave arch-segregationist George Wallace a plurality during the 1968 presidential election. Ironically, black voters actually played a role in the election of Maddox. After Republican candidate Bo Callaway, the clear favorite, refused to court the black vote, local voters' leagues organized a write-in campaign for Ellis Arnall. Even though Callaway received more votes than Maddox, the sixty thousand write-in votes for Arnall were sufficient to stop him from receiving an overall majority, and the Democratic majority state legislature voted that Maddox should be elected governor. [111]

With the removal of the county-unit system and the emergence of genuine two-party elections, voting coalitions in Georgia underwent a radical shift to the detriment of black influence. Previously, as Numan Bartley observed, "the basic alliances in state politics pitted Negroes and the more affluent urban whites against the rural-small-town-lower-status whites." With a substantial number of black votes in many districts across the state, this alliance should have precluded the election of supremacist politicians. Instead, according to Bartley, this alliance threatened to collapse. Moderate white voters in Georgia transferred to the Republican Party during the 1960s, attracted by its economic conservatism. In addition, voters who were conservative on the issue of race were attracted by the Republicans' lily-white strategy in the South. [112]

This statewide picture of a largely impotent black vote, however, masked some important, albeit isolated, local examples of black political empowerment. In 1968, Hancock County in east Georgia became the first county in the United States since Reconstruction to come under black political control. Hancock was a startling exception in Georgia. In 1968, it was the only rural county in Georgia that was carried by Maynard Jackson. By 1975, only five of Georgia's twenty-three black majority counties had black county commissioners and of these, only Hancock County had a majority black county commission. In the nine black majority counties that had elections for local school boards, only six black officials were elected. Four of these six were in Hancock County.[113]

Racial demographics were fundamental to this transfer of power, with blacks constituting over three-quarters of Hancock's population of nine thousand inhabitants. Consequently, blacks formed 66.9 percent of the voting-age population. Although nearly 90 percent of the white community voted in the county elections of 1966, political historian Lawrence Hanks concluded that "because Hancock had so many [black] votes to spare, the election of blacks became a reality there, one on the school board, one on the commission of three."[114]

Local activists built on the opportunity provided by this large black majority. The federal acts of 1964 and 1965 triggered a youth direct action movement and an adult voter registration campaign. Less common was Hancock County's historical tradition of relatively moderate racial mores, partly owing to the unusually high proportion of interracial kinship ties. Consequently, the campaign was able to develop without the vehement backlash characteristic of the black belt. Despite two cross burnings on the night before passage of the Voting Rights Act, Hancock was one of the few southern counties where black applicants stood in line to register to vote on the first day. Using a VEP grant, the Hancock County Democratic Club (HCDC) encouraged 51.8 percent of the black community to register.[115]

Demographics alone did not ensure black political power, for Hancock was the only one of Georgia's twenty-three black majority counties to elect a majority of black county commissioners. The arrival in 1966 and subsequent leadership of John McCown, all observers agreed, was the main reason for the establishment of black political control. Under McCown's inspiration, the HCDC and the local youth movement combined and increased in strength to be able to run a successful slate for the local election of 1968. McCown himself was elected to the county commission.[116]

John McCown was a unique leader in many ways. Both his opponents and supporters echoed Frances Pauley's assessment that "McCown was among the most dynamic personalities in the civil rights movement." Pauley admired McCown's ability to win grants from northern foundations but added that "he was a con artist." Born in North Carolina in 1934, McCown spent his teens in Harlem before joining the air force and moving with his wife, Annie Mae, to Colorado. After acting as the military liaison officer for the local NAACP, McCown left the air force and later joined demonstrations in Atlanta and Selma. In Selma he befriended Stokeley Carmichael. By the time he moved to Hancock, McCown was also experienced in antipoverty programs, having worked as a community organizer with the Southern Rural Action Project. He succeeded Pauley as the head of the Georgia Council on Human Relations in 1967.[117]

McCown's popularity was enhanced by his ability to attract huge financial grants to Hancock County. Before the election of 1968, McCown had already supervised a Headstart education program and secured over twenty Federal Housing Authority loans for local blacks. After his election, McCown persuaded Whitney Young to open a local office of the NUL in the county seat of Sparta. Most dramatically of all, McCown became president of the Georgia Council on Human Relations in 1967 and convinced the organization to concentrate all its resources in one spot—Hancock. By 1974, McCown had brought in a remarkable $10 million of funding to the economic arm of the HCDC, including a Ford Foundation grant to build a 375-acre catfish farm.[118]

Not surprisingly, the story of Hancock County attracted increasing media attention. After the 1968 elections, an *Atlanta Constitution* headline declared, "Negroes Take Over in Hancock Voting." But it was McCown's uncompromising adherence to Black Power that fueled outside publicity. McCown claimed that he had personally been responsible for throwing Mayor Allen off the roof of his car during disturbances in Atlanta (although police records confirmed only that he had been arrested for disturbing the peace). In 1969, McCown was arrested for parading without a permit when leading a march to the white high school. In Sparta, McCown led the takeover of the white Baptist church by over one hundred black residents on Sunday, 12 May 1974. By then, both the Sparta white city government and the Hancock County government had been accumulating rifles and machine guns for self-protection, and Governor Jimmy Carter intervened to try to pacify the arms race.[119]

The Hancock County experiment in economic empowerment fell as quickly as it had risen with the fortunes of John McCown himself. Increasingly adverse publicity from the *Atlanta Constitution* prompted a state audit in April 1974, which revealed financial discrepancies in the HCDC and led to a federal grand jury investigation. All outside funding ceased even before McCown was called to trial for the misappropriation of over one-quarter of a million dollars. As a dramatic postscript, McCown died in January 1976 when his private airplane crashed in suspicious circumstances one week before his trial. Most commentators concluded that it was either suicide or a drunken accident, although many black residents believed that it was a conspiracy. But if the economic experiment collapsed, black political power continued. In 1986, black candidates held all but one of Hancock County's eighteen elective offices. Lawrence Hanks commented that Hancock County "settled down to a very non-eventful existence . . . the bad economy has forced blacks and whites to forget the past and cooperate in attempts to bring industry to the county." [120]

The other major exception to the statewide picture of continued white political dominance was Atlanta. In its 1970 annual report, the VEP observed that, unlike other states, in Georgia "most of the black elected officials came from urban areas." A federal survey concluded that Atlanta provided the major exception to the phenomenon of rural elected officials in the rest of the South.[121]

In many ways, the reasons for black empowerment in Atlanta were the same as those in Hancock County writ large. In both communities demographics played a fundamental role. As a result of white middle-class out-migration, black residents represented over half of Atlanta's voting population by the beginning of 1970.[122] Similar to the HCDC in Hancock County, Atlanta's local leadership, the Citizens' Registration Committee had organized a "crash registration campaign" to take advantage of the 1965 Voting Act. Led by Jesse Hill, the committee represented the generation of business and community leaders who had initially founded the ACCA.

As in Hancock County, a tradition of relatively moderate race relations allowed the registration campaign to prosper. The major problem, Hill reported to the VEP, was not white resistance but simply the restricted hours of registration. With the consent of the city council, registrars agreed to remain open until 9 P.M. on Fridays and opened on Saturdays during April and May 1967. On those two Saturdays alone, nearly three thousand black Atlantans registered to vote. By the end of May 1967, 46,612 black Atlantans had registered to vote, an increase of over 50 percent since 1960.[123]

Political analysts agreed that the city elections of 1969 marked a decisive turning point in Atlanta politics. For the first time, black voters were demonstrably no longer the junior partner in a voting alliance but were sufficient numerically to elect candidates with only limited white assistance. None of the victorious candidates, either black or white, received more than 35 percent support from any particular income group within Atlanta's white voting community. Black accountant Maynard Jackson, grandson of John Wesley Dobbs, was elected vice-mayor with the backing of 97.8 percent of the city's black vote.[124]

In a further twist to the saga of Atlanta's factional black leadership, it emerged that black mayoral candidate Horace Tate might have succeeded with the backing of the ANVL. The Auburn Avenue leaders justified their support for Sam Massell ahead of Tate because they did not believe that Tate could win and they thought it sensible to concentrate on securing a black vice-mayor. T. M. Alexander, however, was one of those who believed that it was more a case that "they did not want any *other* black man to become the first black mayor of Atlanta." Tate himself claimed that he was rejected on account of the extreme darkness of his skin.[125] In the event, Maynard Jackson became the first black mayor of any city in Georgia four years later. Ironically, he also announced his candidature without asking the ANVL.

In contrast to the events in Hancock County, the election of Jackson had a far-reaching impact. Within Atlanta, Jackson's victory was not a short-lived experiment in black power dependent on one man's personality.[126] Jackson remained in office until 1981 before being succeeded by Andrew Young, the same year that Atlanta first had a black majority city council. Jackson's victory also reinforced black middle-class involvement in the city's business and social affairs. Jesse Hill, who was appointed president of Atlanta Life in 1973, became the first black officer at the Atlanta Chamber of Commerce and even served a term as president at the end of the decade.[127]

The emergence of black political control led to a rapid increase in black employment in public departments.[128] Jackson hired Atlanta's first affirmative-action officer, and the proportion of black public employees in professional positions rose from 19.2 percent to 42.2 percent between 1973 and 1978. Similarly, the proportion of black managers more than doubled from 13.5 percent to 32.6 percent. In this Jackson was aided by the 1972 Equal Employment Opportunities Act, which expanded the prohibition against discrimination in the private sector in the 1964 Civil Rights Act to include state and local government jobs.[129]

Jackson's election also influenced black employment beyond public sector appointments. Jackson established the Minority Business Enterprise program to increase the percentage of city contracts going to black firms to about 25 percent, including the building of Atlanta's $750 million new airport. During Jackson's first term, the proportion of city funds paid to black firms soared from 2 to 33 percent. For the first time, some city funds were deposited in black-owned banks, and Jackson withdrew city money from one bank that refused to cooperate on affirmative action. A city ordinance was passed with minority hiring goals for all companies wanting to conduct business with the city. Such developments gave some credence to the long-held beliefs of Jackson's grandfather, John Wesley Dobbs, who had argued during the 1960s that "eventually, and ultimately, most of our problems will be solved and settled at the ballot box." [130]

The election of a black mayor in Georgia's capital city had a broader symbolic significance too. Jackson himself believed that "all of a sudden, I became the mayor not just of Atlanta, but of black people in Georgia and even some neighboring states." Whereas traditionally Georgia's rural conservatism had overshadowed Atlanta's racial moderation, the increasingly ascendant state capital set the tone for the rest of the state. The reason that "Georgia has stood apart from her sister states in the Deep South," the *New South* concluded in 1969, was because "Georgia had Atlanta." [131]

Atlanta's example was followed at the state level in the gubernatorial election of 1970. Lester Maddox's tenure proved to be a brief diversion before the election of Jimmy Carter, from Plains in Sumter County. In his review of Georgia governors, Harold Henderson concluded that Maddox's term was a "fluke that ultimately confirmed rather than deposed the new trends in Georgia political life." Maddox failed to regain the governorship in 1975. In his inaugural address, Carter signaled an end to wool-hat politics by declaring, "I say to you quite frankly that the time for racial discrimination is over. No poor, rural, weak or black person shall ever have to bear the additional burden of being deprived of the opportunity for an education, a job, or simple justice." [132] The contrast with the inauguration speeches of the Talmadges, Vandiver, and Maddox was stark indeed.

Carter's words were reinforced by action. The Georgia historian Donald Grant concluded that "Carter was Georgia's most progressive chief executive yet regarding race relations," appointing dozens of black Georgians to key positions including state senator Horace Ward to Fulton County's civil court. [133] Carter established a biracial civil disorder unit and refused to appoint Roy Harris to the University System Board of Regents and subsequently appointed Jesse Hill as a regent in 1973. In an ostentatious display of his racial moderation, Carter included a black man in his four-man security team and proclaimed 15 January as Martin Luther King Day. In 1974, he even put a portrait of King in the state capitol. [134]

The election of Carter, however, did not signify the triumph of a racially moderate voting majority in Georgia. Maddox was elected lieutenant governor in the same election. In a review of the election, Randy Sanders asserted that Carter's campaign had been tinged with racism reminiscent of his predecessors. Sanders concluded that "at best he had equivocated on the racial issue, and at worst, he had pandered outright to racism." Roy Harris had served as one of Carter's campaign managers. Although Coretta Scott King and Andrew Young subsequently supported Carter's presidential campaign of 1976, other civil rights leaders were less than enthusiastic about Carter's record in Georgia. Julian Bond told reporters that Carter "wouldn't be my first choice, he wouldn't even be my tenth." [135]

Opinion was also divided in Carter's home county, where Carter had been a state senator during the turmoil in Americus during the early 1960s. Rev. Campbell, one of the leaders of the Americus movement, told reporters during the presidential campaign that "when we had our struggle, I don't remember Carter saying anything." [136] But the Barnums interpreted Carter's silence as a "hopeful sign" given that most public officials had vehemently denounced the local movement. Warren Fortson concurred, adding that Carter had actually spoken up for him at a meeting of the county commissioners when Fortson was dismissed. "He caught a lot of unshirted hell by that, and he spent a lot of time trying to patch up his business after that." [137]

Elections of progressive candidates in both the state capital and the state capitol, however, obscured the lack of progress at the local level. By 1980, nearly a generation after the Voting Rights Act, the increase in black voter registration had still not translated into a significant increase in the number of black elected officials. During 1972–80, the proportion of eligible black Georgians who were registered to vote increased by a further 2 percent to 464,783 voters. Although this represented 27 percent of the total number of registered voters in 1980, Georgia's 249 black elected officials represented only 3.7 percent of the state total of 6,660—even less than the average of 5 percent across the South as a whole. Only six of Georgia's 551 municipalities had a black mayor in 1980. [138]

Atlanta and Hancock County may have underlined the potential of the black vote, but they were very much exceptions in Georgia. By 1980, nine of the state's twenty-three majority black counties still had no black elected officials. In his survey of black political empowerment, Lawrence Hanks concluded that "the average number of black elected officials from 1972–80 offers a dismal picture of progress... Georgia had the largest proportion—65%—of counties with no blacks on the major county boards—more than any other southern state with a 20 percent or more black population." [139]

In each city and county across Georgia, therefore, the key issue was not simply registering more voters but changing the system of elections to make the black vote effective. In most cases, this meant challenging at-large electoral systems in the courts. As one local leader in Baldwin County commented, "We've tried many, many times to get blacks elected at-large and we've never been able to do it, even when most everybody turns out to vote. We finally made the decision that the only thing we could do was sue." [140]

In this context, litigation at the local level assumed enormous importance. Just as the *Primus King* decision had increased black political influence during the 1940s, a swath of local litigation played a crucial role in the increase in black political strength during the 1980s. Laughlin McDonald noted that "Georgia has had an extraordinary amount of voting rights litigation at the local level." At least one hundred recorded local lawsuits were filed between 1974 and 1990. The vast majority of these were filed after the 1982 amendment to Section 2 of the Voting Rights Act, which declared that voting practices were in violation of the statute if their "result" was to discriminate on the basis of race or color. Two days later, the Supreme Court ruled in the case of *Lodge v. Burke County, Georgia,* that discriminatory intent need not be proved to make voting practices unlawful if they resulted in discrimination. [141]

While the Justice Department played a key role in the enforcement of Section 5, virtually all litigation was brought by civil rights organizations in conjunction with local leadership. The American Civil Liberties Union, which brought more than fifty of the cases, played a crucial if little publicized role in the struggle for fair electoral systems. By the end of the 1980s, fewer than thirty-five at-large systems remained across Georgia. Over half of the changes from at-large to more representative forms of elections resulted directly from litigation. In many other communities it was the threat or implication of the demands of the minority community that forced change, especially because the losing jurisdiction was required to pay costs. In the Burke County case, for example, the total costs amounted to almost $300,000.

Without doubt, the changes to the electoral systems had a far-reaching impact in Georgia. The ACLU described these changes as Georgia's "quiet revolution." Laughlin McDonald argued that "without electoral changes and the potential empowerment of the black electorate that they provide, very little forward movement in the electoral fortunes of Georgia blacks would have occurred." Linda Meggers, director of the state's reapportionment office, concluded that the phasing out of at-large voting was "the most revolutionary change in Georgia since the Civil War.

You're having a whole new distribution of power."[142] Between 1980 and 1990, the number of black elected officials more than doubled.

Even so, black Georgians represented less than 10 percent of the total number of elected officials. One generation after the Voting Rights Act, the issue of equality of political power remained unresolved. In 1980, incumbent Herman Talmadge lost to Republican Mack Mattingley in his attempt to be reelected to the Senate. The 1980 race marked the end of almost half a century of Talmadge influence in Georgia politics. Maynard Jackson asserted after the election that the result "demonstrates that Afro-American voters cannot any longer be taken for granted in Georgia—you cannot spit in our eye and tell us it's raining." Talmadge's defeat, however, resulted from short-term factors rather than a significant shift in voting patterns. Talmadge had suffered a messy divorce, his alcoholism had become common knowledge, and he had been involved in an acrimonious primary contest with Lieutenant Governor Zell Miller. Above all, as John Lewis has commented, Talmadge "had been troubled by the discovery of a large amount of cash stuffed in one of his overcoats."[143]

The continuing struggle for equality in politics was highlighted again by the controversy over a further reapportionment of Georgia's congressional districts in 1981. Under the plan, Georgia's fifth district would have had a slightly increased proportion of black residents but left a 54 percent white majority among registered voters. The attorney general denied preclearance under Section 5, and the state of Georgia lost its appeal in the Supreme Court.

State senator Julian Bond suggested a revised plan that would make the fifth district 73 percent black. Revealing the intentions of the reapportionment planners, Joe Mack Wilson, chairman of the House Reapportionment Committee, told his colleagues that "I don't want to draw nigger districts." Other senators claimed that the plan would cause white flight and resegregation. Jim Wooten of the *Atlanta Journal* conceded that Bond's plan "acknowledges the reality that within metro-Atlanta, two separate and distinct communities exist and peaceful coexistence, not racial brotherhood, is the true state of affairs."[144] In the event, the House Committee compromised with 65 percent of black residents.[145]

Clearly, black political power was only a part of the struggle for black equality. Across Georgia, elected black politicians found themselves confronted by the seemingly interminable consequences of social and economic deprivation. Judge Edith Ingram, for example, was surprised by the day-to-day realities of her office after her election by Hancock County's black community in 1968. Ingram reflected later,

"I have to write checks for them, pay bills, buy groceries, take them to the doctors, balance checkbooks, certify them for welfare, make doctors' appointments, read letters, answer letters and fix loan papers for houses. A good 85–90% of the work that we do is nonoffice related work, but the people have no one else to depend on." [146]

Urban Protest and Violence

The extensive efforts to gain equality in public accommodations, voting, and education highlighted the continuing struggle for legal rights across Georgia. But these protests had also shown that legal rights in themselves did not guarantee black equality in practice. For many black Georgians caught in economic adversity, however, the irrelevance of changes in the law to the basic issues of black welfare had been apparent far earlier, even before the passage of the federal acts.

The problems of economic deprivation were most apparent in Atlanta. By the beginning of the 1960s, local community leaders in the slum section of Vine City in south Atlanta labeled their home "the forgotten community." Both the student demonstrations and the traditional leadership in Atlanta had overlooked the problems of the Vine City slum. [147] Community leaders also felt that the civil rights legislation had not addressed the issues facing Vine City. After the Civil Rights Act, civic league leaders complained that "the recent civil rights law meant nothing to the average Vine City resident." SNCC staff recorded that in 1965, local civic leagues in south Atlanta "came to us and protested about the way that they are being screwed by the War on Poverty." [148]

Economic statistics highlighted the extent of deprivation in Vine City. The average income of Vine City residents was less than $2,500, over $500 less than the federal poverty level. More than one-third of Vine City residents were unemployed. [149] Economic deprivation was also reflected in poor housing for black Atlantans. In 1960, the Bureau of the Census recorded that one in five black Atlantans lived in rental housing "which does not provide safe and adequate shelter in its present condition and endangers the health, safety and well being of the occupants." [150] By 1968, 83 percent of the public housing units in Atlanta were located in predominantly black districts and all those living in public housing were below the official poverty level. City development projects had exacerbated the problem. A 1963 Fulton County Department of Family and Children Services report noted that bulldozing for highways had pushed many "slum dwellers to the fringes of the areas cleared, making their overcrowded conditions more crowded." The chairman of Atlanta's Housing Authority conceded in 1968 that urban renewal had dislocated 4,590 families, over 95 percent of whom were black.[151]

After touring some of the poorest areas of the Vine City slum, Martin Luther King Jr. lamented that "living conditions were the worst that I have ever seen." King himself lived near Vine City, in what SNCC workers described as a "modest home." But after walking along Markham Street, King admitted that "I had no idea people were living in Atlanta in such conditions. This is a shame on the community." Charles Weltner observed that "South Atlanta is a run down inner-city neighborhood," whose deprivation was all the more poignant because of its location "two miles south of Georgia's gold-domed capitol." Even experienced SNCC workers were shocked. Bill Beardslee, a SNCC member who moved into Vine City, wrote that "there is no barrier against violence here." Beardslee reported that one mother was "a wonderful person, warm and friendly, very hard working . . . and controls the household with a switch." Although poverty affected all races, the fact that over 80 percent of Vine City residents were black meant that the problems of poverty and race were inextricably linked.[152]

In this context, local protest was not aimed at issues of legal rights but simply to gain a basic standard of living. For those caught in economic deprivation, such protests were not so much the beginning of a new struggle as another stage in the long-running battle for an improved standard of living. After a march on the city hall in 1963, civic leaders had presented Mayor Allen with *The City Must Provide,* a pamphlet calling for the provision of community facilities, including over sixty paved sidewalks, twenty traffic lights, and fourteen street sewage systems. In 1966, the Markham Street Area Civic League articulated its grievances succinctly in a pamphlet:

> Because our houses are condemned
> Because we have no heating system
> Because our places are unsanitary
> Because we have rats and roaches
> Because we have holes in the floor.[153]

For all the particular social and economic problems of Vine City, however, Beardslee observed that "the southside of Atlanta is the same as any other city where forgotten Negroes live," albeit magnified in scale compared with other Georgia cities.[154] Across Georgia, a proliferation of urban neighborhood groups addressed the problem of inadequate living standards. What distinguished the Vine City area was the involvement of a major civil rights organization in the struggle.

In 1966, SNCC launched the Atlanta Project, which sought to build "an alternative political model to the conventional one" because, "if this is not done, there is no doubt that the Southern Black Community will become like most Northern Ghettos." For SNCC in Georgia, the Atlanta Project represented another effort to return to local politics to follow on from the faltering Southwest Georgia Project. Within the wider organization, staff workers observed, this shift to local politics "began with the formation of the Freedom Democratic party [in Mississippi] in the summer of 1964 ... and has continued in Alabama as county political parties are being formed in the winter and spring of 1966." [155] What was new, however, was that the Atlanta Project marked the first time that SNCC had begun working in a southern urban ghetto.

Vine City was an obvious target urban ghetto for SNCC. As early as 1963, SNCC workers had asked themselves what they called the obvious question, namely why an area of sixty thousand black residents, including ten thousand registered voters, should be politically impotent, even in the supposedly liberal city of Atlanta. During the same year, SNCC had supported various southside organizations in the march to City Hall protesting economic hardship. SNCC's subsequent failure to be awarded a Voter Education Project grant to canvass the area, coupled with frustration about the ineffectiveness of the ANVL (which had won the grant), fueled determination to work in the area. [156]

The key to the development of SNCC's Atlanta Project was that it built on existing organizations as well as existing disenchantment. SNCC workers who first visited the area in 1963 had met with Rev. Colbert of the South Pryor League, who had called meetings and collated petitions for social improvements during the previous seven years. In 1965, college students living in the region formed the Vine City Improvement Association (VCIA), which tackled projects such as clearing lots to provide playgrounds. Under the leadership of a white Quaker activist, Hector Black, the Vine City Council (VCC) formed in rivalry to supervise a more belligerent task force. [157]

In themselves, the VCIA and VCC had achieved minimal gains before the Atlanta Project. A Southern Regional Council report at the end of 1965 concluded that "not much has changed in Vine City. No real organization has been formed." Often only ten people attended meetings, which could degenerate into a "nightmare of threats, insinuations and chaos." Allegations of financial impropriety undermined the credibility of both organizations, and no worker had been appointed for full-time door-to-door canvassing. For all their failings, however, the Vine City organizations acted as the crucial platform for the development of a neighborhood-wide movement. As the SRC report concluded, "The people have started, however, and have learned something."[158]

Indirectly, it was the Voting Rights Act of 1964–65 that precipitated the Atlanta Project. SNCC communications director Julian Bond had won the 136th state representative district, which was based in Vine City, only to be denied his seat in January 1966 because of his forthright opposition to the war in Vietnam. Consequently, SNCC workers decided to build a tightly knit political organization to reelect Bond at the ensuing special election. Project leader Bill Ware later explained that he saw little point in his civil rights activities if local black elected officials could not freely express their opinions.[159] Using the combination of a highly publicized protest march and an array of neighborhood canvassing techniques, student workers encouraged over seven hundred people to vote.[160] Atlanta's local NBC affiliate described the turnout as spectacular, especially considering that it was snowing, the polling booths had been changed, and Bond was unopposed.[161]

Once involved in the district, SNCC members decided to maintain their presence. Within Atlanta, the project was intended to be a stepping-stone to eventual political control of City Hall. The project was also supposed to act as a regional precedent, one which SNCC members hoped "will have significance for other southern cities where there has been little or no 'movement' up until now." Unlike SNCC's previous urban campaigns, the focus of the project was the black poor, who had "lowered their level of expectation to mere survival."[162]

As in southwest Georgia, SNCC workers actively sought to promote racial pride. Much of the early rhetoric of project workers echoed Sherrod's calls to counter the psychological effects of white supremacy. Project workers organized workshops and produced literature promoting African dignity. The project's newsletter, the *Nitty-Gritty,* was aimed at "the black poor . . . to give people the truth about black people and what they're doing, in an attempt to counteract the 'white lies' of the white press; example Watts rebellion, the Viet Cong, Ghana etc." In contrast to the interracial team in southwest Georgia, however, the Atlanta Project adopted extreme ideas of black separatism. Under the influence of Bill Ware, the project was exclusively run by black field staff. Project reports were filed as black papers. In 1966, Ware denounced local black policemen as "white men with black skins. [They are] as much our enemy as the Ku Klux Klan." In his history of SNCC, Clayborne Carson noted that it was the Atlanta Project that precipitated SNCC's final transition to Black Power.[163]

Although SNCC workers intended to develop a new model of community organizing, unexpected local circumstances precipitated a direct action protest more reminiscent of previous SNCC campaigns. On 26 January 1966, a Markham Street resident named Mrs. Brown was evicted by the notorious local landlord Joe Schaffer, and with nowhere else to go she turned to the project office. Initially, SNCC members hoped to organize a rent strike opposing Schaffer, who owned much of the property in the neighborhood. Schaffer exploited families who could afford only half a normal rent by packing up to five families into individual houses. After a singularly severe spell of cold weather that killed eighteen people across Georgia, however, SNCC joined with the VCC in providing blankets and discovering which homes lacked heating. Shortly after Julian Bond urged Mayor Allen to take action at the end of January 1966, a man froze to death in a Vine City apartment.[164]

It was SNCC's participation in such nitty-gritty action that sparked direct action protest. After Schaffer had Hector Black arrested for trespassing, SNCC and the VCC called mass meetings in an attempt to organize a rent strike. In addition, SNCC contacted American Civil Liberties Union lawyers to file suit against Schaffer. Meanwhile, the visits of Jim Forman, Coretta Scott King, and Martin Luther King Jr. attracted the attention of the city media.[165]

In many ways, the Markham Street affair proved to be a setback for the Atlanta Project. Schaffer was forced to drop the eviction order with the payment of one week's rent, but the courts upheld his legal right to the evictions. Although Mayor Allen offered to move striking residents into public housing, local residents perceived this as another example of public maneuvering to maintain Atlanta's image. Allen refused to support the rent strike and, according to David Harmon, failed "to undertake and sustain the actions necessary to improve the living conditions in the area."[166] Meanwhile, SNCC found its leadership sidelined by the legal tactics of the ACLU and the greater media and official interest in Martin Luther King.

For the Atlanta Project staff, the Markham Street affair marked a tactical shift from political organization to direct confrontation of the practical and psychological exploitation of Vine City residents. This shift became complete after the project severed its links with Julian Bond. After his election, Bond had refused to sack his white secretary or hand over campaign funds to the project, and eventually he decided not to stand for reelection. During the ensuing months, SNCC organized a picket of a local dry cleaning business that had fired its black employees for striking and subsequently replaced them with white workers. Shortly afterward, project workers surrounded the local Twelfth Army Corps building, carrying placards depicting lynchings and bearing captions such as "the Vietcong never called us nigger."[167]

The public belligerence of the project workers masked the increasing isolation of the student group from the wider community. At both the Laundromat and the Army Corps, Atlanta police chief Herbert Jenkins separated the project workers from any bystanders or local allies. The subsequent collapse of the protests once the students were arrested exposed the lack of community support. In the protest against the dry cleaners, the failure of the project to negotiate successfully led to a factional split among local pickets. The project's adoption of extreme Black Power rhetoric, particularly after the mocking of Hector Black as a "White Jesus," further undermined local goodwill. Project workers also formed a list of Uncle Toms and Dr. Thomases that included Martin Luther King Jr., COAHR, and the Vine City Council.[168] When Stokeley Carmichael fired all members of the project because of insubordination in 1967, it was merely the official termination of an already disintegrating protest.

The initial intention of SNCC workers had been to build "an alternative political model," believing that otherwise "the southern Black Community will become like most Northern Ghettos." If SNCC workers failed to build an alternative political model, they were certainly correct in their prediction. With no effective outlet for discontent, Atlanta's poorer black communities did indeed follow the pattern of the northern ghettos as simmering resentment fueled three major racial disturbances across the city during 1966 and 1967. Each disturbance followed a similar pattern of alleged police brutality in a poor neighborhood sparking off a violent reaction. In each case, the arrival of SNCC workers, and particularly Stokeley Carmichael, fomented existing tensions. During the fall of 1966, Carmichael was charged with "inciting to riot" by the Fulton County grand jury and placed on a $10,000 bond.[169]

These outbursts of violence may have tarnished Atlanta's image, but they did not come as a surprise to observers. Both Martin Luther King Jr. and Herman Talmadge had predicted a "long hot summer" of violence in 1967. After noting that forty-three minor racial incidents had occurred during 1965, Mayor Allen had prepared an emergency riot procedure. At a hearing held by the Community Relations Committee in June 1967, one Dixie Hills resident summed up the general consensus when arguing that the "disturbances would come sooner or later, mainly because our kids are on the streets." Although much of the blame in Atlanta's media was leveled at Stokeley Carmichael, Atlanta's Council on Human Relations insisted that "the basic reasons lie with Atlanta's lack of concern over miserable conditions in the slums."

One wide-ranging survey prepared for the National Advisory Committee on Urban Disorders revealed that most black leaders in Atlanta saw the violence as a reflection of poverty and a call for "something to be done about the ghetto."[170]

In many ways, however, the surprising aspect of racial disturbances in Atlanta was not that they occurred but that they remained limited. Quite simply, the "long hot summer" of 1967 failed to materialize. The *New York Times Magazine* described Atlanta's disturbances as "small brushfires compared with the Los Angeles Holocaust." Undoubtedly, Allen's concern to preempt violence prevented the escalation of tensions. In the summer of 1966, Allen swiftly put up $10,000 to catch the murderer of a young black man in a drive-by shooting.[171] When violence did break out, Allen immediately contacted moderate local leaders and ordered the arrest of any SNCC staff who were involved. Allen's swift arrival at the scene of each disturbance, to the extent that he was once thrown from the roof of his car, allowed frustration to be vented verbally.[172]

The disturbances in Atlanta formed part of a more general pattern of racial violence across Georgia after 1965, which ran parallel with the nonviolent efforts to enforce legal rights in the state. Although national media attention focused on northern violence, the evidence of Georgia demonstrates that racial disturbances became a feature of the South too, albeit not on the scale of the most notorious ghetto riots. As in the North, violence was linked to social deprivation, frustration, and a sense of isolation. It also reflected sympathy with some of the extreme Black Power rhetoric. One university investigation into the scenes of violence in Atlanta observed that a "hate-whitey orientation is very prevalent. A deep-seated conviction is that no white person can be trusted."[173]

Atlanta, as the state's largest city, experienced more minor disturbances than any other Georgia city. But even in Rome, where race relations had traditionally been relatively moderate, city police confronted violent protesters after an alleged incident of police brutality in 1971, arresting more than one hundred demonstrators during a week-long curfew. In Columbus, seven black policemen led the protests against an alleged wave of police violence against the black community. In June 1971, the seven policemen picketed their own police headquarters and ripped the American flag shoulder patch from their uniforms. When they were subsequently dismissed, SCLC's Hosea Williams led a protest march of five hundred people. During the summer, Columbus experienced over 150 cases of nighttime arson, including a series of fire bombings, sniper fire, and rock throwing at passing cars.[174]

It was the city of Augusta, despite its tranquil image as the "Garden City of the South," that suffered Georgia's most widespread and violent outburst of racial anger on 9 May 1970. A racial incident that was offensive even by Georgia's standards triggered the outrage. According to attendant prison officers, Charles Oatman, a black teenager awaiting trial, died after falling from his bunk. The undertaker, however, noticed that Oatman had suffered systematic torture, including numerous cigarette burns and skin punctures from a fork. Within hours, an angry crowd rampaged through central streets. By the following morning, over fifty stores had been set aflame, costing an estimated $1.5 million. Six black Augustans were killed, each shot multiple times in the back.[175]

The riot in Augusta followed the pattern of other violent disturbances in Georgia. The SRC observed that "if you took a crayon and colored in the areas of Augusta where there is the lowest income, lowest level of educational achievement, highest incidence of unemployment and underemployment and highest density of Negro residents you would almost perfectly outline the area of chaos on the night of May 9." The reasons why the violence was particularly extensive were the historic lack of communication between races in Augusta, the dearth of effective black leadership, and the Oatman affair, culminating a succession of incidents of police brutality.[176]

Even in the most extreme case of Augusta, however, racial violence did not lead to tangible benefits for black Georgians. Four years after the riot, Ralph Walker, a black professor at Augusta College, concluded a discussion of the violence by stating, "How much better are things since the riots?—politically speaking—not much." In response to the riot, Augusta's predominantly white city council had commissioned a special report by the NUL on racial discrimination in the city. In practice, many of the report's suggestions were sidelined. The Augusta police were exonerated for the deaths of six black Augustans. A decade later, Augusta's sheriff, J. B. Dykes, admitted that his force still suffered from serious problems of racial brutality.[177]

The failure of the riot dampened enthusiasm for violence, even among the extremist minority. "We can gather all the pistols and .22 rifles we want," admitted one Black Panther sympathizer in Augusta in October 1970, "but we can't win in a shoot-out. The establishment has got cannons and bazookas."[178]

The Continuing Struggle

One generation after the civil rights acts, it was clear that there was no longer a uniform or united response to the problems of racial inequality in Georgia. Efforts to secure integration in schools and to increase voter registration ran parallel with community organizing in the slums and outbreaks of violence. It was also clear that the paradigm of protest during the years of direct action protest had become outdated. Integration, the shibboleth of 1960s protest, had been replaced by a more general call for improved black welfare and community development.

If the goals of protest had evolved from the 1960s, the tactics had changed too. Protests were no longer community-wide, all-embracing campaigns but an amalgam of individual groups. At the Hungry Club in 1970, Vernon Jordan observed that "the organization in black communities of groups addressing themselves to specific issues directly affecting them provides a preview of the civil rights arena in years to come." Instead of a coordinated movement or a single goal, Jordan expected to see "welfare groups, tenants' rights associations, co-operatives, domestic unions, poor people's corporations, better-school groups, and health and nutrition organizations. All are developed to focus their energies on the new issues affecting the rights of black people."[179]

In the cities, these new issues centered primarily on the interlinking of economic problems and neighborhood degeneration, poor education, and police brutality. Of course, in many ways these new issues were not particularly new at all; it was simply that set-piece battles for integration of the 1960s had obscured long-running campaigns for black rights at the local level. The campaigns for neighborhood improvements by Benny T. Smith in Atlanta during the 1970s and 1980s, for example, paralleled the efforts of Ruby Blackburn during the 1940s.

Increasingly, the "issues affecting the rights of black people" meant different things for different groups of black Georgians. Nowhere was this more evident than in Atlanta, where there were clearly disparate groups within the city's black community. By 1980, Atlanta was the home to one of the largest concentrations of black millionaires in America and more black Atlantans earned more than $50,000 annually than any other minority group in the South. The city retained its prestige too. *Ebony* magazine in 1973 called Atlanta the "New Mecca for Young Blacks." Nevertheless, one-third of black Atlantans remained under the poverty level in 1980. As Steven Lawson concluded, "The diversity of Atlanta's population, reflected in its class structure, sometimes made it difficult for blacks to unite on behalf of efforts to relieve severe impoverishment."[180]

Consequently, black Atlantans had increasingly diverse concerns. Whereas middle-class black Atlantans sought to overturn residential segregation, Vine City residents were more concerned with decent housing.[181] At times, these interests came into direct conflict. The divergent aspirations of black Atlantans were most vividly exemplified in 1977, when Maynard Jackson decreed that striking black sanitation workers would be fired unless they returned to work. In his review of Atlanta's power structure, Clarence Stone concluded that "neither specifically working class nor neighborhood organizations" among Atlanta's black population has an "irresistible claim on membership in the city's governing regime, and policy is not responsive to the kinds of interests they represent."[182]

Even in the extreme case of Atlanta, however, it would be an oversimplification to draw too sharp a division between the issues affecting different classes of black residents. After his election, Jackson prioritized the problems of urban renewal and affirmative action. To highlight the need for improvement in housing, Jackson spent a weekend in Bankhead Courts, a low-income housing project. Despite the opposition of Atlanta's business leadership, Jackson designated that all of the city's $18.7 million community development fund should be spent on residential neighborhoods, rather than the central business district. Equally, the Atlanta Summit Leadership Conference, acting as an umbrella organization, sought to represent the general interests of Atlanta's black community. Under the leadership of Jesse Hill and Sam Williams, the Summit successfully opposed plans by Atlanta's transit association, MARTA, to expand primarily into white residential districts in 1971. The Summit also pressured MARTA to appoint an affirmative action officer and persuaded the city council to include black representatives in decision making about school desegregation and urban redevelopment.[183]

Away from the cities, local group protests also addressed a wide range of problems, but increasingly the primary issue was the problem of poverty. Where there is poverty, Georgia's NAACP president Robert Flanagan concluded during the 1970s, then even elected black officials could not deliver. "If a crow flew over Stewart County," for example, "it would have to pack a lunch." A common complaint, Flanagan continued, would often be, "you told me to register and told me to vote and, hell, I'm still hungry and I look up there and see the sky through my house."[184]

Problems of rural poverty were typified by the experience of Glascock County in eastern Georgia. In 1970, the median value of the county's housing was only $2,924, in contrast to the national median of $7,344. "One feels there must be an error somewhere in the data or in the interpretation," observed one reporter. Retail purchases in the county averaged $532 per annum, less than half the national average. An editorial in the *Atlanta Inquirer* commented that "one cannot, on learning of such stories, blame the city's new ghetto inhabitants for leaving their earlier homes." Such economic problems were compounded by the hostile attitude of Sheriff James English, who resisted outside assistance with the verdict that "if anyone went to bed hungry at night in Georgia it was because he was sorry as hell." On 3 August 1967, English and a group of angry citizens broke up a meeting between the county commission and two state welfare workers attempting to establish a federal food program. "There'd just be a lot of niggers lined up and that's all it would do," English explained. "We aren't integrated yet." Bob Parris (formerly Bob Moses), commented that "Glascock was not a moral lightning rod but a looking glass into the state of the United States." [185]

Glascock was certainly a looking glass into the state of many areas in Georgia. According to a report in 1967, Georgia had nine of the country's one hundred poorest counties, in which over two-thirds of families had a median income of $1,855, far below the poverty level of $3,000. Although poverty affected Georgians regardless of race, the problems of race and poverty were inextricably linked. In 1970 over two-thirds of Georgia black families had an income lower than the national poverty level of $3,000, compared with only one-quarter of white families. [186]

During the generation after the Civil Rights Act, this situation had barely improved. Between 1960 and 1970, the average black family income had increased from 37 to 52 percent of the average white family income in Georgia. But by 1980, this figure had increased to only 56 percent. At the same time, black unemployment had reached 12.5 percent, almost three times the proportion for whites, and over 55 percent of Georgians in poverty were black. Even in Atlanta, black unemployment was 10.5 percent in 1980, more than double the white unemployment rate of 4.1 percent. Of those employed, seven out of ten black workers had blue-collar jobs. Almost one-third of Atlanta's black families, in contrast to 7 percent of white families, were below the poverty line. Donald Grant concluded that "despite numerous success stories, the overall statistics on the economic and social welfare of black Georgians have been grim." [187]

The problem of poverty was interlinked with the problem of poor education. In 1986, social scientists Douglas Bachtel, Everett Lee, and Hortense Bates pointed out that the average standard of black education had improved very slowly since 1960. Bachtel, Lee, and Bates warned that "without an adequate education, thousands of blacks in Georgia may face a life of minimum wage." [188] Somewhat poignantly, the county that showed the least improvement over time was Taliaferro, with an average of 5.1 completed school years for black children in 1960 rising to only 7.3 in 1980.

Although there was no common trend across the state, it was clear that black Georgians in the southern black belt continued to suffer the most, largely because they lived in the poorest region. By 1980, the concept of "two Georgias" in economic terms had become common parlance. "They say we're the second Georgia down here," one Clay County official told the *Atlanta Journal*, but "it feels like the fifth or sixth to me." Everett Lee noted that "a block of counties with especially low levels of education extends south-eastwards from Athens and continues south of Augusta." An SRC report observed that of the fifty Georgia counties with the most severe poverty in 1980, all but one was in the black belt. The *Atlanta Journal* also pointed out that "only the black-belt has lost jobs because of racial apprehension."[189]

Although the problem of poverty and economic hardship affected communities across the state, there was no common pattern of response by local organizations. In his theoretical overview of black empowerment in Georgia, Lawrence Hanks concluded that no sociological model accurately explained the level of activity of a particular community.[190] For example, agriculture teacher Stine George led a belligerent improvement association in rural Seminole County, forcing a change in the local system of elections. But the activism in Seminole County stood in contrast to the atrophy in surrounding counties that experienced minimal racial change. Various types of black activism in Atlanta and Savannah contrasted with the relative dearth of activity in the cities of Columbus and Augusta.[191]

In fact, the history of Georgia during the tail end of the civil rights movement indicated that the extent and success of local movements for racial progress became increasingly dependent on individual local factors. Preeminent among these factors were the attitude and ability of local black leaders. Camilla in south Georgia, for example, witnessed significant racial change primarily through the leadership of a local mechanic, Ed Brown. After the change to district voting in Camilla, for example, black candidates won two of the three city council seats and two on the county commission. Brown himself was elected mayor in 1978. "Ed had just gotten out of Vietnam," Robert Flanagan observed later, "and he wasn't afraid of nobody." Because he had a job at a Firestone factory out of the county in Albany, Brown had economic independence too.[192]

Local organizations also prospered when focusing on a clear single issue. In Macon, Bill Randall used the incentive of getting streets paved in all-black neighborhoods as the basis for an NAACP voting drive. By the end of the 1970s, just as in the 1940s, one of the key local issues was racial violence. Robert Flanagan admitted that "sometimes I used to say . . . I wish I could hire a white guy to beat a black up down there. Where you don't have a hard white pouncing on blacks it is hard to organize." Similarly, local movements benefited from the technical support of federal programs and statewide human rights organizations. In the sphere of education, the Georgia Leadership Conference on Education had formed as early as March 1965, employing two field secretaries to observe local integration.[193] The ACLU supported the efforts of Stine George and Ed Brown in overturning their local at-large systems of elections. The southern Regional Council organized leadership development programs and provided technical assistance for community organization.[194] In response to letters from local black residents who did not dare to speak out publicly, the GCHR sent four female fieldworkers into Glascock County to supervise emergency free food distribution. In the face of opposition from local merchants who feared loss of trade and despite shootings at their car, the fieldworkers secured a federal Office of Economic Opportunity food and medical program. Indeed, the GCHR played its most significant, if unheralded, role in the movement as a whole during this later phase.[195]

Individual protests were most effective when they combined strong leadership, specific issues, and outside technical support. In Burke County in eastern Georgia, for example, the local movement was particularly effective despite numerous obstacles to black organization. Although it was the second largest county in Georgia, approaching the size of the state of New Hampshire, Burke County had a sparse population of only twenty thousand residents. "These people in the boondocks," movement leader Herman Lodge reflected, "they knew very little about Dr. King and the movement, and they knew very little about the NAACP." [196] During the 1968 election, the majority of black voters backed Talmadge ahead of Jackson because they did not know that Jackson was black.

The problems of a dispersed population in Burke County were compounded by the area's extreme poverty. Once the leading cotton producer of all counties in Georgia, Burke County had become the fifth poorest county in the state in median family income by 1980. In an article in 1986, Christena Bledsoe observed that "poverty abounds . . . entering Waynesboro, the county seat, is entering life away from urban affluence and the inter-states." In common with the rest of the state, this poverty was racially specific. Forty-three percent of blacks lived below the official poverty level compared with 13 percent of whites, while black life expectancy was ten years less than for whites. The average educational level for Burke County blacks was only the sixth grade.[197]

Opposition to racial change was also evident. After the Civil Rights Act, the public swimming pool had been sold to an all-white civic club for one dollar. Shortly after the desegregation of the Burke County high school, the home of one of the first transfer students was shot into twelve times. A private white academy, financially supported by the county board of education, helped circumvent the threat of integrated education. Such actions reflected the prevailing attitude of the county commissioners, one of whom admitted to a radio reporter that "he would head to the hills" if a black candidate was ever elected to the county commission.[198] Although 54 percent of Burke County's population was black, the county commission was still exclusively white by 1980.

Nevertheless, Burke County also had a history of black community action. Herman Lodge, a returning veteran who owned a small hamburger store, founded the Burke County Improvement Association (BCIA) in 1961 after a young black man was imprisoned on a trumped-up charge. The white supremacist reaction was so strong that members of the BCIA initially remained anonymous except for those who held jobs outside the county. The BCIA's first success came through organizing an integrated Headstart program with a budget of $190,000 administered solely by local black residents.[199] In 1967, Lodge received a grant from the VEP to pay fourteen workers $4 a day for three months to facilitate voter registration. Lodge responded by inviting all church leaders to dinner to discuss local problems.

The local movement actually rose to national prominence in 1982 when National Public Radio's legal affairs correspondent Nina Totenburg used Burke County as a case example during a series on the Voting Rights Act. When Burke County movement leaders filed a suit against the at-large system of elections, they backed up their case by transporting thirty-five local blacks to the Supreme Court in a hired bus. The presence of the local delegation undermined the defense's case that the lack of elected officials was owing to black political apathy rather than the at-large system. Justice Sandra Day O'Connor remarked that "if these very poor people came all the way here, that wouldn't be apathy would it?" *Rogers v. Lodge* replaced *Mobile v. Bolden* as the nation's voting rights standard, making it easier to prove discrimination solely on the effects of an electoral system.[200]

Though the county briefly gained publicity, the more fundamental impact was wholly local. In the first election after the Supreme Court decision, some black precincts recorded an almost 100 percent turnout.[201] Within two years Burke County was only the second Georgia county after Hancock County to have a majority black officeholding. Herman Lodge himself was elected to chairman of the county commission.

In contrast to John McCown in Hancock County, Lodge used his political position to initiate a radical economic improvement program rather than build a personal power base. The financial foundation for economic improvements came from the attraction of Georgia Nuclear Power to the county.[202] But central to Lodge's proposals were the racially integrated terms of all improvement programs. Using Georgia Nuclear Power's money, the black majority government proposed a $13.5 million new high school, aimed at drawing some whites back into the 75 percent black school system. Within two years, county commissioners supervised the construction of a forty-five-bed hospital, the doubling of recreational facilities in Waynesboro, and the establishment of a Human Relations Commission. Black family income in the county more than doubled during 1959–79, far in excess of the paltry improvement in the rest of the state.[203]

But if Burke County provided an example of black political and economic progress, it stood in stark contrast to Forsyth County, fifty miles to the north of Atlanta. Ever since 1912, when all local black residents had been violently expelled from the county, Forsyth had remained exclusively white. During the 1960s, billboards warned black visitors "not to let the sun go down on your head." In this way Forsyth County school board officials claimed that they had avoided all "problems" of desegregation and integration. In May 1968, an integrated religious group attempted to stay in Forsyth County, only to be forcibly removed. When the group returned in June, the Georgia Council on Human Relations had alerted the state patrol. Despite the presence of a mob shouting, "Wait until the night comes," the state patrol ensured that the integrated group was able to spend the night in the county, the first such instance for fifty-six years. Nevertheless, white supremacy was swiftly restored. During the late 1970s, even black truck drivers making deliveries to the local chicken dressing plant had to be escorted by GBI agents.[204] By 1980, Forsyth County remained barely challenged by the Georgia civil rights movement.

Forty years after the first statewide protests under Rev. Gilbert, therefore, there was no longer a uniform or united civil rights movement in Georgia. Each community, and often individual groups within each community, had its own independent story to tell. In rural Georgia, the efforts of the local black leadership in Burke County stood in stark contrast to the experiment in black power in Hancock County. It was not simply that some black communities were more active than others but that the dominant racial issues varied between and within communities. The question of unofficial residential segregation in Atlanta, for example, was of a different order than the question of whether a black visitor could sleep in safety in Forsyth County.

Undoubtedly the federal acts of 1964 and 1965 irreversibly changed the context of race relations and racial protest in Georgia. But the separation of the "two Georgias" was also an important development, and consequently it was hardly surprising that black activism across the state should be so diverse. At the start of the century, Du Bois had commented on the divide between Atlanta and the rural black belt. Toward the end of the century, the divide was as stark as ever.

Of course, in many ways there had never been a uniform civil rights protest across Georgia. Local protests had united in opposition to the Talmadges during the 1940s and in response to the direct action protests of the so-called King years. Once the rule of the rustics had been superseded by urban domination in Georgia and Jim Crow ended in the South, however, fewer political issues tied local black activists together. Throughout the state, the goal of securing legal and political civil rights had been replaced by the broader challenge of making rights real, a challenge that varied markedly between communities across Georgia.

In many ways, however, the idea of two Georgias painted too stark a divide for black Georgians because issues of racial discrimination continued to prevail in the generation after the civil rights legislation of 1964 and 1965. Poverty, which affected black Georgians three times as often as whites, was not simply a rural problem. In 1980, one in four black Atlantans lived below the poverty line, which was the second worst rate among the nation's cities. Savannah and Macon also ranked in the bottom ten cities. Meanwhile, issues of equality in education, employment, and elections, not to mention racial prejudice, affected black Georgians in both the cities and the countryside. The Jim Crow era and the antics of the Talmadges may have been receding into history by the 1980s, but race remained a salient and sensitive issue in Georgia, as it did in the South and throughout the United States. Numan Bartley concluded *A History of Georgia* with the statement that in the 1980s, "it appeared that a new generation of problems was available for a new generation of Georgians."[205] It was a particularly apposite comment for those Georgians who were striving for racial equality.

Conclusion

The chronology of protest in Georgia follows the general pattern of protest in Louisiana, Mississippi, and the other southern states. As Fairclough concluded, "The contours of struggle ... bore little resemblance to the Montgomery-to-Selma story." Trezzant Anderson, Georgia correspondent for the *Pittsburgh Courier,* observed in 1961, "The Negro fight against racial discrimination did not begin with the Montgomery bus boycott as some silly folks seem to think."[1]

In Georgia, urban protest in its classical form also occurred outside the Montgomery-to-Selma years. For Aldon Morris, the three most important ways in which successful new local protests "differed from the NAACP and previous protest activity" were charismatic leadership, new decision-making procedures, and the adoption of new tactics.[2] The movement under Ralph Mark Gilbert in Savannah during the 1940s bore many of the hallmarks of this definition. Similarly, new, local protests continued to be initiated in many of the smaller communities into the 1970s and in the larger cities in response to continued discrimination.

What was new about the 1960s was the sheer scale of black protest and the entrance of direct action protest techniques into the political lexicon. The Arnall years had provided a small window of opportunity for black protest. State and national changes provided greater and more widespread opportunities for black protest by 1960. Whereas local movements emerged in certain towns during the 1940s, black protest flourished in most urban centers during the 1960s. The cadre of mostly middle-class black activists of the 1940s had also increased to include large numbers of youths and people from all economic classes. With the addition of boycotts, bloc voting, and neighborhood action, 1960s protest had become a mass movement.

While black activism continued throughout the period, it focused on different issues at different times. During the 1940s, the first upsurge in protest challenged the unfettered nature of Jim Crow. By the end of the decade, black protest organizations outside Atlanta merely hoped to survive. The direct action protests of the 1960s sought to remove Jim Crow, while subsequent protest aimed to translate legal equality into tangible gains. Fairclough's choice of title for his study of Louisiana highlights the fact that the civil rights struggle was not simply about legal discrimination but the broader issue of race and democracy. By the 1970s, black protest in Georgia included education, employment, and economic uplift too. In Burke County, the issue was less racial uplift than the need for the whole community, both black and white, to escape the poverty trap.

The history of black activism in Georgia also sheds light on how local movements emerged and developed. One distinctive feature of Georgia protest was the lack of involvement of national organizations. The story of Georgia protest, therefore, like that of Mississippi, was primarily a story of local people. SCLC and SNCC were not active in the urban protests of the 1960s (with the notable exception of Albany). SCLC's major role came in smaller communities after 1965, and SNCC workers led the less publicized local movements in rural southwest Georgia and Vine City in Atlanta. In Atlanta, opposition from the Auburn Avenue elite and from COAHR restricted the involvement of SCLC and SNCC respectively. Indeed, the Albany movement, which was the only case in which SNCC and SCLC did lead a major Georgia movement, was a conspicuous failure in generating headlines. SNCC and SCLC's participation in the Atlanta Summit Leadership Conference also proved to be ineffective, although in both cases it was not because they were outside organizations but because of a lack of planning and local circumstances.

Over the entire period, and even during the direct action years of the 1960s, the most significant black protest organization in Georgia was the NAACP. During the 1940s, the protest under Gilbert provided a major challenge to Georgia's Jim Crow, especially in the context of often violent white supremacy. NAACP branches also remained active in the generation after the Civil Rights Act. Opponents of black civil rights rated the NAACP as highly influential within Georgia. During the white backlash of the 1940s and 1950s, the NAACP was the favorite target of white supremacist politicians. In 1980, Edward Cashin conducted a survey to assess how Georgians viewed their past. For white Georgians, the NAACP was still "the favorite modern villain in popular history . . . regarded in our sample as an organization bent on agitating Georgia black people who would be satisfied except for such outward interference."[3]

The NAACP played a leading role precisely because it was decentralized. The story of Georgia accords with that of Louisiana, therefore, where Fairclough concluded that "the bedrock strength of the NAACP lay in its local branches." As Raymond Gavins has pointed out, "Studies of southern communities, where the struggle for civil rights was a continuing reality, year in, year out, present a less bureaucratic and more people-oriented NAACP." Before Montgomery, the NAACP was the only black organization that black Georgians could appeal to or local black leaders could affiliate with. NAACP branch movements of the 1960s often ignored the gradualist approach of the national board. After 1960, other organizations rivaled the NAACP in organizing local movements. SCLC workers were often called in by local leaders after 1965. In Glascock County during the 1970s, one black resident wrote to the GCHR in a manner reminiscent of despairing letters to the NAACP of the 1940s: "It wouldn't do for me to put names on this letter because it might get into the wrong hands before it gets to you."[4]

Protests may have been led locally, but they were influenced decisively by national events. The *Smith v. Allwright* decision of 1944 paved the way for an upsurge in local black activism, just as *Brown* did a decade later. The example of Montgomery and Greensboro galvanized the most widespread period of direct action protest in Georgia. Most of the local movements of the late 1960s were in response to the Civil Rights Act of 1964 and the Voting Rights Act of 1965. Supreme Court rulings on education and apportionment fueled black activism at the local level in the generation after the federal laws.

While local protests together had a cumulative impact, some individual protests were vigorous and durable, while other black communities were notable for inactivity. Before the federal acts of 1964–65, an obvious precondition for organized protest was a local environment in which emerging movements were not immediately crushed. The black communities of Savannah and Atlanta, for example, were the major centers for protest during the 1940s. With increasing urbanization and the end of the county-unit system, most cities witnessed racial protest during the years of direct action. By the end of the period, federal and economic changes were such that organized protest could, and did, occur in most areas of the state. Where there was unfettered white supremacy, local protest required outside resources. The state NAACP provided the impetus for numerous local movements during the Arnall years. Similarly, widespread organization occurred in Albany only after the involvement of SCLC and SNCC. Even with the resources of SNCC, the initial achievement of the Southwest Georgia Project was that it withstood racial violence; it did not overturn white supremacy in the region.

The history of Georgia protest provides fewer answers to the question of why particular local movements apparently succeeded and failed. The effectiveness of the direct action movements in the cities of Atlanta and Savannah stand in counterpoint to each other, as do the protests in the cities of Columbus and Macon. The development of a local movement in Burke County contrasts with the lack of progress in Glascock County. In a broader, comparative framework, the SCLC campaign in Albany and SNCC's Southwest Georgia Project failed to make the impact of similar campaigns in Birmingham and Mississippi. Clearly, the historical tradition of protest, the response of the white community, the economic strength of the black community, and support from outside organizations all played a role. Above all, in each local movement in Georgia it was the type of leadership and the extent of support within the black community that proved decisive.

Georgia's civil rights protest does shed light on how local movements were organized. Aldon Morris concluded that the "black church functioned as the institutional center of the modern civil rights movement."[5] The church was indeed important. Many of the leaders were ministers, particularly in the earlier years of protest and during the direct action protests of the 1960s. Rev. Ralph Mark Gilbert in Savannah, Rev. Julius Hope in Brunswick, and Rev. William Holmes Borders and Rev. Martin Luther King Sr. in Atlanta were some of the more prominent civil rights leaders in the state. Church congregations provided a network for civil rights leaders too. Rev. Gilbert contacted churches and colleges before visiting a new town. During the years of white backlash, the black church survived where protest organizations often did not. Dobbs addressed provincial churches on Emancipation Day, and in some of the more dynamic churches, sermons became exhortations for registration. And during the years of direct action, churches were shelters for protesters and a channel for communication. Mass meetings during citywide protests had a liturgy and fervor similar to revival meetings.

In contrast to the churches' network in Alabama, however, the role of the church in Georgia was not paramount. In the first place, churches had a mixed record of involvement. After the burning of the Mt. Olive church, every minister in Terrell County barred SNCC workers from using their churches. The pastor of the Second Baptist Church was Gilbert's most forthright critic in Savannah. In Atlanta, ministers were part of the black establishment that was criticized by students for a gradualist approach. In addition, the role of churches should be placed alongside that of other black networks in the state. During the 1940s, Dobbs and Gilbert also organized through the Masons, unions, and professional groups. In some of the direct action protests in the major cities, it was the colleges rather than the churches that were the primary conduit for communication. The Southwest Georgia Project used professional links from Albany and schools to form a local network. In the generation after the Civil Rights Act, neighborhood and single-issue groups were the main means of organization.

In the same way, ministers were only one part of an emerging group of independent black leaders. In Atlanta, ministers formed only one axis of the black power structure of the Auburn Avenue elite, along with business and educational leaders. The more active civil rights leaders were A. T. Walden, a lawyer, and John Wesley Dobbs, a postal clerk. Other vociferous local secular leaders included postal deliveryman W. W. Law in Savannah, building contractor William Randall in Macon, and John Barnum, who owned a funeral parlor in Americus. After 1965 in particular, most local leaders were employed outside the church.

Histories of the civil rights movement have only recently begun to highlight the role of women.[6] As Nasstrom wrote of Atlanta, "We have inherited a composite portrait of civil rights leadership that has a male face." The story of Georgia reinforces the conclusion of Vicki Crawford, who wrote that the "little-known individual and collective efforts among black women" disguise the fact that "women had a multiplicity of roles in the civil rights movement."[7] During the 1940s, black women in Georgia played an active if unheralded role. Ruby Blackburn was the foremost neighborhood organizer in Atlanta and was recognized by the Auburn Avenue elite. Grace Towns Hamilton was part of the elite and initiated the development of the Atlanta Negro Voters League. In Savannah and across the state, Eloria Sherman Gilbert joined with her husband in pioneering new branches as well as supporting him in his efforts. In each local branch of the NAACP, a woman usually held the important post of secretary. The participation of women in local movements was encouraged by female black voter organizations, such as in Atlanta, and by the formation of women's auxiliaries in local NAACP branches.[8]

At times, the activities of women were so obvious in Georgia protest that it would be a crass oversight to overlook them. This was particularly true among students, who were less tied to traditional gender roles. During the 1940s, Ruth Bacone in Augusta railed against the apathy of a male-dominated NAACP. Spelman College students engaged in protest before the founding of COAHR, and Herschelle Sullivan played a crucial leadership role alongside Lonnie King, her Morehouse counterpart. In Savannah, female protesters often outnumbered their male counterparts. For example, seven of the twelve black students who first sought to enter the hitherto white churches in the first "kneel-in" were women.[9] Female students were also involved in more racially hostile environments. Charles Sherrod recruited women to the Southwest Georgia Project, Robertina Freeman played a leading role in the demonstrations in Americus, and young girls suffered the worst of the incarceration in the Sumter County stockade.

Women also played a distinct supportive role. As Anne Standley concluded, "Black women directed voter registration drives, taught in freedom schools and provided food and housing for volunteers." Usually women led the singing at mass meetings too. Among the adults, observed the *Savannah Herald* in August 1960, "the adage 'behind every great man is a woman' is apropos to the Negroes' fight for freedom in Savannah, for behind this great movement is the courage and the ingenuity of Negro womanhood." Geneva Law, mother of W. W. Law, was one of the many women who took food to the protesters on the downtown picket lines. Her courage in the face of threatening megaphone messages, spotlights at her window, and blazing effigies of her son on the front lawn enabled her son to continue with his forthright leadership. Dolly Raines and Carolyn Daniels were the acknowledged mothers of the movement in southwest Georgia despite violent retribution, and Charles Sherrod noted that it was more often women than men who first supported student protesters.[10]

Women were particularly active in liberal and biracial organizations too. Jean Fairfax and Constance Curry spent a year investigating the integration of schools for the Georgia Conference on Education. Eliza Paschall was the often outspoken leader of the Atlanta Council on Human Relations. Frances Pauley, who led HOPE and the GCHR, was widely regarded as the most influential white supporter of civil rights protest across the state.[11]

Organized black protest in Georgia was not simply the preserve of the black elite. Ruby Blackburn's neighborhood leagues and women's voters' leagues, for example, involved a wide economic spectrum of black Atlantans during the 1940s. In the same period, activists included soldiers and union organizers as well as the emerging group of prosperous black Atlantans. By the 1960s, involvement increased as black communities in urban Georgia grew in size and independence. In some cases, such as in Brunswick and Rome, desegregation settlements were negotiated between the local white and black city leaders. But in Savannah during the 1960s, for example, the NAACP-led movement included diverse groups such as the Hub (for businessmen) and the longshoremen union, as well as students and church members. James Middleton, who worked with the CCCV in Savannah, remembered that Hosea

Williams "mostly worked in most of the slums of the city. Them was the people he wanted to get."[12] Hundreds of protesters from all sections of the community marched in Albany. SNCC workers also involved black Georgians in rural southwest Georgia and the poorer areas of Vine City. After the federal acts of 1964 and 1965, the distinction between elite and popular participation was less clear. Julian Bond from Morehouse College chose to represent Vine City residents. Maynard Jackson, who secured his nomination with support from the Atlanta black power structure, received the vast majority of all black votes in Atlanta and in turn made general economic uplift a major priority.

Protest in Georgia was also not confined to urban areas. The history of Georgia shows that black Georgians in rural areas did respond to the struggle for Jim Crow in innovative and forthright ways. In the context of the 1940s, the often piecemeal attempts to organize an NAACP branch or voter registration were significant acts of protest. Both W. W. Law and Charles Sherrod later highlighted the bravery of D. U. Pullum in Terrell County.[13] During the 1960s, the Southwest Georgia Project may have failed to overturn white supremacy, but it did attract local support. In the later struggle to translate legal rights into practical gains, the battle against poverty and discriminatory education in the countryside ran parallel with similar struggles in the towns.

In fact, the story of Georgia protest demonstrates that the exclusion of rural protest from major overviews of civil rights ignores the uneasy tension that existed between the rural and urban areas. Atlanta aspired to become a liberal economic city but for many years could not escape the shackles of its stubbornly white supremacist hinterland, while this very hinterland was forced to accede to protests for black equality largely because of the successful precedent set in the leading cities.

The story of Georgia protest also sheds light on specific debates within the state. David Garrow wrote that "more than any other single locale, Atlanta, Georgia, was the centerpiece city for the southern black freedom struggle of the 1950s and 1960s." J. Morgan Kousser commented that "a strong civil rights movement centered in Atlanta fanned out across Georgia to register black voters" before the Voting Rights Act of 1965.[14] The importance of Atlanta to Georgia should not be downplayed. As the unofficial capital of the South and as a city with atypically moderate race relations, Atlanta was indeed a center for black protest activity. The Auburn Avenue elite had achieved a reputation outside the state by the 1940s. Atlanta was a crossroads for black protest too. Olen Montgomery, one of the Scottsboro Nine, sought refuge with Atlanta businessman Eugene Martin.[15] At the end of the 1950s, the regional office of the NAACP moved to Atlanta, as did the head offices of SCLC and SNCC during the following decade. The city was also a base for the SRC and ACLU.

The Georgia historian Clifford Kuhn has noted, however, that "there has been a kind of 'Atlanta-centrism' in the scholarship on Georgia black political history from the 1940s through the recent past, that has tended to slight what went on in other communities."[16] The history of black activism in Georgia suggests further that this excessive Atlanta-centrism distorts the true picture of racial protest in Georgia. In the first place, the protest in Atlanta itself was limited in scale and success, particularly in the context of the strength of the black community and the relative racial moderation of the city. The Auburn Avenue elite did secure racial progress but refrained from confronting segregation itself. During the 1960s, the activities of COAHR were eclipsed by other cities in the South. As in the 1950s, it was the very conservatism within the established black leadership that proved the Achilles' heel in developing community pressure. In fact, the most striking years of racial progress in Atlanta were after the federal acts, when voting strength translated into political power.

The history of black activism in the rest of the state not only provides a fuller picture of the statewide story but includes local movements that were far more vigorous than that of the state capital. Atlanta was the leading city in the state, but Savannah was the leading city of protest. During the 1940s, Rev. Gilbert galvanized a tradition of confrontational protest within the city and encouraged similar protests in towns across the state. During the 1960s, too, the direct action movement in Savannah eclipsed protests in Atlanta. Meanwhile, other cities such as Macon, not to mention some of the smaller communities such as in Burke County, provide examples of active local movements.

In many ways, this survey does not do justice to the multifaceted history of black activism in Georgia. Each period and location deserves a far more exhaustive study of its own. Clearly, the 1980s represent a rather arbitrary cutoff point too. Since then, there has been significant change as well as continuity both in Georgia's racial mores and in types of protest. At a national level, increased Republican influence and the shift to the right of the Supreme Court impeded some aspects of the struggle for racial equality. As Kousser has argued, for example, the electoral districting decision *Shaw v. Reno* (1993) and its successors "have threatened to reverse the course of minority political success during the Second Reconstruction."[17] Certainly redistricting in Georgia during the 1990s was to the detriment of black politicians. More locally, the controversy over the flying of the Confederate flag at the 1994 Atlanta Superbowl and even Atlanta's hosting of the Olympic Games two years later provided new issues demanding response. Local demonstrations continued too. In 1987, for example, the SCLC led a March for Brotherhood in Forsyth County. The elevation of Julian Bond to the chairman of the NAACP's Board of Directors encouraged a more active role for the organization in Georgia.[18] Because black protest was not confined to overturning legal discrimination but extended to the more general themes of racial equality and prejudice, the racial struggle in Georgia continues.

Notes

Introduction

1. Du Bois also referred to the history of slavery in Georgia and the large black population in the state. For a full description of Du Bois's journey from Atlanta to Albany, see Du Bois, *Souls of Black Folk*, 91–110; quote on 92. Du Bois believed that Atlanta was "South of the North, yet North of the South" and that it had "something Western, something Southern and something quite its own, in its busy life" (ibid., 63, 92).

2. Norrell, *Reaping the Whirlwind*, ix.

3. See, for example, Chafe, *Civilities and Civil Rights*; Norrell, *Reaping the Whirlwind*; Greene, *Praying for Sheetrock*; Dittmer, *Local People*; Fairclough, *Race and Democracy*; Button, *Blacks and Social Change*; Colburn, *Racial Change and Community Crisis*; Payne, *I've Got the Light of Freedom*.

4. Norrell, for example, "fixes the beginning of the civil rights movement in Tuskegee at 1941," believing that "the story . . . in Tuskegee begins with events in and around the town in 1870" (*Reaping the Whirlwind*, x).

5. Plank and Turner, "Changing Patterns in Black School Politics," 601.

6. Charles Sherrod to Jack Minnis, 9 October 1962, VEP, 2–19, SNCC Microfilm.

7. For a discussion of the value of grassroots history, see the bibliographical essay in Payne, *I've Got the Light of Freedom*, 413–41; Lawson and Payne, *Debating the Civil Rights Movement*.

8. *Savannah Herald Tribune*, 13 October 1960.

9. This point was emphasized in Thornton, "Municipal Politics"; Robinson and Sullivan, eds., *New Directions*, 38–64.

10. Text of speech, n.d. (probably 1938), 2, Ser. 3, Box 26, Folder 16, Josephine Matthewson Papers, Special Collections, Emory University, Atlanta, Ga.

11. See, for example, Dittmer, *Local People*; Fairclough, *Race and Democracy*; Payne, *I've Got the Light of Freedom*; Kirk, "'He Started a Movement,'" 29–44.

12. Interview of Claude Sitton by author.

13. See Tuck, "A City Too Dignified to Hate," 539–59.

14. Garrow, ed., *Atlanta*, vii.

15. See interviews of W. W. Law and Dr. Jamerson Jr. by author.

16. Field Report, David Bell, 5 October 1963, Americus File, Mants Papers, MLK; Perdew, "Southwest Georgia: Problems and Solutions," 28 December 1963, Southwest Georgia File, SNCC Papers, AU.

17. See, for example, Trillin, *Education in Georgia*; McGrath, "Great Expectations." See interview of Flanagan by Josephine Bradley, 11 October 1988, GGDP, GSU, Atlanta, Georgia.

18. "Lopsided Legislatures in Georgia," *New South*, June 1949, 6–7; Key, *Southern Politics*, 59.

19. Dittmer, *Local People*, 19, 25; Fairclough, *Race and Democracy*, 106, 57; Key, *Southern Politics*, 523; Bacote, "Negro in Atlanta Politics," 346–48; Jackson, "Race and Suffrage in the South," 3–4; *New York Times*, 16 July 1946.

20. *Jim Crow* refers to the system of segregation that existed in the South.

21. See Mertz, "Mind Changing Time All Over Georgia," 45.

Chapter 1. First Challenges to Jim Crow after 1940

1. Kuhn, Joye, and West, *Living Atlanta*, 303; *Atlanta Daily World*, 1, 2, 14 January 1940; *Crisis* 47 (February 1940): 55.

2. *Crisis* 47 (February 1940): 44. The *Atlanta Daily World*, 29 February 1940, was summarizing the comments of the white Baptists of Georgia and the Abolish Peonage Committee.

3. Branch, *Parting the Waters*, 55; Raines, *My Soul Is Rested*, 63–64; interview of T. M. Alexander by author.

4. By 1940, forty-seven counties had a majority black population. See Owen, "Rise of Negro Voting in Georgia," Appendix II; Pyles, "Race and Ruralism," 15.

5. Woofter, *Landlord and Tenant*, 20–30; "Understanding Our Neighbors," 1944, 21, SRC Publications, SRC Microfilm. Georgia's total population was just over 3 million people in 1940 (*1940 U.S. Census, Characteristics of the Population, Composition of the Population by Counties*, Table 21, 216–25).

6. Woofter, *Landlord and Tenant*, 24; *1940 U.S. Census, Population*, Vol. 4: *Characteristics by Age*, Part II, Table 4, 186, Table 5, 187, Table 19B, 214; Grant, *The Way It Was*, 472; Hinton, "What's the Matter with Georgia?"; *New York Times*, 7 September 1946.

7. *Atlanta Daily World*, 26 May 1940.

8. Johnson, "New South Georgia and Old South Georgia," vi; Malcolm X, *Autobiography*, 89.

9. Dittmer, *Black Georgia*, 132; NAACP Anti-lynching campaign, 1912–55: Georgia, NAACP Papers on Microfilm; Zangrando, *NAACP Crusade Against Lynching*, 5; Press Clippings, Public Records Office, Mid-Georgia Library, Macon, Georgia; *Atlanta Daily World*, 14 September 1940.

10. Interview of Charles Sherrod by author; "Some Facts Involved in Baker County, Georgia," 17, and Field Report, n.d. (probably 1965), Ser. XV, Reel 37, no. 50, SNCC Microfilm.

11. Interviews of Frances Pauley, Warren Fortson, and John Bertrand by author; *Atlanta Daily World*, 10, 13 October 1940.

12. Interview of John Calhoun by Bernard West, 6 April 1979, 13, Living Atlanta Series, AHC; *Crisis* 53 (July 1946): 201; see also Arnall, *Shore Dimly Seen*.

13. *Pittsburgh Courier*, 23 March 1940; *Atlanta Daily World*, 12 March, 14 January 1940.

14. Johnson, *Patterns of Negro Segregation*, 205, 197; Henderson, *Atlanta Life Insurance Company*, 174.

15. Dittmer, *Black Georgia*, 20–21.

16. Lane, *People of Georgia*, 268; Charles S. Mangum, "Legal Status of the Negro (1940)" and "Sample of Laws on the Separation of the Races," n.d., SRC microfilm, Ser. 16, Reel 218, No. 8, SRC Papers, AU.

17. Three black drivers appealed to Atlanta's mayor to reverse the ordinance, claiming that they were being deprived of both their civil rights and their business. See *Atlanta Daily World*, 9 May, 20 June 1940; Lane, *People of Georgia*, 268; Interviews of T. M. Alexander, J. W. Jamerson, and William Randall Sr. by author.

18. Edwin R. Edwards, "Myrdalian Hypothesis," *Phylon* 15 (Fall 1954): 298; Johnson, *Patterns of Negro Segregation*, 277, 288.

19. Calhoun, "Significant Aspects," 26–27; "Occupational Characteristics of White Collar and Skilled Negro Workers of Atlanta, Georgia," 1937, Works Progress Administration Report no. 165-34-6069, 12, CCMC, AU.

20. In 1870, approximately half of Georgia's blacksmiths and carpenters were black; see Gaston, "History of the Negro Wage Earner in Georgia," 227–28.

21. Coleman, *History of Georgia,* 376; Woofter, *Landlord and Tenant,* 94; *New South,* March 1947, 16.

22. "Understanding Our Neighbors," 24, Publications, 1944–68, SRC Papers, AU; Johnson, *Patterns of Negro Segregation,* 14–15.

23. *Southern Patriot,* January 1946; Coleman, *History of Georgia,* 376; Bachtel, Lee, and Bates, "Georgia's Black Population," 2; *New South,* June 1946, 8–10.

24. Johnson, *Growing Up in the Black Belt,* 59–60, 124; Bunche, *Political Status of the Negro,* 54, 305, 131, 204; 1940 *U.S. Census, Characteristics of the Population: Georgia,* Table 23a, 279.

25. Johnson, *Growing Up in the Black Belt,* 91; Bunche, *Political Status of the Negro,* 263.

26. Bacote, "Negro in Atlanta Politics," 343; see also Calhoun, "Significant Aspects," 4.

27. Bunche, *Political Status of the Negro,* 404.

28. The story was passed down into folklore. See Greene, *Praying for Sheetrock,* 209. See also Bunche, *Political Status of the Negro,* 299.

29. Hamman, "Study of Voting Participation," 3.

30. Calhoun, "Significant Aspects," 11–12; *New York Times,* 24 May 1944.

31. Key, *Southern Politics,* 59.

32. "Lopsided Legislatures in Georgia," *New South,* June 1949, 6–7.

33. Pyles, "Race and Ruralism," 6; Kytle and Mackay, *Who Runs Georgia?,* 99. McGill added that there were a further forty "venal" counties. These were "counties which couldn't be bought for cash but could be had by a crafty bargaining agent." Roy Harris, who orchestrated the gubernatorial campaigns of several successful candidates, including Talmadge, insisted that "there's no tricks to Georgia politics. Ralph McGill thinks so. There's nobody in the state who knows less about politics than Ralph McGill . . . you can't buy a county" (ibid., 261–62).

34. Bunche, *Political Status of the Negro,* 124.

35. Interview of Clarence Bacote by Bernard West, 1978, LAS, 28; *Crisis* 49 (November 1941): 350; "The White Primary, 1944 (With Special Reference to Georgia)," Ser. XVI, Reel 218, no. 16, 2, SRC Microfilm.

36. Henderson and Roberts, *Georgia Governors,* 1–2; Anderson, *Wild Man from Sugar Creek,* xiii. Anderson makes the point that the stereotype of Talmadge as the "redneck racist" overstates his contribution to Georgia's racial mores.

37. Hinton, "What's the Matter?" 15; *Crisis* 48 (December 1940): 375.

38. Coleman, *History of Georgia,* 378; *New York Times,* 21 June, 15 July 1941; Arnall, *Shore Dimly Seen,* 42; Hinton, "What's the Matter?" 51; Henderson and Roberts, *Georgia Governors,* 4; Campbell, *Stem of Jesse,* 29; *New York Herald Tribune,* 17 July 1941, in Politics: Georgia, 1941–52 File, NAACP Papers, LC, Washington, D.C.

39. *New York Times,* 23 July 1941; *New York Herald Tribune,* 17 July 1941.

40. Bullock, *History of Negro Education*, 25; Barnes, *Journey from Jim Crow*, 11; Coleman, *History of Georgia*, 277–78; Hanks, *Struggle for Black Political Empowerment*, 88; Campbell, *Forty Acres and a Goat*, 244.

41. Rolinson, "Universal Negro Improvement Association," 209; Bunche, *Political Status of the Negro*, 301–2; Dittmer, *Black Georgia*, 206; Grant, *The Way It Was*, 311; Spritzer and Bergmark, *Grace Towns Hamilton*, 87.

42. Dittmer, *Black Georgia*, 206–7; Grant, *The Way It Was*, 314.

43. Rolinson, "Universal Negro Improvement Assocation," 202.

44. Ibid., 206, 212.

45. Ibid., 215.

46. Dittmer, *Black Georgia*, 176; Rolinson, "Universal Negro Improvement Association," 220.

47. Rolinson, "Universal Negro Improvement Association," 205, 219.

48. *Atlanta Daily World*, 24 March 1940; Interview of T. M. Alexander by author; Interview of William Holmes Borders by Mary Egan Dalton, 5 March 1976, AAOHC, AARL, Atlanta, Georgia; Grant, *The Way It Was*, 311. APEX, *Sweet Auburn, Street of Pride*, 64.

49. Honey, *Southern Labor and Black Civil Rights*, 54. In Atlanta, six supporters of the Gastonia textile strike were charged by the state of Georgia for inciting insurrection. The insurrection charge was next used in the Herndon case.

50. Martin, *Angelo Herndon Case*, 1–6, quoted in Grant, *The Way It Was*, 343; Branch, *Parting the Waters*, 210 (for the history of the Scottsboro case, see Carter, *Scottsboro*); Grant, *The Way It Was*, 342.

51. Grant, *The Way It Was*, 352; Bunche, *Political Status of the Negro*, 301–2.

52. Patricia Sullivan notes that black citizens of South Carolina and Georgia made an organized effort to vote in 1934 (*Days of Hope*, 4).

53. Johnson, *Patterns of Negro Segregation*, 296.

54. See, for example, Mays, *Born to Rebel*, 285.

55. Kuhn, Joye, and West, *Living Atlanta*, 80; *Pittsburgh Courier*, 3 August 1940.

56. *Southern School News* 4 (February 1958): 4; Kuhn, Joye, and West, *Living Atlanta*, 303, 82; Interview of Benjamin Mays, August 1965, 6, AARL; Dittmer, *Black Georgia*, 17.

57. Interview of Mays, AARL, 13; Alex R. Schmidt, "Episode: A Street Car," *Phylon* 9 (1948): 247.

58. See Kuhn, Joye, and West, *Living Atlanta*, for further examples of individual acts of defiance in Atlanta.

59. An Atlanta maid, Alice Adams, recalled that after work, "we'd dress up and put on our good clothes and go to the show on Auburn Avenue. . . . It was like white folks' Peachtree" (ibid., 39). Similarly, Albany lawyer C. B. King drew attention for his smart suits when he started to practice during the 1950s. See Chapter 5.

60. Kelley, "We Are Not What We Seem," 111–12.

61. Eight hundred black Atlantans attended one ACPL mass meeting during this campaign.

62. Interview of Josie Miller by author.

63. "The White Primary," 3; Sitkoff, "Racial Militancy," 668.

64. Sitkoff, "Racial Militancy," 669; *New York Times*, 11, 12 June 1943; "Report of Investigation at Camp Stewart," 4 June 1943, 1–3, Ralph Mark Gilbert Personal Correspondence, Courtesy W. W. Law, KTC, Savannah, Georgia.

65. Interviews of Ada Kent and Charles Dailey by author.

66. Ralph Mark Gilbert to Walter White, 17 August 1943, Gilbert Correspondence, NAACP Papers, LC.

67. Interviews of A. I. McClung and George Ford by author; *Columbus Ledger-Enquirer*, 24 April 1988; *Crisis* 53 (December 1946): 374; *Macon Telegraph*, 7 June 1942; Memo by Mr. Jones, 27 June 1942, Georgia Branch Files: Macon, 1941–55, NAACP Papers, LC; "White Primary," 12.

68. Kelley, *Race Rebels*, 62; *Pittsburgh Courier*, 30 March, 27 April 1946.

69. McKissack, "Attitudes Towards Negro Political Participation," 46; *Pittsburgh Courier*, 13 April, 16 March 1946; King, *Daddy King*, 134.

70. Dalfiume, "Forgotten Years of the Negro Revolution," 96; *Crisis* 51 (July 1944): 230; *Atlanta Daily World*, 25 May 1940. Sutherland's attorneys did not plead his innocence but contended that the first trial in a federal court, rather than a local court, was invalid. See *Atlanta Daily World*, 21 June 1940.

71. Coleman, *History of Georgia*, 339; Johnson, "Desegregation of Public Education in Georgia," 241; Letter from John Anderson, *Macon Telegraph*, 10 June 1942.

72. Sullivan, *Days of Hope*, 100; Interview of Frances Pauley by author;

73. *Crisis* 50 (May 1943): 136; Interview of Pauley by author; Sullivan, *Days of Hope*, 164, 166.

74. Loveland, *Lillian Smith*, 66, 103; Williamson, *New People*, 136–37. *Strange Fruit* was banned in Boston because of its explicit statements on sex.

75. Talmadge was probably alluding to the use of corncobs as toilet paper in parts of the rural South. See Williamson, *New People*, 137.

76. Cobb, "Politics in a New South City," 96; Henderson and Roberts, *Georgia Governors*, 26.

77. Bartley, *Creation of Modern Georgia*, 180.

78. Brunswick Yard, for example, was revamped by J. A. Jones of Charlotte, South Carolina. See Tindall, *Emergence of the New South*, 696.

79. Coleman, *History of Georgia*, 339–41.

80. The impact of the war on Georgia's economy built on the changes begun during the New Deal. For example, Georgia-born journalist Tom Stokes observed that four-fifths of the fifty-three thousand WPA workers in the state were black (Sullivan, *Days of Hope*, 66).

81. "The South," 15, Ser. XVI, Reel 218, no. 25, SRC Microfilm; Brooks and Parris, *Blacks in the City*, 123, 176; Minchin, *Hiring the Black Worker*, 26.

82. Brooks and Parris, *Blacks in the City*, 307; Bayor, *Race and the Shaping of Twentieth-Century Atlanta*, 107.

83. "Wire to War Manpower Commission," 30 November 1942, Savannah File, NAACP Papers, LC. The wire stated: "Strongly protest lay-off of 800 laborers (including 500 black workers) at SEn shipyards for failure to sign agreement which smacks of collusion between company and union which would deprive workers of rights."

84. *Atlanta Daily World,* 21 June 1942; Clippings, Macon Branch File, NAACP Papers, LC.

85. Daniel, "Going Among Strangers," 899, 909.

86. Du Bois, "Race Relations in America," 236; Tindall, *Emergence of the New South,* 715; Clark Foreman, "Decade of Hope," *Phylon* 12 (Summer 1951): 137; *Crisis* 48 (October 1941): 318; Northrup, *Negro in the Automobile Industry,* 71; Honey, *Southern Labor,* 53.

87. *Southern News Almanac,* 31 July 1941, reported in *Crisis* 48 (October 1941): 318.

88. *Crisis* 48 (October 1941): 318; *South Today,* February–March 1943, 3.

89. Honey, *Southern Labor,* 120, 214, 216.

90. Korstad and Lichtenstein, "Opportunities Found and Lost," 1988–89; see Honey, *Southern Labor;* Griffith, *Crisis of American Labor,* 76, 74.

91. Griffith, *Crisis of American Labor,* 23, 64, 75, 144.

92. Russwurm, *CIO's Left-Led Unions,* 86; Korstad and Lichtenstein, "Opportunities Found and Lost"; *Wall Street Journal,* 24 October 1957; Kornhauser, "Ideology and Interests," 57.

93. Rubin, *Negro in the Longshore Industry,* 94. Rubin recorded that the ILA dominated the waterfront after 1936.

94. Rubin, *Negro in the Longshore Industry,* 96; Lecture by Rev. Samuel Williams, 1 August 1994, St. Phillip's Baptist Church, Savannah, Georgia. The ILA had organized strikes at Savannah and Brunswick as early as the 1890s but had collapsed after a defeated strike in 1921 and remained weak until the revival in 1936.

95. Kornhauser, "Ideology and Interests," 54; B. R. Brazeal to Harold Fleming, "Summary of Laurens County Interviews, 31 August, 1956," 1, Brazeal Correspondence, SRC Papers, AU.

96. Flyer, n.d., and Civic Letter, 4 December 1952, Folder "Handbills, October–November 1952," Charles Matthias Papers, GSU; Ralph Mark Gilbert to Walter White, 2 October 1942, Georgia Branch Files: Savannah, 1941–43, NAACP Papers, LC; King et al., eds., *Negro Employment in Basic Industry,* 71; *Atlanta Journal,* 24 May 1946; Minutes of Meetings of Meat Cutters Local 442, 27 February 1945, 253, Meat Cutters Local Union 442 Minutes, 1938–68, GSU.

97. *Statesman,* 12 July 1951; Hope, "Discrimination in Industry," 267; Griffith, *Crisis of American Labor,* 68.

98. Hope, "Self-Survey of the Packinghouse Union," 28, 34.

99. "Hall of Fame Honorees: John Henry Hall," GSU. These civil rights workers during the 1960s were members of the SNCC Southwest Georgia Project.

100. "1951 Convention Proceedings—12th Annual Convention, 21–23 September 1951, Dempsey Hotel, Macon," Georgia State Industrial Union Council Proceedings, 1948–56, GSU; Photographs 79-34/32 and 79-34/2, Southern Labor Archives, GSU.

101. "Hall of Fame Honorees: John Henry Hall"; Photographs 79-34/32, 79-34/2, and others in series, GSU.

102. "Albany, the Queen of South West Georgia," *Atlanta Daily World,* 14 February 1941.

103. *Atlanta Daily World,* 14 February 1941.

104. Griffith, *Crisis of American Labor,* 75–76.

105. Korstad and Lichtenstein, "Opportunities Found and Lost," 786; "Business Directory, Atlanta: Project to Study Business and Business Education Among Negroes, 1944–45, with

Content Covering 1870–1942," and "Business Directory, Savannah: Project to Study Business and Business Education Among Negroes, 1944–45, with Content Covering 1870–1942," CCMC.

106. U.S. Census 1940, Characteristics of the Population: Georgia, Table 23a, "Non-white Employed Workers 14 Years Old and Over, by Major Occupation Group and Sex, by Counties: 1940," 278–81. See corresponding tables for 1950 for confirmation of this trend in black employment.

107. Interview of R. A. Dent by John Lamar, 2 June 1975, Oral Memoirs of Augusta's Citizens, AOHP, APL, Augusta, Georgia; Interviews of Rev. C. S. Hamilton, Tea Kunney, and James Mays by author; Pierce, *Negro Business and Business Education*, 26–27; "Report to the State Conference: 1946," Dublin Branch File, 1944–56, NAACP Papers, LC.

108. *Pittsburgh Courier*, 16 January 1961; Interviews of W. W. Law, Robert Mants, and Agnew James by author.

109. Campbell, *Stem of Jesse*, 18; *Pittsburgh Courier*, 19 May 1964; Interview of William Randall by author; Interview of Rev. J. Malone, GGDP; Georgia State Conference Reports, 1943–47, NAACP Papers, LC. Numerous interviews, including Al Williams, Amos Holmes, W. W. Law, Charles Sherrod, and J. W. Jamerson by author; Chalfen, "'The Way Out May Lead In,'" 563.

110. McClung, "Dr. Thomas H. Brewer Memorial," 1–4; *Columbus Ledger-Enquirer*, 24 April 1988; Interviews of A. J. McClung and George Ford III by author; *Pittsburgh Courier*, 15 April 1950.

111. *Columbus Ledger-Enquirer*, 24 April 1988; Interview of Primus King by Paul A. Davis, 1979, Tape Recording, SSML, Columbus State College, Columbus, Georgia; Interviews of A. J. McClung, George Ford, and Rev. T. W. Smith by author.

112. Photograph, *Atlanta Daily World*, 1 January 1942; *Atlanta Daily World*, 18 February 1941, 7 June 1940; Calloway, *"Sweet Auburn" Avenue Business History*, 7; Calhoun, "Significant Aspects," 82; Headed title on reverse of handwritten note, 29 February 1952, Box 42, Folder 20, Ser. XIII, Georgia Voters' League Files, A. T. Walden Papers, AHC.

113. Kuhn, Joye, and West, *Living Atlanta*, 106; Penuel, "Analysis of the Treatment of Negro News," 39–40; Rozier, "History of the Negro Press in Atlanta," 22; APEX, *Sweet Auburn*, 42; Blackwell, "Black-Controlled Media in Atlanta," 76; Interview of Horace Tate by author.

114. *Atlanta Daily World*, 15 September 1940. Interview of Calhoun by West.

115. See, for example, transcript of broadcast by Benjamin Mays on radio station WERD, 4 October 1950, 2, Box 43, Folder 20, Ser. XIV, Civil Rights File, Walden Papers, AHC.

116. *Atlanta Daily World*, 15 September, 1 December 1940; see Blackwell, "Black-Controlled Media," 76.

Chapter 2. The Upsurge of Black Protest across Georgia, 1943–1946

1. Dittmer, *Black Georgia*, 19; Fairclough, *Race and Democracy*, xii.

2. Dittmer, *Local People*, 19, 25; Payne, *I've Got the Light of Freedom*, 25; Key, *Southern Politics*, 523; Fairclough, *Race and Democracy*, 106, 57; Lawson, *Black Ballots*, 134.

3. This was also more than a sixfold increase in the number of registered black voters in

1940 (Lawson, *Black Ballots,* 134). Estimates of the exact number of black registered voters vary. V. O. Key estimated 85,000 black voters in *Southern Politics,* 523. Clarence Bacote reported 125,000 black registered voters in "Negro in Atlanta Politics," 346–68; Luther P. Jackson reported 125,000 black registered voters in "Race and Suffrage in the South," 3–4. See also the *Atlanta Daily World,* 7 July 1946; Owen, "Rise of Negro Voting in Georgia," 26. The *New York Times* reported C. A. Scott's estimate of 134,000 registered voters on 16 July 1946. See "Membership Survey, 15 November 1947," Georgia Branch Files, NAACP Papers, LC.

4. Clifford Kuhn, "Two Small Windows of Opportunity: Black Politics in Georgia During the 1940s, and the Pertinent Oral History Sources," 12, paper delivered at the joint meeting of the Georgia Association of Historians and the Georgia Political Science Association, Savannah, Georgia, 29 February 1992. Courtesy Clifford M. Kuhn.

5. The *Smith v. Allwright* case was the culmination of a four-year challenge by the NAACP Legal Committee. See Owen, "Rise of Negro Voting in Georgia," 8; Pyles, "Race and Ruralism," 16. See, for example, *Atlanta Daily World,* 28 August 1940.

6. *Columbus Ledger-Enquirer,* 24 April 1988; Interview of Primus King by Paul A. Davis, 1979, tape recording, SSML; Interviews of A. J. McClung and George Ford by author.

7. Owen, "Rise of Negro Voting in Georgia," 15; Hamman, "Study of Voting Participation," 8, 10; Pyles, "Race and Ruralism," 18; Calhoun, "Significant Aspects," 10; *New South* 3 (June–July 1948): 13. Primus King was pleased to discover that Martin Luther King Jr., as a student, wrote an essay on the *King* case (interview of Primus King by Davis).

8. Talmadge was threatening to cut off money from the University of Georgia because a few Negroes were attending summer school. See Arnall, *Shore Dimly Seen,* 42; Hinton, "What's the Matter with Georgia?" *New York Times Magazine,* 9 February 1947, 51; Henderson and Roberts, *Georgia Governors,* 4; Campbell, *Stem of Jesse,* 29; Egerton, *Speak Now Against the Day,* 225.

9. *Atlanta Journal,* 10 August 1942; Henderson and Roberts, *Georgia Governors,* 34; Arnall, *Shore Dimly Seen,* 96.

10. Mays was also highly critical of Arnall's racist rhetoric during the campaign, and he was angry that Arnall addressed him as Benjamin (rather than Dr. Mays) in a letter (Mays, *Born to Rebel,* 222). See also interview of Benjamin Mays, August 1965, 6, AARL.

11. Interview of Clarence Bacote by Bernard West, 1978, 5, LAS.

12. *Crisis* 52 (March 1945): 73; *Crisis* 53 (July 1946): 201; Chamberlain, "Arnall of Georgia," 69.

13. "The White Primary, 1944 (with Special Reference to Georgia)," Ser. XVI, Reel 218, no. 16, 3, 10, SRC Microfilm; *Crisis* 51 (April 1944): 119; Wilson, "How Dimly Does Ellis Arnall See?" 138.

14. *Crisis* 54 (May 1947): 138; Sullivan, *Days of Hope,* 203; *New York Times,* 4 August 1946; Interviews of Tea Kunney, T. M. Alexander, and William P. Randall by author.

15. Interview of Bacote by West, 39; *New York Times,* 25 January 1947; see Talmadge, *You and Segregation,* 36.

16. Membership Records, Georgia Branch Files, NAACP Papers, LC; Helen Randolph to Roy Wilkins, 31 December 1943, Atlanta, 1944–45 File, NAACP Papers, LC.

17. Gilbert to E. Morrow, New York Head Office, 13 January 1942, Georgia Branch Files: Savannah, 1942–43, NAACP Papers, LC.

18. Baker to Black, 20 November 1942, Donald Jones to Baker, 26 November 1943, Georgia Branch Files: Savannah, 1942–43, NAACP Papers, LC.

19. "Business Directory, Savannah Project to Study Business and Business Education Among Negroes, 1944–45, with Content Covering 1870–1942," CCMC; Interview of W. W. Law by Cliff Kuhn and Tim Crimmins, 15, 16 November 1990, 28–29, GGDP; *Pittsburgh Courier,* 30 March 1946.

20. Interview of Tea Kunney by author; Memo, "New members," n.d., Memo, 12 January 1945, Memo, "Go to School Drive, September 1944," n.d., memo, "Cancer control," April 1945, Georgia Branch Files: Savannah, 1944–45, NAACP Papers, LC.

21. See Tuck, "A City Too Dignified to Hate," 550; Simms, *First Colored Baptist Church in North America;* Barnes, *Journey from Jim Crow,* 11; Campbell, "Profit, Prejudice, and Protest," 197–231.

22. Tuck, "A City Too Dignified to Hate," 556; Bunche, *Political Status of the Negro,* 301; Gilbert to White, 29 June 1942, Georgia Branch Files: Savannah, 1942–43, NAACP Papers, LC.

23. Gilbert to Gloster Current, 20 January 1947, Georgia State Conference 1947 File, NAACP Papers, LC; Interview of J. W. Jamerson by author; Thurgood Marshall to Joseph Wright, 13 April 1943, Georgia Branch Files: Savannah, 1942–43, NAACP Papers, LC.

24. *Congressional Record,* Senate, 10 May 1945, 4474; Senator Bilbo to Ralph Mark Gilbert, 7 June 1945, Gilbert to Bilbo, 13 July 1945, Georgia Branch Files: Savannah, 1944–45, NAACP Papers, LC.

25. See Smyth, "Segregation in Charleston,"and Pat Watters, "Brunswick," SRC Publications, 1944–76, SRC Papers, AU; Gilbert to Baker, 22 May 1944, Georgia Branch Files: Savannah, 1944–45, NAACP Papers, LC; Jones to Baker, 17 November 1943, ibid., 1942–43.

26. Bunche, *Political Status of the Negro,* 301; Interviews of W. W. Law, J. W. Jamerson, Eugene Gadsden, and Tena Rhodes by author.

27. Bilbo to Gilbert, 30 June 1945, Georgia Branch Files: Savannah, 1944–45, NAACP Papers, LC; J. W. Jamerson to Current, 20 December 1947, *Pittsburgh Courier,* 15 April 1950.

28. Baker to Black, 20 November 1942, Georgia Branch Files: Savannah, 1942–43, NAACP Papers, LC; *Crisis* 50 (February 1943): 58; Baker to Black, 20 November 1942, Gilbert to Robert Weaver, 29 June 1942, Georgia Branch Files: Savannah, 1942–43, NAACP Papers, LC.

29. *Savannah Herald,* 9 May 1946; Interview of W. W. Law by Cliff Kuhn and Tim Crimmins, 28, GGDP; *Pittsburgh Courier,* 30 March 1946.

30. Interview of W. W. Law by Kuhn and Crimmins, GGDP; *Crisis* 50 (February 1943): 58.

31. Gilbert to Baker, 4 March 1943, Georgia Branch Files: Savannah, 1942–43, NAACP Papers, LC; Bunche, *Political Status of the Negro,* 301; Gilbert to White, 29 June 1942, Georgia Branch Files: Savannah, 1942–43, NAACP Papers, LC.

32. *New York Times,* 7 September 1946.

33. Gilbert to Fred Wessels, 21 October 1942, W. H. Sillwell to Gilbert, 26 October 1942, and reply, November 1942, Gilbert to White, 29 June 1942, Georgia Branch Files: Savannah, 1942–43, NAACP Papers, LC; *Savannah Tribune,* 15 March 1945.

34. *New York Times,* 7 September 1946; *New South* 3 (June–July 1948): 22; Current to White, 15 December 1947, Georgia Branch Files: Savannah, 1944–47, NAACP Papers, LC.

35. *New York Times,* 26, 27 June 1948; Mozell Hill and Alexander Miller, "Safety, Security and the South," 8–10, Ser. XVI, Reel 218, no. 9, SRC Publications 1944–76, SRC Microfilm.

36. Memo, Current to Walter White, 15 December 1947, Georgia State Conference File, NAACP Papers, LC.

37. Jones to Baker, 26 November 1943, Georgia Branch Files: Savannah, 1942–43, NAACP Papers, LC.

38. Gilbert to Wilkins, 27 August 1942, Gilbert, "Report on the Georgia State Conference," for *Crisis,* 22 January 1943, Georgia Branch Files: Savannah, 1942–43, NAACP Papers, LC; *Crisis* 50 (March 1943): 90.

39. Gilbert to Baker, 25 January 1944, Georgia State Conference, 1943–46 File, NAACP Papers, LC; Gilbert to White, 4 June 1945, Georgia Branch Files: Savannah, 1944–45, NAACP Papers, LC; Walter Dawkins to Baker, 20 May 1946, Georgia Branch Files: Donaldsonville, 1944–52, ibid.

40. Interview of W. W. Law by Kuhn et al., 24–25; Gilbert to White, 4 June 1945, Georgia Branch Files: Savannah, 1944–45; Gilbert to Current, 9 October 1946, Georgia State Conference, 1943–46 File, ibid.; William M. Boyd to Daisy Lampkin, 12 February 1944, Georgia Branch Files: Fort Valley, 1944–45, ibid.; Black to Gilbert, 19 April 1946, Georgia State Conference, 1943–46 File, ibid.

41. Gilbert to Current, 9 October 1946, Georgia State Conference, 1943–46 File, NAACP Papers, LC; Interviews of Tea Kunney, William Randall, and Al Williams by author.

42. Interviews of W. W. Law and J. W. Jamerson by author; Gilbert to Current, 9 October 1946, Georgia State Conference, 1943–46 File, NAACP Papers, LC; Ben Armstrong to Gilbert, 18 December 1947, Georgia Branch Files: Hazelhurst, 1947, ibid.

43. Morris, *Origins of the Civil Rights Movement,* 13; Ruth L. Bacone to Hurley, 24 May, 6 July 1945, Georgia Branch Files: Augusta, 1941–55, NAACP Papers, LC.

44. Raymond Gavins paints a similar picture of NAACP membership in North Carolina in "NAACP in North Carolina," 120.

45. Such professions included skilled artisans, ministers, salesmen, morticians, and insurance agents. See Membership Report, 30 March 1948, Georgia Branch Files: Fitzgerald, 1948–50, NAACP Papers, LC; Membership Report, n.d., Georgia Branch Files: Cairo, 1940–44, ibid.

46. Campbell, *Stem of Jesse,* 18.

47. Current to White, 15 December 1947, Georgia State Conference, 1947, NAACP Papers, LC; La Grange NAACP to Georgia Senators, 21 February 1944, Georgia Branch Files: La Grange, 1940–55, NAACP Papers, LC; *Macon Telegraph,* 10 June 1942.

48. Lucille Black to J. M. Atkinson, 25 February 1942, Atkinson to New York Office, 11 March 1942, Georgia Branch Files: Brunswick, 1942, NAACP Papers, LC; *Macon Telegraph,* 7 June 1942; Memo, Mr. Jones, 27 June 1942, Georgia Branch Files: Macon, 1941–55, NAACP Papers, LC; *Atlanta Daily World,* 21 June 1942; *Macon Telegraph,* 10 June 1942.

49. *Macon Telegraph,* 10 June 1942; Gilbert to White, 4 June 1945, Georgia Branch Files:

Savannah, 1944–45, NAACP Papers, LC; J. T. Atwater to Current, 20 June 1947, Georgia Branch Files: Polk County, 1946–51, and Baker to E. M. Martin, 31 August 1945, Georgia Branch Files: Macon, 1941–55, NAACP Papers, LC.

50. William Henrie Browne to NAACP, received 21 November 1949, Legal Department and Central Office Records, 1940–55: Discrimination in the Criminal Justice System, 1910–55 File, NAACP Microfilm.

51. Sanders Kendrick to NAACP, 9 September 1946, Legal Department and Central Office Records, 1940–55: Discrimination in the Criminal Justice System, 1910–55 File, NAACP Microfilm; M. O. Smith to NAACP Legal Department, 10 September 1946, Dover Carter to New York Office, 18 September 1948, Legal File: Atlanta Voting, 1944–47, NAACP Microfilm.

52. Dover Carter to Baker, 24 May 1946, and NAACP News Release, 2 December 1948, Georgia Branch Files: Ailey, 1946–52, NAACP Papers, LC; Interviews of W. W. Law, Charles Sherrod, and James Mays by author. In Texas, an active state NAACP conference was also at the forefront of voter registration activities. Michael L. Gillette wrote that "in the late 1930s an extraordinary group of black Texans began to organize and direct the state's civil rights movement. As they revived the five languid branches of the NAACP, they built a state-wide organization... which ultimately included more than 170 local chapters" ("Rise of the NAACP in Texas," 393). In Arkansas, by contrast, the voter registration drive was led by the Committee on Negro Organizations. The CNO formed because an "entrenched conservative elite still wielded considerable influence and still dominated [NAACP] activities" during the early 1940s. See Kirk, "'He Started a Movement,'" 32.

53. See Lynch, _Black Urban Condition;_ Coleman, ed., _History of Georgia,_ 343; Holloway, _Politics of the Southern Negro,_ 190; Pierce quoted in Coleman, ed., _History of Georgia,_ 344.

54. Mays, _Born to Rebel,_ 276; Holden, "Race and Politics," 85; _Pittsburgh Courier,_ 24 January 1948.

55. This figure is the combined total of black residents of DeKalb and Fulton Counties, which made up Atlanta. See 1940 U.S. Census, Characteristics of the Population: Georgia, Composition of the Population by Counties, Table 21, 218–19.

56. See Alexander, _Beyond the Timberline;_ "Business Directory, Atlanta: Project to Study Business and Business Education Among Negroes, 1944–45, with Content Covering 1870–1942," CCMC.

57. Milton also founded a major pharmacy chain with Clayton Yates, another of the leading businessmen from this period. Yates and Milton Pharmacy was managed by Rose Milton and Mae Yates. See Calloway, _"Sweet Auburn" Avenue Business History,_ 10.

58. Pierce, _Negro Business and Business Education,_ 16; _Atlanta Daily World,_ 1 January 1946; Thiebolt and Fletcher, "Negro in Insurance," 40.

59. APEX, _Sweet Auburn,_ 46; Dittmer, _Black Georgia,_ 13.

60. Meier and Lewis, "History of the Negro Upper Class in Atlanta," 13; See Hunter, _Community Power Structure._

61. By 1940, over a third of black Atlantans lived on the west side, in segregated communities. The formation of the Atlanta University Center, in 1929–30, consolidated the city's black colleges on the west side. Between the wars several Auburn Avenue businesses started branches on Hunter Street on the west side (Kuhn, Joye, and West, _Living Atlanta,_ 40, 45).

62. "America's Tenth Man," 21, Ser. XVI, Reel 218, no. 15, SRC Microfilm; Branch, *Parting the Waters,* 53; Bunche, *Political Status of the Negro,* 490.

63. The high proportion of black-owned churches in Atlanta was typical of many southern towns. See Morris, *Origins of the Civil Rights Movement,* 5.

64. Interview of William Holmes Borders by Bernard West, 29 November 1978, 8, LAS.

65. Range, *Rise and Progress of Negro Colleges in Georgia,* 227–35; Hinton, "What's the Matter with Georgia?" 15; Garrow, ed., *Atlanta,* vii; *Crisis* 47 (April 1940): 251. For more information about the formation of Atlanta University, see Bacote, *Story of Atlanta University;* Spritzer and Bergmark, *Grace Towns Hamilton,* 43–44.

66. Alexander, *Beyond the Timberline,* 59; Interview of William Holmes Borders by Mary Egan Dalton, 5 March 1976, AAOHC; Interview of B. R. Brazeal by Marcus Barksdale, 1 February 1978, LAS.

67. Interview of John Calhoun by Bernard West, 6 April 1979, 13, LAS; Du Bois, "Race Relations in America," 239; Henderson, *Atlanta Life Insurance Company,* 168; Branch, *Parting the Waters,* 54; Interview of T. M. Alexander by author.

68. For more detail, see Harmon, "Beneath the Image."

69. The Top Hat became the first desegregated nightclub in Atlanta (Calloway, *Sweet Auburn Avenue,* 10).

70. The Women's Club was organized by the Atlanta Urban League. See *Atlanta Daily World,* 14 July, 1 November 1940.

71. Interview of T. M Alexander by author. The YMCA was also the venue for meetings of other groups, such as the Negro Chamber of Commerce. See *Atlanta Daily World,* 15 January 1940.

72. Spritzer and Bergmark, *Grace Towns Hamilton,* 79; Nasstrom, "Down to Now," 126.

73. E. M. Martin to Ruby Blackburn, 19 June 1945, Program for Meeting, 23 March 1947, Ruby Blackburn Papers, AARL. Letters from people in Oklahoma, Chicago, and Washington asking advice about training schools point to the national reputation of Blackburn's school. See also *New York Times,* 26 December 1945.

74. Helen Randolph to Roy Wilkins, 31 December 1943, Atlanta, 1944–45 File, NAACP Papers, LC; E. M. Martin to Ruby Blackburn, 19 June 1945, Blackburn Papers, AARL; *New York Times,* 26 December 1945. Randolph also mentions that "outstanding white women" spoke at the meetings, although she does not list them by name.

75. Spritzer and Bergmark, *Grace Towns Hamilton,* 79; Bacote, "Negro in Atlanta Politics," 343; Interviews of Bacote and Calhoun by West, LAS; Harmon, "Beneath the Image," 26; Interview of T. M. Alexander by author; Calhoun, "Significant Aspects," 81.

76. Program for Seventh Anniversary of Dixie Hills Political and Civic Club, held at Wheat Street Baptist Church, 15 October 1952, 4, Blackburn Papers, AARL.

77. Helen Randolph to Wilkins, 31 December 1943, Georgia Branch Files: Atlanta, 1944–45, NAACP Papers, LC; Willis A. Sutton, Superintendent of Schools, to Blackburn, 7 October 1943, Blackburn Papers, AARL; Brooks and Parris, *Blacks in the City,* 307.

78. Mae Yates and E. M. Martin were also on the NAACP committee in 1940. See *Atlanta Daily World,* 27 November 1940.

79. Henderson, *Atlanta Life Insurance Company,* 171. Other leading members of this cadre

were Jesse Blayton, a drugstore owner, L. D. Milton, and Geneva Haughabrooks, owner of a funeral parlor. Warren Cochrane, head of the YMCA, was a strong supporter of A. T. Walden and a leading Democratic organizer in his own right.

80. For a detailed discussion of Hamilton's career, see Mullis, "The Public Career of Grace Towns Hamilton." Spritzer and Bergmark make the point that Hamilton "did not set out to be a race leader . . . what she had going for her was 'class' as white culture defined the word" (*Grace Towns Hamilton*, 74–75).

81. Helen Randolph to Roy Wilkins, 31 December 1943, Atlanta, 1944–45 File, NAACP Papers, LC; Interview of T. M. Alexander by author; *Atlanta Daily World*, 14 January, 22, 26 May 1940; Jim Daniel to New York Office of NAACP, received 9 August 1944, Office Files: Atlanta, 1944–45, NAACP Papers, LC; Bunche, *Political Status of the Negro*, 488, 490.

82. Spritzer and Bergmark, *Grace Towns Hamilton*, 57–58. Hamilton was descended from George Washington Towns, Georgia's governor between 1847 and 1851 (ibid., xiii–xiv).

83. Bacote, "Negro in Atlanta Politics," 346; Gilbert to Baker, 25 January 1944, Georgia State Conference, 1943–46 File, NAACP Papers, LC.

84. Helen Randolph to Roy Wilkins, 31 December 1943, Atlanta, 1944–45 File, NAACP Papers, LC.

85. Interviews of Julian Bond and T. M. Alexander by author; Branch, *Parting the Waters*, 53–55; *Atlanta Daily World*, 2 January 1946.

86. Calhoun to Hurley, 2 June 1952, Georgia Branch Files: Atlanta, 1951–53, NAACP Papers, LC; Mason, *Going Against the Wind*, 120; *Atlanta Daily World*, 14 July, 30 August 1940.

87. Meier, "History of the Negro Upper Class," 8; Interview of Bacote by West, 26, LAS; Galphin and Shavin, *Atlanta*, 258; Interview of Warren Cochrane by Bernard West, 15 November 1978, 15, LAS; Interview of Bacote by West, 5, LAS.

88. Grant, *The Way It Was*, 375–76; Harmon, "Beneath the Image," 117.

89. Interview of T. M. Alexander by author.

90. The fifth district consisted of urban Fulton and DeKalb Counties and rural Rockdale County. Special elections did not require a primary and were therefore, in theory, open to both races. In addition, this special election was fought on a popular vote basis rather than using the county-unit system. See Holden, "Race and Politics," 18.

91. Interview of Bacote by West, 10, LAS; Bacote, "Negro in Atlanta Politics," 344; Kuhn, Joye, and West, *Living Atlanta*, 333–34; see Spritzer, *Belle of Ashby Street*, 65–80.

92. During the 1950s, Hugh Carl Owen and Anna Holden concluded that Mankin had not sought the black vote. See Owen, "Rise of Negro Voting in Georgia," 18, and Holden, "Race and Politics," 29, as cited by Spritzer, *Belle of Ashby Street*, 164. Oral interviews conducted by Spritzer and for the LAS revealed that Mankin had solicited black support, albeit under "cover of darkness"; see Kuhn, "Two Small Windows of Opportunity," 9.

93. *Pittsburgh Courier*, 13, 23 February 1946; Holden, "Race and Politics," 42; *Atlanta Daily World*, 13 February 1946; *New York Times*, 14 February 1946; *Time*, 23 February 1946, 22; *Newsweek*, 25 February 1946, 28; Interview of Bacote by West, 7, LAS.

94. Bacote, "Negro in Atlanta Politics," 345–46; Program for the Seventh Anniversary of Dixie Hills Political and Civic Club, held at Wheat Street Baptist Church, 15 October 1952, 13, Blackburn Papers, AARL.

95. Interview of Bacote by West, 13, LAS; Stone, *Regime Politics*, 28; Bacote, "Negro in Atlanta Politics," 346–48; Kuhn, Joye, and West, *Living Atlanta*, 335; *Pittsburgh Courier*, 28 August 1948; McKissack, "Attitudes Towards Negro Political Participation," 44.

96. Nasstrom, "Down to Now," 125. There are no statistics available to assess whether women registered to vote on the same scale as men, but as Nasstrom points out, "the photographic record of the drive attests to the likelihood that they did" ("Down to Now," 120).

97. *Atlanta Daily World*, 20 February 1946, quoted in Nasstrom, "Down to Now," 122–23; ibid., 124.

98. *Atlanta Daily World*, 8, 30 April 1948; "Report on the Grievances of Black Firemen to the Board of Masters, City of Atlanta," by the Community Relations Commission, 29 December 1969, 1; Galphin and Shavin, *Atlanta*, 258.

99. Owen, "Rise of Negro Voting in Georgia," 19.

100. *Atlanta Daily World*, 7 June 1940; Lucille Black to Harper, 14 October 1948, Branch Files: Atlanta, 1946–48, NAACP Papers, LC; G. V. Kimbers to White, 12 November 1941, Georgia Branch Files: La Grange, 1940–55, ibid.; Griffin County, Democratic Clubs, Walden Papers, AHC; Henderson, *Atlanta Life Insurance Company*, 185.

101. Thomas Jones to Marshall, 22 June 1942, Georgia Branch Files: Cairo, 1940–44, NAACP Papers, LC; *Atlanta Daily World*, 2 February 1946.

102. *New York Times*, 4 July 1944; "White Primary," 5; Calhoun, "Significant Aspects," 89.

103. The Bipartisan League sponsored demonstrations of voting machines and gave instructions in their use. See interview of Jake Henderson, LAS.

104. *Savannah Herald*, 14, 21 March, 23 April 1946; Gilbert, "Report of Georgia State Conference," for *Crisis*, 22 January 1943, Georgia Branch Files: Savannah 1942–43, NAACP Papers, LC.

105. *New South* 3 (June–July 1948): 19; Owen, "Rise of Negro Voting in Georgia," 47–48.

106. *Pittsburgh Courier*, 30 March 1946; *New York Post*, 17 April 1945; *New South* 3 (June–July 1948): 22; *New York Times*, 18 April 1946; *Southern Patriot*, 27 April 1946; McCoy, "Historical Sketch of Black Augusta," 81.

107. *Crisis* 53 (July 1946): 201.

108. Key, *Southern Politics*, 127.

109. Pyles, "Race and Ruralism," 18; *New York Times*, 19, 21 July 1946; *Atlanta Constitution*, 19 July 1946. By including the votes cast for the other minor candidates, all of whom accepted the end of the white primary, Lorraine Spritzer believed that "it seemed that four out of seven Georgians in 1946 could be called racial moderates. The state's popular inclination in that critical year was toward a new accommodation with blacks" (*Belle of Ashby Street*, 107).

110. Bernd, "White Supremacy," 492–93, 500, 510; *New York Times*, 12 July 1946.

111. Roche, *Restructured Resistance*, 12; Clarence Jordan to NAACP, 29 January 1948, Legal File: General Georgia Voting, 1944–49, NAACP Microfilm; *Columbus Ledger-Enquirer*, 24 April 1988; *New York Times*, 18 July 1946.

112. Watters and Cleghorn, *Climbing Jacob's Ladder*, 30; Interview of Osgood Williams by Cliff Kuhn, 12 May 1988, 10–13, GGDP.

113. Sosna, *In Search of the Silent South*, 160, quoted in Spritzer, *Belle of Ashby Street*, 108; ibid., 106.

114. Mays, *Born to Rebel*, 223.

115. *New South* 1 (August 1946): 6; White, *A Man Called White*, 322; *New York Times*, 4 August 1946; E. M. Martin to White, 19 August 1946, Anti-Lynching Campaign: Georgia, 1912–55; NAACP Microfilm.

116. Transcript from *P.M.*, 28, 29 July 1946, 1, Anti-Lynching Campaign: Walton County, Georgia, NAACP Microfilm; *New York Times*, 4 August 1946.

117. E. M. Martin to Walter White, 19 August 1946, NAACP Anti-Lynching Campaign, 1912–55, Ser. A, Part 7, Reel 28, NAACP Microfilm; Anderson, *Wild Man*, 130–31.

118. The fourteen delegates to the committee included six from Fulton County, six from DeKalb County, and two from Rockdale County, in accordance with the county-unit representation. Under previous incumbent Robert Ramspeck, the committee had chosen the popular vote method of voting rather than the county-unit system.

119. Helen Mankin's brother, for example, insisted that in one Fulton County booth the stack of votes for Mankin appeared to be double that for Davis, but the official count gave Mankin 86 votes to nearly 3,000 for Davis.

120. Spritzer, *Belle of Ashby Street*, 90–96, 106–7, 127–28.

121. *New York Times*, 15 August 1948. For more details on the "three governors Crisis," see Egerton, *Speak Now Against the Day*, 384–88, and Henderson and Roberts, *Georgia Governors*, 5–6.

122. Under a constitutional provision, when no candidate received a majority of the votes, the Georgia Assembly chose the governor from among the top two write-in candidates in the general election. Fearing Eugene's ill health, the Talmadge camp organized a write-in campaign for Herman and subsequently argued that the provision was applicable in the 1946 election because the winner was unavailable to take office. Unexpectedly, Herman came in third among the write-in candidates at first count, hence the discovery of new votes in Telfair County. For more details, see Roche, *Restructured Resistance*, 14, and Harold P. Henderson, "The 1946 Gubernatorial Election in Georgia" (M.A. thesis, Georgia Southern College, 1967).

123. Memo from Robert Carr to the president of the Committee for Civil Rights, 16 April 1947, 8, Committee on Civil Rights Correspondence, 1946–47, Box 3, no. 539, Dorothy Tilly Papers, EU.

124. Payne, *I've Got the Light of Freedom*, 27; Egerton, *Speak Now Against the Day*, 374; Grant, *The Way It Was*, 366; Robert Carr to Dorothy Tilly, 24 July 1947, Box 3, no. 539, Tilly Papers, EU.

125. "Negro Children in Georgia-Harris County," report 1947, 1–7, 9, Committee on Civil Rights Misc. Materials, Box 4, no. 539, Tilly Papers, EU.

126. Numerous interviews, including Tea Kunney and William Randall by author; *Pittsburgh Courier*, 13 November 1948; *Time*, 20 September 1948; NAACP News Release, 2 December 1948, Ailey, 1946–52, Georgia Branch Files, NAACP Papers, LC; George S. Mitchell, "Georgia 1949," *New South* 4 (October 1949): 8; *Pittsburgh Courier*, 1 January 1949; 18 September 1948; Membership review, 15 November 1947, Georgia State Conference Files, 1947, NAACP Papers, LC.

127. Harper statement, n.d., Branch Files: Atlanta, 1946–48, NAACP Papers, LC; Gilbert to Current, 13 November 1946, Georgia State Conference, 1943–46, NAACP Papers, LC.

128. Current to Gilbert, 8 June 1947, Gilbert to Current, 20 January 1947, Georgia State Conference, 1947 File, NAACP Papers, LC; Black to Mr. Cummings, 20 August 1946, Cummings to Black, 25 July 1946, Georgia Branch Files: Dublin, 1945–55, NAACP Papers, LC; Newspaper clipping, n.d., Georgia State Conference, 1947 File, NAACP Papers, LC.

129. Current to Jamerson, 15 December 1947, Gilbert to Black, 17 October 1949, Current to Gilbert, 29 December 1949, Georgia Branch Files: Savannah, 1946–55, NAACP Papers, LC.

130. Franklin Williams to Roy Wilkins, 26 November 1948, Georgia State Conference, 1948–49 File, NAACP Papers, LC.

131. Sullivan, "Southern Reformers," 99; Interviews of Charles Sherrod and John Perdew by author.

132. Memo, Amos Holmes to Brunswick NAACP, 26 August 1958, Amos Holmes Correspondence, Office Files, NAACP Papers, LC.

Chapter 3. The Effects of the White Supremacist Backlash on Black Protest, 1948–1960

1. Kytle, "A Long, Dark Night for Georgia?" 55; *Time,* 20 September 1948, 10.

2. There were 13,595 members in 1946 and 11,941 members in 1948. See C. T. Perkins to Gloster Current, 13 July 1953, Georgia State Conference, 1950–55 File, NAACP Papers, LC.

3. Boyd to Current, 5 February 1949, Georgia State Conference, 1948–49 File, NAACP Papers, LC.

4. Dittmer, *Black Georgia,* 34; Gavins, "NAACP in North Carolina," 110; Fairclough, *Race and Democracy,* 135.

5. *New South* 4 (June 1949): 5, 7; Key, *Southern Politics,* 121.

6. Pyles, "Race and Ruralism," 11; *New South* 7 (October–November 1952): 2; Interview of Clarence Bacote by West, 1978, 21, 27, LAS; Talmadge, *You and Segregation,* 31–32; *Pittsburgh Courier,* 3 February 1951.

7. *New York Times,* 15 August 1948; 13 January 1949; Mitchell, "Georgia 1949," 7; *Pittsburgh Courier,* 21 August 1948.

8. *New York Times,* 19 February, 18 December 1948, 13 January, 5, 6 February 1949; *Pittsburgh Courier,* 7, 24, 31 January 1948, 5 February 1949.

9. Joyce, "Atlanta Black Crackers," 198; *New York Times,* 15 January, 15 February 1949.

10. *Pittsburgh Courier,* 5 February 1949; Fite, *Richard B. Russell,* 244; Potenziani, "Striking Back," 274. Russell admitted privately that he did not expect the bill to succeed, but he thought that "it will at least enable us to put our finger on the hypocrites" (Fite, *Richard B. Russell,* 244).

11. *New South* 6 (May–June 1951): 1, April 1958, 4; Henderson and Roberts, *Georgia Governors,* 9.

12. *Pittsburgh Courier,* 5 May 1951; *Southern School News* 1 (September 1954): 5.

13. *Brown v. Board of Education, Topeka, Kansas,* was a case sponsored by the NAACP to test the doctrine of separate but equal in education.

14. *Pittsburgh Courier,* 13 January, 10, 24 February 1951; *Southern Patriot,* November 1954, 1; Transcript of broadcast by Benjamin Mays on radio station WERD, 4 October 1950, 2, Box 43, Folder 20, Ser. XIV, Civil Rights File, Walden Papers, AHC; Mays, "Why an Atlanta School Suit?" *New South* 5 (September–October 1950): 2.

15. Current speech to meeting in Savannah, 12 December 1948, Georgia State Conference, 1950–55 File, NAACP Papers, LC; *New York Times,* 16, 29 June, 19 August 1949, 28 March 1948; Talmadge, *You and Segregation,* 44; Interview of Herman Talmadge by author; *Pittsburgh Courier,* 13 November, 7 January 1948; Payne, *I've Got the Light of Freedom,* 27.

16. *New South* 4 (March 1949): 3–4; *New South* 4 (October 1949): 8; *New York Times,* 3, 14, 28 March 1948; *Pittsburgh Courier,* 18 September, 13 November 1948, 1 January 1949; *Time,* 20 September 1948; NAACP News Release, 2 December 1948, Ailey, 1946–52, Georgia Branch Files, NAACP Papers, LC; Mitchell, "Georgia 1949," 8.

17. *Pittsburgh Courier,* 22 January 1949; 7 April, 30 June 1951; *New York Times,* 12 January 1949; *New South* 4 (July 1949): 8, January 1952, 7; *Atlanta Daily World,* 28 October 1948.

18. Flyer for registration meeting, 3 September 1951, Southeast Region of Association of Citizens' Democratic Clubs, Ser. XIII, Georgia Voters' League, Box 42, Folder 9, Walden Papers, AHC; Owen, "Rise of Negro Voting in Georgia," 60; Brazeal, "Summary of Early County Interviews and Findings About Negro Participation in Politics," 31 August 1956, Brazeal Papers, SRC Papers, AU; Elliott, *Rise of Guardian Democracy,* 87.

19. Charles Greenlea to Walden, 14 April 1948, Ser. XIII, Box 42, Folder 4, Walden Papers, AHC; Brazeal, "Summary of Early County Interviews"; L. G. Chance to Walter White, 15 July 1953, Current to Chance, 30 October 1946, Georgia Branch Files: Camden County, 1946–54, NAACP Papers, LC.

20. *Atlanta Daily World,* 31 October 1948; *Pittsburgh Courier,* 18 September 1948.

21. Georgia Association of Citizens' Democratic Clubs, Minutes, 11 October 1950, Box 42, Folder 9, Ser. XIII, Georgia Voters' League Files, Walden Papers, AHC; Price, "The Negro Voter in the South," September 1957, 33, SRC Publications, 1944–76, SRC Papers, AU; Johnson, "Southern Negro's View of the South," 5; *Pittsburgh Courier,* 3 March 1951. In contrast, Georgia writer Lillian Smith had predicted that "within the next ten years Southern segregation will have disappeared, that is as far as the law is concerned" (*Pittsburgh Courier,* 26 May 1951).

22. See B. R. Brazeal, "Summary of Peach County Interviews and Findings About Negro Participation in Politics," 31 August 1956, Brazeal Papers, SRC Papers, AU.

23. "Report of Secretary for the Month of September," 13 October 1953, Reel 2, Supplement 1951–55, Part I, NAACP Microfilm. The editor was Robert Brown. See *Pittsburgh Courier,* 3 March 1956.

24. Johnson, "Desegregation of Public Education in Georgia," 235; "Report of Secretary for the Month of September," 13 October 1953, Reel 2, Supplement 1951–5, Part I, NAACP Microfilm; *Southern School News* 1 (February 1955): 6; *Pittsburgh Courier,* 28 April 1951.

25. *Pittsburgh Courier,* 12, 19, 26 May 1951.

26. Bartley, *From Thurmond to Wallace,* 58.

27. *Pittsburgh Courier,* 17 March 1951; Interview of John Bertrand by author; B. R. Brazeal, "Summary of Floyd County Interviews," and "Findings About Negro Participation in Politics," 31 August 1956, 2, Brazeal Papers, SRC Papers, AU.

28. Brazeal, "Summary of Floyd County," 1; Price, "Negro Voter," 48; *Pittsburgh Courier,* 17 March 1951.

29. *Pittsburgh Courier,* 17 March 1951; Brazeal, "Summary of Floyd County," 3.

30. Calhoun, "Significant Aspects," 4–5; Price, *Negro and the Ballot,* 14.

31. Owen, "Rise of Negro Voting in Georgia," 53; B. R. Brazeal, "Summary of McIntosh County Interviews and Findings About Negro Participation in Politics," 31 August 1956, Brazeal Papers, SRC Papers, AU. See Greene, *Praying for Sheetrock*, 8, 117.

32. Brazeal, "Summary of McIntosh Interviews." One explanation for this racial moderation was that the coastal plains had experienced far less plantation slavery.

33. Owen, "Rise of Negro Voting in Georgia," 53.

34. *Atlanta Daily World*, 31 October 1948.

35. Bartley, *From Thurmond to Wallace*, 58; Jackson, "Race and Suffrage," 4; Sullivan, *Days of Hope*, 257. Sullivan notes that canvassers for the Progressive Party campaign were run out of Columbus and Augusta. One contemporary observation was that the campaign was akin to "guerilla warfare" in the face of what Sullivan described as "escalating terror."

36. *New York Times*, 9 May 1948; *Pittsburgh Courier*, 21 May 1949; *New South* 4 (September 1949): 9, *New South* 7 (September 1952): 6, *New South* 8 (October–November 1953): 6; *New York Times*, 15 February 1949; Interview of Joe Hendricks by author.

37. Price, "Negro Voter," 48.

38. *Pittsburgh Courier*, 14 May 1949.

39. *New York Times*, 28 June 1948; Carter, *Southern Legacy*, 92. For an account of Wallace's southern campaign, see Sullivan, *Days of Hope*, 249–75.

40. Sullivan, *Days of Hope*, 253; *Pittsburgh Courier*, 25 April 1953.

41. *Crisis* 58 (October 1951): 526–28, 535; *Pittsburgh Courier*, 1 April 1950.

42. *Columbus Ledger-Enquirer*, 8 May 1988; Amos Holmes Field Report, September 1958, Amos Holmes Correspondence, Office Files, NAACP Papers, LC.

43. "Brunswick 1956," Annual Reports, Georgia, 1956–65, NAACP Papers, LC; Amos Holmes Field Report, November 1958, Amos Holmes Correspondence, Office Files, NAACP Papers, LC.

44. Garrow, ed., *Atlanta*, vii; McPheeters, *Negro Progress in Atlanta*, 1; *Southern School News* 2 (June 1956): 9.

45. *Journal of Negro Education* 23 (Summer 1954): 227–28; *New York Times*, 9 April 1949; Joyce, "Atlanta Black Crackers," 199–200; *Pittsburgh Courier*, 16 April 1949; Robinson also stole home to score a run.

46. *Pittsburgh Courier*, 25 March 1950; *New York Times*, 3 May 1949. Ironically, Jenkins had been in the Ku Klux Klan when he joined the police force.

47. Bayor, *Race and the Shaping of Twentieth-Century Atlanta*, 108; "Negro Municipal Workers," compiled by Industrial Relations Department, Richmond Urban League, in *New South* 6 (May–June 1951): 1; Spritzer and Bergmark, *Grace Towns Hamilton*, 98–99.

48. It is easy to paint too stark a picture of moderates and segregationists as implacable enemies. A reporter on the *Atlanta Constitution*, Hunter James, was surprised to discover that Roy Harris and Ralph McGill met socially. According to James, Harris explained that "we used to be real good friends, Ralph and I. It's just that he went wrong on the Negro question" (*They Didn't Put That on the Huntley-Brinkley!* 93).

49. The Georgia Council was the state affiliate of the Southern Regional Council. See Blumberg, *One Voice*, 112.

50. Stone, *Regime Politics*, 28; Martin, *William Berry Hartsfield*, 49; Interview of Bacote by

West, 5, LAS; Interview of Warren Cochrane by Bernard West, 15 November 1978, 15, LAS; Calhoun, "Significant Aspects," 92, 94.

51. Hartsfield to Walden, 15 September 1949, Georgia Association of Democratic Clubs, Box 42, Folder 3, Walden Papers, AHC; *Southern Patriot,* November 1947, 3. For a more detailed discussion of the Freedom Train, see John White, "Civil Rights in Conflict: The 'Birmingham Plan' and the Freedom Train, 1947," *Alabama Review* 52 (April 1999): 121–41.

52. Newspaper clipping, 1950s n.d., Blackburn Papers, AARL; *Pittsburgh Courier,* 7 July 1951; Galphin and Shavin, *Atlanta,* 259; Martin, *William Berry Hartsfield,* 87; Interview of Cochrane by West, 13, LAS.

53. Hope, "Discrimination in Industry," 267. In 1953, the UPWA decided to force locals to accept federal antidiscrimination policies.

54. *Southern Patriot,* January 1955, 1; *Pittsburgh Courier,* 3 December 1960.

55. Hamman, "Study of Voting Participation," 21; Calhoun, "Significant Aspects," 21–22, 87; Jackson, "Voting Registration in Georgia," January 1953, 8, SRC Publications, SRC Microfilm; *New York Times,* 7 September 1949.

56. Kuhn, Joye, and West, *Living Atlanta,* 39; APEX, *Sweet Auburn,* 45; Hamman, "Study of Voting Participation," 46, 55. The primary reason given for voting was to improve conditions generally, rather than specifically to improve the standing of black Atlantans.

57. APEX, *Sweet Auburn,* 48, 51.

58. Program for the Seventh Anniversary of the Atlanta Cultural League, 27 April 1952, Blackburn Papers, AARL; Nasstrom, "Down to Now," 124; *Atlanta Daily World,* 11 September 1956.

59. Interview of John Calhoun by Bernard West, 6 April 1979, LAS.

60. Interview of Calhoun by West. The ACRC was under the authority of the local NAACP, which was led by Dobbs's close ally C. A. Harper at the time.

61. Calhoun, "Significant Aspects," 93; McPheeters, *Negro Progress in Atlanta,* 2; Interview of Cochrane by West, 7, LAS; Interview of Bacote by West, 14, LAS.

62. Stone, *Regime Politics,* 28; *New York Times,* 7 September 1949; McPheeters, *Negro Progress in Atlanta,* 3; Interview of Cochrane by West, 42, LAS; Bacote, "Negro in Atlanta Politics," 349.

63. Interview of Bacote by West, 14, LAS; Goldfield, *Black, White, and Southern,* 46.

64. Calhoun, "Significant Aspects," 99, 12; Bacote, "Negro in Atlanta Politics," 349; Hamman, "Study of Voting," 11; *New South* 8 (June 1953): 6; Interview of Cochrane by West, 7, LAS.

65. "Georgia State Conference Report," 3 December 1949, Box C42, Georgia Conference, 1948–49, NAACP Papers, LC; *Pittsburgh Courier,* 1 January 1949, 6 January 1951.

66. Spritzer and Bergmark, *Grace Towns Hamilton,* 75; "Annual Report 1950," Atlanta, Georgia, 1950 File, NAACP Papers, LC.

67. *Pittsburgh Courier,* 23 June, 17, 24 February, 7 July 1951.

68. Confidential memo to Wilkins, Current, and Marshall from White, 9 August 1950, Anonymous letter to Wilkins, received 29 September 1950, Memo, Robert L. Carter to White, Marshall, and Current, 21 September 1950, Georgia Branch Files: Atlanta, 1950, NAACP Papers, LC; Statement by Calhoun on death of Harper, June 1955, ibid., Atlanta 1954–55; Calhoun to Hurley, 2 June 1952, ibid., 1951–53.

69. R. R. Reed to Rev. R. T. Newbold, 15 November 1950, *Business Bulletin* 4 (June 1950), Memo, Robert L. Carter to Walter White, Thurgood Marshall, and Gloster Current, 21 September 1950, Georgia Branch Files: Atlanta, 1950, NAACP Papers, LC.

70. Memo, Current to White, 13 July 1950, ibid.

71. Calhoun and Harper were also close allies of Dobbs.

72. Memo, Robert L. Carter to Walter White, Thurgood Marshall, and Gloster Current, 21 September 1950, Georgia Branch Files: Atlanta, 1950, NAACP Papers, LC.

73. Ibid.; *Pittsburgh Courier,* 27 January 1951; Calhoun to Harper, 10 February 1951, Atlanta, 1951–53 File, NAACP Papers, LC.

74. R. R. Reed to Rev. R. T. Newbold, 15 November 1950, Georgia Branch Files: Atlanta, 1950, NAACP Papers, LC; King, *Daddy King,* 125; Hamman, "Rise of Negro Voting in Georgia," 37. Registered blacks were more likely to vote because of interest in a particular candidate or to use the privilege of full citizenship.

75. "Atlanta Business League, Annual Report 1952," 2, Blackburn Papers, AARL; Bayor, *Race and the Shaping of Twentieth-Century Atlanta,* 108.

76. Harmon, "Beneath the Image," 120.

77. See Hunter, *Community Power Structure; Reporter,* 14 December 1967, 34; Stone, *Regime Politics,* 36; Telegram, 17 August, no year, Ser. XIII, Georgia Voters' League, Walden Papers, AHC.

78. Alexander, *Beyond the Timberline,* 76; Charles S. Rooks, "The Atlanta Elections of 1969," June 1970, 1, SRC Publications, Ser. XVI, Reel 220, no. 166, SRC Microfilm; Martin, *William Berry Hartsfield,* 68, 49; *Atlanta Daily World,* 30 April 1948; Interview of Bacote by West, 32, LAS; Stone, *Regime Politics,* 31.

79. Weiss, *Whitney M. Young,* 63; Henderson, *Atlanta Life Insurance Company, 165.* Hill rose to chief actuary by the end of the decade.

80. Weiss, *Whitney M. Young,* 64.

81. Trillin, *Education in Georgia,* 8; see Atlanta Committee on Cooperative Action, *A Second Look: The Negro Citizen in Atlanta* (Atlanta Committee on Cooperative Action, 1960); Harmon, "Beneath the Image," 189; Paschall, *It Must Have Rained,* 18.

82. *New York Times,* 14 February 1960.

83. Paschall, *It Must Have Rained,* 53; *New York Times,* 14 February 1960.

84. King, *Daddy King,* 123.

85. Interview of Bacote by West, 14, LAS; King, *Daddy King,* 124.

86. *Southern School News* 2 (March 1956): 10; Baldwin, *Nobody Knows My Name,* 102; *Southern School News* 2, no. 6, 10; *Atlanta Journal,* 16 February 1959.

87. Weiss, *Whitney M. Young,* 63; Thornton, "Challenge and Response in the Montgomery Bus Boycott," 163–235.

88. *Atlanta Daily World,* 14 April 1948; Shadron, "Popular Protest and Legal Authority in Post–World War II Georgia," 236; Press Release, 2 December 1948, Georgia Conference, 1948–49 File, NAACP Papers, LC; *New York Times,* 12 January 1949.

89. Press Release, 2 December 1948, Georgia Conference, 1948–49 File, NAACP Papers, LC.

90. B. R. Brazeal, "Summary of Walton County Interviews and Findings About Negro Participation in Politics," 31 August 1956, Brazeal Papers, SRC Papers, AU; *Pittsburgh Courier,* 7 January 1950, 16 August 1958; Preface to *A Second Look,* January 1960, Ser. XIV, Box 44, Folder 3, Walden Papers, AHC.

91. "Georgia State Conference Report," 3 December 1949, Box C42, Georgia Conference 1948–49, NAACP Papers, LC; Law to Current, 13 November 1950, Georgia Branch Files: Savannah, 1946–55, NAACP Papers, LC; *Pittsburgh Courier,* 18 July 1953.

92. W. W. Law to Jack Greenberg, 25 April 1955, Discrimination in the Criminal Justice System, 1910–55, Part 8, Reel 16, Ser. B: Legal Department and Central Office Records 1940–55, NAACP Microfilm; Dennis Roberts, "Georgia Justice," *Progressive,* March 1964, 17; Branch, *Parting the Waters, 525;* Bolster, "Civil Rights Movement," 158.

93. McGrath, "Great Expectations," 79–81; Bolster, "Civil Rights Movement," 156.

94. These lawyers included E. E. Robinson and Howard Moore.

95. Interviews of Donald Hollowell, Horace Tate, Amanda Perdew, Warren Fortson, and Rev. Samuel Wells by author; McGrath, "Great Expectations," 80–81.

96. By 1957, the NAACP Legal Defense Fund, headed by Thurgood Marshall, and the NAACP had become distinct entities, with organizational independence.

97. *Brown* was also the culmination of nine years of education cases which represented the NAACP's strategy to overturn Jim Crow.

98. Klarman, "How *Brown* Changed Race Relations," 91.

99. "The South and Supreme Court's School Decisions," 2, Ser. XVI, Reel 220, no. 198, SRC Microfilm; *Southern School News* 1 (June 1955): 3; Roche, *Restructured Resistance,* 28; *Southern School News* 1 (February 1955): 6.

100. *Southern School News* 2 (March 1956): 9; *New South,* March 1956.

101. *New South* 11 (March 1956); *Southern Patriot,* November 1955, 1, March 1956, 4; *Southern School News* 3 (December 1956): 9, 11; *Greensboro Daily News,* 31 December 1957; *Delta-Democrat Times,* 19 October 1955; *Southern School News* 2 (August 1955): 4; *Atlanta Journal,* 12 August 1955.

102. The state paid Charles J. Bloch $5,000 to file a "friendly" segregation suit. See "Valdosta report," 2, Ser. III, Box 28, Folder 6, Walden Papers, AHC.

103. *Atlanta Constitution,* 30 August 1956.

104. *Southern School News* 2 (July 1955): 11; McGrath, "Great Expectations," 79; Minutes of Macon Meeting, 13 August 1955, Executive Committee Meeting Minutes, 31 August 1955, Georgia State Conference File, 1950–55, NAACP Papers, LC.

105. The city branches were in Atlanta, Augusta, Columbus, Macon, Savannah, Valdosta, and Waycross. The rural exception was in Liberty County, where there was a tradition of more moderate race relations.

106. Current to Law, 9 August 1955, Georgia State Conference File, 1950–55, NAACP Papers, LC; Johnson, "Desegregation of Public Education in Georgia," 248. Numerous black activists criticized the Georgia Teachers and Education Association for failing to take a more decisive stand against Jim Crow. In 1940, for example, John Wesley Dobbs urged teachers to register, asking, "How can you teach boys and girls something that you are not yourself?" (*Atlanta Daily World,* 6 April 1940). In 1955, Benjamin E. Mays spoke to the association confer-

ence on the "Tragedy of Fear." See Johnson, "Desegregation of Public Education in Georgia," 248.

107. *Southern School News* 4 (February 1958): 4; McGrath, "Great Expectations," 56. For more details on the course of the Atlanta case, see *Vivian Calhoun et al. v. A. C. Latimer et al.,* Civil Action no. 20273, U.S. Court of Appeals Fifth Circuit.

108. Various members of the Atlanta elite also competed to recruit potential transfer students.

109. McGrath, "Great Expectations," 112.

110. Klarman, "How *Brown* Changed Race Relations," 92; Fairclough, *Race and Democracy,* 196; Dittmer, *Local People,* 70.

111. *Pittsburgh Courier,* 25 February 1956.

112. McGrath, "Great Expectations," 100.

113. *Atlanta Journal,* 29 December 1958; Pyles, "Race and Ruralism," 102; *Atlanta Constitution,* 2 September 1958; see Mertz, "Mind Changing Time All Over Georgia," 45.

114. *New York Times,* 13 December 1959; Meyer quoted in Galphin and Shavin, *Atlanta,* 272; *Charleston News and Courier,* 12 January 1959; *Southern Patriot,* March 1960, 4.

115. Helen Fuller, "Atlanta Is Different," 15–16, *New Republic,* n.d., Wilkins Papers, EU. Also see *Southern Patriot,* February 1959, 1; *Southern School News* 5 (January 1959): 5; *Atlanta Constitution,* 23 December 1958; *Southern Patriot,* May 1959, 2; Calhoun to McGill, 10 October 1957, Georgia Branch Files, Atlanta, 1957–58, NAACP Papers, LC; HOPE handbill, December 1963, Ser. XVI, Reel 219, no. 121, SRC Microfilm; Mertz, "Mind Changing Time All Over Georgia," 41.

116. "Education," 1961 U.S. Commission on Civil Rights Report, 60, 76; see also discussion at end of Chapter 4 and in the conclusion.

117. Henderson and Roberts, *Georgia Governors,* 10; "A Report on School Desegregation for 1960–61," 1 April 1961, 33, Ser. XVI, Reel 220, no. 219, SRC Microfilm; Roche, *Restructured Resistance,* 95; Mertz, "Mind Changing Time All Over Georgia," 53; *Atlanta Journal,* 27 January 1959.

118. This was the majority view of the commission. An official minority view in favor of closing the schools was also presented. See Mertz, "Mind Changing Time All Over Georgia," 55; HOPE handbill, December 1963, Ser. XVI, Reel 219, no. 121, SRC Microfilm.

119. Roche, *Restructured Resistance,* 168. For many black Georgians, speaking up against segregation at a commission hearing was an intimidating prospect. In Sylvania, to a chorus of boos, W. W. Law supported integration and insisted that he spoke for thousands of Georgians who "are silent because they dare not say what is really and truly in their hearts" (ibid., 140).

120. "Education," 1961 U.S. Commission on Civil Rights Report, 76.

121. Charlayne Hunter-Gault, Foreword, in Trillin, *Education in Georgia,* x. Within a week of desegregation, Hamilton Holmes's father, Alfred Holmes, had his business sales tax investigated by state officials. Alfred Holmes had never previously been challenged by state officials. See *Pittsburgh Courier,* 18 October 1960.

122. McGrath, "Great Expectations," 182; Interviews of T. M. Alexander, Donald Hollowell, and Leroy Johnson by author; Roche, *Restructured Resistance,* 181.

123. *Southern Patriot,* March 1960, 4.

124. Calvin Trillin, "Reporter at Large," *New Yorker,* 13 July 1963, 30.

125. "Southern Justice: An Indictment," 18 October 1965, 9, Ser. XVI, Reel 220, no. 234, SRC Microfilm; *Pittsburgh Courier,* 7, 14, 21 October 1961; "Monthly Report of the General Counsel," March 1964, Ser. III, NAACP, Walden Papers, AHC; "Progress Report in Reference Preston Cobb Jr.," 1–2, November 1961, Georgia Legal File, NAACP Papers, LC; T. V. Anderson, draft report to *Pittsburgh Courier,* 1 August 1963, *Courier* Roving Reporter, 1962–63 File, T. V. Anderson Papers, CCMC; Interview of Donald Hollowell by author.

126. Weltner, *Southerner,* 27; Henderson and Roberts, *Georgia Governors,* 10; Galphin and Shavin, *Atlanta,* 281; Pyles, "Race and Ruralism," 10–11; Davidson and Grofman, *Quiet Revolution in the South,* 72–73; *New Yorker,* 13 July 1963, 31.

127. See, for example, Robinson, *Montgomery Bus Boycott and the Women Who Started It.*

128. *Southern School News* 3 (February 1957): 9; Interview of William Holmes Borders by Mary Egan Dalton, 5 March 1976, AAOHC; *Pittsburgh Courier,* 19 January 1957; Barnes, *Journey from Jim Crow,* 125–26.

129. *Pittsburgh Courier,* 16 March 1957; 9 April 1960.

130. Bolster, "Civil Rights Movement," 170; McGrath, "Great Expectations," 194–95.

131. Field Report, Amos Holmes, July 1958, NAACP Papers, LC; *Macon Telegraph,* 1 April 1954; *Pittsburgh Courier,* 6 September 1958; B. R. Brazeal, "Summary of Laurens County Interviews and Findings About Negro Participation in Politics," 31 August 1956, 1–2, Brazeal Papers, SRC Papers, AU.

132. Johnson, "Desegregation of Public Education in Georgia," 237.

Chapter 4. Direct Action Protest in Georgia's Cities, 1960–1965

1. For a detailed narrative of this phase of black protest, see Branch, *Parting the Waters.*

2. Levine, "Civil Rights," 9, unpublished manuscript, 1988, courtesy John Bertrand, Rome, Georgia; "Student Protest Movement: September 1961," Ser. XVI, Reel 220, no. 223, SRC Microfilm. According to the SRC report, these cities were Atlanta, Savannah, Macon, Augusta, Columbus, and Marietta. More than twenty students had also been arrested at the New Varsity in Athens during March 1960 (*Atlanta Constitution,* 20 March 1960).

3. According to the Georgia Voters' League, black voter registration increased by over eighty thousand between 1962 and 1964. See Kousser, *Colorblind Injustice,* 211.

4. *Atlanta Journal,* 8 April 1963; Kousser, *Colorblind Injustice,* 211.

5. Rural Development 2, U.S. Bureau of the Census; Walker, "Sit-ins in Atlanta," in Garrow, ed., *Atlanta,* 60; Johnson, "Desegregation of Public Education in Georgia," 231.

6. *Southern School News* 4 (April 1958): 13; Henderson and Roberts, *Georgia Governors,* 10; Galphin and Shavin, *Atlanta,* 281; Pyles, "Race and Ruralism," 10–11; Davidson and Grofman, *Quiet Revolution in the South,* 72–73.

7. Norrell, *Reaping the Whirlwind,* ix.

8. Trezzant Anderson, the Georgia correspondent for the *Pittsburgh Courier,* commented that "it looks like every time handsome cigar-smoking Donald Hollowell becomes counsel in

a civil rights case down here in Dixie his side wins the case" (*Pittsburgh Courier,* 23 April 1961). See also *Chattanooga Times,* 2 April 1963; Rome Council on Human Relations Newsletter, 10 February 1964, courtesy John Bertrand; *Pittsburgh Courier,* 28 May 1960, 6 April 1961.

9. *Pittsburgh Courier,* 9 April, 24 September 1960. By May 1961, the NAACP had twelve branches in Georgia. Another three branches were chartered by October 1961 (*Pittsburgh Courier,* 18 April, 10 June 1961). The NAACP also held statewide conferences; see "NAACP State-Wide Rally Report," 15 May 1960, Ser. III, Box 30, Folder 8, Walden Papers, AHC. Randolph Blackwell reported in 1963 that "it was a pleasure to observe the extent to which [the Georgia Voters' League] has affiliates across the state" (Blackwell to Branton, 4 November 1963, VEP, SRC Papers, AU). But the league did not have a far-reaching impact. See, for example, "Report of Rev. Amos O. Holmes," 20 September 1962, Ser. XIII, Box 42, Folder 1, Walden Papers.

10. *Pittsburgh Courier,* 27 February, 14 October 1960, 25 November 1961; "Student Protest Movement: Winter 1960," Ser. XVI, Reel 220, no. 217, SRC Microfilm. See also Webb, "Charles Bloch," 267–92.

11. *Sewanee Herald Tribune,* 13 October 1960. In Savannah, for example, Ezell Blair, one of the Greensboro four, spoke on 20 August 1960.

12. Georgia State Conference Resolutions, 13 November 1961, Georgia State Conference, 1960–62, NAACP Papers, LC; Lomax, *Negro Revolt,* 101–4.

13. See, for example, Ricks, "'De Lawd' Descends and Is Crucified"; Norrell, *Reaping the Whirlwind;* Chafe, *Civilities and Civil Rights;* Eskew, *But for Birmingham;* Colburn, *Racial Change and Community Crisis.*

14. Interview of Lonnie King by John Britton, 29 August 1967, 24, CRDP, Howard University (HU); Interview of Julian Bond by John Britton, 22 January 1968, 4, CRDP, HU; *Student Voice,* June 1960, 4; Walker, "Sit-ins," 68; Interview of Ben Brown by John Britton, 16 August 1967, 3, CRDP, HU.

15. Interview of Charles Black by John Britton, 1, CRDP, HU; Interview of Brown by Britton, 1, CRDP, HU; *Pittsburgh Courier,* 8 October 1960, 23 September 1961.

16. Sitton, "Atlanta's Example," 22.

17. *Look,* 25 April 1960, quoted in Martin Luther King Jr. and Wyatt T. Walker, "SCLC Voter Registration Prospectus 1961," 7, Box 43, Folder 29, Ser. XIV, Civil Rights File, Walden Papers, AHC; Sitton, "Atlanta's Example," 123; Confidential Minutes, "Plans and Procedures Committee Meeting Held Wednesday, March 22, 1961: 3:30 P.M. 14 Floor, Commerce Building," 1, Ser. XIV, Civil Rights File, Walden Papers, AHC; *New South* 17 (June 1962): 11; Interview of Adelaide Taitt by Robert Martin, 20 August 1968, 34, CRDP, HU.

18. Allen, *Mayor,* 82; *Pittsburgh Courier,* 7 October 1961; Gwendolyn Isles to Ivan Allen, 14 March 1963, Ser. XV, no. 43, Reel 32, SNCC Microfilm; *Student Voice,* 16 December 1963; Harmon, "Beneath the Image," 325.

19. Interview of Julian Bond by author.

20. *Student Voice,* August 1960, 5; *Pittsburgh Courier,* 30 July 1960; Vanlandingham, "In Pursuit of a Changing Dream," 75; Mays, *Born to Rebel,* 292; Walker, "Sit-ins," 73; Holloway, *Politics of the Southern Negro,* 202; *Pittsburgh Courier,* 28 May 1960.

21. Walker, "Sit-ins," 75; *Atlanta Inquirer,* 14 August 1960; Vanlandingham, "In Pursuit of a Changing Dream," 77.

22. T. V. Anderson report to *Pittsburgh Courier,* Draft copy, n.d., T. V. Anderson Papers, CCMC. According to the *Student Voice,* fifty-seven protesters were arrested. The *Pittsburgh Courier* recorded fifty-two. See *Student Voice,* October 1960, 1; *Pittsburgh Courier,* 29 October 1960.

23. *Student Voice,* October 1960, 1; Vanlandingham, "In Pursuit of a Changing Dream," 76; T. V. Anderson report to *Pittsburgh Courier,* Draft copy, untitled and n.d., Anderson Papers, CCMC.

24. *Pittsburgh Courier,* 6 April 1960; Interview of John Gibson by John Britton, 26 April 1968, 19, CRDP, HU; *Student Voice,* December 1960; *New South* 21 (Fall 1966): 75–76.

25. *New York Times,* 4 December 1960; *Student Voice,* January 1961; Interview of Gibson by Britton, 26, CRDP, HU.

26. Raines, *My Soul Is Rested,* 89; Carson, *In Struggle,* 29.

27. Harmon, "Beneath the Image," 295.

28. Walker, "Sit-ins," 88; Interview of Carl Holman by John Britton, 32, CRDP, HU; Interview of Lonnie King by Britton, 44, CRDP, HU; *Pittsburgh Courier,* 25 March 1961.

29. Ten of Atlanta's thirty movie theaters had desegregated (*New South* 17 [September 1962]: 11; Margaret Long, "Strictly Subjective," *New South* 19 [February 1964]: 5).

30. Harmon, "Beneath the Image," 305; Grant, *The Way It Was,* 400; *New York Times,* 31 January 1964.

31. *Nation,* 17 February 1964; *New York Times,* 12, 28 January 1964; *Student Voice,* 18 November 1963.

32. *Brown Daily Herald,* 3 February 1964.

33. News Releases, 11, 16, 20 January 1964, Ser. XV, no. 43, Reel 32, SNCC Microfilm.

34. *Student Voice,* 27 January 1964; *Jet,* 13 February 1964; *New York Times,* 27 January 1964.

35. *New York Times,* 29 January 1964; *Florida Times-Union,* 3 February 1964; James Forman, statement, 24 December 1964, SNCC Microfilm.

36. *Student Voice,* 3 February 1964, 16 December 1963; *New York Times,* 31 January 1964; Harmon, "Beneath the Image," 337.

37. Nelson, "Georgia"; Interviews of Don Hollowell, Frances Pauley, Willie Bolden, Rev. C. S. Hamilton, Lawrence Hanks, and others by author.

38. Mays, *Born to Rebel,* 275; Interview of Taitt by Martin, 25, 34–35, CRDP, HU.

39. Sitton, "Atlanta's Example," 22, 123; Jones, *They Didn't Put That on the Huntley-Brinkley!* 80; Interview of William Holmes Borders by Mary Egan Dalton, 5 March 1976, AAOHC; Allen, *Mayor,* 105–8, 96.

40. Freedgood, "Life in Buckhead," 192; *Wall Street Journal,* 24 August 1961.

41. Mays, *Born to Rebel,* 282.

42. Garrow, ed., *Atlanta,* vii; Branch, *Parting the Waters,* 345; Raines, *My Soul Is Rested,* 85.

43. Interview of Brown by Britton, 21, CRDP, HU; Interview of Bond by Britton, 9, CRDP, HU.

44. *Pittsburgh Courier,* 29 July 1961; Lewis, *Walking with the Wind,* 122; Zinn, *SNCC,* 17; Bond, "Autobiography," 22; Interview of Lonnie King by Britton, 33, 31, CRDP, HU; Interview of Gibson by Britton, 23, CRDP, HU; Interview of Brown by Britton, 14–15, CRDP, HU.

45. Vanlandingham, "In Pursuit of a Changing Dream," 67–68; Interview of Taitt by Martin, 3, 5–6, 12.

46. Interview of Taitt by Martin, 8, CRDP, HU.

47. Long, "Strictly Subjective," 2; *New South* 19 (February 1964); Harmon, "Beneath the Image," 325; Jones, *They Didn't Put That on the Huntley-Brinkley!* 16.

48. Interview of Taitt by Martin, 14, CRDP, HU; Mays, *Born to Rebel*, 293, 296.

49. Branch, *Parting the Waters*, 395–96; Allen, *Mayor*, 103.

50. Paschall, *It Must Have Rained*, 1, 18, 173.

51. See, for example, Lewis, *Walking with the Wind*, 117, 132.

52. Branch, *Parting the Waters*, 355.

53. Other divisions included rivalry within the Auburn Avenue elite, and Julian Bond recalled SNCC's jealousy of COAHR's influence.

54. Interview of John Gibson by Britton, 31, CRDP, HU; Interview of Black by Britton, 8, CRDP, HU; Harmon, "Beneath the Image," 273; *Pittsburgh Courier*, 4 June 1960; Vanlandingham, "In Pursuit of a Changing Dream," 76; Hornsby, "Georgia," 138–39; Interview of Gibson by Britton, 30, CRDP, HU.

55. Interview of Lonnie King by Britton, 37, CRDP, HU; Raines, *My Soul Is Rested*, 86.

56. This claim is denied by Benjamin Mays, who wrote in his autobiography that "the six presidents in the Center were in full sympathy with the students, and the Council of Presidents never tried to overpersuade, let alone dictate to them" (*Born to Rebel*, 288).

57. Interview of Holman by Britton, 16, CRDP, HU.

58. *Pittsburgh Courier*, 28 February 1961; Interview of Bond by Britton, 8, CRDP, HU.

59. *Student Voice*, 18 November 1963, 4; Ralph Moore, Executive Secretary COAHR, to Walden, 24 June 1963, Ser. III, Box 30, Folder 16, Walden Papers, AHC; *Pittsburgh Courier*, 4 June, 29 October 1960; Interview of Lonnie King by Britton, 24, CRDP, HU.

60. Interview of Black by Britton, 7, CRDP, HU; Interview of Lonnie King by Britton, 37, CRDP, HU; 35; Walker, "Sit-ins," 85.

61. Walker, "Sit-ins," 74; Branch, *Parting the Waters*, 381; Harmon, "Beneath the Image," 305.

62. Interview of Black by Britton, 7, CRDP, HU; Johnson, *Patterns of Negro Segregation*, 205; Walker, "Sit-ins," 77, 72; Interview of Bond by Britton, 46, CRDP, HU.

63. Interview of Holman by Britton, 40, 24, CRDP, HU; *Pittsburgh Courier*, 20 February 1960.

64. *New York Times*, 12 March 1961; Walker, "Sit-ins," 89; Interview of Bond by Britton, 14, CRDP, HU; Branch, *Parting the Waters*, 397; Interview of Lonnie King by Britton, 45, CRDP, HU; Newsom and Gorden, "A Stormy Rally in Atlanta," in Garrow, ed., *Atlanta*, 108.

65. Interview of Black by Britton, 22, CRDP, HU; Interview of Holman by Britton, 38–40, CRDP, HU; *New York Times*, 12 March 1961; Newsom and Gorden, "A Stormy Rally in Atlanta," 110; Galphin and Shavin, *Atlanta*, 266; Interview of Lonnie King by Britton, 45, CRDP, HU; Branch, *Parting the Waters*, 397.

66. Walker, "Functions of Disunity," 28.

67. Interview of Holman by Britton, 34, CRDP, HU; *Pittsburgh Courier*, 25 March 1961; Interview of Bond by Britton, 8, CRDP, HU.

68. Interview of Lonnie King by Britton, 40, CRDP, HU; Interview of Black by Britton, 13, 6. CRDP, HU

69. Interview of Bond by Britton, 7, CRDP, HU; Walker, "Sit-ins," 70, 78; Harmon, "Beneath the Image," 334.

70. Harmon, "Beneath the Image," 323.

71. Fairclough, *To Redeem the Soul of America*, 176.

72. See Hornsby, "Negro in Atlanta Politics," 7–33. For a useful selection of articles about black activism in Atlanta during the 1960s, see Garrow, ed., *Atlanta*.

73. *Atlanta Inquirer*, 7 August 1965. See Chapter 6.

74. For a much more detailed survey of black protest in Savannah, see Stephen Tuck, "The Civil Rights Movement in Savannah" (Undergraduate thesis, University of Cambridge, 1992).

75. Reel recording of speech, 1 January 1964; Raines, *My Soul Is Rested*, 443; *Atlanta Journal*, 3 October 1963.

76. Nevertheless, Georgia as a whole, and thus Savannah, lagged behind many other areas of the South. See *Atlanta Journal*, 7 July 1961.

77. Field Report, 29 January 1963, Newspaper clipping, VEP 2–25, SRC Papers, AU. Further pressure led to Savannah becoming one of the first cities to introduce district, rather than citywide, elections, allowing the election of black officials starting with Bobby Hill in 1966. See *Savannah Morning News*, 18 March 1966.

78. *Atlanta Journal*, 4 July 1963; Interview of Judson Ford by author; Bolster, "Civil Rights Movement," 199.

79. Interview of Malcolm Maclean by author; *Savannah Herald*, 1 April 1961.

80. *Savannah Herald*, 28 March 1960.

81. Interviews of W. W. Law, Hosea Williams, Earl Shinholster, James Alexander, and Malcolm Maclean by author.

82. Williams to Wiley Branton, 8 November 1962, VEP 2–25, SRC Papers, AU. The Political Action Council (PAC), led by lawyer Eugene Gadsden, superseded the CCCV as the political arm of the NAACP, continued the earlier work, and also selected black candidates for the new district elections.

83. For a more detailed analysis of the context of Savannah, see Tuck, "A City Too Dignified to Hate," 539–59.

84. *Atlanta Journal*, 22 June 1960.

85. U.S. Census, 1960. PC (1) 12B, Table 21, 63, 12C, Table 73, 230, Table 74, 235, Table 76, 245, Table 77, 249; Chatham County Statistics, VEP 2–25, SRC Papers, AU.

86. *Atlanta Journal*, 14 June 1963; Interviews of Geneve Law, Eugene Gadsden, and J. W. Jamerson by author.

87. Interview of Maclean by author; Smyth, "Segregation in Charleston," 28; *New York Times*, 4 August 1963; see also Tuck, "A City Too Dignified to Hate."

88. See Chafe, *Civilities and Civil Rights*; Interview of Maclean by author.

89. Interviews of Gadsden and Henry Brownlee by author; Jacoway and Colburn, eds., *Southern Businessmen and Desegregation*, 11.

90. *Atlanta Journal*, 22 June 1960. Savannah's median family income of $4,761 was the tenth highest out of the thirty-two towns in the state. For comparison, this income would have placed Savannah third out of eighteen towns in Mississippi. See U.S. Census 1960, PC (1) 12C, 242–45, Table 76, and PC (1) 26C, 155–56, Table 76.

91. *New York Times,* 6 August 1964.

92. Ibid.; *Savannah Morning News,* 1 October 1974, 22 October 1960; Interviews of Tena Rhodes, Carolyn Quilloin, Ulysses Bryan, Judson Ford, and Charles Dailey by author.

93. *Atlanta Journal,* 22 April 1960.

94. *Savannah Morning News,* 14 May 1961; *Pittsburgh Courier,* 12 August 1960.

95. *Crisis* 68 (August–September 1961): 438–49; *Pittsburgh Courier,* 1, 21 October 1961; *South Carolina Times,* 28 October 1961.

96. *Jet,* 31 August 1961; *Crisis* 68 (October 1961): 507–8; *Pittsburgh Courier,* 21 October 1961; *South Carolina Times,* 23 September 1961; *New York Times,* 9 November 1961; *Flax-Times Union,* 18 November 1961.

97. *Pittsburgh Courier,* 12 March 1961.

98. Interview of Rankin Jaudon by author.

99. *Pittsburgh Courier,* 10 August 1960.

100. *Crisis* 68 (October 1961): 507; Interview of Jamerson by author; *Crisis* 67 (August–September 1960): 412.

101. *Chicago Defender,* 7 May 1960, 1; quoted in Weisbrot, *Freedom Bound,* 41; *Charleston News and Courier,* 4 January 1961.

102. Raines, *My Soul Is Rested,* 436.

103. Interviews of Law, Gadsden, Curtis Cooper, and Jamerson by author; Bolster, "Civil Rights Movement," 242; Memo, Jordan to Branton, 23 February 1962, VEP 2–25, SRC Papers, AU; Fairclough, *To Redeem the Soul of America,* 94.

104. Vernon Jordan Field Report, 23 December 1963, VEP 2–25, SRC Papers, AU.

105. Fairclough, *To Redeem the Soul of America,* 141; *Atlanta Journal,* 14 June, 26 July 1963; Interviews of Ford, Sage Brown, Brownlee, and McLean by author; *Savannah Morning News,* 12 July 1963.

106. Telfair Academy, *We Ain't What We Used to Be,* 28; *New York Times,* 4 August 1963; *Savannah Morning News,* 8 July 1963.

107. *Atlanta Constitution,* 8 July 1963; *New York Times,* 4 August 1963.

108. Interview of Arthur Gordon by author; William Brophy, "Active Acceptance—Active Containment: The Dallas Story," in Jacoway and Colburn, eds., *Southern Businessmen and Desegregation,* 150.

109. The cities were Atlanta, Savannah, Albany, Augusta, Brunswick, Columbus, Macon, and Rome.

110. Vernon Jordan, Georgia Field Secretary, Monthly Report, 23 January 1963, NAACP Papers, LC; *Atlanta Journal,* 8 February 1963; "Brunswick," Synopsis of Recent Civil Rights Developments, Parts I–IV, 25 June–31 December 1963, Ser. XVI, Reel 219, no. 122, SRC Microfilm; *New York Times,* 31 August 1963; Watters, "Brunswick," SRC Publications, 1944–76, SRC Papers, AU, 3.

111. *Atlanta Journal,* 27 June 1962; *New York Times,* 31 August 1963; Vernon Jordan, Georgia Field Secretary, Monthly Report, 10 November 1961, Vernon Jordan to Gloster Current, Field Report, 17 August 1962, Brunswick Annual Report 1962, Annual Reports, Georgia, 1956–65 File, NAACP Papers, LC. Hope was greatly assisted in his leadership of NAACP activities and the youth council by NAACP branch secretary Geneva Lyde.

112. Watters, "Brunswick," 7; *New York Times,* 31 August 1963.

113. Watters, "Brunswick," 25; *New York Times,* 31 August 1963.

114. *Atlanta Journal,* 8 February 1963; Vernon Jordan, Georgia Field Secretary, Monthly Report, 23 January 1963, NAACP Papers, LC.

115. Watters, "Brunswick," 27.

116. Ibid., 27–28.

117. Ibid., 63; Vernon Jordan, Georgia Field Secretary, Monthly Report, 23 January 1963, NAACP Papers, LC.

118. *Chattanooga Times,* 2 April 1963; *Southern Patriot,* 4 April 1963; "Rome," Synopsis of Recent Civil Rights Developments, Parts I–IV, 25 June–31 December 1963, Ser. XVI, Reel 219, no. 122, SRC Microfilm; B. R. Brazeal, "Summary of Floyd County Interviews and Findings About Negro Participation in Politics," 31 August 1956, 1–4, Brazeal Papers, SRC Papers, AU; B. R. Brazeal to Mozell Hill, Associate Director, Georgia Council on Human Relations, "Confidential Appraisal of Status of the Rome, Georgia, Committee on Interracial Co-operation," 13 November 1956, 1, CCMC, AU.

119. Brazeal to Hill, "Confidential Appraisal of Status of the Rome, Georgia, Committee," 1; Directory of members of the Rome Council on Human Relations, property of John Bertrand.

120. John R. and Annabel H. Bertrand, "Rome Council on Human Relations, 1962–1988: Historical Survey Based on Documentary Sources," 1 December 1988, 2; "Events in Berry College's Race Relations Since 1959: A Statement by John R. Bertrand, president, Berry College, Mount Berry, Georgia," 1–2; John R. and Annabel H. Bertrand, "History of Rome Council on Human Relations," 1, Box 14, Folder 17, Pauley Papers, EU; Hutzler, "History of Rome, Georgia," 100–101.

121. *Chattanooga Times,* 2 April 1963; *Southern Patriot,* 4 April 1963; "Rome," Synopsis of Recent Civil Rights Developments, Parts I–IV, 25 June–31 December 1963, Ser. XVI, Reel 219, no. 122, SRC Microfilm; "Report of Secretary for April," NAACP report, 13 May 1963, 9, Ser. III, Box 29, Folder 14, Walden Papers, AHC; Levine, "Civil Rights," 10; Field Report, John Calhoun, 9 March 1963, John Calhoun Field Reports, VEP, SRC Papers, AU; "Synopsis of Recent Civil Rights Developments: Rome," 4–5, 25 June–31 December 1963, Ser. XVI, Reel 219, no. 122, SRC Microfilm; *Atlanta Daily World,* 29 March 1963.

122. Doss, "Homegrown Movement," 3; Draft reports to *Pittsburgh Courier,* 26 December 1962, *Courier* Roving Reporter, 1962–63 File, CCMC, AU; Law to Anderson, 13 March 1962, T. V. Anderson Papers, CCMC, AU.

123. *Pittsburgh Courier,* 11 November 1961.

124. The first sit-ins on the buses were as early as March 1961, one year before the bus boycott. See *Student Voice,* March 1961; *Macon Telegraph,* 1 November 1961, 16 February 1962; *Pittsburgh Courier,* 11 November 1961; Vernon Jordan, Georgia Field Secretary, Monthly Report, 10 November 1961, NAACP Papers, LC.

125. Doss, "Homegrown Movement," 9; Draft reports to *Pittsburgh Courier,* 12 May 1962, *Courier* Roving Reporter, 1962–63 File, CCMC, AU; *Baltimore Afro-American,* 5 January 1963.

126. *Macon Telegraph,* 19 May 1964, 3, 5 July 1962; Doss, "Homegrown Movement," 1–3, 6–10.

127. Campbell, *Stem of Jesse,* 21–22. Trezzant Anderson was impressed that Macon leaders

used mass meetings to target particular stores rather than to raise money. See Draft reports to *Pittsburgh Courier,* 26 December 1962, *Courier* Roving Reporter, 1962–63 File, CCMC, AU.

128. Vernon Jordan, Georgia Field Secretary, Monthly Report, 20 November 1962, NAACP Papers, LC.

129. *New York Times,* 3 March 1962; Doss, "Homegrown Movement," 6; *Baltimore Afro-American,* 5 January 1963; *Pittsburgh Courier,* 2 April 1962; *Southern School News,* April 1963, 15.

130. Interview of William Randall by author; *Macon Telegraph,* 16 February 1962, 6 April 1964; "Synopsis of Recent Civil Rights Developments: Macon, 25 June–31 December 1963," 4, Ser. XVI, Reel 219, no. 135, SRC Microfilm.

131. Interview of William Randall by Clifford Kuhn and Duane Stuart, 4 February 1989, 29, GGDP; Interview of Joe Hendricks by author. This charge was widely reported at the time.

132. Campbell, *Stem of Jesse,* 107, which also provides a detailed survey of the desegregation of Mercer.

133. Ibid., 191, 40, 173; Holmes, *Ashes for Breakfast,* 99, 100, 109.

134. Interview of William Randall by Clifford Kuhn and Duane Stewart, GGDP; *Macon Telegraph,* 3 June 1961; Doss, "Homegrown Movement," 5.

135. For example, according to NAACP field secretary Amos Holmes, Alphonzo Sirmon could not get people to join him in demonstrating in Dublin, so Sirmon decided to "stage sit-ins alone" (Holmes, Monthly report for November 1960, quoted in Bolster, "Civil Rights Movement," 204).

136. Vernon Jordan, Georgia Field Secretary, Monthly Report, 17 August 1961, NAACP Papers, LC; "Columbus," Synopsis of Recent Civil Rights Developments, Parts I–IV, 25 June–31 December 1963, Ser. XVI, Reel 219, no. 122, SRC Microfilm; *Birmingham News,* 10 July 1963.

137. T. V. Anderson report to *Pittsburgh Courier,* Draft copy, "Will They Act in Crisis," Anderson Papers, CCMC, AU; "Columbus," Synopsis of Recent Civil Rights Developments, Parts I–IV, 25 June–31 December 1963, Ser. XVI, Reel 219, no. 122, SRC Microfilm.

138. Blackwell to Branton, 19 November 1963, Randolph Blackwell Field Reports, VEP Files, SRC Microfilm.

139. Ibid.

140. Report, Helen Hayes, October 1964, John Calhoun, Field Report, 16 January, 1 February 1963, John Calhoun Field Reports, John Gibson to Branton, 18 August 1964, Blackwell to Branton, 25 August 1963, Blackwell Field Reports, VEP, SRC Microfilm.

141. "Columbus," Synopsis of Recent Civil Rights Developments, Parts I–IV, 25 June–31 December 1963, Ser. XVI, Reel 219, no. 122, SRC Microfilm; Blackwell to Branton, 19 November 1963; Watters, "Augusta, Georgia, and Jackson State University: Southern Episodes in a National Tragedy," 4, SRC Publications, SRC Papers, AU.

142. *Pittsburgh Courier,* 26 March 1960; *Student Voice,* August 1960, February 1961; *Atlanta Journal,* 14 December 1960. Roy Harris was a stockholder of Augusta Bus Company (*Pittsburgh Courier,* 28 May 1960).

143. The students carried signs that read, "Lincoln . . . Emancipation!!! Ike . . . Civil Rights????" See *Pittsburgh Courier,* 31 December 1960; *Student Voice,* December 1960.

144. *Student Voice,* January, December 1961, March 1962. On 3 June 1961, the *Pittsburgh Courier* reported that "the Augustans are relying on their students to fight their battles." See also *Student Voice,* December 1960.

145. Grant, *The Way It Was,* 418–19. The Citizens' Voters' League was accused of accepting bribes by the more recently established Augusta–Richmond County Voters' League. See Field report, 11 February 1963, Calhoun Reports, VEP, SRC Papers, AU.

146. Vernon Jordan, Georgia Field Secretary, Monthly Report, 8 October 1962, NAACP Papers, LC.

147. Vernon Jordan by author; Georgia Field Secretary, Monthly Report, 13 April 1962, NAACP Papers, LC; *Pittsburgh Courier,* 31 December 1960; *Southern Patriot,* August 1962.

148. Interview of C. S. Hamilton, Vernon Jordan, Georgia Field Secretary, Monthly Report, 3 May 1962, NAACP Papers, LC.

149. *New York Times,* 6 October 1962.

150. "Augusta," Synopsis of Recent Civil Rights Developments, Parts I–IV, 25 June–31 December 1963, Ser. XVI, Reel 219, no. 122, SRC Microfilm; Vernon Jordan, Georgia Field Secretary, Monthly Report, 3 May 1962, NAACP Papers, LC.

151. Ricks, "'De Lawd,'" 3.

152. Walker, "Albany," *New South* 18 (June 1963): 3; Chappell, *Inside Agitators,* 138.

153. *Pittsburgh Courier,* 9 March 1963; *New Republic,* 20 July 1963, 218; *New York Times,* 5, 22 August 1962.

154. Zinn, *SNCC,* 130; Ricks, "'De Lawd,'" 3, 12; *New York Times,* 17 July 1962.

155. Carson, "SNCC and the Albany Movement," 18. See also Reagon, "In Our Hands."

156. Oates, "Albany Movement," 29.

157. *New York Times,* 3 February 1962.

158. *Pittsburgh Courier,* 9 March 1963; *New Republic,* 20 July 1963, 16.

159. Ricks, "'De Lawd,'" 9; Moberly, "Testing the Bonds of Segregation," 88.

160. Young quoted in White, *Martin Luther King, Jr.,* 18; Ricks, "'De Lawd,'" 14; *New Republic,* 20 July 1963, 16; Lewis, *King,* 119.

161. *New York Times,* 5 August 1962; *New Republic,* 20 July 1963, 18.

162. Interview of Charles Sherrod by author.

163. Lewis, *Walking with the Wind,* 186; Ricks "'De Lawd,'" 14.

164. Zinn, *SNCC,* 124. See Chapter 5.

165. Carson, *In Struggle,* 59; Moberly, "Testing the Bonds of Segregation," 15. Moberly points out that Gray was a college friend of Joseph Kennedy and "fostered close relationships with his sons."

166. King, *Walking with the Wind,* 186; *New York Times,* 5 August 1962; David L. Lewis, "Martin Luther King, Jr., and the Promise of Non-violent Populism," in Franklin and Meier, eds., *Black Leaders of the Twentieth Century,* 282; Oates, "Albany Movement," 32.

167. *Peace News* (London), no. 1366, 31 August 1962; Lewis, *Walking with the Wind,* 186; Chalfen, "The Way Out," 583; *New South* 18 (February 1963): 9.

168. *New York Times,* 15 November 1962; *Nation,* 1 December 1962; Moberly, "Testing the Bonds of Segregation," 103.

169. Chalfen, "The Way Out," 567. Somewhat cryptically, Wyatt T. Walker accepted that the "defeat" of Albany was a "penalty in necessary demonstration and suffering" ("Albany," 8).

170. Chalfen, "The Way Out," 561, 592; *Jet,* 4 July 1963; *Atlanta Journal,* 6 June 1963; *Student Voice,* 28 April 1964, 3, 5 May 1964, 2, 20 July 1964, 1. Albany also attracted outside protesters. In January 1964, over twenty marchers on the Quebec-Washington-Guantanamo Peace Walks were arrested (Barbara Deming, "Prison Notes," 26, *Liberation,* February 1965).

171. *Peace News* (London), no. 1366, 31 August 1962.

172. Morris, *Origins of the Civil Rights Movement,* 280.

173. White, *Martin Luther King, Jr.,* 9; Fairclough, *To Redeem the Soul of America,* xix.

174. *Pittsburgh Courier,* 23 April 1960; August Meier, "Negro Protest Movements and Organizations," in Bracey, Meier, and Rudwick, *Conflict and Competition,* 25–26.

175. Sitkoff, *Struggle for Black Equality,* 95. Minnie Finch, after researching the national files, devoted only a single chapter out of twelve to the organization's role during the years of direct action. See Finch, *The NAACP and Its Fight for Justice.*

176. Lomax, *Negro Revolt,* 101–4; *Savannah Herald,* 19 February, 13 August 1961.

177. *Pittsburgh Courier,* 3 June 1961; Report, Helen Hayes, October 1964, VEP 4–29, SRC Microfilm.

178. Jacoway and Colburn, eds., *Southern Businessmen and Desegregation,* 14; Bartley, *Rise of Massive Resistance.*

179. Campbell, *Stem of Jesse,* 21; *Pittsburgh Courier,* 23 April 1960. For Joe Hendricks, this "argument" took the form of hate mail, threats, and a cross burning in his front yard. See Campbell, *Stem of Jesse,* 20–21.

180. Chappell, *Inside Agitators,* xv.

181. Ibid., 49.

182. Ibid., 123; Ricks, "'De Lawd,'" 12; Marion King, "Reflections on the Death of a Child," 10, *New South* 18 (February 1963).

Chapter 5. Protest in Rural Georgia: SNCC's Southwest Georgia Project, 1962–1967

1. Greene, *Praying for Sheetrock,* 8; Mitchell, *I'm Somebody Important,* 186, 239. For example, one VEP report noted that southeast Georgia voter registration depended on one personality, Hosea Williams, who was aided by Ben Clark. "This is a very effective team in Savannah, but in Savannah and not in the remainder of the South East Georgia region" (John Due, Field Report, 1 September 1964, VEP Files).

2. "History of the Project," 1967, and John Perdew, "Introduction to Southwest Georgia," 1, Box 1, Folder 3, Battle Papers, MLK.

3. *Southern Patriot* 20 (December 1962): 3; *Pittsburgh Courier,* 21 June 1958; *New York Times,* 12 September 1965; Perdew, "Introduction to Southwest Georgia," 1.

4. Field Report, John Perdew, 1 August 1965, SNCC Papers, MLK.

5. "Some Facts Involved in the Political Status of Negro Residents in Baker County, Geor-

gia," B. R. Brazeal to Harold Fleming, 27 May 1959, 13–14; Field Report, Charles Sherrod, 27 July 1965, Ser. XV, Reel 37, no. 50, SNCC Microfilm.

6. *Pittsburgh Courier,* 21 June 1958, 28 February 1959, 6 September 1958; *Washington Post,* 8 June 1958.

7. Carson, *In Struggle,* 66, 74; Forman, *Making of Black Revolutionaries,* 266; "History of the Project," 1967, 1; *Student Voice,* Spring 1964.

8. *Pittsburgh Courier,* 4 August 1962.

9. See, for example, Belfrage, *Freedom Summer;* MacAdam, *Freedom Summer;* Cobb, *Most Southern Place on Earth;* Dittmer, *Local People;* and Payne, *I've Got the Light of Freedom.*

10. Interview of Julian Bond by author; Dittmer, *Local People,* 244.

11. See Zinn, *SNCC;* Stoper, *Student Nonviolent Coordinating Committee;* Forman, *Making of Black Revolutionaries.*

12. Carson, *In Struggle,* 74.

13. Watters and Cleghorn, *Climbing Jacob's Ladder,* 171; Zinn, *SNCC,* 142; Levy, ed., *Let Freedom Ring,* 100.

14. Carson, *In Struggle,* 74, 57; Interview of Sherrod by author.

15. Charles Sherrod to Jack Minnis, 9 October 1962, VEP 2–19, SNCC Microfilm.

16. Sherrod to Wiley Branton, 9 October 1962, ibid.

17. Stoper, *Student Nonviolent Coordinating Committee,* 28; Interviews of John Perdew and Sherrod by author; Carson, *In Struggle,* 72–73.

18. Sherrod to Wiley Branton, 9 October 1962, VEP 2–19, SNCC Microfilm; "Terrell County, Georgia: A Statistical Profile," 9 April 1963, and "Lee County: Statistical Profile," 1963, SNCC Microfilm; *Southern Patriot* 20 (December 1962): 1.

19. *New York Times,* 5, 6 September 1958; Kousser, *Colorblind Injustice,* 201; Grant, *The Way It Was,* 371; *Pittsburgh Courier,* 28 February 1961.

20. *Student Voice,* 20 January 1962.

21. Ibid.

22. Field Report, Jack Chatfield, 28 November 1962, Box 1, Folder 11, Battle Papers, MLK, and VEP, SRC Papers, AU.

23. Levy, *Let Freedom Ring,* 100; *Southern Patriot* 20 (December 1962): 3.

24. *Southern Patriot* 20 (December 1962): 3.

25. Interview of Sherrod by author; Field Report, John Churchville, 28 December 1962, VEP 2–19, SNCC Microfilm.

26. Interview of Claude Sitton by author; Branch, *Parting the Waters,* 619–20; King, *Freedom Song,* 244.

27. Press Releases, 30 June 1964, 17 September 1962, Ser. VIII, SNCC Papers, MLK; Forman, *Making of Black Revolutionaries,* 276; *Atlanta Constitution,* n.d., Sherrod Papers, Box 2, File 24; *Atlanta Journal,* 16 August 1962; McCullar, *This Is Your Georgia,* 611.

28. Field Report, Jack Chatfield, 8 January 1963, Box 1, Folder 12, Battle Papers, MLK; Field Report, Ralph Allen, 6 April 1963, Box 1, Folder 13, ibid.; *New York Post,* 3 August 1962; Chatfield to Branton, 11 December 1962, VEP, SRC Papers, AU; Watters and Cleghorn, *Climbing Jacob's Ladder,* 169.

29. Field Report, Jack Chatfield, 8 January 1963, Box 1, Folder 12, Battle Papers, MLK.

30. Press Release, 23 December 1963, Ser. VIII, SNCC Papers, AU; Watters and Cleghorn, *Climbing Jacob's Ladder,* 139.

31. Field Report, Ralph Allen, 6 April 1963, "Lee County Report," Larry Rubin, December 1962, VEP, SRC Papers, AU.

32. Field Report, Ralph Allen, 6 April 1963, Box 1, Folder 13, Battle Papers, MLK; Field Reports, Jack Chatfield, 2 November, 4 December 1962, 4, Box 1, Folder 11, ibid.

33. Field Reports, Jack Chatfield, 16, 20, 22 December 1962, Box 1, Folder 11, Battle Papers, MLK.

34. Field Report, Jack Chatfield, 2 November 1962, 4; Field Report, John Churchville, 23 January 1963, Box 1, Folder 12, Battle Papers, MLK; Field Report, John Churchville, 27 January 1963, ibid.

35. Field Report, Jack Chatfield, 4 December 1962, VEP 2−19, SNCC Microfilm.

36. "Southwest Georgia Project: Report on Rural Counties," Wendy Mann and Bob Cover, 7 October 1963, 4, SNCC Microfilm; Field Report, Ralph Allen, 6 April 1963, Box 1, Folder 13, Battle Papers, MLK; Field Report, Jack Chatfield, 2 January 1963, Box 1, Folder 12, Battle Papers, MLK.

37. "Southwest Georgia Project: Report on Rural Counties," 4.

38. Stoper, *Student Nonviolent Coordinating Committee,* 146; Field Report, Prathia Hall, 6 April 1963, VEP 2−19, SNCC Microfilm.

39. "Terrell County, Georgia: A Statistical Profile," 9 April 1963, and "Lee County: Statistical Profile," 1963, SNCC Microfilm.

40. *Southern Patriot* 20 (December 1962): 3; Field Report, Herman Kitchens, 28 February−21 July 1964, Ser. VI, Reel 182, no. 352, VEP, SRC Microfilm; Interviews of Sherrod, Wells, and James Mays by author.

41. Interview of Bob Mants by author; "Lee County Summer Project," Ernest McMillan, VEP, SNCC Microfilm; Field Report, Carolyn Daniels, 1 February 1963, Box 1, Folder 12, Battle Papers, MLK.

42. Field Report, Faith Halseart, 6 March 1963, VEP 2−19, SNCC Microfilm; Field Report, Jack Chatfield, 2 November 1962.

43. Interview of W. W. Law by author; *Pittsburgh Courier,* 16 January 1961; Carson, *In Struggle,* 75.

44. Statement by Agnew James, 15 February 1963, Leesburg, Box 1, no. 8, Battle Papers, MLK; *Atlanta Daily World,* 6 September 1962; Press Release, 8 December 1963, Ser. VIII, SNCC Papers, AU; Zev Aeloney to Jim Marcia et al., 10 August 1963, Box 87, Folder Georgia, Americus File, CORE Papers, MLK; Stoper, *Student Nonviolent Coordinating Committee,* 147.

45. *Southern Patriot* 20 (December 1962): 3; Sherrod to Branton, 8 February 1963, VEP 2−19, SNCC Microfilm.

46. Field Report, Charles Sherrod, n.d., Sherrod Papers, MLK; Interview of Sherrod by author; Sherrod to Branton, 8 February 1963, VEP 2−19, SNCC Microfilm; Southwest Georgia Report, 6, Roy Shields, Project Director, February 1965, Ser. VIII, SNCC Papers, AU; *Student Voice,* 25 February 1964; Branton to Forman, 20 November 1962, VEP 2−19, SNCC Microfilm.

47. Field Report, Bob Cover, Wendy Mann, and R. B. King, 22 November−8 December

1963, Box 1, Folder 14, Battle Papers, MLK; Field Report, George Bess and Bob Cover, 1 January–8 January 1964, Box 1, Folder 15, ibid.

48. "SNCC in Southwest Georgia," 19; A. Bradley Schrade, Draft copy of "Southwest Georgia," 18, courtesy of John Inscoe, University of Georgia, Athens, Georgia.

49. Sherrod to Wiley Branton, 9 December 1962, VEP, SRC Papers, AU; Field Report, John Churchville, 11 February 1963, 6, VEP, SRC Microfilm; Sherrod to Branton, 8 February 1963, VEP 2–19, SNCC Microfilm; Watters and Cleghorn, *Climbing Jacob's Ladder,* 186.

50. Field Report, probably by Randolph Battle, 24–27 January 1963, Box 1, Folder 2, Battle Papers, MLK.

51. Forman, *Making of Black Revolutionaries,* 276; Memo from Prathia Hall to Jean Fairfax, 4 May 1965, TCP, AFSC, University of Pennsylvania, Philadelphia; Carson, *In Struggle,* 75.

52. Field Report, Jack Chatfield, 4 December 1962; Press Release, 8 December 1963, Ser. VIII, SNCC Papers; Memo from Prathia Hall to Jean Fairfax, 4 May 1965.

53. Field Report, Jack Chatfield, 4, 17 December 1962, Box 1, Folder 11, Battle Papers, MLK; Field Report, Charles Sherrod, February 1962, Reel 37, SNCC Microfilm; Carson, *In Struggle,* 195; Field Report, John Churchville, 11 February 1963, 8.

54. *Atlanta Constitution,* 29 April 1963; Zinn, *SNCC,* 138; Sherrod to Branton, 8 February 1963, VEP 2–19, SNCC Microfilm; Field Report, Carolyn Daniels, 1 February 1963.

55. There were almost three thousand white voters in Terrell County at the end of 1961 (Grant, *The Way It Was,* 413).

56. Carver Neblett to Wiley Branton, 11 December 1962, VEP, SRC Papers, AU; Field Report, Jack Chatfield, 29 March 1963.

57. Field Report, Jack O'Neal and Rubin, n.d. (probably 1964), VEP 2–19, SNCC Microfilm; Field Report, Charles Sherrod, April 1963, quoted in Watters and Cleghorn, *Climbing Jacob's Ladder,* 158.

58. Field Report, Bob Cover, Wendy Mann, and R. B. King, 22 November–8 December 1963, Box 1, Folder 14, Battle Papers, MLK.

59. John Perdew to Mr. Jackson, WPRS Radio (Warner-Robins), 24 August 1963, Ser. VIII, SNCC Papers, AU; SNCC Fact Sheet, n.d., "Americus 1965" Folder, *Newsweek* Files, EU; *Atlanta Journal,* 3 October 1963. In fact, the Supreme Court had voided the statute thirty years previously after the Angelo Herndon case (Grant, *The Way It Was,* 414).

60. SNCC Southwest Georgia Office Staff, Spring 1963, Ser. VII, SNCC Files, AU. Aelony was based at Koinonia Farm.

61. *Collegiate Press Service,* 30 September 1963.

62. Grant, *The Way It Was,* 414; *New York Times,* 29 September 1963; Field Report, David Bell and Robert Mants, 24 September 1963, 3, Americus File, Mants Papers, MLK.

63. Field Report, Bell and Mants, 24 September 1963, 3.

64. Field Report, Ralph Allen, n.d., SNCC Papers, AU; Field Report, David Bell, 5 October 1963, Field Report, Bob Mants, 30 September–5 October 1963, Field Report, David Bell, 10 October 1963, Field Reports—Georgia, Americus, Ser. VII, SNCC Papers, AU.

65. Interviews of Rev. Campbell and Sammy Mahone by author.

66. *New York Times,* 29 July 1975, 29 September 1963.

67. Field Report, Ralph Allen. n.d. (but clearly during the early weeks of July 1963), 5, SNCC Papers, AU; Sherrod to Branton, 8 February 1963, VEP 2–19, SNCC Microfilm; *Connecticut Daily Campus News,* 14 October 1963; Interviews of Mants, Sherrod, and Perdew by author; Field Report, John Churchville, 11 February 1963.

68. Frady, *Southerners,* 229–30; Donald Harris interview in Stoper, *Student Nonviolent Coordinating Committee,* 161.

69. *New York Times,* 28, 29 September 1963; Marshall Frady to WVX New York, "Americus 1965" Folder, *Newsweek* Files, EU; *Southern Patriot* 23 (November 1965): 2; Marshall Frady typescript, n.d., "Americus" Folder, *Newsweek* Files, EU; Frady, *Southerners,* 231; Pauley, "Stories of Struggle and Triumph," 4.

70. Frady to WVX New York; Field Report, 11 August 1963, Americus File, Mants Papers, MLK; Press Releases, 9, 31 August, 11, 24 September 1963, Ser. VIII, SNCC Papers, AU; Lena Turner Affidavit, 29 August 1963, Americus File, Mants Papers, MLK; *New York Times,* 28 September 1963; "Fact Sheet on Americus," n.d., Americus File, Mants Papers, MLK; *Atlanta Constitution,* 19 August 1963; Affidavits: Henrietta Fuller, 13 September 1963, Robertina Freeman, 13 September 1963, Ser. XV, Reel 37, no. 15, SNCC Microfilm.

71. Andrew S. Chancey, "The Communal Vision of Koinonia Farm," in Inscoe, ed., *Georgia in Black and White,* 256, 262; *New York Times,* 29 September 1963; Lee, *Cotton Patch Evidence,* 35.

72. The campaign started in response to a local news article that reported Jordan's support for two black students seeking to enroll in Georgia State College of Business in Atlanta. As an alumnus of the university system, Jordan acted as one of the two signatories required for each application. In fact, Jordan was ruled ineligible because he had graduated from a different school in the system. See Lee, *Cotton Patch Evidence,* 105–6.

73. Ibid., 112, 106–8; *Southern Patriot,* October 1956, 3.

74. Transcript of tape-recording of a meeting held at Koinonia Farm on Sunday afternoon (May 26, 1957) at 2:30 P.M. between members of Koinonia and a group of ten citizens of Americus and Sumter County, 2, 11, Koinonia Files, Americus, Georgia; *Greensboro Daily News,* 8 August 1965.

75. Field Report, 24–27 January 1963, Sasser, Georgia, Box 1, Folder 2, Mants Papers, MLK; "Fact Sheet on Americus."

76. *Atlanta Journal,* 4 December 1963; Interview of Amanda Bowens by author.

77. *Southern Patriot* 23 (November 1965): 2; "Koinonia: 20 summer workers orientation, June 11–15, 1963," SNCC Papers, AU; Tracy Elaine K. Meyer, "Koinonia Farm: Building the Beloved Community in Postwar Georgia" (Ph.D. diss., University of North Carolina, 1993), 244; *Southern Patriot* 23 (November 1965): 2; Sherrod to Branton, 8 February 1963, VEP 2–19, SNCC Microfilm.

78. *Southern Patriot* 23 (November 1965); Interview of Sam Mahone by author.

79. Interview of Mahone by author.

80. Plains, Desoto, and Andersonville were the largest settlements, although each had only a few hundred inhabitants.

81. Field Report, Don Harris, 27 March 1964, Ser. VI, Reel 182, no. 352, VEP 4-4, SNCC Microfilm; *Voice of Americus,* Summer 1964, 1.

82. "Evaluation of Sumter County Project," David E. Bell and Robert Mants, 24 September 1963, 3, Americus File, Mants Papers, MLK.

83. Field Report, Don Harris, 27 March 1964, Ser. VI, Reel 182, no. 352, VEP 4-4, SNCC Microfilm; Memo, n.d., Georgia Council on Human Relations File, Box 11, Folder 1, Ser. 5, Pauley Papers, EU; Field Report, Bob Mants, 30 September–5 October 1963, Field Reports—Georgia, Americus, Ser. VII, SNCC Papers, AU, and in Americus File, Mants Papers, MLK; Mahone to Harris, 2 September 1964, Ser. VI, Reel 182, no. 352, VEP 4-4, SNCC Microfilm.

84. "Who Runs Southwest Georgia?" SNCC Research, 17 April 1965, Ser. VIII, SNCC Microfilm; Interview of J. Frank Myers by author.

85. Field Report, Don Harris, 27 March 1964, and Leaflet, n.d. (probably 1964), Ser. VI, Reel 182, no. 352, VEP 4-4, SNCC Microfilm; "Southwest Georgia SNCC Field Report," 22 November 1965, 1.

86. Field Report, n.d. (probably late 1963), Americus File, Mants Papers, MLK.

87. *Southern Patriot* 22 (October–November 1964); "Introduction to Southwest Georgia," n.d., Ser. VIII, SNCC Microfilm.

88. Roy Shields to Reggie Robinson, 30 June 1965, Ser. XV, SNCC Microfilm; Press Release, 25 May 1965, Ser. VIII, SNCC Papers, AU; *Voice of Americus,* 16 June 1965. Brown and Freeman's attorney, Warren Fortson, believed that the arrests were intended to quash student protest. Fortson was not sure whether the charges were true or false, but he made the point that the police did not choose to arrest any of the other numerous couples who were "fornicating" in the park during the summer (Interview of Warren Fortson by author).

89. Press Release, 9 May 1965, Ser. VIII, SNCC Papers, AU; Roy Shields to Reggie Robinson, 30 June 1965, Ser. XV, SNCC Microfilm.

90. Letter from Gloria Wise, Mary Bell, Mamie Campbell, and Lena Turner, 24 July 1965, Americus File, SCOPE, MLK, quoted in Bolster, "Civil Rights Movement," 307.

91. Initially, Williams's team came to Americus to register voters to take advantage of the Voting Rights Act, which was expected to pass Congress in July. When the act was not passed, Williams switched tactics to mass demonstrations with a view to speeding the passage of the legislation. See Press Release, 26 July 1965, Hosea Williams File, SCOPE Papers, MLK.

92. *Greensboro Daily News,* 8 August 1965.

93. Watters and Cleghorn, *Climbing Jacob's Ladder,* 259–60; *New York Times,* 7 August 1965.

94. Handwritten notes, n.d., Americus File, *Newsweek* clippings, EU.

95. *Southern Patriot* 23 (November 1965); Field Report, John Perdew, 1 August 1965.

96. Frady, *Southerners,* 232–33; Kousser, *Colorblind Injustice,* 219; Interview of Fortson by author; *Southern Patriot* 23 (August 1965): 3.

97. Handwritten notes, n.d., Americus File, *Newsweek* clippings, EU; Frady, *Southerners,* 233; *Voice of Americus,* 19 June 1965.

98. Handwritten notes, n.d., Americus File, *Newsweek* clippings, EU; Frady, *Southerners,* 237–39.

99. *Southern Patriot* 23 (August 1965): 3; Nicholas Von Hoffman, for News World Service, n.d., "Americus 1965" Folder, *Newsweek* Files, EU.

100. *Atlanta Constitution,* 5 August 1965; Handwritten notes, n.d., Americus File, *Newsweek* clippings, EU.

101. *New York Times,* 2 August 1965; Handwritten notes by Marshall Frady, n.d., "Americus 1965" Folder, *Newsweek* Files, EU; Ralph McGill editorial, 16 September 1963, Ralph McGill Files, EU.

102. Carson, *In Struggle,* 208–9; Bolster, "Civil Rights Movement," 304.

103. *Atlanta Journal,* 29 July 1965; Interview of Willie Ricks by author; *Greensboro Daily News,* 8 August 1965.

104. *Greensboro Daily News,* 8 August 1965; *Atlanta Journal and Constitution,* 8 August 1965; *New York Times,* 1, 2, 6 August 1965; *Atlanta Constitution,* 9 August 1965; Williford, *Americus Through the Years,* 365.

105. Marshall Frady report for *Newsweek,* n.d., "Americus 1965" Folder, *Newsweek* Files, EU; Bolster, "Civil Rights Movement," 310; *Atlanta Constitution,* 30 July 1965.

106. *Atlanta Journal,* 9 March 1966.

107. *Atlanta Journal,* 9 March 1966; Press Release, 12 March 1964, Research Department, 1959–67, Ser. VIII, SNCC Papers, AU; *Voice of Americus and South West Georgia,* 5 June 1964, ibid.

108. Interview of Willie Bolden by author; Field Report, Don Harris, 27 March 1964, Ser. VI, Reel 182, no. 352, VEP 4-4, SNCC Microfilm; "Southwest Georgia–Problems and Solutions," 23 December 1963, 2, Ser. XV, SNCC Papers, AU.

109. Sherrod to Branton, 9 October 1962, VEP 2–19, SNCC Microfilm; Field Report, Charles Sherrod, 27 July 1965, Ser. XV, Reel 37, no. 50, SNCC Microfilm.

110. *Atlanta Inquirer,* 6 November 1965; Forman, *Making of Black Revolutionaries,* 267; Field Report, Charles Sherrod, 27 July 1965, Ser. XV, Reel 37, no. 50, SNCC Microfilm; Charles Sherrod, "From the Gator's Stronghold," 16 September 1965, 1–6, Box 3, Folder 2, "Georgia: Baker County," Sherrod Papers, MLK.

111. SRC Report, ix–x, Ser. XVI, Reel 221, no. 237, SRC Microfilm; "Public Assistance: To What End?," November 1967, 8, Ser. XVI, Reel 221, no. 240, SRC Microfilm; "Some Facts in Baker County, Georgia," Brazeal to Fleming, 27 May 1959, 6–12, SRC Papers.

112. *New York Times,* 12 September 1965; *Washington Post,* 20 December 1965.

113. "Baker County," 4 October 1965, Box 3, Folder 2, Sherrod Files, MLK; *Atlanta Inquirer,* 6 November 1965.

114. "Southwest Georgia SNCC Field Report," 22 November 1965, 7.

115. *New York Times,* 26 June 1966, 23 February 1969, 12 December 1968; *New South* 21 (Summer 1966): 93, *New South* 24 (Winter 1969): 62; *Atlanta Inquirer,* 21 December 1968; *Nation,* 3 February 1969; Interview of Rev. Wells by author.

116. Bob Pfefferman, "Summary of Cordele Boycott and Background," n.d., Ser. XV, Reel 37, no. 52, SNCC Microfilm; "The Other Side," September 1967, Georgia: Southwest Georgia File, Mants Papers, MLK; "Southwest Georgia Report," 4, Roy Shields, Project Director, February 1965, Ser. VIII, SNCC Papers, AU; *Student Voice,* 5 March 1963; Herman Kitchens, "A New Direction," 15 February 1965, Ser. XV, Reel 37, no. 55, SNCC Microfilm; *Voice of Americus,* 20 February 1965, Box 87, "CORE GA: Americus Newsletter Sept 64–Mar 65," CORE Papers, MLK; "Southwest Georgia Project Newsletter," n.d. (but referring to events of summer 1967), Box 1, Folder 5, Battle Papers, MLK.

117. "Southwest Georgia Report," Roy Shields, Project Director, February 1965, Ser. VIII, SNCC Papers, AU; *Student Voice,* 15 July 1964.

118. "Southwest Georgia SNCC Field Report," 22 November 1965, 6; "Evaluation of UNITAS Summer Project 1967 Workshop for Christian Involvement," Joe Pfister, 15, Box 1, Folder 7, Battle Papers, MLK.

119. Roy Shields to Reggie Robinson, 30 June 1965, Ser. XV, SNCC Microfilm; Marvin Wall to Curtis Thomas, 16 August 1966, Reel 185, VEP 66–58, SRC Microfilm; McCullar, *This Is Your Georgia,* 620.

120. Kitchens to Don Harris, 15 August 1964, Ser. VI, Reel 182, no. 352, VEP 4–4, SRC Microfilm.

121. Herman Kitchens, "A New Direction and the Key to Freedom," 15 February 1965, 4, Ser. XV, Reel 37, no. 55, SNCC Microfilm; Battle Field Report, 7 September 1968, Box 1, Folder 7, Battle Papers, MLK.

122. "Who Runs Southwest Georgia?" 17 April 1965, 2, Ser. VIII, Reel 37, SNCC Microfilm; John Perdew, "Southwest Georgia: Problems and Solutions," 28 December 1963, 2.

123. Donald Harris interview in Stoper, *Student Nonviolent Coordinating Committee,* 152; Field Report, David Bell, 5 October 1963; Forman, *Making of Black Revolutionaries,* 344.

124. Field Report, David Bell, 10 October 1963.

125. Field Report, n.d., no signature, 3, VEP, SNCC Microfilm.

126. John Perdew, "Southwest Georgia: Problems and Solutions," 28 December 1963, 2; Harris to Cortland Cox, 17 July 1964, SNCC Papers, AU; Lewis, *Walking with the Wind,* 291–92.

127. Hanks, *Struggle for Black Political Empowerment,* 128. Sherrod later founded the Southwest Georgia Community Education Project, which was the successor to the Southwest Georgia Project but was entirely local and independent.

128. Field Report, Bob Cover, Wendy Mann, and R. B. King, 22 November–8 December 1963, Box 1, Folder 14, Battle Papers, MLK; Report, Charles Sherrod, n.d., Box 2, "Centres of Renewal" Folder, Sherrod Papers, MLK; Baker County Memo for "Drafting Committee for Baker County Project, 26 September 1966," Ser. XIV (Community Organization Project), Reel 214, no. 4, SRC Microfilm.

129. Interview of Frances Pauley by author; Baker County Memo for "Drafting Committee for Baker County Project, 26 September 1966"; *Southwest Georgia Project Newsletter* 2 (15 April 1968): 3; L. Regier to Sherrod, 15 June 1966, Box 2, Folder 3, Sherrod Papers, MLK.

130. *Southwest Georgia Project Newsletter* 1 (20 January 1968): 1.

Chapter 6. Black Protest after the Federal Civil Rights Legislation of 1964–1965

1. James, *They Didn't Put That on the Huntley-Brinkley!* 82.

2. The Civil Rights Act also created the Equal Employment Opportunities Commission to outlaw job discrimination. For more details, see Cook, *Sweet Land of Liberty,* 148.

3. Spritzer and Bergmark, *Grace Towns Hamilton,* 161.

4. Speech by A. T. Walden on Irwin Co. Case, 22 October 1949, Ser. III, Box 28, Folder 4, Walden Papers, AHC; Talmadge, *You and Segregation,* 44, 46–49; Interview of Talmadge by author.

5. Privately, Talmadge had already made a rapprochement with A. T. Walden and many of the Auburn Avenue elite. Shortly after Vandiver was elected as governor, he was invited to

Talmadge's home and was introduced to some of the Auburn Avenue leadership. See Roche, *Restructured Resistance*, 73. Talmadge also invited Leroy Johnson to his farm shortly after Johnson's election (*Atlanta Journal*, 2 May 1963).

6. "Talmadge," *New South* 21 (Winter 1966): 75–76.

7. Interview of Robert Flanagan by Josephine Bradley, 11 October 1988, 67, GGDP.

8. Kyle, "Model of Political Revolution," 55; Henderson and Roberts, *Georgia Governors*, 13–14; Coles, "Maddox of Georgia," 20–21; Sherrill, "Strange Decorum of Lester Maddox," 553.

9. Coleman, *History of Georgia*, 369.

10. *New South* 21 (Fall 1966): 101.

11. *Atlanta Inquirer*, 29 April 1967; Henderson, *Atlanta Life Insurance Company*, 185.

12. Chafe, "The End of One Struggle, the Beginning of Another," 127.

13. See, for example, Ralph, *Northern Protest*.

14. Demonstrations in support of strikers at the Scripto Plant in Atlanta became national news in 1965, the *International Chemical Worker* reported, because it represented a "unique alliance of labor and civil rights leaders." The *Atlanta Inquirer* pointed out that even if black employees worked for eight hours a day for every day of the year, they would still earn $400 below the poverty level, even before reductions. A national boycott, publicized by SCLC, further pressured Scripto to adopt an integrated apprentice training program (*Atlanta Inquirer*, 5 December 1964). As was the case throughout Georgia's history, however, the limited extent of unionization precluded the possibility of a significant class alliance. According to a U.S. Department of Labor estimate, only 12.7 percent of Georgia's nonagricultural workers belonged to a union in 1966 (*Southern Patriot* 23 [February 1965]: 4; Numan Bartley, "Unions," *New South Writer* 25 [Winter 1970]: 31).

15. Fairclough, *To Redeem the Soul of America*, 275.

16. Carmichael had been banned from speaking on campus by the college president. See Harding, "When Stokeley Met the President," 4–6.

17. *New South* 22 (Winter 1967): 99; Fairclough, *To Redeem the Soul of America*, 253.

18. Fairclough, *Race and Democracy*, 384; Lawson, *Running for Freedom*, 146. As early as February 1965, the black activist Bayard Rustin predicted that direct action techniques were being subordinated to a strategy calling for the building of community institutions or power bases.

19. Dittmer, *Local People*, 363; Fairclough, *Race and Democracy*, 384.

20. Joe Hendricks, who had supported the meeting on the condition that it would be open to all students, went to the bank the following morning to stop the check. See Campbell, *Stem of Jesse*, 148.

21. *Atlanta Inquirer*, 28 April 1969; *New South* 24 (Spring 1969): 65–66.

22. King criticized many of his recent predecessors, claiming that "the NAACP has not in recent years addressed itself to the majority of black people in this town" (*Atlanta Inquirer*, 1 February 1969).

23. *Atlanta Inquirer*, 19 June 1965.

24. *Nation*, 21 December 1964; *Rome News-Tribune*, 6 September 1964.

25. *New York Times*, 31 December 1967; Harmon, "Beneath the Image," 438.

26. Interviews of Joe Hendricks, Rudy Hayes, and William Randall by author. According to Will Campbell, "Ronnie Thompson is remembered by many Mercerians of the 1960s as being the most vehement racist mayor in Mercer's history" (Campbell, *Stem of Jesse,* 187).

27. *Chicago Sun-Times,* 8 March 1965; *Atlanta Daily World,* 19 July 1964.

28. *Nation,* 21 December 1964.

29. *Pittsburgh Courier,* 15 August 1964; *Atlanta Inquirer,* 26 June 1965, 15 March 1969; Constance Covington to Constance Curry, Memorandum, 13 July 1965, TCP, AFSC Files; *Atlanta Daily World,* 16 January 1964.

30. *Southwest Georgia Newsletter* 1 (21 October 1967), Box 1, Folder 5, Battle Papers, MLK.

31. Fairclough, *To Redeem the Soul of America,* 266.

32. *Atlanta Inquirer,* 19 June 1965.

33. "Georgia: Statistics," Box 170, Folder 12, SCOPE Papers, MLK; Fairclough, *To Redeem the Soul of America,* 264; "Assignment Lists," Box 168, Folder 3, SCOPE Papers, MLK. Nonetheless, some SCOPE workers did make an impact at the local level. Willie Levanthal, a SCOPE worker in Macon, claimed to have been the first white member of an integrated baseball team in the city (Interview of Willie Levanthal by author).

34. *New South* 25 (Winter 1970): 5; Fairclough, *To Redeem the Soul of America,* 269; *Atlanta Inquirer,* 16 October 1965.

35. For example, SCLC staffers led campaigns in Social Circle, Barnesville, Sandersville, Monroe County, and Twiggs County, all in different areas of the state. See *Atlanta Inquirer,* 17 June, 1 July 1967, 24 February 1968; Interviews of D. F. Glover, Willie Bolden, James Orange, Tyrone Brooks, and Thaddeus Olive by author.

36. *New South* 24 (Winter 1969): 62; *Atlanta Inquirer,* 21 October 1968.

37. Campbell, *Forty Acres and a Goat,* 247, 239; Interviews of John Goolsby and Joe Hendricks by author.

38. *Atlanta Constitution,* 24 June 1909, quoted in Campbell, *Forty Acres and a Goat,* 244; Interviews of Hendricks, Goolsby, and Linda Matthews by author.

39. After the demonstrations in Talbot County, numerous communities experienced widespread protests that included many of the tactics characteristic of the 1960s. In McIntosh County, for example, black leaders called for a boycott of white stores in 1976. See Greene, *Praying for Sheetrock,* 195–97.

40. Interviews of Hendricks, Goolsby, and Linda Mitchell by author; Campbell, *Forty Acres and a Goat,* 243–48, 250.

41. *Southern School News* 11 (September 1964): 15. These school systems were in the largest cities in Georgia: Albany, Americus, Athens, Atlanta, Augusta, Brunswick, Columbus, Macon, Marietta, and Savannah. The desegregation of Americus, a city noted for white supremacy, highlights the significant role played by Warren Fortson.

42. *Southern School News* 9 (June 1963): 1; ibid., 11 (December 1964): 7. Over 90 percent of all transferred children were from Atlanta and Savannah.

43. *Southern School News* 11 (May 1965): 2–3.

44. *New South* 22 (Spring 1967): 94, (Spring 1966, 85): "School Desegregation," December 1966, Ser. XVI, Reel 221, no. 238, SRC Microfilm.

45. *New York Times,* 20 December 1965, 2 April 1966; "Baker County," *New South* 22 (Winter 1967): 73.

46. Interview of Constance Curry by author.

47. The telephone conversation was overheard by Rev. Oliver W. Holmes, one of the field secretaries for the Ten Communities Project.

48. Constance Curry to Jean Fairfax, Memorandum, "The 'Goods' on Claude Purcell," 4 May 1965, AFSC Files.

49. Fairfax, "The 'Goods' on Claude Purcell." Field reports from the Ten Communities Project during 1965–66 supported Fairfax's conclusion. See interview of Constance Curry, Constance Curry correspondence, and TCP in AFSC Files, including Curry to Francis Keppel, U.S. Commissioner of Education, HEW, 6 May 1965; Fairfax and Barbara Moffett, "Ten Communities Project: Developments in Georgia," 3 June 1965, TCP, AFSC Files; Interview of Martha Fay by author.

50. Constance Curry to Francis Keppel, U.S. Commissioner of Education, 6 May 1965, TCP, AFSC Files.

51. "Atlanta Schools," *New South* (20 February 1965): 9; Moeser and Silver, *Separate City,* 121–22; Noyes Collinson to Jean Fairfax, Memorandum, 26 May 1965, TCP, AFSC Files.

52. Winifred Falls to Francis Keppel, U.S. Commissioner of Education, 1 July 1965, TCP, AFSC Files; *New York Times,* 16 May 1965.

53. Winifred Falls to Francis Keppel, U.S. Commissioner of Education, 1 July 1965, TCP, AFSC Files.

54. *Atlanta Constitution,* 7 October 1965; *Atlanta Inquirer,* 9 October 1965; *Birmingham News,* 14 October 1965.

55. *Atlanta Constitution,* 16 October 1965; *Atlanta Journal and Constitution,* 10 October 1965; *St. Petersburg Times,* editorials, 16 October 1965, 6.

56. *Atlanta Constitution,* 6 October 1965.

57. Charles Hamilton of the Ten Communities Project noted in April 1965 that local officials had tried to stop a Head Start program, and that "considerable pressure is now exerted to keep more Negroes from registering" (Charles Hamilton to Jean Fairfax, Memorandum, 30 April 1965, TCP, AFSC Files; *Atlanta Constitution,* 19 October 1965).

58. *New York Times,* 31 October 1965; *Washington Post,* 11 October 1965; *Atlanta Journal,* 13, 14 October 1965; *Birmingham News,* 14 October 1965; *Atlanta Constitution,* 13, 15, 17 October 1965.

59. *Atlanta Inquirer,* 9 October 1965; *Birmingham News,* 14 October 1965; *Atlanta Constitution,* 7 October 1965; *State* (Columbus, S.C.), 4 October 1965.

60. *Atlanta Constitution,* 15, 19 October 1965; *St. Petersburg Times,* 16 October 1965.

61. *Atlanta Constitution,* 15 October 1965; Metcalf, *From Little Rock to Boston; Atlanta Journal,* 17 November 1965.

62. Constance Curry to Jean Fairfax, Memorandum, 23 July 1965, TCP, AFSC Files.

63. Jean Fairfax to Barbara Moffat, Report of Visit: 15–16 April 1965, Jean Fairfax to Barbara Moffat, "Report; Developments in Georgia," 3 June 1965, Charles Hamilton to Jean Fairfax, Memorandum, 30 April 1965, Constance Covington to Constance Curry, Memorandum, 7 July 1965, TCP, AFSC Files.

64. This was true in a wide range of institutions that desegregated. For example, for the desegregation of the textile industry in Georgia, see Minchin, *Hiring the Black Worker,* 246.

65. Winifred Falls to Francis Keppel, U.S. Commissioner of Education, 1 July 1965, TCP, AFSC Files; Phone conversation with Joe Tucker, field secretary NAACP, 30 September 1965, AFSC Files. According to Tucker, the uncle was so afraid that he had not reported the incident.

66. Prathia Hall to Jean Fairfax, Visit to Terrell County, 2, 3 April 1965, TCP, AFSC Files.

67. Jean Fairfax to Francis Keppel, U.S. Commissioner of Education, 23 September 1965, TCP, AFSC Files; *Southern School News* 11 (September 1964): 15; (November 1964): 5.

68. Interviews of Ulysses Bryan and Sadie Wiley by author; *Savannah Morning News,* 2 September 1963; Memo, 12 October 1963, NAACP Files, Savannah.

69. Messages on cover of school yearbook, in possession of Ulysses Bryan.

70. The interviewees who volunteered this information wish to remain confidential.

71. Grant, *The Way It Was,* 524; *New York Times,* 20 July, 23 October 1969; Moeser and Silver, *Separate City,* 122; McGrath, "Great Expectations," 339; *Atlanta Inquirer,* 21 December 1968; 15 February 1969.

72. Circuit Justice J. Black stated that "in my opinion, there is no reason why such a wholesale deprivation of constitutional rights should be tolerated another minute" (*Beatrice Alexander et al. v. Holmes County Board of Education et al.,* 396 U.S. 1218).

73. *New York Times,* 23 October, 19 December 1969; *Congressional Record,* 19 December 1969; *Atlanta Journal,* 16 December 1969; *Washington Post,* 18 December 1969. For the subsequent appeals see 5 Cir., 1970, 428 F.2d 377; 5 Cir., 1971, 445 F.2d 303; 5 Cir., 1972, 466 F.2d 197.

74. *New York Times,* 25 February, 23 October 1969, 14 January 1970; *New South* 24 (Fall 1969): 90.

75. *New York Times,* 14 January 1970; *Atlanta Journal,* 16 December 1969; Horace N. Baker Jr., "Athens: Where Busing Works," 61–62, in "The South and Her Children: School Desegregation 1970–71," March 1971, Ser. XVI, Reel 220, no. 193, SRC Microfilm; Grant, *The Way It Was,* 525.

76. *New York Times,* 20 July 1969, 14 January 1970; Interviews of Sammy Mahone and Ferrell Malone by author; Grant, *The Way It Was,* 527.

77. *Atlanta Inquirer,* 26 August 1967.

78. Interview of Glover by author; *New South,* Summer 1969, 96; D. F. Glover, "Positive Facts About Negro Teachers and Schools," *GTEA Herald,* Fall 1967, 1.

79. *New South* 24 (Summer 1969): 96–97; Interviews of Bolden and Glover by author; *Atlanta Inquirer,* 28 June 1969.

80. Baker, "Athens," 56–57.

81. Ibid., 61–62, 67; *Athens Banner Herald,* 31 May 1970, quoted in Baker, "Athens," 66.

82. McGrath, "Great Expectations," 333, 335, 339.

83. Moeser and Silver, *Separate City,* 123.

84. Plank and Turner, "Changing Patterns in Black School Politics," 601.

85. Ibid., 603.

86. "Voting Rights Act, Ten Years After," A Report of the United States Commission on

Civil Rights, January 1975, 127; Bellamy, "Whites Sue for Desegregation," 317, 336; *Macon Telegraph,* 6 April 1972; Grant, *The Way It Was,* 448.

87. Bachtel, Lee, and Bates, "Georgia's Black Population," 2; Davidson and Grofman, eds., *Quiet Revolution,* 75.

88. *New South* 21 (Summer 1966): 83.

89. Fairclough, *To Redeem the Soul of America,* 265; *New South* 21 (Summer 1966): 83; "Political Participation," U.S. Commission on Civil Rights, Washington D.C., May 1968, 169.

90. Davidson, *Quiet Revolution,* 76. New Communities was the successor to the Southwest Georgia Project.

91. *New South* 22 (Spring 1967): 95.

92. The *Atlanta Journal* noted on 8 April 1963 that "major spurts in Negro registration came chiefly in the larger cities such as Savannah, Albany, Columbus, Atlanta, Macon and Augusta."

93. Progress Report of VEP Savannah Branch of the NAACP by Curtis Cooper, 18 April 1966, VEP 66–31, SRC Microfilm.

94. Davidson, *Quiet Revolution,* 75; "Negro Vote in Georgia," *New South* 24 (Summer 1969): 79–83; "Political Participation," 12; "Voting Rights Act, Ten Years After," 42.

95. Davidson, *Quiet Revolution,* 76.

96. "Voting Rights Act, Ten Years After," 89–90, 193–95; *New South* 24 (Summer 1969): 87.

97. King was assisted in his campaign by Tyrone Brooks of the SCLC (Interview of Laughlin McDonald by author).

98. Watters, "Democracy in the South," *New South* 21 (Spring 1966): 77.

99. "Voting Rights Act, Ten Years After," 113; Rev. F. R. Rowe to Thaddeus Olive, 6 October 1967, VEP 67–105, SRC Microfilm; Curtis Thomas to Vernon Jordan, 11 November 1966, Courtesy Curtis Thomas.

100. VEP Annual Report 1971, Jesse Hill to Wiley Branton, 31 May 1962, VEP Annual Report 1970, VEP Report, 24 July 1970, Reel 185, VEP, SRC Microfilm; Vernon Jordan to Houston Stallworth, 2 August 1966, VEP 66–103, SRC Microfilm.

101. Interview of Thaddeus Olive by author; Jordan to Eugene Gadsden, 11 April 1966, Reel 185, VEP 66–31, SRC Microfilm; Jordan to Sherrod, 10 June 1966, James Bulloch, report to VEP, 21 April 1966, Reel 185, VEP 66–63, SRC Microfilm; Jordan to Pullum, 12 July 1967, Reel 186, VEP 67–12, SRC Microfilm; Request from Non-partisan Voters' League, 31 March 1966, Reel 185, VEP 66–57, SRC Microfilm; Branton to Blackwell, 25 August 1964, Reel 184, VEP 4–31, SRC Microfilm; Field Reports, John Calhoun, 16 January, 1 February, 20 March 1963, John Calhoun Field Reports, VEP, SRC Papers, AU; Interviews of George Ford and A. J. McClung by author.

102. "Black Elected Officials in Southern States," 8 January 1969, iii, Ser. XVI, Reel 219, no. 175, SRC Microfilm; "National Roster of Black Elected Officials February 1970," Ser. XVI, Reel 220, no. 188, SRC Microfilm.

103. "Voting Rights Act, Ten Years After," 50–52; *Southern Patriot,* April 1965, 1; SRC News Release, 22 May 1964, Ser. VI, Reel 175, no. 101, SRC Microfilm.

104. *New South* 24 (Summer 1969): 84.

105. Kousser, *Colorblind Injustice,* 197, 228, 242.

106. Davidson, *Quiet Revolution,* 82. After these counties had been forced by legal action to return to single-member district elections, 17 percent of the county commissioners elected were black.

107. Ibid.

108. For a full report of the Supreme Court's ruling on the Georgia House of Representatives reapportionment proposals, see *Georgia v. United States,* 411 U.S. 526.

109. Objection letter, 11 February 1972, quoted in "Voting Rights Act, Ten Years After," 231.

110. Quoted in Davidson, *Quiet Revolution,* 85.

111. Bartley, "Atlanta Elections," 25; *New South* 22 (Winter 1967): 72; Mays, *Born to Rebel,* 233; Interview of Eugene Gadsden by author.

112. Bartley, *From Thurmond to Wallace,* 107–9; Bartley, "Atlanta Elections," 28–29. At the state level, the election of Lester Maddox bucked the trend toward the Republican Party. In the longer term, Georgia was one of the few southern states where the Democratic Party remained dominant in statewide elections.

113. Rozier, *Black Boss,* 48; "Voting Rights Act, Ten Years After," 255.

114. Watters and Cleghorn, *Climbing Jacob's Ladder,* 302; Rozier, *Black Boss,* 2, 6; Hanks, *Struggle for Black Political Empowerment,* 51, 63.

115. Schultz, "Interracial Kinship Ties"; Hanks, *Struggle for Black Political Empowerment,* 52, 146, 58; Rozier, *Black Boss,* 7.

116. *New South,* Summer 1969, 83; Hanks, *Struggle for Black Political Empowerment,* 64; Rozier, *Black Boss,* 46.

117. Interview of Frances Pauley by author; Rozier, *Black Boss,* 36. For a brief biography of McCown, see ibid., 20–33.

118. Lawson, *Running for Freedom,* 123; Hanks, *Struggle for Black Political Empowerment,* 67, 77; Rozier, *Black Boss,* 51, 62, 68–69.

119. *Atlanta Constitution,* 8 November 1968; *New South,* Fall 1969, 91; Rozier, *Black Boss,* 28, 86–87; Hanks, *Struggle for Black Political Empowerment,* 79.

120. Hanks, *Struggle for Black Political Empowerment,* 94, 86.

121. "VEP Annual Report 1970," VEP, SRC Papers, AU; "Voting Rights Act, Ten Years After."

122. Stone, "Race and Regime in Atlanta," 126; Lawson, *Running for Freedom,* 166.

123. "Report, Atlanta All Citizens Registration Committee," VEP 2–1, SRC Papers, AU.

124. Rooks, "Atlanta Elections," 1, 34; Bartley, "Atlanta Elections," 67, 25; Lawson, *Running for Freedom,* 165.

125. Alexander, *Beyond the Timberline,* 79; Interview of Horace Tate by author.

126. Clarence Stone noted a decade later that "blacks hold governmental power in Atlanta" ("Race and Regime in Atlanta," 126).

127. Bill Schamel, "Atlanta," *New South* 27 (Spring 1972): 64; Conyers, "Negro Leaders in Atlanta," in Crawford, Gates, and Conyers, "Civil Aggression and Urban Disorders," 182–83.

128. For example, although the fire department had introduced an open hiring policy in 1963, six years later the department had 234 white officers and no black officers. After Massell's election in 1969, the Community Relations Commission recommended the appointment of a

full-time black recruitment officer and automatic promotion for longevity of service. Once again these provisions proved inadequate. By 1979, however, the fire department had set percentage goals for the hiring and promotion of black and white firefighters and plans for objective tests that would be developed by an outside company. See "Report on the Grievances of Black Firemen to the Board of Masters, City of Atlanta," by the Community Relations Commission, 29 December 1969, 1–3; Bayor, *Race and the Shaping of Twentieth-Century Atlanta*, 187.

129. Bayor, *Race and the Shaping of Twentieth-Century Atlanta*, 122. In 1974, the EEOC put forward a case charging widespread discrimination in hiring. Nonetheless, by 1982, black Georgians filled less than 4 percent of top administrative positions. In the same year, the Office of Fair Employment Practices claimed that the majority of state agencies had "forgotten or ignored" affirmative action targets. See Grant, *The Way It Was*, 469.

130. Fayer and Hampton, *Voices of Freedom*, 632; Lawson, *Running for Freedom*, 167; Bayor, *Race and the Shaping of Twentieth-Century Atlanta*, 49, 52, 123.

131. Fayer and Hampton, *Voices of Freedom*, 629; Wall, "Maynard Jackson and Voting in Georgia," 80.

132. Henderson and Roberts, *Georgia Governors*, 14; Sanders, "'The Sad Duty of Politics,'" 612.

133. Grant, *The Way It Was*, 436. Ward had been an assistant to Donald Hollowell.

134. Henderson, *Atlanta Life Insurance Company*, 182; Henderson and Roberts, *Georgia Governors*, 15.

135. Sanders, "'The Sad Duty of Politics,'" 620, 627, 629, 612; *New South* 24 (Winter 1969): 59; Grant, *The Way It Was*; Interview of Julian Bond by author.

136. Campbell added that he would vote for Carter nevertheless in preference to Ford.

137. *New York Times*, 1 August 1976.

138. Davidson, *Quiet Revolution*, 76; Weisbrot, *Freedom Bound*, 158; Grant, *The Way It Was*, 448.

139. Hanks, *Struggle for Black Political Empowerment*, 43.

140. Davidson, *Quiet Revolution*, 78.

141. Interview of McDonald by author; Davidson, *Quiet Revolution*, 81, 83.

142. Davidson, *Quiet Revolution*, 80–81; see also "Columbus, Georgia," report 1971, courtesy A. J. McClung; *Atlanta Constitution*, 26 August 1984, quoted in Davidson, *Quiet Revolution*, 84.

143. Schulman, *From Cotton Belt to Sunbelt*, 214; Coleman, *History of Georgia*, 405; Lewis, *Walking with the Wind*, 430.

144. Robert A. Holmes, "Reapportionment Politics in Georgia," *Phylon*, September 1984, 183.

145. In an acrimonious campaign in 1986, Julian Bond lost the election to his former SNCC colleague John Lewis. See, for example, Lewis, *Walking with the Wind*.

146. Quoted in Lawson, *Running for Freedom*, 159, and in Hanks, *Struggle for Black Political Empowerment*, 69–70.

147. This was partly because many Vine City residents were recent migrants to the city from rural Georgia. When Mayor Allen asked Martin Luther King Sr. to calm tensions during an outbreak of violence, King had to admit that "these people are not my people." See Harmon, "Beneath the Image," 420.

148. "A City Slum," n.d., 6, SRC Publications ca. 1966, Ser. XVI, Reel 219, SRC Microfilm; "The Battle Against New Welfare," 2, Ser. XV, Reel 37, no. 42, SNCC Microfilm.

149. Crawford, Gates, and Conyers, "Civil Aggression," 3; "South-wide Conference of Black Elected Officials, 11–14 December 1968," 8, SRC Publications, Ser. XVI, Reel 219, no. 174, SRC Microfilm.

150. Adams, "Blueprint for Segregation," 81. Only one in twenty white Atlantans lived in similar conditions.

151. Harmon, "Beneath the Image," 363.

152. *Jet*, February 1966, quoted in "History of the Project," 5; Weltner, *John Willie Reed*, 8; Beardslee, "Self Respect in the Alley," 10; Conyers, "The Negro Leader in Atlanta, the Poverty Program and Related Concerns," 11–12, in Crawford, Gates, and Conyers, "Civil Aggression."

153. "'The City Must Provide.' South Atlanta: The Forgotten Community," 1–2, Ser. XV, Reel 37, SNCC Microfilm; *Atlanta Daily World*, 6 August 1963; "Statement to Mayor," 1, Ser. XV, Reel 37, no. 41, SNCC Microfilm.

154. "Introduction to the 'Forgotten Side of Atlanta,'" 1, Ser. XV, Reel 37, no. 45, SNCC Microfilm.

155. "History of the Atlanta Project," 5–6, Ser. XV, Reel 37, no. 45, SNCC Microfilm; "Purpose of the Atlanta Project," SNCC News Service, Ser. XV, Reel 37, SNCC Microfilm.

156. "Introduction to the 'Forgotten Side of Atlanta,'" 2–3; *Atlanta Daily World*, 6 August 1963; "South Atlanta Project: Critical Analysis," 15 August 1963, 1–2, Ser. XV, Reel 37, no. 45, SNCC Microfilm.

157. Memorandum, 8 January 1955, and memorandum, n.d., 1954, Blackburn Papers, AARL; "Introduction to the 'Forgotten Side of Atlanta,'" 1; Field Report, Debbie Amis, October 1963, Ser. XV, Reel 37, SNCC Microfilm.

158. "A City Slum," 19, 12.

159. "History of the Atlanta Project," 1; "Purpose of the Atlanta Project," 1; Interview of Julian Bond by Britton, 22 January 1968, 71, CRDP, HU; Carson, *In Struggle*, 192.

160. These canvassing techniques included the establishment of a baby-sitting rota for voting mothers, driving people to the polls, and using Atlanta University students to call constituents.

161. "History of the Atlanta Project," 4.

162. Ibid., 7.

163. Ibid.; SNCC Black Paper, 25 August 1966, 6, Ser. XV, SNCC Microfilm; Carson, *In Struggle*, 240–41. See also Lewis, *Walking with the Wind*, 364–65.

164. "History of the Atlanta Project," 13; "The Markham Street Affair," 1, Ser. XV, Reel 37, no. 45, SNCC Microfilm; Bond to Allen, 31 January 1966, Ser. XV, Reel 37, no. 41, SNCC Microfilm.

165. *Atlanta Inquirer*, 13 November 1965; "The Markham Street Affair," 2.

166. "History of the Atlanta Project," 17, 19; Harmon, "Beneath the Image," 405.

167. "History of the Atlanta Project," 11–12; "The Markham Street Affair," 9; "Account of the One Hour Valet Movement," 1, Ser. XV, Reel 37, no. 45, SNCC Microfilm; SNCC Black

Paper, 25 August 1966, 2, Ser. XV, Reel 37, no. 38, SNCC Microfilm.

168. "Account of the One Hour Valet Movement," 2; *New South* 21 (Summer 1966): 93; "Report," 4, Ser. XV, Reel 37, no. 42, SNCC Microfilm; "Uncle Toms and Dr. Thomas," Atlanta Project reports, Ser. XV, Reel 37, no. 41, SNCC Microfilm.

169. "History of the Atlanta Project," 5–6; *Atlanta Journal,* 11 September 1966, 30 June 1967; *Atlanta Journal and Constitution,* 18 September 1966, 30 July 1967; "Description of Riot," by R. D. Robinson, and Miscellaneous Reports, Ser. XV, Reel 37, no. 42, SNCC Microfilm; *New South* 21 (Fall 1966): 101.

170. *Atlanta Journal,* 21 June 1970, 7 September 1966; Harvey Gates and Fred Crawford, "The Civil Aggression Study Team," 1, in Crawford, Gates, and Conyers, "Civil Aggression"; Allen, *Mayor,* 181–82; Harmon, "Beneath the Image," 437; *New South* 21 (Fall 1966): 101; Conyers, "Negro Leaders in Atlanta," 15.

171. Crawford, Gates, and Conyers, "Civil Aggression," Appendix, 1; Gates, "Civil Aggression Study Team," 1; *New York Times Magazine,* 14 October 1966, 137; *New South* 21 (Fall 1966): 101.

172. Allen, *Mayor,* 181–82; Crawford, Gates, and Conyers, "Civil Aggression," 8. Lester Maddox argued that Allen had nothing to fear because he had been voted in by the "Negroes" anyway (*New South* [Fall 1966]: 101).

173. Crawford, Gates, and Conyers, "Civil Aggression," 3.

174. *Rome News-Tribune,* 19 September 1971; *New York Times,* 22 June, 18, 27 July 1971.

175. Smith, "Riot of May 1970," 106; *Atlanta Constitution,* 17 May 1970; Terrell and Terrell, *Black in Augusta,* 34; Cashin, *Story of Augusta,* 302; Watters, "Augusta, Georgia, and Jackson State University: Southern Episodes in a National Tragedy" (Atlanta: Southern Regional Council, 1971).

176. See also Cobb, "Politics in a New South City"; Garrison, "Augusta Black Community Since World War II"; Harvey, "The 'Terri,'" 70–71; Smith, "Riot of May 1970," 106; Cashin, *Story of Augusta,* 302; Terrell and Terrell, *Black in Augusta,* 34; Watters, "Augusta, Georgia, and Jackson State University"; Interview of James Beck by John Smith, 11 March 1974, quoted in Smith, "Riot of May 1970," 108; Interview of R. A. Dent by John Lamar, 2 June 1975, AOHP; *Atlanta Constitution,* 17 May 1970; *New York Times,* 1 September 1963.

177. Walker, "Reaction," 120; *Atlanta Constitution,* 14 May 1970; Grant, *The Way It Was,* 511.

178. *Atlanta Constitution,* 11 October 1970.

179. Vernon Jordan, "Civil Rights in Georgia, Focus on the Future of Georgia," quoted in Bolster, "Civil Rights Movement," 324.

180. Adams, "Blueprint for Segregation," 74; *Ebony,* September 1973, 62; Lawson, *Running for Freedom,* 168–69.

181. See, for example, Adams, "Blueprint for Segregation."

182. Lawson, *Running for Freedom,* 167; Stone, "Race and Regime," 138.

183. Harmon, "Beneath the Image," 578; Bayor, *Race and the Shaping of Twentieth-Century Atlanta,* 124.

184. Interview of Robert Flanagan by Cliff Kuhn and Josephine Bradley, 9 January 1989, GGDP.

185. Pounders, "Glascock County," *New South* 25 (Winter 1970): 48, 51; *Atlanta Inquirer,* 19 August 1967; "The People's Voice," 5 July 1968, 2, GCHR Publication, Box 4, Folder 4, Battle Papers, MLK.

186. "Public Assistance: To What End?," November 1967, 8, Ser. XVI, Reel 221, no. 240, SRC Microfilm; SRC Report, 1970, x, Ser. XVI, Reel 221, no. 237, SRC Microfilm.

187. Interviews of Horace Tate, Willie Bolden, Thaddeus Olive, and Don Hollowell by author; Grant, *The Way It Was,* 460–61, 487; Bayor, *Race and the Shaping of Twentieth-Century Atlanta,* 124–125.

188. Bachtel, Lee, and Bates, "Georgia's Black Population," 4.

189. Interview of Herman Lodge and Ed Brown by author; Bachtel, Lee, and Bates, "Georgia's Black Population," 4; "Georgia Vital Statistics," Georgia Department of Human Resources, Atlanta, Georgia; Hope A. Harvey, "Poverty and the 'Two Georgias,'" *Georgia Poverty Journal* 1 (Fall 1986): 23. See *Atlanta Journal* 16–20 November 1986, quoted in Grant, *The Way It Was,* 461.

190. See Hanks, *Struggle for Black Political Empowerment.*

191. Interview of Stine George, 14 October 1989, by Cliff Kuhn, GGDP, GSU; Interview of Rev. C. S. Hamilton by author; see Cobb, "Politics in a New South City."

192. Interview of Flanagan by Kuhn et al., GGDP; Interview of Ed Brown by author.

193. William P. Randall to Jordan, n. d. (after 1966), Reel 185, VEP, SRC Microfilm; Interview of Flanagan by Kuhn et al.; Barbara Moffat and Jean Fairfax, "Ten Communities Project: Georgia, March 31, 1965," TCP, AFSC Files.

194. "SRC Annual Report 1974," May 1975, 12, Ser. XVI, Reel 220, no. 195, SRC Microfilm. For example, in 1974, the SRC gave assistance to "the unincorporated black community of Newtown." Three-quarters of this population was rural and widely dispersed, leading to difficulties for education, especially because of the need to travel.

195. Pounders, "Glascock County," 50; Interviews of Pauley, Law, Rev. Samuel Wells, and John Bertrand by author.

196. Donald Ross, "Black Belt Schools: Beyond Desegregation," 5–6, November 1965, Ser. XVI, Reel 219, no. 143, SRC Microfilm; Interview of Lodge, GGDP, GSU, 72.

197. Wallace H. Warren, "'The Best People in Town Won't Talk': The Moore's Ford Lynching of 1946 and Its Cover-Up," 270, in Inscoe, ed., *Georgia in Black and White;* "General Characteristics of the 100 Poorest Counties," SRC Ser. XVI, Reel 221, no. 240, SRC Microfilm; Bledsoe, "Burke County Today," 7, 14.

198. Constance Curry and Winifred Falls to Jean Fairfax, 6 October 1965, Ten Communities Project, AFSC Files; Interview of Herman Lodge by author; Bledsoe, "Burke County Today," 9.

199. Jordan to Lodge, 15 June 1967, Lodge to Jordan, 1 August 1967, Reel 185, VEP 67–61, SRC Microfilm; Field Report "Conclusion for S. E. GA VEP," John Due, 9 January 1964, VEP, SRC Microfilm; Bledsoe, "Burke County Today," 9.

200. Davidson, *Quiet Revolution,* 83.

201. Greene, *Praying for Sheetrock,* 172; Interview of Lodge by author; Bledsoe, "Burke County Today," 14.

202. The Burke County East Georgia Farmers Co-operative formed at the end of the 1960s. See Grant, *The Way It Was*, 465.

203. Bledsoe, "Burke County Today," 15–16; Bachtel, Lee, and Bates, "Georgia's Black Population," 3.

204. Interviews of Hosea Williams and Bolden by author; Rozier, *Black Boss*, 45–46; Grant, *The Way It Was*, 554–55.

205. Coleman, *History of Georgia*, 407.

Conclusion

1. Fairclough, *Race and Democracy*, xii; *Pittsburgh Courier*, 23 September 1961.

2. Morris, *Origins of the Civil Rights Movement*, 46.

3. Cashin, "Will the Real Georgia History Rise and Be Recognized?" 5.

4. Fairclough, *Race and Democracy*, xv; Gavins, "NAACP in North Carolina," 106; Pounders, "Glascock County," 50.

5. Morris, *Origins of the Civil Rights Movement*, 4.

6. See, for example, Brown, ed., *Ready from Within*; Mills, *This Little Light of Mine*; Payne, *I've Got the Light of Freedom*. See also Gilmore, *Gender and Jim Crow*.

7. Nasstrom, "Down to Now," 115; Crawford, Rouse, and Woods, eds., *Women in the Civil Rights Movement*, xvii, xxi.

8. *Savannah Herald*, 12 October 1960.

9. *Savannah Morning News*, 22 August 1960.

10. Anne Standley, "The Role of Black Women in the Civil Rights Movement," in Crawford, Rouse, and Woods, *Women in the Civil Rights Movement*, 184; Interviews of Geneva Law, W. W. Law, and Charles Sherrod by author.

11. Interviews of W. W. Law, Charles Sherrod, John Bertrand, and Joe Hendricks by author.

12. Interviews of William Randall and Sherrod by author; Interview of James Middleton in Telfair Academy, *We Ain't What We Used to Be*, 61.

13. Interviews of W. W. Law and Sherrod by author.

14. Garrow, ed., *Atlanta*, vii; Kousser, *Colorblind Injustice*, 3.

15. Montgomery was then escorted to his home in Monroe, Georgia, where he wrote *Scottsboro Boy*. See Grant, *The Way It Was*, 342.

16. Clifford M. Kuhn, "Two Small Windows of Opportunity: Black Politics in Georgia During the 1940s, and the Pertinent Oral History Sources," paper delivered at the joint meeting of the Georgia Association of Historians and the Georgia Political Science Association, Savannah, Georgia, 29 February 1992, 13. Courtesy Clifford M. Kuhn.

17. Kousser, *Colorblind Injustice*, 2.

18. See, for example, Julian Bond's address on 12 July 1998 to the NAACP Convention in Atlanta, entitled "The NAACP: Yesterday, Today and Tomorrow."

Bibliography

Manuscript Collections

APEX Museum, Auburn Avenue, Atlanta: "Sweet Auburn" Video presentation.

Atlanta History Center: Georgia Voters' League Files; Living Atlanta Series and Interviews; Grace Hamilton Papers; A. T. Walden Papers.

Auburn Avenue Research Library on African-American Culture and History, Atlanta: "Education," U.S. Commission on Civil Rights, Washington, D.C., 1961; "Political Participation," U.S. Commission on Civil Rights, Washington, D.C., 1968; "The Voting Rights Act: Ten Years After," U.S. Commission on Civil Rights, Washington, D.C., 1975.

Augusta Regional Public Library, Augusta, Georgia: Oral Memoirs of Augusta's Citizens.

Central Georgia Archives, Macon, Georgia: *Macon Telegraph* Clippings File.

Countee Cullen Memorial Collection, Atlanta University: Trezzant V. Anderson Files; Georgia Council on Human Relations Papers (uncataloged); "Report on the Grievances of Black Firemen to the Board of Masters, City of Atlanta," by the Community Relations Commission, 29 December 1969; Southern Regional Council Papers; Voter Education Project Files, Field Reports and Office Files, 1960–68.

Georgia Historical Society, Savannah: Race Relations Clippings File.

Howard University, Washington, D.C.: Civil Rights Documentation Project.

King-Tisdell Cottage, Savannah: Grand Songs of the NAACP "Freedom Now" Movement, 1964; NAACP, Savannah Branch, Miscellaneous Documents, Letters, Papers, and Records, 1950–76; Freedom Fund Dinner Reports, 1984–89; Newspaper Clippings File. Savannah NAACP Clippings File.

Koinonia Farm, Americus, Georgia: Koinonia Files (by permission).

Library of Congress, Washington, D.C.: NAACP Papers.

Martin Luther King Center for Nonviolent Social Change, Atlanta: Randolph Battle Papers; Congress on Racial Equality Papers; Robert Mants Papers; Southern Christian Leadership Conference Papers; Student Nonviolent Coordinating Committee Papers; Summer Community Organizing Project Files; Video, "Be Somebody," produced by Fred Hoffman, edited by John Rapoport.

Rome Carnegie Library, Rome, Georgia: Race-Relations File; *Rome Herald Tribune* Clippings File.

Simon Schwab Memorial Library, Columbus State University, Columbus, Georgia: *Columbus Ledger Enquirer* Clippings File.

Southern Labor Archives, Pullen Library, Georgia State University, Atlanta: Georgia State Industrial Union Council Proceedings, 1948–56; Charles Matthias Papers.

Special Collections, Auburn Avenue Research Library on African-American Culture and History, Atlanta: T. M. Alexander Papers; Moses and Miles G. Amos Papers; Ruby Blackburn Papers; Ella Mae Brayboy Papers; Student Nonviolent Coordinating Committee Papers on Microfilm; Southern Regional Council Papers on Microfilm.

Special Collections, Emory University, Atlanta: John Adams Sibley Papers; Facts on Film, Southern Education Reporting Service, Nashville, Microfilm Copy; Ralph McGill Papers; *Newsweek* Clippings File; Eliza Paschall Papers; Frances Pauley Papers; Sibley Commission on Education Report, 1960; Claude Sitton Papers; Dorothy Tilly Papers; Josephine Wilkins Papers.

Special Collections, Pullen Library, Georgia State University, Atlanta: Georgia Government Documentation Project Interviews.

University Library, Cambridge, England: NAACP Papers, Microfilm Copy; United States Census of the Population, 1940, 1960.

University of Georgia, Athens, Georgia: Lillian Smith Papers.

University of Pennsylvania, Philadelphia: American Friends Service Committee Papers; Constance Curry Correspondence; "Ten Communities Project" File.

Personal Papers, Photographs, Correspondence, and Unpublished Materials

John Bertrand, Rome: John R. and Annabel H. Bertrand, "Rome Council on Human Relations, 1962–1988 Historical Survey Based on Documentary Sources," 1 December 1988; "Events in Berry College's Race Relations Since 1959: A Statement by John R. Bertrand, President, Berry College, Mount Berry, Georgia"; "Beyond Racism: A Talk by John R. Bertrand, 28 April 1961"; Rose Levine, "Civil Rights," 1980.

Dorothy Bolden, Atlanta.

Paul Bolster, Atlanta: Interview with Ruby Hurley.

Tyrone Brooks, Atlanta.

Calvin Craig, Clayton County: "Martin Luther King . . . At Communist Training School" (leaflet, 1963).

W. W. Law, Savannah.

A. J. McClung, Columbus: A. J. McClung, "Dr. Thomas H. Brewer Memorial" transcript, n.d.; "Columbus, Georgia," report of the workings of Columbus government, 1971.

Benny T. Smith, Atlanta.

Larry Stell, Savannah: Recording of Speech by Martin Luther King in Savannah, 1 January 1964.

Curtis Thomas, Thomasville.

Interviews

Atlanta-Fulton Public Library Oral Collection, Archives and Manuscripts Division, Auburn Avenue Research Library, Atlanta: Ivan Allen; Dorothy Blackshear; Dorothy Bolden; W. H. Borders; John C. Calhoun; Ben Fortson; John Letson; Sam Massell; Dr. Benjamin E. Mays; Lorimer Douglas (L. D.) Milton; Cornelius Adolphus (C. A.) Scott; Pat Watters; Charles Yates

Augusta Oral History Collection, Augusta Regional Public Library, Augusta: C. Dent; R. A. Dent; Roy Harris

Civil Rights Documentation Project, Howard University, Washington, D.C.: Charles Black; Julian Bond; Benjamin Brown; John Calhoun; Clarence Coleman; John Gibson; Carl Holman; Lonnie King; Adelaide Taitt; P. Q. Yancey; Whitney Young

Georgia Government Documentation Project, Georgia State University, Atlanta: Stine George; Grace Hamilton; Robert Flanagan; Jake Henderson; W. W. Law; Herman Lodge; William Randall Sr.; William Randall Jr.; Robert Thompson

Living Atlanta Series, Atlanta History Center, Atlanta: Clarence Bacote; Mrs. J. B. (Ivella) Blayton; William Holmes Borders; B. R. Brazeal; M. A. "Peanut" Brown; John Calhoun; Estelle Clemmons; Warren Cochrane; John Griffin; Herbert Jenkins; Benjamin Mays; L. D. Milton; Eliza Paschall; Arthur Raper; C. A. Scott

Simon Schwab Memorial Library, Columbus State University, Columbus: Primus King

Interviews by Stephen Tuck, 1991–94

Copies of interviews labeled KT are at the King-Tisdell Cottage, Savannah. Copies of interviews labeled GGDP will be held as part of the Georgia Government Documentation Project, Georgia State University, Atlanta.

John Alexander, KT; T. M. Alexander, GGDP; Mabel Barnum, GGDP; Jean Benton, GGDP; John Bertrand, GGDP; Charlie Bloodworth, KT; Willie Bolden, GGDP; Dorothy Bolton, GGDP; Julian Bond, GGDP; Amanda Bowen Perdew, GGDP; Ella May Brayboy, GGDP; Tyrone Brooks, GGDP; Ed Brown, GGDP; Sage Brown, KT; Henry "Trash" Brownlee, KT; Ulysses Bryan, KT; Sam Burrell, GGDP; Attorney Aaron Buschbaum, KT; Olga Bynes, KT; Ed Cashin, GGDP; Frank Chester, GGDP; Curtis Cooper, GGDP; Rev. Eugene Cooper, GGDP; Calvin Craig, GGDP; Constance Curry, GGDP; Charles Dailey, KT; Martha Fay, KT; George Ford, GGDP; Judson Ford, KT; Warren Fortson, GGDP; Rev. Robert Lee Freeman, GGDP; Judge Eugene Gadsden, GGDP; John Goolsby, GGDP; Arthur Gordon, KT; Philip and Mildred Greer, GGDP; Rev. C. S. Hamilton, GGDP; Clifford Hardwick, GGDP; Rudy Hayes, GGDP; Beverly Hearn (née Brown), KT; Joe Hendricks, GGDP; Rev. Clyde Hill Sr., GGDP; Lucius Holloway, GGDP; Donald Hollowell, GGDP; Amos Holmes, GGDP; Edna Jackson, KT; Agnew James, GGDP; Dr. J. W. Jamerson Jr., KT; Dr. Rankin Jaudon, KT; Leroy Johnson, GGDP; Myrtle Jones, GGDP; Ada Kent, KT; Tea Kunny, GGDP; Geneva Law, KT; Westley (W. W.) Law, KT; Bob Leonard, GGDP; Willie Leventhal, GGDP; John Lipscomb, GGDP; Herman Lodge,

GGDP; Lawrence Young Lumpkin, GGDP; Laughlin MacDonald, GGDP; Malcolm Maclean, KT; Sammy Mahone, GGDP; Ferrell Malone, GGDP; Robert Mants, GGDP; James Mays, GGDP; A. J. McClung, GGDP; Josie Miller, GGDP; Louis Milton, KT; Linda Mitchell, KT; Mable Morris-Hudson, KT; Judge Victor Mulling, KT; J. Frank Myers, GGDP; Thaddeus Olive, GGDP; James Orange, GGDP; Frances Pauley, GGDP; John Perdew, GGDP; William Randall, GGDP; Tena Rhodes-Butler, KT; Willie Ricks, GGDP; Charles Sherrod, GGDP; Mary Shipp, GGDP; Earl Shinholster, KT; Claude Sitton, GGDP; Rev. Larry Stell, KT; Herman Talmadge, GGDP; Al Thompson, GGDP; Albert Turner, GGDP; Clarence White, GGDP; Margaret and Charles Whitworth, GGDP; Sadie Wiley, KT; Al Williams, GGDP; Hosea Williams, GGDP; Sam Williams, KT; Bill Winn, GGDP; Deacon William Winters, KT; Lawrence Young, GGDP

Newspapers and Periodicals

Atlanta Daily World, 1939–70.

Atlanta Inquirer, 1960–69.

Atlanta Journal and Constitution, 1940–80.

Crisis (official journal of the NAACP), 1938–64.

Herald (journal of the Georgia Teachers and Education Association), 1952–70.

New South, 1946–72.

New York Times, 1938–64.

Pittsburgh Courier, 1940–65.

Race Relations Law Reporter, 1960–66.

Savannah Herald Tribune, 1952–61.

Savannah Morning Press and Evening News, 1954–66.

Southern Patriot, 1944–65.

Southern School News, 1958–70.

South Today, 1942–45.

Student Voice, 1960–65.

Books, Articles, Dissertations, and Theses

Abernathy, Ralph David. *And the Walls Came Tumbling Down.* New York: Harper & Row, 1989.

Adams, Samuel L. "Blueprint for Segregation." *New South,* Spring 1967.

Alexander, Theodore Martin (T. M.), Sr. *Beyond the Timberline.* Edgewood, Md.: M. E. Duncan, 1992.

Allen, Ivan. *Mayor: Notes on the Sixties.* New York: Simon and Schuster, 1971.

Ambrose, Andrew M. "Redrawing the Color Line: The History and Patterns of Black Housing in Atlanta, 1940–1973." Ph.D. diss., Emory University, 1992.

Anderson, William F. *The Wild Man from Sugar Creek.* Baton Rouge: Louisiana State University Press, 1975.

APEX. *Sweet Auburn: Street of Pride. A Pictorial History.* Atlanta: African-American Panoramic Experience, 1988.

Arnall, Ellis Gibbs. *The Shore Dimly Seen.* Philadelphia: J. B. Lippincott, 1946.

Atlanta Committee for Cooperative Action. *A Second Look: The Negro Citizen in Atlanta.* Atlanta: Atlanta Committee for Cooperative Action, 1960.

Bachtel, Douglas C., Everett Lee, and Hortense L. Bates. "Georgia's Black Population." *Issues Facing Georgia* 2 (December 1986): 1–5.

Bacote, Clarence A. "The Negro in Atlanta Politics." *Phylon* 16 (1955): 333–50.

———. "The Negro Voter in Georgia Politics Today." *Journal of Negro Education* 26 (Summer 1957): 307–18.

———. *The Story of Atlanta University: A Century of Service, 1865–1965.* Atlanta: Atlanta University, 1969.

Badger, Anthony. "Segregation and the Southern Business Elite." *Journal of American Studies* 18 (April 1984): 105–9.

Badger, Anthony, and Brian Ward, eds. *The Making of Martin Luther King and the Civil Rights Movement.* London: Macmillan, 1996.

Baldwin, James. *Nobody Knows My Name: More Notes of a Native Son.* 1964. Reprint. London: Penguin, 1991.

Barnes, Catherine. *Journey from Jim Crow: The Desegregation of Southern Transit.* New York: Columbia University Press, 1983.

Barnum, Richard L., John C. Howard, Richard L. Rowan, and Herbert Northrup, eds. *Negro Employment in Southern Industry.* Philadelphia: University of Pennsylvania, Wharton School of Industrial Research Unit, 1970.

Bartley, Numan. "Atlanta Elections and Georgia Political Trends." *New South* 25 (Winter 1970): 24–30.

———. *The Creation of Modern Georgia.* 2d ed. Athens: University of Georgia Press, 1990.

———. *From Thurmond to Wallace: Political Tendencies in Georgia, 1948–68.* Baltimore: Johns Hopkins Press, 1970.

———. *The Rise of Massive Resistance: Race and Politics in the South During the 1950s.* Baton Rouge: Louisiana State University Press, 1969.

Bass, Jack, and Walter Devries. *The Transformation of Southern Politics: Social Change and Political Consequences Since 1945.* New York: Basic Books, 1976.

Bayor, Ronald H. *Race and the Shaping of Twentieth-Century Atlanta.* Chapel Hill: University of North Carolina Press, 1996.

Beardslee, Bill. "Self Respect in the Alley." *New South* 20 (November 1965): 10–12.

Bederman, Sanford Harold. "Black Residential Neighbourhoods and Job Opportunity Centers in Atlanta, Georgia." Ph.D. diss., University of Minnesota, 1973.

Belfrage, Sally. *Freedom Summer.* New York: Viking Press, 1965.

Bellamy, Donnie D. "Whites Sue for Desegregation in Georgia: The Fort Valley State College Case." *Journal of Negro History* 64 (1979): 316–36.

Bernd, Joseph L. "White Supremacy and the Disenfranchisement of Blacks in Georgia, 1946." *Georgia Historical Quarterly* 66 (1982): 492–513.

Binford, Michael B., Ken Johnson, and Laughlin McDonald. "Georgia." In C. Davidson and B. Grofman, eds., *Quiet Revolution in the South: The Impact of the Voting Rights Act 1965–90.* Princeton: Princeton University Press, 1994.

Black, Earl. *Southern Governors and Civil Rights.* Cambridge, Mass.: Harvard University Press, 1976.

Blackwell, Gloria. "Black-Controlled Media in Atlanta, 1960–70: The Burden of the Message and the Struggle for Survival." Ph.D. diss., Emory University, 1973.

Bledsoe, Christena. "Burke County Today." *Georgia Poverty Journal* 1 (Fall 1986): 6–14.

Bloom, Gordon F., F. Marion Fletcher, and Charles R. Perry, eds. *Negro Employment in the Retail Trade.* Philadelphia: University of Pennsylvania, Wharton School of Industrial Research Unit, 1974.

Blumberg, Janice Rothschild. *One Voice: Rabbi Jacob M. Rothschild and the Troubled South.* Macon: Mercer University Press, 1985.

Bolster, Paul. "Civil Rights Movement in Twentieth Century Georgia." Ph.D. diss., University of Georgia, 1972.

Bond, Julian. "Autobiography: Memoirs of a Southern Gentleman." *Ramparts,* January and February 1967.

———. "Black Candidates: Southern Campaign Experiences." Southern Regional Council Publications, 1944–76.

Bracey, John H., August Meier, and Elliott Rudwick. *Conflict and Competition: Studies in the Recent Black Protest Movement.* Belmont, Calif.: Wadsworth, 1971.

———. *The Rise of the Ghetto.* Belmont, Calif.: Wadsworth, 1971.

Branch, Taylor. *Parting the Waters: America in the King Years, 1954–73.* New York: Simon and Schuster, 1988.

Brooks, Lester, and Guiehard Parris. *Blacks in the City: History of the National Urban League.* Boston: Little, Brown, 1971.

Brown, Cynthia Stokes, ed. *Ready from Within: Septima Clark and the Civil Rights Movement.* Trenton, N.J.: Africa World Press, 1990.

Browning, Rufus P., Dale Rogers Marshall, and David H. Tabb. *Racial Politics in American Cities.* New York: Longman, 1990.

Bullock, H. A. *A History of Negro Education.* Cambridge, Mass.: Harvard University Press, 1967.

Bunche, Ralph. *The Political Status of the Negro in the Age of F.D.R.* Edited by Dewey W. Grantham. Chicago: University of Chicago Press, 1973.

Button, James. *Blacks and Social Change: Impact of the Civil Rights Movement in Southern Communities.* Princeton: Princeton University Press, 1989.

Calhoun, John. "Significant Aspects of Some Negro Leaders' Contributions to the Progress of Atlanta, Georgia." M.A. thesis, School of Business Administration, Atlanta University, 1968.

Calloway, W. L. *The "Sweet Auburn" Avenue Business History, 1900–88.* Atlanta: Central Atlanta Progress, 1988.

Campbell, Walter E. "Profit, Prejudice, and Protest: Utility Competition and the Generation of Jim Crow Streetcars in Savannah, 1905–1907." *Georgia Historical Quarterly* 70 (Summer 1986): 197–231.

Campbell, Will D. *Forty Acres and a Goat.* Atlanta: Peachtree Publishers, 1986.

———. *The Stem of Jesse: The Costs of Community at a 1960s Southern School.* Macon: Mercer University Press, 1995.

Carson, Clayborne. *In Struggle: SNCC and the Black Awakening of the 1960s.* Cambridge, Mass.: Harvard University Press, 1981.

———. "SNCC and the Albany Movement." *Journal of Southwest Georgia History* 2 (Fall 1984): 16–25.

Carter, Dan T. *Scottsboro: A Tragedy of the American South.* Baton Rouge: Louisiana State University Press, 1979.

Carter, Hodding. *Southern Legacy.* Baton Rouge: Louisiana State University Press, 1950.

Cashin, Edward. *The Story of Augusta.* Augusta: Richmond County Board of Education, 1980.

———. "Will the Real Georgia History Rise and Be Recognized?" *Georgia Historical Quarterly* 65 (Spring 1981): 1–6.

Chafe, William H. "The End of One Struggle, the Beginning of Another." In *The Civil Rights Movement in America,* edited by Charles Eagles. Jackson: University Press of Mississippi, 1986.

———. *Civilities and Civil Rights: Greensboro, North Carolina, and the Black Struggle for Freedom.* New York: Oxford University Press, 1980.

———. *The Unfinished Journey: America Since World War II.* 2d ed. New York: Oxford University Press, 1991.

Chalfen, Michael. "'The Way Out May Lead In': The Albany Movement Beyond Martin Luther King, Jr." *Georgia Historical Quarterly* 79 (Fall 1995): 560–98.

Chamberlain, John. "Arnall of Georgia." *Life,* 6 August 1945.

Chambers, David. *Hooded Americanism: History of the Ku Klux Klan.* Durham: Duke University Press, 1987.

Chancey, Andrew S. "Race, Religion and Agricultural Reform: The Communal Vision of Koinonia Farm." In *Georgia in Black and White: Explorations in the Race Relations of a Southern State, 1865–1950,* edited by John Inscoe. Athens: University of Georgia Press, 1994.

Chappell, David L. *Inside Agitators: White Southerners in the Civil Rights Movement.* Baltimore: Johns Hopkins University Press, 1994.

Clayton, Xenona, with Hal Gulliver. *I've Been Marching All the Time: An Autobiography.* Atlanta: Longstreet Press, 1991.

Cleghorn, Reese. "Epilogue in Albany: Were the Mass Marches Worthwhile?" *New Republic,* 20 July 1963.

Cobb, James C. *The Most Southern Place on Earth: The Mississippi Delta and the Roots of Regional Identity.* New York: Oxford University Press, 1992.

———. "Polarization in a Southern City: The Augusta Riot and the Emerging Character of the 1970s." *Southern Studies* 20 (Summer 1981): 185–200.

———. "Politics in a New South City: Augusta, Georgia, 1946–71." Ph.D. diss., University of Georgia, 1975.

Colburn, David. *Racial Change and Community Crisis: St. Augustine, Florida, 1877–1980.* New York: Columbia University Press, 1985.

Coleman, Kenneth, ed. *History of Georgia.* Athens: University of Georgia Press, 1977.

Coles, Robert. "Maddox of Georgia." *New Republic,* 5 August 1967.

Conway, Alan. *The Reconstruction of Georgia.* Minneapolis: University of Minnesota Press, 1966.

Conyers, James E., and William J. Farmer. *Black Youth in a Southern Metropolis*. Atlanta: Southern Regional Council Publications, 1968.

Cook, Robert. *Sweet Land of Liberty: The African American Struggle for Civil Rights in the Twentieth Century*. London: Longman, 1997.

Cotman, John Walton. *Birmingham, J. F. Kennedy, and the Civil Rights Act of 1963: Implications for Elite Theory*. New York: Peter Lang, 1989.

Crawford, Fred, Harvey Gates, and James Conyers. "Civil Aggression and Urban Disorders: Atlanta, Georgia, 1967." 21 November 1967. Prepared for the National Advisory Commission on Civil Disorders.

Crawford, Vicki, Jacqueline Rouse, and Barbara Woods, eds. *Women in the Civil Rights Movement: Trailblazers and Torchbearers, 1941–65*. New York: Carlson, 1990.

Dalfiume, Richard M. *Desegregation of the U.S. Armed Forces: Fighting on Two Fronts, 1939–1953*. Columbia: University of Missouri Press, 1969.

———. "The Forgotten Years of the Negro Revolution." *Journal of American History* 55 (June 1968): 90–106.

Daniel, Pete. "Going Among Strangers: Southern Reactions to World War II." *Journal of American History* 77 (December 1990): 886–911.

Davidson, Chandler, and Bernard Grofman, eds. *Quiet Revolution in the South: The Impact of the Voting Rights Act, 1965–90*. Princeton: Princeton University Press, 1994.

Dewey, Thomas. "Negro Employment in Southern Industry." *Journal of Political Economy* 60 (August 1952): 279–93.

Dittmer, John. *Black Georgia in the Progressive Era, 1900–1920*. Urbana: University of Illinois Press, 1980.

———. *Local People: The Struggle for Civil Rights in Mississippi*. Urbana: University of Illinois Press, 1994.

Doss, George A., Jr. "Homegrown Movement in Macon." *New South* 18 (April 1963): 3–10.

Drago, Edmund. *Black Politicians and Reconstruction in Georgia: A Splendid Failure*. Baton Rouge: Louisiana State University Press, 1982.

Du Bois, W. E. B. "Race Relations in America, 1917–47." *Phylon* 9 (1948): 234–46.

———. *The Souls of Black Folk*. New York: Penguin, 1989.

Egerton, John. *Speak Now Against the Day*. New York: Knopf, 1994.

Elliott, Ward. *The Rise of Guardian Democracy: The Supreme Court's Role in Voting Rights Disputes, 1845–1969*. Cambridge, Mass.: Harvard University Press, 1974.

Eskew, Glenn. *But for Birmingham: The Local and National Movements in the Civil Rights Struggle*. Chapel Hill: University of North Carolina Press, 1997.

Fairclough, Adam. "Historians and the Civil Rights Movement." *Journal of American Studies* 24 (1990): 387–98.

———. *Race and Democracy: The Civil Rights Struggle in Louisiana*. Athens: University of Georgia Press, 1995.

———. *To Redeem the Soul of America: The Southern Christian Leadership Conference and Martin Luther King, Jr*. Athens: University of Georgia Press, 1987.

Fayer, Steve, and Henry Hampton. *Voices of Freedom: An Oral History of the Civil Rights Movement from the 1950s Through the 1980s*. New York: Bantam Books, 1990.

Finch, Minnie. *The NAACP and Its Fight for Justice.* Metuchen, N.J.: Scarecrow Press, 1981.

Fite, Gilbert C. *Richard B. Russell, Jr., Senator from Georgia.* Chapel Hill: University of North Carolina Press, 1991.

Fletcher, Linda P., and Armand Thiebolt, eds. *Negro Employment in Finance.* Philadelphia: University of Pennsylvania, Wharton School of Industrial Research Unit, 1974.

Ford, James, and John M. Gries, eds. *Negro Housing.* New York: Negro University Press, 1932.

Forman, James. *The Making of Black Revolutionaries.* Washington, D.C.: Open Hand, 1972.

Fortune Magazine. *The Negro and the City.* New York: Time-Life Books, 1968.

Frady, Marshall. "Discovering One Another in a Georgia Town." *Life,* 12 February 1971.

———. *Southerners: A Journalist's Odyssey.* Indianapolis: New American Library, 1980.

Franklin, John Hope, and August Meier, eds. *Black Leaders of the Twentieth Century.* Urbana: University of Illinois Press, 1982.

Freedgood, Seymour. "Life in Buckhead." *Fortune,* September 1961.

Galphin, Bruce, and Norman Shavin. *Atlanta: Triumph of a People.* Atlanta: Capricorn, 1982.

Garrison, Joseph Yates. "The Augusta Black Community Since World War II." Master's thesis, University of Miami, 1971.

Garrow, David. *Bearing the Cross: Martin Luther King and the Southern Christian Leadership Conference.* New York: William Morrow, 1986.

———. *Protest at Selma: Martin Luther King, Jr., and the Voting Rights Act of 1965.* New Haven: Yale University Press, 1978.

———, ed. *Atlanta, Georgia, 1960–1961.* Brooklyn: Carlson, 1989.

Gaston, Edward Aaron, Jr. "A History of the Negro Wage Earner in Georgia, 1890–1940." Ph.D. diss., Emory University, 1957.

Gavins, Raymond. "The NAACP in North Carolina During the Age of Segregation." In *New Directions in Civil Rights Studies,* edited by Armstead L. Robinson and Patricia Sullivan. Charlottesville: University Press of Virginia, 1991.

Gillette, Michael L. "The Rise of the NAACP in Texas." *Southwestern Historical Quarterly* 81 (April 1978): 393–416.

Gilmore, Glenda Elizabeth. *Gender and Jim Crow: Women and the Politics of White Supremacy in North Carolina, 1896–1920.* Chapel Hill: University of North Carolina Press, 1996.

Goldfield, David R. *Black, White, and Southern: Race Relations and Southern Culture, 1940 to the Present.* Baton Rouge: Louisiana State University Press, 1990.

Good, Paul. *The Trouble I've Seen.* Washington, D.C.: Howard University Press, 1975.

Grant, Donald L. *The Way It Was in the South: The Black Experience in Georgia.* New York: Birch Lane Press, 1983.

Greene, Melissa Fay. *Praying for Sheetrock: A Work of Nonfiction.* London: Secker and Warburg, 1992.

Gregory, Dick (and Robert Lipsyte). *Nigger: An Autobiography.* New York: Pocket Books, 1964.

Griffith, Barbara S. *The Crisis of American Labor: Operation Dixie and the Defeat of the C.I.O.* Philadelphia: Temple University Press, 1988.

Hamman, William Charles. "A Study of Voting Participation, 1945–55, in All Negro Precincts in Atlanta, Georgia." M.A. thesis, Emory University, 1955.

Hanks, Lawrence. *The Struggle for Black Political Empowerment in Three Georgia Counties.* Knoxville: University of Tennessee Press, 1987.

Harding, Vincent. "When Stokeley Met the President: Black Power and Negro Education." *Motive,* January 1967.

Harmon, David. "Beneath the Image: The Civil Rights Movement and Race Relations in Atlanta, Georgia, 1946–81." Ph.D. diss., Emory University, 1992.

Harvey, Diane. "The 'Terri,' Augusta's Black Enclave." *Richmond County History* 5 (Summer 1973): 70–74.

Harvey, Hope A. "Poverty and the 'Two Georgias.'" *Georgia Poverty Journal* 1 (Fall 1986): 23–26.

Henderson, Alexa Benson. *Atlanta Life Insurance Company: Guardian of Black Economic Dignity.* Tuscaloosa: University of Alabama Press, 1990.

Henderson, Harold P., and Gary L. Roberts. *Georgia Governors in an Age of Change: From Ellis Arnall to George Busbee.* Athens: University of Georgia Press, 1988.

Hinton, Harold B. "What's the Matter with Georgia?" *New York Times Magazine,* 8 February 1947.

Holden, Anna. "Race and Politics: Congressional Elections in the Fifth District of Georgia, 1946–52." Master's thesis, University of North Carolina, 1955.

Holloway, Harry. *The Politics of the Southern Negro.* New York: Random House, 1969.

Holmes, Thomas J. *Ashes for Breakfast.* Valley Forge: Judson Press, 1969.

Honey, Michael K. *Southern Labor and Black Civil Rights: Organizing Memphis Workers.* Urbana: University of Illinois Press, 1993.

Hope, John III. "Efforts to Eliminate Discrimination in Industry, with Particular Reference to the South." *Journal of Negro Education* 23 (Summer 1954): 262–72.

———. "The Self-Survey of the Packinghouse Union." *Journal of Social Issues* 9 (1953): 28–36.

Hornsby, Alton, Jr. "Georgia." In *The Black Press of the South, 1865–1979,* edited by Henry Suggs. Westport, Conn.: Greenwood Press, 1983.

———. "The Negro in Atlanta Politics, 1961–73." *Atlanta Historical Bulletin* 21 (1973): 7–33.

Hunter, Floyd. *Community Power Structure.* Chapel Hill: University of North Carolina Press, 1953.

Hutzler, Helen C. "History of Rome, Georgia, Carnegie Library, 1911–61." Master's thesis, Catholic University of America, 1963.

Inscoe, John C., ed. *Georgia in Black and White: Explorations in the Race Relations of a Southern State, 1865–1950.* Athens: University of Georgia Press, 1994.

Jackson, Luther P. "Race and Suffrage in the South Since 1940." *New South* 3 (June–July 1948): 3–10.

Jacoway, Elizabeth, and David Colburn, eds. *Southern Businessmen and Desegregation.* Baton Rouge: Louisiana State University Press, 1982.

James, Hunter. *They Didn't Put That on the Huntley-Brinkley! A Vagabond Reporter Encounters the New South.* Athens: University of Georgia Press, 1993.

Jenkins, Welborn Victor. *The "Incident" at Monroe.* Atlanta: Robinson Printing Company, 1918.

Johnson, Charles S. *Growing Up in the Black Belt: Negro Youth in the Rural South*. Washington, D.C.: American Council on Education, 1941.

———. *Patterns of Negro Segregation*. London: Victor Gollancz, 1944.

———. "A Southern Negro's View of the South." *Journal of Negro Education* 26 (Winter 1957).

———. *To Stem This Tide: A Survey of Racial Tension Areas in the U.S.* Boston: Pilgrim Press, 1943.

Johnson, Jerah. "New South Georgia and Old South Georgia: Towards a Definition of Two Regional Cultures." *Journal of Southwest Georgia History* 4 (Fall 1986): v–vi.

Johnson, R. O. "Desegregation of Public Education in Georgia." *Journal of Negro Education* 24 (Summer 1955): 228–47.

Jordan, Clarence. "Impractical Christianity." *Young People's Quarterly* (1948): 2.

Joyce, Allen Edward. "The Atlanta Black Crackers." Master's thesis, Emory University, 1975.

Kelley, Robin. *Race Rebels: Culture, Politics, and the Black Working Class*. New York: Free Press, 1996.

———. "We Are Not What We Seem: Rethinking Black Working Class Opposition in the Jim Crow South." *Journal of American History* 80 (June 1993): 75–112.

Key, V. O. *Southern Politics in State and Nation*. New York: Knopf, 1949.

King, Carl B., Herbert Northrup, William Quay Jr., Howard W. Risher Jr., and Richard L. Rowan, eds. *Negro Employment in Basic Industry*. Philadelphia: University of Pennsylvania, Wharton School of Industrial Research Unit, 1970.

King, Martin Luther, Sr., with Clayton Riley. *Daddy King, an Autobiography*. New York: William Morrow, 1980.

King, Mary. *Freedom Song: A Personal Story of the 1960s Civil Rights Movement*. New York: Morrow, 1987.

King, Slater. "Report from Albany." *Peace News*, No. 1366, 31 August 1962.

Kirk, John. "'He Started a Movement': W. H. Flowers, the Committee on Negro Organizations and the Origins of Black Activism in Arkansas, 1940–57." In *The Making of Martin Luther King and the Civil Rights Movement* edited by Anthony Badger and Brian Ward. London: Macmillan, 1996.

Klarman, Michael J. "How *Brown* Changed Race Relations: The Backlash Thesis." *Journal of American History* 81 (June 1994): 81–118.

Kolmar, Karen. "Southern Black Elites and the New Deal: A Case Study of Savannah." *Georgia Historical Quarterly* 65 (Winter 1981): 341–55.

Kornhauser, William. "Ideology and Interests." *American Journal of Social Issues* 9 (1953): 49–60.

———. "Negro Union Official: A Study of Sponsorship and Control." *American Journal of Sociology* 57 (March 1952): 443–52.

Korstad, Robert, and Nelson Lichtenstein. "Opportunities Found and Lost: Labor, Radicals and the Early Civil Rights Movement." *Journal of American History* 75 (1988–89): 786–811.

Kousser, J. Morgan. *Colorblind Injustice: Minority Voting Rights and the Undoing of the Second Reconstruction*. Chapel Hill: University of North Carolina Press, 1999.

Kuhn, Clifford M., Harlon E. Joye, and E. Bernard West. *Living Atlanta: An Oral History of the City, 1914–48*. Athens: University of Georgia Press, 1990.

Kyle, Samuel Boyles, III. "A Model of Political Revolution—The Black Revolution in the South: A Case Study." Master's thesis, Georgia State University, 1974.

Kytle, Calvin. "A Long, Dark Night for Georgia?" *Harper's* 197 (September 1948): 55−64.

Kytle, Calvin, and James A. Mackay. *Who Runs Georgia?* Athens: University of Georgia Press, 1998.

Lamis, Alexander. *The Two Party South*. New York: Oxford University Press, 1984.

Lane, Mills B. *The People of Georgia*. Savannah: Beehive Press, 1992.

Lawson, Steven F. *Black Ballots: Voting Rights in the South, 1944−1969*. New York: Columbia University Press, 1976.

———. "Freedom Then, Freedom Now: The Historiography of the Civil Rights Movement." *American Historical Review* 96 (1991): 456−71.

———. *Running for Freedom: Civil Rights and Black Politics in America Since 1941*. Philadelphia: Temple University Press, 1981.

Lawson, Steven F., and Charles M. Payne. *Debating the Civil Rights Movement, 1945−68.* Lanham, Md.: Rowman and Littlefield, 1998.

Lee, Dallas. *The Cotton Patch Evidence: The Story of Clarence Jordan and the Koinonia Farm Experiment*. New York: Harper & Row, 1971.

Leventhal, Will. "A Personal Odyssey." *New South* 27 (Fall 1962): 73−78.

Levy, Peter B., ed. *Let Freedom Ring*. New York: Praeger, 1992.

Lewis, David Levering. *King: A Biography*. Urbana: University of Illinois Press, 1978.

Lewis, John, with Michael D'Orso. *Walking with the Wind: A Memoir of the Movement*. New York: Simon and Schuster, 1998.

Lincoln, C. E. "The Strategy of a Sit-In." *Reporter,* 5 January 1961.

Lomax, Louis. "Georgia Boy Goes Home." *Harper's* 230 (April 1965): 152−59.

———. *The Negro Revolt*. London: Hamish Hamilton, 1963.

Loveland, Anne C. *Lillian Smith: A Southerner Confronting the South*. Baton Rouge: Louisiana State University Press, 1986.

Lynch, Hollis R. *The Black Urban Condition*. New York: Thomas R. Crowell, 1975.

MacAdam, Doug. *Freedom Summer*. New York: Oxford University Press, 1988.

Martin, Charles H. *The Angelo Herndon Case and Southern Justice*. Baton Rouge: Louisiana State University Press, 1976.

Martin, Harold H. *William Berry Hartsfield: Mayor of Atlanta*. Athens: University of Georgia Press, 1988.

Mason, Herman "Skip." *Going Against the Wind*. Atlanta: Longstreet Press, 1992.

Mays, Benjamin E. *Born to Rebel*. 1971. Reprint. Athens: University of Georgia Press, 1982.

McCoy, Carl Levert. "A Historical Sketch of Black Augusta, Georgia, from Emancipation to the *Brown* Decision: 1865−1954." Master's thesis, University of Georgia, 1984.

McCullar, Bernice. *This Is Your Georgia*. Montgomery: Viewpoint Publications, 1972.

McDonald, Laughlin. "*Holder vs. Hall:* Trail of Voting Rights Act." Draft Article, courtesy Laughlin McDonald.

McGill, Ralph. *South and the Southerner*. Athens: University of Georgia Press, 1992.

McGrath, Susan. "Great Expectations: The History of School Desegregation in Atlanta and Boston, 1954–1990." Ph.D. diss., Emory University, 1992.

McKissack, Rosetta Sangster. "Attitudes Towards Negro Political Participation in Georgia, 1940–47." Master's thesis, Atlanta University, 1954.

McMillan, George. "Talmadge: The Best Southern Governor." *Harper's* 209 (December 1954): 34–40.

McPheeters, Annie L. *Negro Progress in Atlanta, Georgia, 1950–60: A Selective Bibliography on Human Relations from Four Atlanta Newspapers.* Atlanta: West Hunter Branch Atlanta Public Library, 1964.

Meier, August, and David Lewis. "History of the Negro Upper Class in Atlanta, Georgia, 1890–1958." *Journal of Negro Education* 28 (Spring 1959): 128–39.

Mertz, Paul E. "Mind Changing Time All Over Georgia: HOPE, Inc., and School Desegregation, 1958–61." *Georgia Historical Quarterly* 77 (Spring 1993): 41–61.

Metcalf, George R. *From Little Rock to Boston: The History of School Desegregation.* Westport, Conn.: Greenwood Press, 1983.

Mills, Kay. *This Little Light of Mine: The Life of Fannie Lou Hamer.* New York: Dutton, 1993.

Minchin, Timothy J. *Hiring the Black Worker: The Racial Integration of the Southern Textile Industry, 1960–1980.* Chapel Hill: University of North Carolina Press, 1999.

Mitchell, George. *I'm Somebody Important: Young Black Voices from Rural Georgia.* Urbana: University of Illinois Press, 1973.

Moberly, Richard E. "Testing the Bonds of Segregation: The Civil Rights Movement in Albany, Georgia." Master's thesis, Emory University, 1991.

Moeser, John, and Christopher Silver. *The Separate City: Black Communities in the Urban South, 1940–68.* Lexington: University Press of Kentucky, 1995.

Morris, Aldon. *Origins of the Civil Rights Movement: Black Communities Organizing for Change.* New York: Collier Macmillan, 1984.

Mullis, Sharon Mitchell. "The Public Career of Grace Towns Hamilton: A Citizen Too Busy to Hate." Ph.D. diss., Emory University, 1976.

Murphy, James Burford. "A Study of the Editorial Policies of the *Atlanta Daily World:* 1952–55." Master's thesis, Emory University, 1961.

Nasstrom, Kathryn L. "Down to Now: Memory, Narrative and Women's Leadership in the Civil Rights Movement in Atlanta, Georgia." *Gender and History* 11 (April 1999): 113–44.

Neary, John. *Julian Bond: Black Rebel.* New York: William Morrow, 1971.

Nelson, Robert. "Georgia: 'High Ground.'" *Christian Science Monitor,* 30 August 1962.

Norrell, Robert. *Reaping the Whirlwind: The Civil Rights Movement in Tuskegee.* New York: Knopf, 1985.

Northrup, Herbert R. *The Negro in the Automobile Industry.* Philadelphia: Industrial Research Unit, Wharton School, University of Pennsylvania, 1968.

Northrup, Herbert, Lester Rubin, and William S. Swift, eds. *Negro Employment in the Maritime Industries.* Philadelphia: Industrial Research Unit, Wharton School, University of Pennsylvania, 1974.

Northrup, Robert. "The Negro and the United Mine Workers of America." *Southern Economic Journal* 9 (July 1942–April 1943): 313–26.

Oates, Stephen B. "The Albany Movement: A Chapter in the Life of Martin Luther King Jr." *Journal of Southwest Georgia History* 2 (Fall 1984): 26–39.

Owen, Hugh Carl. "The Rise of Negro Voting in Georgia, 1944–50." Master's thesis, Emory University, 1951.

Paschall, Eliza. *It Must Have Rained.* Atlanta: Center for Research in Social Change, Emory University, 1975.

Pauley, Frances. "Stories of Struggle and Triumph." *Hospitality* 12 (May 1993): 3–4.

Payne, Charles M. *I've Got the Light of Freedom: The Organizing Tradition and the Mississippi Freedom Struggle.* Berkeley: University of California Press, 1995.

Penuel, Peggy Irene. "An Analysis of the Treatment of Negro News in the *Atlanta Journal* and the *Atlanta Constitution* from 1900 to April 1, 1951." Master's thesis, Emory University, 1951.

Perdue, Robert. *The Negro in Savannah, 1865–1900.* New York: Exposition Press, 1973.

Pierce, Joseph A. *Negro Business and Business Education.* New York: Harper and Brothers, 1947.

Plank, David N., and Marcia Turner. "Changing Patterns in Black School Politics: Atlanta, 1872–1973." *American Journal of Education* 56 (August 1987): 584–602.

Polenziana, David D. "Striking Back: Richard B. Russell and Racial Relocation." *Georgia Historical Quarterly* 65 (Fall 1981): 263–75.

Price, Margaret. *The Negro and the Ballot in the South.* Atlanta: SRC Publications, 1959.

———. "The Negro Voter in the South." SRC Publications, September 1957.

Pyles, Charles B. "Race and Ruralism in Georgia Elections 1948–66." Ph.D. diss., University of Georgia, 1968.

Raines, Howell. *My Soul Is Rested: Movement Days in the Deep South Remembered.* 1977. Reprint. New York: Bantam Books, 1983.

Ralph, James R., Jr. *Northern Protest: Martin Luther King, Jr., Chicago, and the Civil Rights Movement.* Cambridge, Mass.: Harvard University Press, 1993.

Range, Willard. *Rise and Progress of Negro Colleges in Georgia, 1865–1949.* Athens: University of Georgia Press, 1951.

Reagon, Bernice. "In Our Hands: Thoughts on Black Music." *Sing Out!* January–February 1976.

Reed, John Shelton. *One South: An Ethnic Approach to Regional Culture.* Baton Rouge: Louisiana State University Press, 1982.

Ricks, John A., III. "'De Lawd' Descends and Is Crucified: Martin Luther King Jr. in Albany, Georgia." *Journal of Southwest Georgia History* 2 (Fall 1984): 3–14.

Robinson, Armstead L., and Patricia Sullivan, eds. *New Directions in Civil Rights Studies.* Charlottesville: University Press of Virginia, 1991.

Robinson, Jo Ann Gibson. *The Montgomery Bus Boycott and the Women Who Started It: The Memoir of Jo Ann Robinson Gibson.* Edited by David J. Garrow. Knoxville: University of Tennessee Press, 1987.

Roche, Jeff. *Restructured Resistance: The Sibley Commission and the Politics of Desegregation in Georgia.* Athens: University of Georgia Press, 1998.

Rogers, Kim Lacy. "Oral History and the History of the Civil Rights Movement." *Journal of American History* 75 (September 1988): 567–76.

Rolinson, Mary Gambrell. "The Universal Negro Improvement Association in Georgia: Southern Strongholds of Garveyism." In *Georgia in Black and White: Explorations in the Race Relations of a Southern State, 1865–1950,* edited by John C. Inscoe. Athens: University of Georgia Press, 1994.

Rooks, Charles S. *The Atlanta Elections of 1969.* Atlanta: SRC Publications, 1970.

Rozier, John Wiley. "A History of the Negro Press in Atlanta." Master's thesis, Emory University, 1947.

Rozier, John. *Black Boss: Political Revolution in a Georgia County, the Story of John McCown and Hancock County.* Athens: University of Georgia Press, 1982.

Rubin, Lester. *The Negro in the Longshore Industry.* Philadelphia: Industrial Research Unit, Wharton School, University of Pennsylvania, 1974.

Ruchames, Louis. *Race, Jobs and Politics.* New York: Columbia University Press, 1953.

Russwurm, Steve, ed. *The CIO's Left-Led Unions.* New Brunswick: Rutgers University Press, 1992.

Sanders, Randy. "'The Sad Duty of Politics:' Jimmy Carter and the Issue of Race in His 1970 Gubernatorial Campaign." *Georgia Historical Quarterly* 76 (Fall 1992): 612–38.

Schrade, A. Bradley. "'Bad' Baker, 'Terrible' Terrell, and Pritchett's Albany: SNCC and the Interplay Between Rural and Urban Civil Rights Movements in Southwest Georgia." Master's thesis, University of Georgia, 1995.

Schuck, Patrick, and Harrison Wellford. "Democracy and the Good Life in a Country Town: The Case of St. Marys Georgia." *Harper's* 244 (May 1972): 56–71.

Schulman, Bruce J. *From Cotton Belt to Sunbelt: Federal Policy, Economic Development, and the Transformation of the South, 1938–1980.* Durham, N.C.: Duke University Press, 1994.

Schultz, Mark R. "Interracial Kinship Ties and the Emergence of a Rural Black Middle Class: Hancock County, Georgia, 1865–1970." In *Georgia in Black and White: Explorations in the Race Relations of a Southern State, 1865–1950,* edited by John C. Inscoe. Athens: University of Georgia Press, 1994.

Shadron, Virginia. "Popular Protest and Legal Authority in Post–World War II Georgia: Race, Class and Gender Politics in the Rosa Lee Ingram Case." Ph.D. diss., Emory University, 1991.

Sherrill, Robert G. "Strange Decorum of Lester Maddox." *Nation,* 1 May 1967.

Simms, James Meriles. *The First Colored Baptist Church in North America.* Philadelphia: J. B. Lippincott, 1888.

Sitkoff, Harvard. "Racial Militancy and Interracial Violence in the Second World War." *Journal of American History* 58 (December 1971): 661–81.

———. *The Struggle for Black Equality.* New York: Hill and Wang, 1981.

Sitton, Claude. "Atlanta's Example: Good Sense and Dignity." *New York Times Magazine,* 6 May 1962.

Smith, David M. "Inequality in Atlanta, Georgia, 1960–1980." Dissertation, Department of Geography and Earth Science, Queen Mary College, University of London, 1985.

Smith, John M. "Riot of May 1970." *Richmond County History* 7 (Summer 1975): 103–16.

Smyth, William. "Segregation in Charleston in the 1950s: A Decade of Tradition." *South Carolina Historical Magazine* 92 (April 1991): 99–123.

Sosna, Morton. *In Search of the Silent South: Southern Liberals and the Race Issue.* New York: Columbia University Press, 1977.

Spero, S. D., and A. L. Harris. *The Black Worker: The Negro and the Labor Movement.* New York: Atheneum, 1969.

Spritzer, Lorraine Nelson. *The Belle of Ashby Street: Helen Douglas Mankin and Georgia Politics.* Athens: University of Georgia Press, 1982.

Spritzer, Lorraine, and Jean B. Bergmark. *Grace Towns Hamilton and the Politics of Southern Change.* Athens: University of Georgia Press, 1997.

Stone, Clarence N. "Race and Regime in Atlanta." In *Racial Politics in American Cities,* edited by Rufus Browning, Dale Rogers Marshall, and David M. Tabb. New York: Longman, 1990.

———. *Regime Politics: Governing Atlanta, 1946–1988.* Lawrence: University Press of Kansas, 1989.

Stoper, Emily. *The Student Nonviolent Coordinating Committee: The Growth of Radicalism in a Civil Rights Organization.* Brooklyn: Carlson, 1989.

Suggs, Henry, ed. *The Black Press of the South, 1865–1979.* Westport, Conn.: Greenwood Press, 1983.

Sullivan, Patricia. *Days of Hope: Race and Democracy in the New Deal Era.* Chapel Hill: University of North Carolina Press, 1996.

———. "Southern Reformers, the New Deal and the Movement's Foundation." In *New Directions in Civil Rights Studies,* edited by Armstead L. Robinson and Patricia Sullivan. Charlottesville: University Press of Virginia, 1991.

Taeuber, Karl, and Alma F. Taeuber. *Negroes in Cities: Residential Segregation and Neighborhood Change.* Chicago: Aldine, 1965.

Talmadge, Herman E. *You and Segregation.* Birmingham, Ala.: Vulcan Press, 1955.

Telfair Academy. *We Ain't What We Used to Be.* Savannah: Telfair Academy of Arts and Sciences, 1983.

Terrell, Lloyd, and Marguerite S. C. Terrell. *Black in Augusta: A Chronology, 1741–1977.* Augusta: Preston Publications, 1977.

Thiebolt, A. J. *Negro Employment in Finance.* Philadelphia: University of Pennsylvania, 1970.

Thornton, J. Mills III. "Challenge and Response in the Montgomery Bus Boycott of 1955–56." *Alabama Review* 33 (July 1980): 163–235.

———. "Municipal Politics and the Course of the Movement." In *New Directions in Civil Rights Studies,* edited by Armstead L. Robinson and Patricia Sullivan. Charlottesville: University Press of Virginia, 1991.

Tilly, Charles. *From Mobilization to Revolution.* Reading, Mass.: Addison-Wesley, 1978.

Tindall, George B. *Emergence of the New South.* Vol. 10. Baton Rouge: Louisiana State University Press, 1967.

Trillin, Calvin. *An Education in Georgia.* 1964. Reprint. Athens: University of Georgia Press, 1991.

Tuck, Stephen. "A City Too Dignified to Hate: Civic Pride, Civil Rights, and Savannah in Comparative Perspective." *Georgia Historical Quarterly* 79 (Fall 1995): 539–59.

Vanlandingham, Karen. "In Pursuit of a Changing Dream: Spelman College Students and the Civil Rights Movement, 1955–62." M.A. thesis, Emory University, 1983.

Walker, Jack L. "The Functions of Disunity: Negro Leadership in a Southern City." In *Atlanta, Georgia, 1960–1961,* ed. David Garrow. New York: Carlson, 1989.

———. "Protest and Negotiation: A Case Study of Negro Leadership in Atlanta." In *Atlanta, Georgia, 1960–1961,* ed. David Garrow. New York: Carlson, 1989.

Walker, Ralph. "Reaction." *Richmond County History* 7 (Summer 1975): 117–18.

Walker, Wyatt T. "Albany." *New South* 18 (June 1963): 3–8.

Wall, Marvin. "Maynard Jackson and Voting in Georgia." *New South* 24 (Summer 1969): 80–87.

Washington, C. I. "Reactions." *Richmond County History* 7 (Summer 1975): 119.

Watters, Pat. "Atlanta: Tokenism." *Nation,* 17 February 1964.

Watters, Pat, and Reese Cleghorn. *Climbing Jacob's Ladder: The Arrival of Negroes in Southern Politics.* New York: Harcourt, Brace & World, 1967.

Webb, Clive. "Charles Bloch, Jewish White Supremacist." *Georgia Historical Quarterly* 83 (Summer 1999): 267–92.

Weisbrot, Robert. *Freedom Bound: A History of America's Civil Rights Movement.* New York: Norton, 1990.

Weiss, Nancy J. *Whitney M. Young, Jr., and the Struggle for Civil Rights.* Princeton: Princeton University Press, 1989.

Weltner, Charles Longstreet. *John Willie Reed: An Epitaph.* Atlanta: SRC Publications, 1969.

———. *Southerner.* Philadelphia: J. B. Lippincott, 1966.

White, John. *Martin Luther King, Jr., and the Civil Rights Movement in America.* South Shields: British Association for American Studies, 1991.

White, Walter. *A Man Called White.* Bloomington: Indiana University Press, 1948.

Williams, Juan, ed. *Eyes on the Prize: America's Civil Rights Years, 1954–65.* New York: Viking Penguin, 1987.

Williamson, Joel. *New People: Miscegenation and Mulattoes in the United States.* New York: Free Press, 1980.

Williford, William Bailey. *Americus Through the Years: The Story of a Georgia Town and Its People, 1832–1975.* Atlanta: Cherokee, 1975.

Wilson, Ruth Danehower. "How Dimly Does Ellis Arnall See?" *Crisis* 54 (May 1947): 138–39.

Winn, Billy. "The Color of Justice." *Columbus Ledger-Enquirer,* 19, 26 May, 2 June 1991.

Wood, Betty. *Slavery in Colonial Georgia, 1730–1775.* Athens: University of Georgia Press, 1984.

Woodward, C. Vann. *The Strange Career of Jim Crow.* 3d rev. ed. New York: Oxford University Press, 1974.

Woofter, T. J., Jr. *Landlord and Tenant on the Cotton Plantation.* 1936. Reprint. New York: Da Capo Press, 1971.

Wyn, Craig Wade. *The Fiery Cross: The Ku Klux Klan in America.* New York: Simon and Schuster, 1987.

X, Malcolm (with the assistance of Alex Haley). *The Autobiography of Malcolm X.* New York: Penguin Books, 1965.

Zangrando, Robert L. *The NAACP Crusade Against Lynching, 1909–50.* Philadelphia: Temple University Press, 1980.

Zinn, Howard. "Albany." Atlanta: Southern Regional Council Publication, 8 January 1962.

———. "The Albany Cases: Upside Down Justice." SCEF Publication, 1964.

———. *SNCC: The New Abolitionists.* Boston: Beacon Press, 1964.

Index